# Arizona

**Rob Rachowiecki**

**Jennifer Rasin Denniston**

LONELY PLANET PUBLICATIONS
Melbourne • Oakland • London • Paris

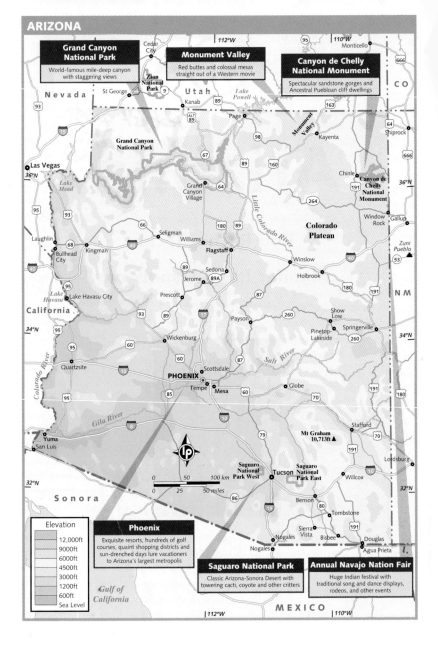

# ARIZONA

**Grand Canyon National Park**
World-famous mile-deep canyon with staggering views

**Monument Valley**
Red buttes and colossal mesas straight out of a Western movie

**Canyon de Chelly National Monument**
Spectacular sandstone gorges and Ancestral Puebloan cliff dwellings

**Phoenix**
Exquisite resorts, hundreds of golf courses, quaint shopping districts and sun-drenched days lure vacationers to Arizona's largest metropolis

**Saguaro National Park**
Classic Arizona-Sonora Desert with towering cacti, coyote and other critters

**Annual Navajo Nation Fair**
Huge Indian festival with traditional song and dance displays, rodeos, and other events

Nevada
Utah
CO
NM
California
Sonora
MEXICO

Cedar City
Zion National Park
St George
Kanab
Page
Lake Powell
Monticello
Shiprock
Grand Canyon National Park
Kayenta
Chinle
Canyon de Chelly National Monument
Las Vegas
Lake Mead
Window Rock
Gallup
Zuni Pueblo
Grand Canyon Village
Colorado Plateau
Laughlin
Bullhead City
Kingman
Seligman
Williams
Flagstaff
Winslow
Holbrook
Jerome
Sedona
Prescott
Lake Havasu City
Lake Havasu
Payson
Show Low
Springerville
Pinetop-Lakeside
Quartzsite
Wickenburg
Scottsdale
**PHOENIX**
Tempe
Mesa
Globe
Salt River
Gila River
Yuma
San Luis
Mt Graham 10,713ft ▲
Stafford
Lordsburg
Saguaro National Park West
Tucson
Saguaro National Park East
Willcox
Benson
Tombstone
Nogales
Sierra Vista
Bisbee
Douglas
Agua Prieta
Nogales
Gulf of California

## Elevation
12,000ft
9000ft
6000ft
4500ft
3000ft
1200ft
600ft
Sea Level

0   50   100 km
0   25   50 miles

Little Colorado River
Colorado River
Monument Valley

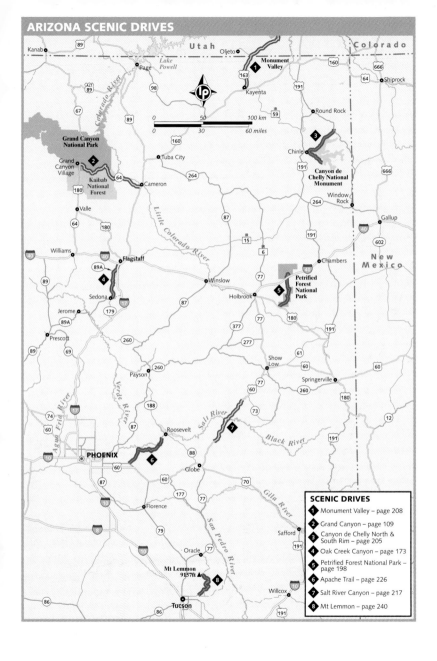

# ARIZONA SCENIC DRIVES

**SCENIC DRIVES**

1. Monument Valley – page 208
2. Grand Canyon – page 109
3. Canyon de Chelly North & South Rim – page 205
4. Oak Creek Canyon – page 173
5. Petrified Forest National Park – page 198
6. Apache Trail – page 226
7. Salt River Canyon – page 217
8. Mt Lemmon – page 240

**Arizona**
**1st edition** – September 2002

**Published by**
**Lonely Planet Publications Pty Ltd**  ABN 36 005 607 983
90 Maribyrnong St, Footscray, Victoria 3011, Australia

**Lonely Planet Offices**
**Australia** Locked Bag 1, Footscray, Victoria 3011
**USA** 150 Linden St, Oakland, CA 94607
**UK** 10a Spring Place, London NW5 3BH
**France** 1 rue du Dahomey, 75011 Paris

**Photographs**
Many of the images in this guide are available for licensing from
Lonely Planet Images.
**W** www.lonelyplanetimages.com

**Front cover photograph**
Saguaro cacti, Saguaro National Park (Richard Cummins)

ISBN 1 74059 458 4

text & maps © Lonely Planet Publications Pty Ltd 2002
photos © photographers as indicated 2002

Printed by The Bookmaker International Ltd
Printed in Malaysia

# Contents

## TUCSON & SOUTHERN ARIZONA                                   228

## SOUTHEASTERN ARIZONA                                         262

## INDEX                                                         280

## MAP LEGEND                                                     288

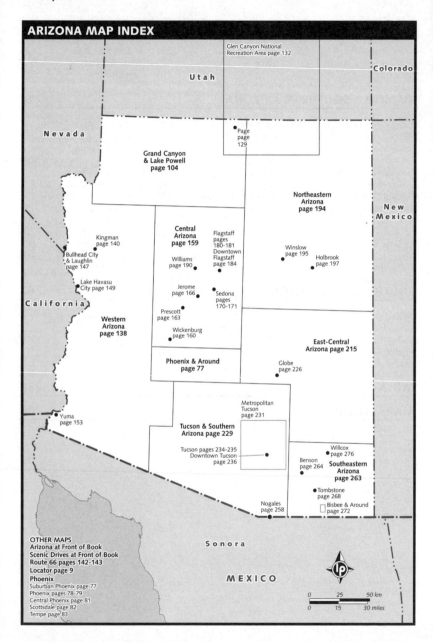

## ARIZONA MAP INDEX

Glen Canyon National
Recreation Area page 132

Utah

Colorado

Nevada

Page
page
129

Grand Canyon
& Lake Powell
page 104

Northeastern
Arizona
page 194

New
Mexico

Central
Arizona
page 159

Flagstaff
pages
180-181
Downtown
Flagstaff
page 184

Kingman
page 140

Bullhead City
& Laughlin
page 147

Williams
page 190

Winslow
page 195

Holbrook
page 197

Lake Havasu
City page 149

California

Jerome
page 166

Sedona
pages
170-171

Prescott
page 163

Western
Arizona
page 138

Wickenburg
page 160

East-Central
Arizona page 215

Phoenix & Around
page 77

Globe
page 226

Metropolitan
Tucson
page 231

Yuma
page 153

Tucson & Southern
Arizona 229

Tucson pages 234-235
Downtown Tucson
page 236

Willcox
page 276

Benson
page 264

Southeastern
Arizona
page 263

Tombstone
page 268

Nogales
page 258

Bisbee & Around
page 272

OTHER MAPS
Arizona at Front of Book
Scenic Drives at Front of Book
Route 66 pages 142-143
Locator page 9
Phoenix
Suburban Phoenix page 77
Phoenix pages 78-79
Central Phoenix page 81
Scottsdale page 82
Tempe page 83

Sonora

MEXICO

0        25        50 km
0        15        30 miles

# The Authors

### Rob Rachowiecki

Rob was born in London and became an avid traveler as a teenager. He has visited places as diverse as Greenland and Thailand and is the author of Lonely Planet's guides to Ecuador, Peru and Costa Rica. Rob is an active member of the Society of American Travel Writers. Since 1989, he has lived in Tucson, Arizona, with his wife, Cathy, and children, Julia, Alison and David. He finds Tucson to be an ideal base from which to explore what he considers to be the most beautiful region of the USA.

### Jennifer Rasin Denniston

Jennifer began traveling independently as a teenager and, by age 21, had visited Africa, Australia, Europe, Vietnam, Japan and China. Born and raised in the American Midwest, she lived in Albuquerque for several years and calls New Mexico her second home. She lives in Mt Vernon, Iowa, with her husband, Rhawn, dog, Cyril, and baby, Anna Salinas, and studies the American West and visual culture as an American Studies PhD candidate at the University of Iowa.

## FROM THE AUTHORS

**Rob Rachowiecki** I dedicate this book to my son, David, who loves to play in the desert.

**Jennifer Rasin Denniston** Thank you to Rob, whose excellent research and writing is an inspiration. Also, thanks to David – your infinite patience, sense of humor and guidance make it a pleasure to work with you. I appreciate the support and encouragement you have both given me. Finally, thank you to Rhawn for starting me on this road and then traveling with me along it.

# This Book

For this 1st edition of *Arizona,* author Jennifer Denniston updated text originally written by Rob Rachowiecki for Lonely Planet's *Southwest.* Rob pitched in with his expertise and support during the updating process.

## FROM THE PUBLISHER

This book was edited in Lonely Planet's US office in Oakland, California, by Wade Fox, with help from senior editor David Zingarelli. The index was created by Ken DellaPenta.

Margaret Livingston designed the color pages and laid out the book, and Candice Jacobus designed the cover.

The original maps were drawn by Justin Colgan and the crew that worked on the 3rd edition of *Southwest.* The maps were updated for this book by Bart Wright and Annette Olson.

Thanks to everyone involved. It was a pleasure working with you.

# Foreword

## ABOUT LONELY PLANET GUIDEBOOKS

The story begins with a classic travel adventure: Tony and Maureen Wheeler's 1972 journey across Europe and Asia to Australia. There was no useful information about the overland trail then, so Tony and Maureen published the first Lonely Planet guidebook to meet a growing need.

From a kitchen table, Lonely Planet has grown to become the largest independent travel publisher in the world, with offices in Melbourne (Australia), Oakland (USA), London (UK) and Paris (France).

Today Lonely Planet guidebooks cover the globe. There is an ever-growing list of books and information in a variety of media. Some things haven't changed. The main aim is still to make it possible for adventurous travelers to get out there – to explore and better understand the world.

At Lonely Planet we believe travelers can make a positive contribution to the countries they visit – if they respect their host communities and spend their money wisely. Since 1986 a percentage of the income from each book has been donated to aid projects and human rights campaigns, and, more recently, to wildlife conservation.

## UPDATES & READER FEEDBACK

Things change – prices go up, schedules change, good places go bad and bad places go bankrupt. Nothing stays the same. So, if you find things better or worse, recently opened or long-since closed, please tell us and help make the next edition even more accurate and useful.

Lonely Planet thoroughly updates each guidebook as often as possible – usually every two years, although for some destinations the gap can be longer. Between editions, up-to-date information is available in our free, quarterly *Planet Talk* newsletter and monthly email bulletin *Comet*. The *Upgrades* section of our website (W www.lonelyplanet.com) is also regularly updated by Lonely Planet authors, and the site's *Scoop* section covers news and current affairs relevant to travelers. Lastly, the *Thorn Tree* bulletin board and *Postcards* section carry unverified, but fascinating, reports from travelers.

**Tell us about it!** We genuinely value your feedback. A well-traveled team at Lonely Planet reads and acknowledges every email and letter we receive and ensures that every morsel of information finds its way to the relevant authors, editors and cartographers.

Everyone who writes to us will find their name listed in the next edition of the appropriate guidebook and will receive the latest issue of *Comet* or *Planet Talk*. The very best contributions will be rewarded with a free guidebook.

We may edit, reproduce and incorporate your comments in Lonely Planet products such as guidebooks, websites and digital products, so let us know if you don't want your comments reproduced or your name acknowledged.

**How to contact Lonely Planet:**
Online: e talk2us@lonelyplanet.com.au, W www.lonelyplanet.com
**Australia:** Locked Bag 1, Footscray, Victoria 3011
**UK:** 10a Spring Place, London NW5 3BH
**USA:** 150 Linden St, Oakland, CA 94607

# Introduction

Mention Arizona and distinct images leap to mind: thick arms of the saguaro cactus, howling coyotes, stunning ancient Indian sites tucked against cliffs, the changing colors of the Grand Canyon. Deserts, mountain ranges covered in forest, high mesas and plateaus are all engulfed in the vast sky, yet more than a magnificent geographical terrain, Arizona also exists as a cultural phenomenon.

The first people in the region were the ancestors of today's Native American tribes. Archaeologists have excavated fragments of their villages, hunting sites and irrigation ditches, and have found petroglyphs and pictographs. Visitors to Arizona can learn about these ancestors of today's tribes through the fascinating ancient pueblos that have been preserved

throughout the state, and in several excellent museums.

Spanish conquistadors and missionaries searching for gold, land, slaves and converts arrived in the 1600s. But the Indian tribes had no gold and held land communally. After centuries of overt and covert resistance to the Spanish, many tribes succeeded in maintaining their cultural identity, and all learned the lessons they would rely upon when confronted with the next wave of newcomers – the Anglo Americans.

After the Mexican War of 1846 to 1847, the US assumed control over what was to be called the New Mexico Territory, which included most of Arizona and New Mexico. In 1853 the Gadsden Purchase brought southern Arizona into US hands. The government soon sent troops to 'clear' the

lands of the Native Americans, establishing massive reservations that still cover large parts of the Southwest. Cattle wranglers and miners arrived in the middle of the nineteenth century, and the railroads brought tourists drawn to the sunny weather and awesome landscape. Indeed, in lieu of ancient cathedrals and classic art, spectacular national parks like the Grand Canyon in Arizona and Yellowstone in Wyoming became the young United State's national treasures.

Today, Arizona has the third largest Native American population of the 50 states (after California and Oklahoma) and the two largest Indian reservations in the country (the Navajo and the Tohono O'odham). About 26% of the state is reservation land. Many tribes have retained much of their cultures, languages and traditions, all of which differ from tribe to tribe. Some of their ancient dances and ceremonies are open to the public, but many are not. However, all visitors can experience the Indian cultures in the villages, trading posts and crafts stores that dot the reservations, and in the Indian fairs, powwows and rodeos held regularly throughout the state.

The southern reaches of the state have particularly close ties to Mexico. Architecture, cuisine and language in Arizona are a mix of Mexican, Native American and Spanish cultures. The Spanish heritage can be discovered in the centuries-old missions of southern Arizona established by Padre Kino and in the historic barrios of Tucson, where Spanish is as commonly heard as English. Tucson has a wonderful selection of Mexican restaurants that are as good as those in Mexico itself.

Visitors interested in natural history can spot numerous species in Arizona found nowhere else in the USA. Southeastern Arizona is the undisputed hummingbird capital of the country, and many other rarities fly in from Mexico, including two species of tropical trogons. The tall, majestic saguaro and organ-pipe cacti are found only in parts of southern Arizona and in Mexico. These cacti provide nests and shelter for many desert birds and animals. Arizona is one of three states where the wild pigs (javelinas) and the raccoonlike coatis are regularly glimpsed in the wild. The country's only poisonous lizard, the gila monster, lives here too.

The Grand Canyon State offers much more than canyons. Take the time to explore an old mining town, visit the cliff dwellings of Canyon de Chelly or other Native American sites, follow the path of migrants on Route 66 or ride through the desert on a horse. You'll see why, under the famously blue skies, the land, the people and the history of Arizona have lured tourists for over a hundred years, making Arizona one of the top tourist destinations in the United States.

# Facts about Arizona

## HISTORY
### The First Americans

The history of the sun-baked Southwest, a region that includes Arizona, Utah, New Meixco and Nevada, begins not with sun but with ice. For it was during the last ice age, roughly 25,000 years ago, that the first people reached the North American continent from Asia by way of the Bering Strait. These first Americans were hardy nomadic hunters who, armed with little more than pointed sticks and the courage born of hunger, pursued Ice Age mammals such as mammoths, cave bears and giant sloths.

As the climate warmed, the glaciers that covered much of North America receded and the nomads began moving south. In the 1920s, workers in Folsom and Clovis, New Mexico, found stone spear points embedded in the bones of extinct mammals dated to over 11,000 years ago. This is the earliest evidence of the first inhabitants of the Southwest, although people probably arrived earlier.

Indian oral histories offer various other scenarios. One cosmic origin myth describes how the first arrivals, four men and three women, came from the Man Carrier (an Indian name for the Big Dipper constellation) 50,000 years ago. There are many other tribal beliefs.

After many large Ice Age mammals became extinct, people began hunting smaller animals such as deer and rabbits. Hunters built simple traps and used a throwing device called an 'atlatl' to propel hunting spears. Gathering wild food (berries, seeds, roots and fruits) bolstered diets. Baskets used to collect food were so tightly woven that they held water and could be used for cooking when heated stones were dropped into the water. Stone metates were developed to grind hard seeds and roots. Archaeological sites near Cochise County in southeastern Arizona have yielded the remains of baskets and stone cooking implements, so Southwestern hunter-gatherers of this early period (7000 BC to 500 BC) have been named the Cochise people.

After 3000 BC, contacts with farmers from farther south (now central Mexico) led to the beginnings of agriculture in the Southwest. The first crops were minor additions to diets of people continuing their nomadic hunter-gatherer lifestyles. Eventually, people started reusing the same plots of land for their crops and spending more time in these areas. Primitive corn was one of the first crops. By 500 BC, beans and squash were also being cultivated, and cotton followed soon afterward. Finally, around 300 BC to AD 100, distinct groups began to settle in semipermanent villages throughout the Southwest.

## Ancient Southwestern Cultures

By about AD 100, three dominant cultures were emerging in the Southwest: the Hohokam of the desert, the Mogollon of the central mountains and valleys, and the Ancestral Puebloan (formerly known as the Anasazi) of the northern plateaus. In addition, several other groups were either blendings of or offshoots from the three main cultures – these smaller groups are still the subject of controversy among archaeologists. Examples are the Hakataya, Fremont, Salado and Sinagua traditions.

These groups are discussed below, but there is debate and disagreement about these matters. Clearly, neither the three dominant cultures nor the smaller ones existed in isolation, and much blending and fusion of lifestyles took place. By the mid-15th century, and earlier in some cases, most of these cultures had disappeared, their villages abandoned. The reasons for this are unclear, although many theories have been suggested. Most likely was a combination of factors including a devastating drought near the end of the 12th century, climate changes, overhunting, soil erosion, disease and the arrival of new groups.

## Petroglyphs

Throughout the Southwest, rocks, boulders and cliffs may be darkened with a blue-black layer called 'desert varnish.' The dark color is caused by iron and manganese oxides that leach out of the rock over many centuries, leaving a thin and slightly shiny polish that sometimes streaks cliffs from top to bottom. Ancient Indians chipped away the varnish to expose the lighter rock beneath, thus creating the rock art known as petroglyphs.

**Hohokam** This culture existed in the southern and central deserts of Arizona from 300 BC to AD 1450. These people created an advanced irrigation system based on the Gila, Salt and Verde Rivers and became well adapted to desert life. Apart from farming, they collected wild desert food such as saguaro cactus fruit and mesquite tree beans – a practice that can still be observed among desert Indians such as the Tohono O'odham tribe.

Their irrigation system was quite incredible. Using stone tools, the people dug many miles of canals, some of which were 15 feet deep and twice as wide.

The people lived in simple mud or stick shelters over shallow depressions in the earth. As time passed, this culture developed low earthen pyramids, which may have been temples, and sunken ball courts with earthen walls in which games were played. These features clearly point to a Hohokam connection with the cultures of Mexico and Guatemala. The dead were cremated, and so archaeologists today learn comparatively little by excavating burial sites. A rich heritage of pottery, however, attests to Hohokam artistry, and their ceramics and other artifacts can be seen in such places as the Arizona State Museum in Tucson. Hohokam sites can be visited in the Pueblo Grande Museum, Phoenix, and the Casa Grande Ruins National Monument, between Phoenix and Tucson.

Around 1450, the Hohokam disappeared. Why? We don't know. Today's Pima and Tohono O'odham (formerly called Papago) Indians appear to be descended from the Hohokam, but the links are not clear.

**Mogollon** The Mogollon (pronounced 'mo-guh-YOHN') culture is named after the mountains of the same name in western New Mexico and the Mogollon Rim in eastern Arizona. The region south of these mountainous areas as far as the Mexican border and east to the flatlands of eastern New Mexico was the province of the Mogollon culture, which existed here from 200 BC to AD 1450.

The Mogollon people settled in small communities, often elevated on an isolated mesa top. Their houses were simple pit dwellings. They did some farming but depended more on hunting and foraging than did their contemporaries of other cultures. As the Mogollon people developed, their villages grew bigger and often featured a kiva (a circular underground chamber used for ceremonies and other purposes).

Later, the Mogollon people began to depend on farming to a greater extent. There are many signs that by about the 13th or 14th century the Mogollon were being peacefully incorporated by the Ancestral Puebloan groups from the north. The beautiful black-on-white Mimbres pottery (from the Mimbres River area in southwestern New Mexico) has distinctive animal and human figures executed in a geometric style reminiscent of Puebloan ware.

**Ancestral Puebloan** These people inhabited the Colorado Plateau (also called the Four Corners area), comprising parts of northeastern Arizona, northwestern New Mexico, southwestern Colorado and southeastern Utah. This culture left us by far the richest heritage of archaeological sites and ancient settlements that are still inhabited in the Southwest. Until recently, this culture was called the Anasazi, a Navajo term meaning 'enemy ancestors.' The Navajo, however, were late arrivals on the scene (see Later Cultures, below), and modern Pueblo people prefer the more accurate term Ancestral Puebloan. Texts written prior to the mid-1990s used 'Anasazi.'

Like the Hohokam and Mogollon cultures, the earliest Ancestral Puebloans were hunter-gatherers who slowly added farming to their repertoire of methods of obtaining food. The people lived in pit houses. They gathered food in baskets, and the excellence of their basket weaving has led archaeologists to refer to these as the Basket Maker periods. Toward the end of the Basket Maker III period (AD 400 to AD 700), pottery became increasingly important.

The Pueblo periods, which followed the Basket Maker periods, saw much development in pottery and architecture. Larger villages, some with over 100 rooms, were built, many of them in shallow caves under overhanging cliffs. One of the most important Ancestral Puebloan sites in the Southwest can be seen at Canyon de Chelly National Monument in northeast Arizona.

Today, the oldest links with the Ancestral Puebloans are found among the Hopi tribe of northern Arizona. Here, perched on a mesa top, the village of Old Oraibi has been inhabited since the 1100s, making it the oldest continuously inhabited settlement in North America.

By about AD 1450, the Hohokam had mysteriously disappeared and the Mogollon people had been more or less incorporated into the Ancestral Puebloans, who themselves began to leave many of their ancient pueblos in the 1400s and, by the 1500s, had mainly moved to the pueblos now found along the Rio Grande in New Mexico.

**Smaller Groups** The Hakataya is the general term for several small groups that once lived in western and central Arizona and were contemporaries of the Ancestral Puebloans. The best known of these groups is the Sinagua, who left various interesting and attractive sites such as those at the Montezuma Castle, Tuzigoot, Walnut Canyon and Wupatki National Monuments

in central Arizona. Lesser-known groups existed west of the Sinagua and included the Prescott, Cohonina, Cerbat and Laquish peoples.

The Salado culture exhibits influences from both the Ancestral Puebloan and Mogollon peoples, and the culture appears to have influenced some late Hohokam sites. Salado remains are found in central Arizona, in an area where all three of the major cultural groups overlapped to some extent. The best Salado site is seen at the Tonto National Monument.

## Later Cultures

The cultures described above can be traced back in the Southwest for two millennia or longer. Many of the tribes living in the Southwest today, however, are comparatively recent arrivals. Nomadic bands of Indians from two distinct language groups, the Shoshonean and the Athapaskan, straggled into the Southwest from the north between AD 1300 and AD 1600.

Shoshonean tribes found in the Southwest today live mainly in Utah and make up only a small part of the population. They include the Southern Paiutes in southwestern Utah (and into Nevada and Arizona).

The Navajo and various Apache tribes are of Athapaskan descent; they now make up a substantial part of Arizona's and New Mexico's populations. The Navajos moved into the Four Corners area, especially northeastern Arizona.

These late arrivals didn't conquer the Pueblo and Hopi descendants of the Ancestral Puebloans but rather coexisted with them. Certainly, there were occasional skirmishes and raids, but generally the Pueblo peoples took advantage of the hunting skills of the newcomers, and the Apache and Navajo learned about pottery, weaving and agriculture from the Pueblo tribes. Then the Europeans arrived in the Southwest, bringing a lifestyle completely foreign to the Native Americans. Mother Earth and Father Sky, bows and arrows, ritual dances and sweatlodges, foot travel, spiritual oneness with the land – all these were to be challenged by the new concepts of Christ and conquest, gunpowder and sword, European civilization and education, horses and a grasping desire for land.

## The Spaniards

For the next three centuries, it was the Spanish who wrought the greatest changes in the region. After brief incursions into the region by small Spanish groups in 1536 and 1539, a major expedition was launched in 1540 led by Francisco Vásquez de Coronado. He set off from Mexico City with 336 Europeans, 1000 Indians and 1100 pack and riding animals. The expedition's goal was the fabled, immensely rich 'Seven Cities of Cibola.'

For two years, they traveled through Arizona, New Mexico and as far east as Kansas, but instead of gold and precious gems, the expedition found Indian pueblos of adobe bricks. Some of the leaders took contingents to explore the Hopi mesas and the Grand Canyon, among other areas. During the harsh winters, the expedition expropriated some of the pueblos for its own use, burned one and killed dozens of Indians. This ferocity was to prove typical of the behavior of many of the Europeans who were yet to come. Finally, the expedition returned home, penniless and broken. Coronado had failed to become rich or find the fabled cities, and for the next 50 years, Spanish exploration focused on areas outside the Southwest.

The dreams of fabulously rich cities were revived periodically by small groups making minor forays. In 1598, Juan de Oñate, a Spaniard born in Mexico, headed north from Mexico and up the Rio Grande. With a large force of 400 European men and an unknown number of Indians, women and children, accompanied by 7000 head of various livestock and 83 oxcarts, he called the land north of El, Paso Texas New Mexico and claimed it for Spain. He set up San Gabriel as the first capital of New Mexico (it was moved to Santa Fe in 1609), and Spanish efforts to settle and farm the land and bring the Indians into the Catholic Church were marked with bloodshed and brutality. For most of the 17th century, there was little European exploration of other parts of the Southwest.

Less brutal incursions were made into Arizona by the Jesuit priest Eusebio Kino, who has garnered almost mythical status as the bringer of God to what is now (mainly) southern Arizona. He began his travels in Mexico in 1687 and spent over two decades in the Arizona-Sonora area. His approach to being a missionary was, certainly by the standards of the day, humane, and this distinguished him from many of his contemporaries. He established missions at Tumacácori and San Xavier del Bac (both south of Tucson); these sites can be visited today, although the present buildings were erected about a century after Kino was there.

After Kino's departure, conditions for the Indians deteriorated and led to the short-lived Pima Revolt of 1751 and the Yuma Massacre of 1781, when the Yuma killed colonizers in their area.

The Europeans brought with them diseases to which the Indians had no resistance and caused terrible epidemics within the tribes. By some accounts, 80% of Native Americans died from disease in the 16th century, and the history of North America may have been very different if epidemics had not taken such a terrible toll.

## Arizona Becomes a US Territory

In 1803, the Louisiana Purchase resulted in the USA's acquiring a huge tract of land (from Louisiana to the Rocky Mountains) from the French, doubling the size of the young country. The Spanish colonies of the Southwest now abutted, for the first time, US territory, and the two countries maintained an uneasy peace.

When Mexico became independent from Spain in 1821, the newly independent Mexicans welcomed US traders and a major trade route was established. This was the famous Santa Fe Trail between Missouri and Santa Fe, a trail traversed by thousands of people until the railway arrived in 1879. Few Anglos (as non-Hispanic whites from the USA were called), however, ventured beyond the Santa Fe Trail. Some who did were the 'mountain men' – hunters and trappers who explored all over the West.

In 1846, the United States declared war on Mexico, and two years later, the land north of the Gila River was claimed by the USA and incorporated into the New Mexico Territory, which then included Arizona. The USA soon realized that the best route from the Mississippi River to the burgeoning territory of California lay south of the Gila River, passing through the Mexican town of Tucson. US diplomat James Gadsden arranged for the USA to purchase the land between the present international border and the Gila River from Mexico. In 1854, the USA annexed the territory and Americans began to cross the area en route to California.

Many of the settlers were from southern states, and when the American Civil War broke out in 1861, Arizona declared itself a Confederate state. This resulted in the westernmost battle of the Civil War, when a small Confederate force was defeated by Union troops at Picacho Peak in 1862. The Confederate forces killed three Union soldiers before retreating to Tucson and dispersing, aware that they would soon be greatly outnumbered.

Arizona was designated as a separate territory the following year. Territories differed from states in that they were not allowed to elect their own senators and representatives to the US Congress in Washington, DC. Territories were headed by an elected governor, with little power in the nation's capital. Though Tucson was the largest town, Prescott was chosen as the territorial capital because Tucson was perceived as a bastion of Confederate loyalty. From 1867 to 1877, however, Tucson held the position of territorial capital, after which it was returned to Prescott and finally moved to the Anglo-founded town of Phoenix in 1889, where it has remained. Historians, Hispanic and non-Hispanic alike, attribute this to the anti-Hispanic sentiment then prevalent in US politics.

**Indian Wars & Reservations** Since the early nineteenth century, US military forces had been pushing west across the continent,

fighting the Indian wars, protecting settlers and wresting the land from the Indians, who had little use for European concepts of land ownership. The Americans settled the new territories much more aggressively than the Spaniards had, killing or forcibly moving whole tribes of Indians who were in their way. All of the many tribes in the Southwest resisted the westward growth of the USA to a greater or lesser extent.

The best-known incident is the forceful relocation of many Navajos in 1864. US forces, led by Kit Carson, destroyed Navajo fields, orchards and houses and forced the people into surrendering or withdrawing into remote parts of the Canyon de Chelly in northeastern Arizona. Eventually, they were starved out and 9000 Navajos were rounded up and marched 400 miles east to a camp at Bosque Redondo, near Fort Sumner in New Mexico. Hundreds of Indians died from sickness, starvation or gunshot along the way. The Navajos call this 'The Long Walk,' and it remains an important part of their history.

Life at Bosque Redondo was harsh, with inadequate resources for 9000 people; over 2000 Navajos died. Even from the Anglo point of view, this relocation was not working and, after four years, the surviving Navajos were allowed to return to their lands in northeastern Arizona and allotted over 5000 sq miles for their reservation. Since the 1868 treaty, the reservation has grown to encompass over 20,000 sq miles in Arizona, New Mexico and Utah; it is the largest in the USA, and the Navajo people are the largest tribe.

The last serious conflicts were between US troops and Apaches. This was partly because raiding was the essential and honorable path to manhood for Apaches. Young Apache men were required to demonstrate raiding skills in order to marry well, and then to provide for an extended family and to be considered a leader. As US forces and settlers moved into Apache land, they became obvious targets for the raids that were part of the Apache way of life. These continued under the leadership of Mangas Coloradas, Cochise, Victorio and, finally, Geronimo, who surrendered in 1886 after being promised that he and the Apaches would be imprisoned for two years and then allowed to return to their homeland. As with many promises made during these years, this one, too, was broken. The Apaches spent the next 27 years as prisoners of war.

By the time of Geronimo's surrender, which ostensibly marked the end of the US Army's Indian Wars, there were many Indian reservations in the Southwest, each belonging to one or sometimes a few tribes. Although the wars were over, Indian people continued to be treated like second-class citizens for many decades. Non-Indians used legal loopholes and technicalities to take over reservation land. Many children were removed from reservations and shipped off to boarding schools where they were taught in English and punished for speaking their own languages or behaving 'like Indians' – this practice continued into the 1930s. Older Indians were encouraged to lose their culture and customs. Despite the history of cultural oppression, Indians today still practice spiritual customs and other beliefs that predate US expansion. Many native languages are still spoken, and a majority of Navajos learn their tribal language before English.

Indians fought alongside Americans in WWI but were not extended US citizenship until 1924 and were not given voting rights in Arizona until 1948. Most tribes have their own governments and laws that are applicable to people living on or visiting their reservations. Federal laws are also applicable to reservations, but normally state and other local laws do not apply.

WWII prompted the first large exodus of Indians from the reservations, when they joined the US war effort. The most famous unit was the Navajo Code Talkers – 420 Navajo marines who used a code based on their language for vital messages in the Pacific arena. This code was never broken by the Japanese. Today, the surviving code talkers are among the most revered of Navajo elders and are often honored in public events.

Currently, about half of the Indians in the US live off reservations, but many maintain strong ties with their tribes.

## Mining, Cowboys & the Wild West

The nation's first transcontinental railroad line was completed in northern Utah in 1869. By the late 1880s, the railway connected Arizona with the rest of the country, and the arrival of more people and resources via the railroad led to further exploration of the land, and the frequent discovery of mineral deposits. The 1870s and 1880s saw the foundation of many mining towns, and they were wild and dangerous places. New mining towns, mushrooming overnight near the richest mines, often had more saloons and bordellos than any other kind of building. Newly rich miners would come into town to brawl, drink and gamble, sometimes being fleeced by professional cardsharps. It is no surprise that law and order were practically nonexistent in many parts of the Southwest during the latter part of the 19th century. Desperate tales of gunslingers and cattle rustlers, outlaws and train robbers are all part of the legend of the Wild West.

Cattle trails, along which cowboys drove many thousands of head of cattle, letting them feed as they went, sprang up in the 1860s and 1870s. The Chisholm Trail, which branched off from the Goodnight-Loving Trail near Roswell, New Mexico, directed cattle west into Arizona. Cattle ranching remains a mainstay of Arizona's economy, and the cowboy is very much alive throughout the state.

One of the most legendary Wild West figures is Wyatt Earp. In 1881, Wyatt Earp, along with his brothers Virgil and Morgan and Doc Holliday, shot dead Billy Clanton and the McLaury brothers in a blazing gunfight at the OK Corral in Tombstone, Arizona – the showdown took less than a minute. Both sides accused the other of cattle rustling, but the real story will never be known. Today, reenactments of the gunfight take place regularly in Tombstone.

Such reenactments are the closest you'll get to those lawless frontier days. Several towns have them daily or for annual festivals.

By the dawn of the 20th century, some semblance of law and order had arrived in Arizona, and the days of gunslingers were over. Mining, and copper mining in particular, remains an important part of Arizona's economy.

## From Dams to Statehood

At the end of the nineteenth century, with the railroads bringing more and more Anglos, the mining towns thriving and the Indians pushed away onto reservations, the territory began to petition for statehood. The federal government in Washington, DC, didn't take these petitions very seriously; Arizona's reputation as a wild and lawless desert territory led politicians to suspect that statehood would prove a constant financial drain on the federal coffers.

This opinion began to change after President Theodore Roosevelt visited Arizona in 1903 and, by way of the Reclamation Act of 1902, which called for construction of dams to resist the wildest of floods, promoted the damming of the territory's rivers. The Theodore Roosevelt Dam on the Salt River was finished in 1911, providing year-round water for irrigation and drinking. This readily available water finally paved the way to statehood, and Arizona became the 48th state on February 14, 1912.

Over the next few decades, more dams were built, and copper mining flourished. Some mines prospered, while others went bust and their accompanying towns dwindled to ghost towns. Irrigation increased crop yields, and cotton and cattle were important products. Tourists, who had begun arriving at the end of the nineteenth century, continued to arrive, seeking the desert sun and awe-inspiring landscape. In 1908, the Grand Canyon was designated a national monument, and in 1919 it became a national park. Resorts and guest ranches for the wealthy began to appear in the Phoenix area in the '20s and '30s. Growth was steady but slow until WWII, when the population swelled with an influx of military personnel

training for war in the deserts of Africa and other hot regions.

After the war, air-conditioning became increasingly available, and many veterans who had trained in Arizona decided to return and settle in what appeared to be a land of new opportunity. Growth was phenomenal, and the small towns of Phoenix and Tucson quickly grew into the important cities they are today, with all the accompanying big-city problems of air pollution, urban crime and sprawling suburban growth. The warm climate has also attracted large numbers of retirees, some of whom spend winters in Arizona and summers in their northern home states. These 'snowbirds' are an important part of the socioeconomic fabric of the state.

## GEOGRAPHY

Travelers find that vast canyons and steep bluffs, buttes, mesas and mountains often make it difficult to get from here to there. Although the varied topography may hinder travel, it is also one of the attractions that lure travelers to Arizona in the first place. The scenery is literally breathtaking.

The northern part of Arizona is part of the Colorado Plateau, a series of plateaus, between 5000 and 8000 feet in elevation, separated by deep canyons, among them the world-famous Grand Canyon. The plateaus are topped by buttes, mesas and other topographical features that give the landscape its distinctive character. The Four Corners region, so named because Arizona, New Mexico, Utah and Colorado share a common boundary point here, is the only place where four US states meet. Much of this area is part of the Navajo Indian Reservation, the largest in the USA.

Southwest of the Colorado Plateau, Arizona's terrain drops in a rugged cliff called the Mogollon Rim, reaching a height of 2000 feet in some places and stretching a third of the way across Arizona. Beyond lies a broad belt of mountain ranges, getting progressively lower to the southwest.

The southwestern and south-central parts of Arizona belong to the desert Basin and Range province. Desert basins alternate with mountain ranges, many topped by forests and most running north to south. It's in these arid basins that Arizona's major cities, Phoenix and Tucson, are found, supported by massive irrigation projects from the Colorado, Gila and Salt Rivers. This is part of the Arizona-Sonora Desert.

## GEOLOGY

Approximately 1.7 billion years ago, during the Precambrian Era, what is now the Southwest formed the western edge of the North American continent (tectonic plates would later mash themselves onto western North America, extending it to the west). Tectonic plates crashed against North America, buckling the crust and producing magma that cooled to form large bodies of granite. Oceans flooded the region, depositing thick layers of marine sediments that formed shales, siltstones and sandstones. As the Precambrian ended, the seas gradually withdrew, and for hundreds of millions of years the region was slowly beveled by erosion. Beautifully exposed in the lower portions of the Grand Canyon, this Great Unconformity removed over one billion years of geologic history from much of the Southwest.

At the start of the Paleozoic, about 570 million years ago, North America was joined with Europe, Asia, Africa and Antarctica into a supercontinent named Pangaea. Seas again advanced across western Pangaea, depositing another thick sequence of sediments. The Mesozoic, or Age of the Dinosaurs, began with arid conditions that created expanses of sand dune–covered desert but ended with humid floodplains and swampy lowlands. During the final segment of the Mesozoic, the ocean swept in yet again, forming a long, north-south trending sea called the Cretaceous Seaway, which extended as far north as Canada. In the late Cretaceous, another tectonic collision, named the Laramide Orogeny, resulted in the birth of the modern Rocky Mountains, uplifted the Colorado Plateau (with little tilting or folding) and led to another round of volcanic eruptions that led to the formation of gold, silver and copper deposits in Arizona.

Approximately 15 to 8 million years ago, the crust began to stretch to the east and west throughout western Arizona, western Utah and southern New Mexico, cracking the crust into long, north-south mountains (ranges) and valleys (basins). This geologic province, called the Basin and Range, forms a distinctive Southwestern landscape. By the time it finished, rifting had extended the crust 50 miles. Separating the Basin and Range from the Colorado Plateau is a northwest-southeast band of mountains, called the Central Highlands, that crosscuts Arizona and western New Mexico.

## CLIMATE

Southwestern and south-central Arizona is below 3000 feet in elevation and is often the hottest part of the USA. High temperatures exceed 100°F for weeks on end and occasionally surpass 120°F. The humidity is low, however, and evaporation helps to cool the body. Dry air does not hold heat like humid air does, and so nighttime temperatures drop by 20° or 30°F. Winter temperatures occasionally will drop below freezing, but only for a few hours. Yuma, at 200 feet in the southwestern corner of Arizona, is the driest part of Arizona, and indeed one of the driest in the Southwest. The rest of Arizona is

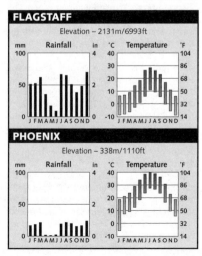

higher, and because of that, cooler; the state's average elevation is 4100 feet.

In the driest areas of southwestern Arizona, almost no rain falls from April to June. The highest rainfall here is during the monsoons of July and August, when rains tend to be brief, heavy downpours falling mainly in the afternoon. In the wetter areas, it can rain at any time, but even so, few areas have more than five wet days in any month.

The areas of greatest precipitation (more than 20 inches) are mostly in the high mountains of central Arizona.

Conditions can be extreme, and every year people die from lightning, dehydration and flash floods. For more information, see the 'Flash Floods' boxed text in the Outdoor Activities chapter.

## ECOLOGY & ENVIRONMENT

The current environment of Arizona is related to the history of modern settlement and the accompanying development of water use in the arid Southwest in general. The climate, dry for months and then subject to sudden heavy rainstorms, made rivers difficult to control for early settlers. Reduced to a trickle or drying completely during the dry months, rivers could change into tremendous torrents in a matter of hours after a monsoon storm. Interestingly enough, the ancient Hohokam people had learned how to irrigate large parts of central and southern Arizona, but their system is long abandoned and silted up.

From the 1870s until the early 1900s, ranchers along the Salt and Pecos Rivers and settlers in river valleys throughout the Southwest built makeshift dams to control and divert the waters for irrigation. Time after time, floods swept away the dams, which would be rebuilt. Following the completion of the Theodore Roosevelt Dam in 1911, dam after dam was constructed and constant disagreements and rancorous debates raged as to who should be allowed to use the dammed river water. Colorado River water rights, however, were an even bigger matter – seven states and Mexico had claims to the water. In 1922, US secretary of commerce (later president) Herbert Hoover united the states in the Colorado River Compact and engineered a scheme to divide water rights, with California getting the largest share.

Although Arizona refused to ratify the compact until 1944, the 1922 legislation laid the groundwork for a series of major dams on the Colorado River. Despite the seeming bounty of water created by modern technology, there were and are many water problems, not the least of which were ethical ones – the huge lakes formed by the dams flooded canyons containing hundreds of ancient Indian sites that are now lost. Furthermore, thousands of people were forced to relocate when their homes and land were flooded by the creation of the dams. Technical problems have included the inaccurate measurement of water flow by early gauges; what to do with the silt that drops out of the water when it comes to a halt behind a dam; and how to deal with drought.

Nevertheless, water has become available in Arizona, and with it, towns have grown. More water means more people who need more water still – a vicious cycle that has reached crisis proportions. Phoenix is a noteworthy example. Founded in 1870, the city had 5500 inhabitants in 1900. It has more than 1.3 million today, making it the sixth largest city in the country. Including those in adjoining towns, 3.3 million people live in the metropolitan area. There is simply not enough water to continue supplying all these people.

Recent additions to the Southwest's water supply are underground water reserves, or aquifers, which are are 'mined' – in other words, water is extracted from them at a faster rate than it can naturally be replenished. Despite legislation to limit using water from aquifers, they are rapidlyg being depleted. Water-thirsty golf courses, irrigated farms and increasing populations play a part in making water the Southwest's major ecological concern. In the 1990s, the Central Arizona Project (CAP) enabled Tucson and southeastern Arizona to receive water from the Colorado River.

Cattle ranching is also a concern. Many federal lands are leased inexpensively to ranchers to graze cattle. This can result in degradation of riparian areas when cattle trample the edges of streams in efforts to find water. This trampling doesn't allow plants to grow and deteriorates the banks so that they are washed away. Over 90% of riparian habitats have disappeared in Arizona over the past century.

Finally, the mining industry also plays a controversial environmental role. Huge copper mines scar the earth's surface and strip-mining for coal is also a contentious issue.

## FLORA & FAUNA

Arizona wildlife is unique and fascinating, and much of it can easily be seen and experienced. Forests of the giant saguaro (pronounced 'sa-WA-roh') cactus cover

many slopes of southern Arizona, and the coyote, the wily trickster of Navajo legend, is often seen darting across the highways or skulking off the road. Vultures wheel through the air; poisonous lizards and venomous snakes are occasionally glimpsed; tarantulas and scorpions scuttle along the ground; and jackrabbits bound along with prodigious leaps. Southeastern Arizona is a mecca for birders, with 16 species of hummingbird recorded (eight are commonly seen).

Clearly, there is plenty of life in this desert – the question is, which desert? What was once called the Great Southwestern Desert by early travelers is now divided into four different deserts – the Arizona-Sonora Desert, Chihuahua Desert, the Mojave Desert and the Great Basin Desert (the

### Cacti of the Southwest

Researchers cannot agree on exact numbers, but more than a hundred species of cactus are found in the Southwest. They are superbly adapted to survival in the arid environment. The succulent pads that form the body of the plant are actually modified stems, and their waxy 'skin' helps retard moisture loss. The leaves, which in other plants normally allow a lot of water to escape through transpiration, have been modified into spines that not only lose little moisture, but also protect the plant against herbivores looking for water. Evaporation is further reduced because the plant keeps its pores closed during the day and open only at night. These remarkable plants are further enhanced by their often splendid flowers.

Cacti are legally protected. You need a permit to collect any kind of cactus from the wild. It is also illegal to damage or destroy a cactus. A famous (and true) story you may hear is of a man who was shooting at a saguaro from close range. One of the huge arms of the cactus toppled over and killed him. Let that be a lesson to you.

**Identification** It is fairly easy to identify the six most common types of Southwestern cactus. These are prickly pear, pincushion, cholla, giant columnar, barrel and hedgehog cacti.

Prickly pears are often of the genus Opuntia and are distinguished by the flattened cross-section of their pads. If the pads are cylindrical, read on.

Pincushion cacti, often of the genus Mammilaria, are small and cylindrical in cross-section, and don't have ribs running from top to bottom. Spine clusters grow out of nipplelike bumps on the stems – hence the scientific name. Many species have hooked spines.

Cholla (pronounced 'CHOY-uh') cacti are also cylindrical and lack ribs, but are much taller and have branches. Like the prickly pears, they belong to the genus Opuntia. They can range from pencil chollas, with extremely thin branches; to teddybear chollas, which look warm and fuzzy but have wickedly barbed spines; to large jumping chollas, which have fruits hanging in loose chains. Brushing a jumping cholla lightly often results in part of the chain becoming attached to your

continent's most northerly desert). A brief overview of the three deserts that extend into Arizona introduces you to the diversity of plants and animals in the state.

## The Arizona-Sonora Desert

This area covers most of southern Arizona and much of the northern part of Mexico's state of Sonora, most of Baja California and the southeastern corner of California. It is a subtropical desert with two distinct wet seasons: the summer monsoons and the winter rains. Generally low-lying and extremely hot, it has a greater diversity of wildlife than the other deserts. This is partly because the rainfall pattern allows for both a spring and a winter flowering season and also because tropical regions have more species than do temperate ones.

More than any other region, the Arizona-Sonora Desert is characterized by cacti, especially the giant saguaro cactus, huge columnar cacti with uplifted arms, that is found in southern Arizona but nowhere else in the USA. The organ-pipe cactus and the senita cactus are other giants found in southern Arizona near the Mexican border. Dozens of other species are here too: prickly pear, barrel, fishhook, hedgehog and teddybear cholla are the most typical cacti of this desert.

The Arizona-Sonora Desert also has the greatest variety of trees, which tend to be short and spiny with small leaves. The Arizona state tree, the blue paloverde, as well as the yellow and Mexican paloverdes are common here. *Paloverde* is Spanish for 'green stick' and refers to the color of the

## Cacti of the Southwest

body – almost as if it had jumped onto you. Jumping chollas often grow in thick stands. The chollas have some of the sharpest and most difficult to remove spines – if you are stuck, it may be easier to cut the spines with scissors and then remove them one by one with tweezers.

The remaining three main types are all cylindrical in cross-section and ribbed. If they are also very tall (from 15 to 50 feet high), they are giant columnar cacti and most likely to be a saguaro cactus (Cereus giganteus), which has branches high off the ground (and is found only in southern Arizona and northern Mexico). In a few places in southern Arizona, you might see large cacti branching from the ground. These are either organ-pipe or senita cacti. (Organ-pipes have 10 or more ribs and lack the white or gray hairs of the senita. You can see them at Organ Pipe Cactus National Monument.) There are many more species of columnar cacti across the border in Mexico.

Finally, smaller cylindrical cacti with ribs are likely to be hedgehog or barrel cacti. Hedgehog cacti, often of the genus Echinocereus, are small, with the main pad less than 4 inches in diameter. When they bloom, the flowers grow from the sides. Barrel cacti, often of the genus Ferocactus, are over 5 inches in diameter and their flowers grow from the top. The largest examples can grow to 10 feet in height, although this is unusual.

All six types are commonly found in southern Arizona. The other Southwestern deserts lack the giant columnar cacti. The Great Basin Desert tends to have just the smaller species.

bark, which is capable of photosynthesis. The ironwood, a tree with very dense wood that sinks in water, is also typical of this desert.

Animals are easily seen, especially many species of lizard and, sometimes, several snake species, including various rattlesnakes and the highly venomous Arizona coral snake. Commonly seen mammals are coyotes, several rabbit species and various species of ground, rock and antelope squirrel. Birds include the quaint Gambel's quail, with its question-mark-shaped head plume, the roadrunner and the ubiquitous cactus wren.

The superb Arizona-Sonora Desert Museum in Tucson provides visitors with an excellent introduction to this region.

## The Chihuahua Desert

This desert is found in southern New Mexico, western Texas, the extreme south-eastern corner of Arizona and the Mexican state of Chihuahua. Although at a similar latitude to the Arizona-Sonora Desert, it lies at a generally higher elevation and is therefore cooler. On average, more rain falls in summer, and most flowers bloom in late summer and early fall.

The desert's most striking plants are the agaves (pronounced 'a-GAH-vees') and yuccas. The agaves, of which there are several species (some found in the other desert regions), have a rosette of large, tough, spiny swordlike leaves out of which shoots an amazing flowering stalk, often reaching as high as 15 feet, covered with thousands of tiny flowers. After flowering for a few weeks, the plant dies.

Some yuccas resemble agaves with rosettes of tough leaves and tall flower stalks; others are more shrublike. Unlike the agave, however, the yucca flowers annually. The flowers are pollinated at night by yucca moths, which lay their eggs inside the flowers. The moth larvae then feed on the developing fruit and thus both plant and animal benefit.

Creosote bush dominates the ground cover of the Chihuahua Desert, and is found in the Arizona-Sonora and Mojave Deserts

as well. Although this low, straggly bush is not much to look at, it produces complex oils and resins that make it taste bad to most animals. When it rains, these chemicals are released and give the air a characteristically astringent but not unpleasant smell.

The ocotillo is a common plant of both the Chihuahua and Arizona-Sonora Deserts. During dry months, this plant looks like a bunch of skinny, spiny stems. After rain, the stems are covered by many tiny green leaves and tipped by clusters of small, bright red flowers.

Both the Chihuahua and Arizona-Sonora Deserts are home to mammals that are typical of Mexico but not frequently seen by visitors to the USA. For eample, if you enjoy hiking and backcountry camping, you may well see javelina or coati. Javelinas are piglike mammals that travel in small groups or occasionally herds of up to 60, feeding on cacti and making quiet grunting sounds.

## The Mojave Desert

This desert spreads across parts of southern Nevada, southeastern California, north-western Arizona and extreme southwestern Utah. The Mojave is the smallest, driest and hottest of the country's deserts, and it is also thought of as a transition desert between the Arizona-Sonora and Great Basin Deserts.

Much of this desert is low-lying. It includes the lowest point in the Western Hemisphere: Death Valley (282 feet below sea level). The lowest areas are characterized by widely spread shrubby vegetation or empty sand dunes and dry lake beds. In Arizona the elevations are higher, and the dominant plants are the eerie Joshua trees. These 30- to 40-foot-high plants, believed to live up to 1000 years, are the largest species of yucca and are members of the lily family.

Spring can bring a carpet of about 250 species of flower, of which 80% are endemic to the Mojave Desert. Cacti are quite common, although they are generally smaller than the ones of the Arizona-Sonora Desert. Creosote bushes are seen in great and odorous quantities, and many lizards and desert birds are present.

## Higher Life Zones

Biologists divide the elevations of the mountains into a series of life zones that, despite being somewhat arbitrary and imprecise in regards to their altitude, are useful tools for making sense of the sudden changes in flora and the associated fauna. The following is a popular zonation.

**Lower Sonoran Zone**: Elevations below 4500 feet, encompassing most of the deserts discussed above

**Upper Sonoran Zone**: Elevations of 4500 to 6500 feet. This supports evergreen trees such as small junipers and the piñon pine.

**Transition Zone**: 6500 to 8000 feet. This falls between the desert basins and the high mountains, and includes much of the Colorado Plateau. The most notable vegetation is the ponderosa pine. There are fewer species of reptiles, but animals that live in this zone include squirrels, chipmunks, Black bears, mountain lions, white-tailed deer and elk.

**Canadian Zone**: Elevations of 8000 to 9500 feet. The predominant trees are Douglas firs and aspens, and the shading of these thick forests precludes the growth of many other plants.

**Hudsonian, or Subalpine, Zone**: Elevations from 9500 to 11,500 feet. Conifers including Engelmann spruce, subalpine fir and bristlecone pine dominate. This zone receives heavy winter snows, and few mammals are found here in winter.

**Alpine Zone**: Above the tree line (11,500 feet), characterized by small tundra-like plants.

## GOVERNMENT & POLITICS

The federal government has three branches: the legislative branch, makes the laws of the land; the executive branch executes these laws; and the judicial branch studies and interprets both the Constitution and the laws.

The legislative branch is made up of the bicameral Congress, composed of the Senate and the House of Representatives. The Senate has two senators from each of the 50 states, and the House has several members from each state, depending on the size of that state's population. Arizona has six representatives. In contrast, California, the most populous state, has 52 representatives. The executive branch consists of the

president, the 14-member cabinet and various assistants. The president serves four years and may serve only two terms. The judicial branch is headed by the Supreme Court, with nine justices who are appointed for life by presidents and approved by the Senate.

Each of the 50 states has its own government, run along similar lines to the national government, with some differences. The head of each state is the governor. National (federal) laws apply to all states, although there are often conflicts between federal and state interests. Additionally, each state enacts its own laws that visitors should be aware of.

Traditionally, most Western states are Republican, and the generally conservative state of Arizona is no exception. In a land where water is a scarce resource and the population is increasing more rapidly than in the country as a whole, it is not surprising that the most contentious issues in the region concern the use of water and land (see Ecology and Environment).

## ECONOMY

Historically, Arizona's economy is based on the 'Four Cs' – copper, cattle, cotton and citrus. Nicknamed the Copper State, the state has been the USA's largest producer of the mineral since 1907. Copper was the main product of the $2.5 billion 1999 nonfuel mineral production in Arizona.

Citrus and cotton in the midst of the Southwestern desert is more of a surprise – irrigation from the Gila River has provided the necessary moisture. Cotton continues to be the most important crop, but citrus appears to have been replaced by several other 'C' crops – carrots, cauliflower, corn and celery – as well as other vegetables. The 1999 value of all farm marketings was $2.18 billion, of which about 55% was crops and 45% livestock and related products.

Indeed, much of Arizona's economy has been directly linked to the scarcity of water and projects to divert water to agricultural areas and population centers. Where farmers and ranchers can tap water reserves, crops such as cotton, citrus fruits, grains, lettuce and broccoli thrive, and cattle and dairy products are major farm products. In the less arid central and northern areas, extensive forests, owned primarily by the US government, produce large lumber yields.

Today, all these have been surpassed by manufacturing, construction and tourism. Major products include aircraft and missiles (Hughes Missile System Co employs many thousands in Tucson), electronics, metals, foods, clothes and the printing and publishing industry. Tourism now brings in about $9 billion annually. This growth has led to an expanded construction industry in the major metropolitan areas, and the value of construction in 1997 was $10 billion.

For Arizonans, more than 70% of jobs are in the service, trade and government sectors. Unemployment was 4.4% in 1999. Per capita income in 1999 was about $25,300 per year.

## POPULATION & PEOPLE

The US Census Bureau takes a census of the population every 10 years. The April 2000 census found that from 1990 to 2000 Nevada, Arizona, Colorado and Utah experienced the greatest population growth of all the states.

Arizona is the 20th most populous state, with 5,130,632 inhabitants, and has a rich Hispanic heritage. Its comparatively high population density is skewed by the presence of the greater Phoenix metropolitan area, which accounts for over 60% of the state's inhabitants.

It has the third largest Native American population of the 50 states (Oklahoma and California have the largest), over half of which are Navajo. Other tribes include various Apache groups, Havasupai, Hopi, Hualapai, Tohono O'odham, and a host of smaller groups. The African American and Asian/Pacific Islander populations are very small.

Arizona is commonly perceived as having a tricultural mix of Indian, Hispanic and Anglo cultures, but all three cultures make their mark in differing degrees depending on the region. The Indians predominantly live in the Four Corners area, especially on the Navajo and Hopi Reservations of northeastern Arizona. There are large Apache reservations in mountainous eastern Arizona, the Tohono O'odham Reservation in the southern desert of Arizona and a scattering of smaller reservations elsewhere in the region. None of these places can be considered truly tricultural. However, reservation culture is definitely bicultural – Indian and Anglo – in most respects.

Southern Arizona has much Hispanic influence. The architecture and arts, among other things, reflect this heritage. In the border areas, many Hispanic people are of Mexican-American heritage and proudly call themselves Chicano. Some still do not recognize the legality of the US claim of Mexican land in 1848 after the US-Mexican war and the Gadsden Purchase in 1853; they refer to the land affected as Aztlan.

Anglos dominate the scene in many fast-growing cities of Arizona, particularly the Phoenix metropolitan area and the towns along the Colorado River in western Arizona.

## ARTS

Phoenix and Tucson have their own symphony orchestras, and Phoenix also is home to the Arizona Opera Company and Ballet Arizona. Every city of any size has theaters, art galleries and museums.

Hispanic and Native American influences have helped create a distinctive local arts scene. Much of this aesthetic is evident in the region's pottery, paintings, weavings, jewelry, sculpture, wood carving and leatherwork.

Many visitors are eager to see Native American art: Navajo rugs, Hopi kachina dolls, Zuni silverware, Tohono O'odham basketry and Pueblo pottery are some of the best known. Excellent examples of Southwestern Native American art can be seen in many museums, especially Phoenix's Heard Museum. Contemporary Native American art is easy to buy, and both traditional and modern work is available in hundreds of galleries.

The Southwest's music scene, too, has its Hispanic and Native American influences. Of course, you can hear anything from jazz to hip-hop in the major cities, but you can also catch *mariachis* (typically dressed in dark, ornately sequined, body-hugging costumes and playing predominantly brass instruments and guitars), especially in towns close to the Mexican border. Native American dances and music are performed throughout Arizona and the Southwest.

## RELIGION
Christians make up the religious majority, and Arizona's Jewish population is about 2%, the national average.

Native American tribes have the oldest North American religions, which may have changed, however, since contact with Europeans. Some, like the Native American Church, which uses hallucinatory peyote buttons as a sacrament, are partly pan-Indian responses to encroachment by Anglo culture.

Various Native American religions are closely followed by tens of thousands of people. In any discussion of Indian religious beliefs, several points are worth bearing in mind. First, different tribes often have particular creation stories, rituals and practices, which means that there are dozens of unique and carefully prescribed spiritual ways of life. Second, Indians usually maintain a strict sense of privacy about their most important ceremonies, and thus books written by even the most respected outsiders, such as anthropologists, usually contain some inaccuracies when describing Indian religion. Third, the Indian ways are beliefs that Indians feel and know essentially because they are Indians – it's not something that non-Indians can properly understand or convert to.

## LANGUAGE
Although American English is spoken throughout the USA, there are regional variations. Over 20% of Arizonians speak a language other than English (usually Spanish or one of the numerous Indian languages) at home.

You are likely to hear 'Spanglish,' in which speakers switch smoothly between Spanish and English, even within the same sentence. You might be invited to 'vamos a mi house' (come to my house), or hear Spanglish patter on the radio.

There are plenty of Spanish-language radio stations, many broadcasting from Mexico. In the Four Corners area, KTTN radio station, broadcasting out of Window Rock on 660 AM, has many programs in Navajo.

Visitors to Indian reservations should remember that silence is almost like a statement. If you say something to an Indian and are met by silence, this doesn't indicate that the person you are talking to is ignoring you. Indians speak their minds when they disagree with the speaker and may remain silent when they agree with the speaker or have no special opinion.

# Facts for the Visitor

## PLANNING
### When to Go

In northern Arizona, summer is the high season, coinciding with school vacations in both North America and Europe. Traditionally, Memorial Day weekend (end of May) to Labor Day weekend (beginning of September) is the vacation season; expect higher prices and more crowds except in hot southern Arizona, where luxury resorts cut their prices in half. Hotels in Phoenix, Tucson and other southern Arizona towns consider winter (Christmas to May) their high (and more expensive) season. While the rest of the country is buried under snowdrifts, southern Arizonans enjoy T-shirt weather most days.

### Maps

Free state maps are available from state tourist information offices and welcome centers. Members of the American Automobile Association (AAA) and its foreign affiliates (see the Getting Around chapter) can receive free state and city maps from AAA offices, as well as their *Indian Country* map, which covers the Four Corners area in excellent detail. AAA maps are available to nonmembers for a few dollars. City maps are often provided by local chambers of commerce for free or at nominal cost.

National parks provide free maps after you pay the entrance fee. US Forest Service (USFS) ranger stations sell maps of their national forest lands. Topographic maps published by the US Geological Survey (USGS) are sold at camping stores, US National Park visitor centers and USFS ranger stations. 1:62,500 (approximately 1 inch=1 mile) or 1:24,000 maps are ideal for backcountry use.

Many outdoor equipment stores sell the DeLorme Mapping series of individual state atlases that contain detailed topographic and highway maps at a scale of 1:250,000.

## What to Bring

Arizona generally has a casual attitude, and people's clothing reflects that. Few restaurants expect men to wear ties or jackets. Southern Arizonans wear shorts and T-shirts all summer long, but if you are heading into the highlands, you'll need some warmer clothes for the evening, even in midsummer. For much of the year, severe sunburn is a real possibility, so bring plenty of strong sunblock. A broad-brimmed hat and sunglasses are important, too.

## TOURIST OFFICES

The Arizona Office of Tourism State (☎ 602-230-7733, 800-842-8257, 888-520-3433), 2702 N Third St, Suite 4015, Phoenix, AZ 85004, can send you informative brochures about the state's main attractions. These free brochures are updated annually and contain addresses and telephone numbers of chambers of commerce, hotel lists and other useful information.
website: www.arizonaguide.com

## VISAS & DOCUMENTS
### Passport & Visas

Canadians must have proper proof of Canadian citizenship, such as a citizenship card with photo ID or a passport. Visitors from other countries must have valid passports, and many must have a US visa. All visitors should bring their driver's licenses and any health-insurance or travel-insurance cards.

There is a reciprocal visa-waiver program in which citizens of certain countries may enter the USA for stays of 90 days or less with a passport but without first obtaining a US visa. Ask a travel agent if your country is part of this program. Other travelers will need to obtain a visa from a US consulate or embassy. In some countries the process can be done by mail.

Your passport should be valid for at least six months longer than your intended stay in the USA. The US State Dept has a Visa Services page online that contains a good deal of information on various kinds of visas (www.travel.state.gov/visa_services .html). It also includes a list of embassy phone and fax numbers and addresses.

For information on work visas and employment in the US, see Work, later in this chapter.

**Visa Extensions & Reentry** If you want, need or hope to stay in the USA longer

---

## HIV & Entering the USA

Everyone entering the USA who isn't a US citizen is subject to the authority of the Immigration & Naturalization Service (INS). The INS can keep someone from entering or staying in the USA by excluding or deporting them. This is especially relevant to travelers with HIV. Though being HIV-positive is not grounds for deportation, it is 'grounds for exclusion,' and the INS can invoke it to refuse admission.

Although the INS doesn't test people for HIV at customs, it may try to exclude anyone who answers 'yes' to this question on the non-immigrant visa application form: 'Have you ever been afflicted with a communicable disease of public health significance?' INS officials may also stop people if they seem sick, are carrying AIDS/HIV medicine or, sadly, if the officer happens to think the person 'looks gay,' though sexual orientation is not legally grounds for exclusion.

It's imperative that visitors know and assert their rights. Immigrants and visitors who may face exclusion should discuss their rights and options with a trained immigration advocate before applying for a visa. For legal immigration information and referrals to immigration advocates, contact the National Immigration Project of the National Lawyers Guild (☎ 617-227-9727), 14 Beacon St, Suite 506, Boston, MA 02108, or Immigrant HIV Assistance Project, Bar Association of San Francisco (☎ 415-267-0795), 685 Market St, Suite 700, San Francisco, CA 94105.

---

than the date stamped on your passport, go to the local Immigration & Naturalization Service (INS) office *before* the stamped date to apply for an extension. (To locate the nearest INS office, look in the blue section of the local white pages telephone directory under 'US Government' or call ☎ 800-755-0777.)

### Travel Insurance

No matter how you're traveling, make sure you take out travel insurance. This should cover you not only for medical expenses and luggage theft or loss, but also for cancellations or delays in your travel arrangements, and everyone should be covered for the worst possible case, such as an accident that requires hospital treatment and a flight home. Coverage depends on your insurance and type of ticket, so ask both your insurer and your ticket-issuing agency to explain the finer points. STA Travel and Council Travel offer travel insurance options at reasonable prices. Ticket loss is also covered by travel insurance.

### International Driving Permit

An international driving permit is a useful accessory for foreign visitors in the USA. Local traffic police are more likely to accept it as valid identification than an unfamiliar document from another country. Your national automobile association can provide one for a nominal fee. They're usually valid for one year.

### Other Documents

If you plan on doing a lot of driving in the USA, it would be beneficial to join your national automobile association or the American Automobile Association. See the Getting Around chapter for more information.

Most hostels in the USA are members of Hostelling International–American Youth Hostel (HI-AYH). Hostelling International is managed by the International Youth Hostel Federation (IYHF). You can purchase membership on the spot when checking in or purchase it before you leave home.

If you're a student, get an international student ID or bring along your school or

university ID card to take advantage of the discounts available to students.

All people over the age of 65 get discounts throughout the USA. All you need is an ID with proof of age. There are organizations, such as the AARP (see Senior Travelers, later), that offer membership cards for discounts and extend coverage to citizens of other countries.

You will need a photo ID to prove you are over 21 to get into most bars and to buy alcohol.

## Copies

Before you leave home, you should photocopy all important documents (passport data page and visa page, credit cards, travel insurance policy, air/bus/train tickets, driver's license, etc). Leave one copy with someone at home and keep another with you, separate from the originals.

It's also a good idea to store details of your vital travel documents in Lonely Planet's free online Travel Vault in case you lose the photocopies or can't be bothered with them. Your password-protected Travel Vault is accessible online anywhere in the world – create it at www.ekno.lonely planet.com.

## EMBASSIES & CONSULATES
## US Embassies & Consulates

Some US diplomatic offices abroad include the following:

**Australia**
(☎ 2-6270-5900) 21 Moonah Place, Yarralumla ACT 2600
(☎ 2-9373-9200) Level 59 MLC Centre 19-29 Martin Place, Sydney NSW 2000
(☎ 3-9526-5900) 553 St Kilda Rd, Melbourne, Victoria

**Canada**
(☎ 613-238-5335) 490 Sussex Dr, Ottawa, Ontario K1N 1G8
(☎ 604-685-4311) 1095 W Pender St, Vancouver, BC V6E 2M6
(☎ 514-398-9695) 1155 rue St-Alexandre, Montréal, Québec

**France**
(☎ 01 43 12 48 76) 2 rue Saint Florentin, 75001 Paris

**Germany**
(☎ 30-8305-0) Neustädtische Kirschstr.4-5, 100117 Berlin

**Ireland**
(☎ 1-668-8777) 42 Elgin Rd, Ballsbridge, Dublin 4

**Israel**
(☎ 3-519-7575) 71 Hayarkon St, Tel Aviv 63903

**Japan**
(☎ 3-224-5000) 10-5 Akasaka Chome, Minato-ku, Tokyo 107-8420

**Mexico**
(☎ 5-209-9100) Paseo de la Reforma 305, Colonia Cuauhtémoc, 06500 Mexico City

**Netherlands**
(☎ 70-310-9209) Lange Voorhout 102, 2514 EJ, The Hague
(☎ 20-575-5309) Museumplein 19, 1071 DJ Amsterdam

**New Zealand**
(☎ 644-722-2068) 29 Fitzherbert Terrace, Thorndon, Wellington

**United Kingdom**
(☎ 20-7499-2000) 24 Grosvenor Sq, London W1A 1AE
(☎ 31-556-8315) 3 Regent Terrace, Edinburgh EH7 5BW
(☎ 28-9032-8239) Queens House, 14 Queen St, Belfast BT1 6EQ

## Foreign Embassies & Consulates in the US

Most nations' main consuls or embassies are in Washington, DC. To find the telephone number of your embassy or consul, call Washington, DC, directory assistance (☎ 202-555-1212). Phoenix has Mexican, Dutch, German and Swiss consuls, and Tucson has a Mexican consul. These lists change often and are found in the yellow pages of telephone directories under 'Consulates.' There is a consulate for the UK in Los Angeles, California (☎ 310-477-3322).

## CUSTOMS

US Customs allows each person over the age of 21 to bring 1 liter of liquor and 200 cigarettes duty-free into the USA. US citizens are allowed to import, duty-free, $400 worth of gifts from abroad, and non-US citizens are allowed to bring in $100 worth. Should you be carrying more than $10,000 in US and foreign cash, traveler's checks, money orders or the like, you need to declare the excess amount. There is no legal restriction on the amount that may be imported, but undeclared sums in excess of $10,000 may be subject to confiscation.

## MONEY
### Currency & Exchange Rates

The US dollar ($) is divided into 100 cents (¢). Coins come in denominations of 1¢ (penny), 5¢ (nickel), 10¢ (dime), 25¢ (quarter), 50¢ (half-dollar) and $1 (dollar); the latter two are infrequently seen. Quarters are the most useful in vending machines and parking meters.

Bills (paper currency) are all the same size and color, regardless of denomination; bills come in $1, $2 (rare), $5, $10, $20, $50 and $100.

At press time, exchange rates were:

| country | unit | | US dollar |
|---------|------|---|-----------|
| Australia | A$1 | = | $0.53 |
| Canada | C$1 | = | $0.63 |
| EU | €1 | = | $0.88 |
| Hong Kong | HK$1 | = | $0.13 |
| Japan | ¥100 | = | $0.76 |
| New Zealand | NZ$1 | = | $0.44 |
| United Kingdom | UK£1 | = | $1.44 |

### Exchanging Money

**Cash & Traveler's Checks** Some banks exchange cash or traveler's checks in major foreign currencies, though banks in outlying areas do this infrequently and it may take them some time. Traveler's checks offer greater protection from theft or loss; American Express and Thomas Cook are widely accepted, though people in small towns my look at you askance and not exchange them. Be sure to always carry some cash as well. You'll save yourself trouble and expense if you buy traveler's checks in US dollars, as restaurants, hotels and most stores accept US-dollar traveler's checks as if they were cash.

**Credit & Debit Cards** Major credit and charge cards are widely accepted by car-rental agencies and most hotels, restaurants, gas stations, shops and larger grocery stores. It's virtually impossible to rent a car without a credit card, and the cards are useful for hotel reservations and ticket agencies. The most commonly accepted cards are Visa, MasterCard and, to a lesser extent, American Express.

Places that accept Visa and MasterCard are also likely to accept debit cards. Unlike a credit card, a debit card deducts payment directly from the user's bank account. Sometimes a minimal fee is charged for the transaction. Check with your bank to confirm that your debit card will be accepted in other states; debit cards from large commercial banks can often be used worldwide.

**ATMs** Most banks, airports, shopping malls and many grocery stores and gas stations have ATMs, usually open 24 hours a day. For a nominal service charge, you can withdraw cash from an ATM using a credit or debit card. Credit card companies usually charge a 2% fee ($2 minimum), but cards linked to your personal checking account usually give fee-free cash advances from any branch of your bank.

**Costs** The best way to get around is by car, because intercity buses, trains and planes are not very cheap and do not go to the out-of-the-way places. Car rental is available in most towns of any size (see Getting Around chapter). Gas (petrol) is cheap, ranging from about $1.40 to over $2 for a US gallon, depending on the location, grade of fuel and international economic factors.

There is an incredibly wide range of accommodations and eating options in Arizona. Ubiquitous camping opportunities and cheap Mexican restaurants are convenient for those on a tight budget (see Accommodations later in this chapter).

**Tipping** In restaurants and bars, wait staff are paid minimal wages and rely upon tips for their livelihoods. Tip 15% unless the service is terrible (in which case a complaint to the manager is warranted) or up to 20%

if the service is great. Don't tip in fast food, take-out or buffet-style restaurants where you serve yourself. Taxi drivers expect 10% to 15%, and baggage carriers receive $1 for the first bag and 50¢ for each additional bag carried, or more if they go a long way. In better hotels, housekeeping staff get $1 or $2 a day, and parking valets get $1 or $2 upon delivering your car.

**Taxes** Almost everything you pay for in the USA is taxed. Occasionally, the tax is included in the advertised price (eg, gas, drinks in a bar, transportation tickets and museum or theater entrance tickets). Restaurant meals and drinks, motel rooms and most other purchases are taxed, and this is not included in the rates quoted in this book.

You'll pay different taxes in every town. Most restaurants add 6% to 8% to the bill; most hotels add 9% to 14%; and most car-rental companies add 10% to 15%, though those at airports add over 20%. The prices given in this book do not reflect local taxes; always ask.

## POST & COMMUNICATIONS
### Postal Rates
Postage rates increase every few years. At the time of this writing, 1st-class mail within the USA cost 37¢ for letters up to 1 ounce (23¢ for each additional ounce) and 23¢ for postcards.

International airmail rates (except for Canada and Mexico) are 60¢ for a half-ounce letter and 40¢ for each additional half ounce. International postcard rates are 50¢. Letters to Canada are 48¢ for a half-ounce letter and 45¢ for a postcard. Letters to Mexico are 40¢ for a half-ounce letter, 40¢ for a postcard. Aerogrammes are 60¢.

The cost for parcels airmailed anywhere within the USA is $3.20 for 2lb or less, increasing up to $6.50 for 5lb. For heavier items, rates differ according to the distance mailed. Books, periodicals and computer disks can be sent by a cheaper 4th-class rate. For rates, office address and zip code information, call ☎ 800-275-8777 or check www.usps.com.

### Sending Mail
If you have the correct postage, you can drop your mail into any blue mailbox. However, to send a package of more than 16 ounces, to buy stamps or weigh your mail, go to a post office. Usually, post offices in main towns are open 8 am to 5 pm Monday to Friday and from 8 am to 3 pm on Saturday.

### Receiving Mail
You can have mail sent to you care of General Delivery at any post office that has its own 5-digit zip (postal) code. Mail is usually held for 10 days before it's returned to sender; you might request that your correspondents write 'hold for arrival' on their letters. Mail should be addressed like this:

Name
c/o General Delivery
Anytown, AZ 85747

Alternatively, have mail sent to the local American Express or Thomas Cook representative. Both companies provide mail service for their customers.

### Telephone
The Phoenix metropolitan area and surrounding Maricopa County use the ☎ 602, 480 and 623 area codes. Most of southeastern Arizona (including Tucson) uses the ☎ 520 area code, and the rest of the state uses the new ☎ 928 area code.

For local directory assistance, dial ☎ 411. For directory assistance outside your area code, dial ☎ 1 + 411, which can give you numbers nationwide. Directory assistance calls cost up to 95¢.

The 800, 888 or 877 area codes are for toll-free numbers within the USA, and may work from Canada. These might not be available if dialing locally. Call ☎ 800-555-1212 to request a company's toll-free number.

The 900 area code is for numbers for which the caller pays a premium rate.

**Rates** Local calls usually cost 50¢ at pay phones. Many mid-range and top end hotels add a service charge of 50¢ to $1 for local calls made from a room phone and also have hefty surcharges for long-distance calls. A new long-distance alternative is phone debit cards, which allow purchasers to pay $5, $10, $20 or $50 in advance, with access through an 800 number.

Long-distance rates vary depending on the destination and which telephone company you use – call the operator (☎ 0) for rates information. Don't ask the operator to put your call through, however, because operator-assisted calls are much more expensive than direct-dial calls. Generally, nights (11pm to 8am), all day Saturday and from 8am to 5pm Sunday are the cheapest (60% discount) times to call.

**eKno** There's a wide range of local and international phone cards. Lonely Planet's eKno Communication Card is aimed specifically at independent travelers and provides budget international calls, a range of messaging services, free email and travel information.

Check the eKno website at www.ekno .lonelyplanet.com for membership information, access numbers from other countries, and updates on super budget local access numbers and other new features.

**International Calls** To make an international call direct, dial ☎ 011, then the country code, followed by the area code and the phone number.

### Fax

Fax machines are easy to find in the US at shipping companies like Mail Boxes Etc, photocopy stores and hotel business service centers, but be prepared to pay high prices (over $1 a page).

### Email & Internet Access

Free Internet access is available at most public libraries during library hours. In large towns, photocopy centers such as Kinko's are open 24 hours and charge 20¢ per minute. Internet cafés are limited to larger or popular towns and charge around 10¢ a minute. Hotel business centers and major

airports charge about $4 for 15 minutes. If you have a laptop and modem, you can connect with the Internet from most hotel rooms.

## INTERNET RESOURCES

There's no better place to start your Web explorations than the Lonely Planet website (www.lonelyplanet.com). Here you'll find succinct summaries on traveling to most places on Earth, postcards from other travelers and the Thorn Tree bulletin board, where you can ask questions before you go or dispense advice when you get back. You can also find travel news and updates for many of our most popular guidebooks. The subWWWay section links you to the most useful travel resources available elsewhere on the Web.

For general Arizona information, visit the state's official website, www.az.gov. Here travellers will find links to hundreds of other Internet resources that feature anything from cities to hotels to events and activities.

Road closures and other transportation-related resources can be found online at www.dot.state.az.us. Information on the state parks is at www.pr.state.az.us. You can search the state yellow pages at www.access arizona.com. The Arizona Game & Fish Department's website is www.gf.state.az.us, and the state Bureau of Land Management (BLM)'s website is www.az.blm.gov.

The National Park Service has a website with links to sites for every park and monument at www.nps.gov. To make reservations for any US Forest Service campground, go to www.reserveusa.com.

Thousands of Arizona businesses, hotels and other organizations have websites; many are mentioned in appropriate parts of the book. Don't forget to add 'http://' to the beginning of the URLs given throughout this book.

## BOOKS

Tens of thousands of books have been written about Arizona and the Southwest, and many have comprehensive indexes that will lead you as far as you want to go. For books dealing specifically with outdoor activities, see the recommendations under the appropriate headings in the Outdoor Activities chapter.

## Lonely Planet

*Rocky Mountains, Southwest* and *USA* will give plenty of information for travels outside of Arizona, and *Las Vegas* is full of details about that gritty and glamorous city. Outdoorsy types should check out *Hiking in the USA*. If you're heading south, get a copy of *Mexico*.

## Archaeology & History

*Those Who Came Before,* by Robert H and Florence C Lister, is an excellent source of readable information about the prehistory of the Southwest and about the archaeological sites of the national parks and monuments of this area. It is extensively indexed.

The best general history is *The Southwest,* by David Lavender. It has a detailed (if dated) index. *The Smithsonian Guide to Historic America – The Desert States,* by Michael S Durham, is a nicely illustrated guide to the historic sites of the region.

*Arizona: A History,* by Thomas E Sheridan, covers the area from prehistoric times through the early 1990s.

## Geology

*Basin and Range,* by John McPhee, is as much a journey as a popular geological text. It covers Nevada as well as Utah and is a recommended read.

*Roadside Geology of Arizona,* by Halka Chronic, is a good guide for the curious nongeologist. It describes the geology along major roads and is well illustrated.

## Natural History

A tremendous variety of books will help you identify Arizona's plants and animals, tell you where you can see them and give you insight into their biology. The Peterson Field Guide series has over forty titles and is recommended. The National Geographic Society's *Field Guide to the Birds of North America* and the series of Audubon Society Field Guides (covering birds, plants and animals) are recommended. The Audubon Society Nature Guide *Deserts,* by James A MacMahon, gives a fine overview of all four Southwestern deserts, as well as being a field guide to the most important plants and animals of these regions. An excellent series of pocket books published by the Southwest Parks & Monuments Association in Tucson helps you identify the region's plants.

Birders may want to supplement their field guides with *Birds in Southeastern Arizona,* by William A Davis and Stephen M Russell, which describes the seasonal distribution and abundance of birds in what is one of the premier birding 'hot spots' in the country, and gives directions on how to travel to scores of the best birding areas.

*Arizona Wildlife Viewing Guide,* by John N Carr, lists scores of places to see wildlife. It includes information on access and on the probability of seeing the most important species at specific sites.

Several excellent books about Arizona natural history are designed to be read rather than used as field guides. These include John Alcock's very readable *Sonoran Desert Spring* and *Sonoran Desert Summer. Gathering the Desert,* by Gary Paul Nabhan, describes in splendid and fascinating detail 12 desert plants and their importance to Native Americans.

Ann Zwinger writes eloquently in *The Mysterious Lands: A Naturalist Explores the Four Great Deserts of the Southwest.*

## Native Americans

The best introduction for the serious student is the 20-volume Handbook of North American Indians (Smithsonian Institution). The volumes that cover this region are *Volume 9: Southwest* and *Volume 10: Southwest,* edited by Alfonso Ortiz.

An even better introduction for the generalist is *The People: Indians of the Southwest,* by Stephen Trimble. The author traveled among the area's many tribes, photographing and interviewing them for almost a decade. Much of the book is in the words of the Indians themselves.

Some introductions to Southwestern Indian arts and crafts include *Navajo Rugs: How to Find, Evaluate, Buy and Care for Them*, by Don Dedera; *Hopi Kachinas: The Complete Guide to Collecting Kachina Dolls*, by Barton Wright; and *Hopi Silver: The History and Hallmarks of Hopi Silversmithing*, by Margaret Wright.

*Native*Roads*, by Fran Kosik, subtitled *The Complete Motoring Guide to the Navajo and Hopi Nations*, does an excellent job describing the history, and native cultures to be experienced, along the highways through and around these reservations.

Native American writers are mentioned in the section on fiction.

## Fiction

Early novels of note include Zane Grey's westerns, of which *Riders of the Purple Sage* is the best known. Grey spent years living in Arizona. Oliver La Farge won a Pulitzer Prize for his 1929 *Laughing Boy*, a somewhat romantic portrayal of Navajo life.

Tony Hillerman, an Anglo, writes award-winning mystery novels that take place on the Navajo, Hopi and Zuni Reservations. Even Indians find his writing true to life. Following the adventures of Navajo policemen Jim Chee and Joe Leaphorn is a lot of fun, particularly when you are driving around the reservations of the Four Corners area.

*The Monkey Wrench Gang*, by Edward Abbey, is hugely fun to read, which is more than can be said of many classic novels, and this one certainly is a classic. It's a fictional and comic account of real people who become 'eco-warriors'; their plan is to blow up Glen Canyon Dam before it floods Glen Canyon.

An acclaimed recent Southwestern novelist is Barbara Kingsolver, whose novels are superb portrayals of people living in the Arizona. *The Bean Trees* echoes the author's own life – a young woman from rural Kentucky moves to Tucson. *Animal Dreams* gives wonderful insights into the lives of people from a small Hispanic village near the Arizona–New Mexico border and

from an Indian pueblo. Don't miss these books.

## Author Picks

Though not about Arizona specifically, *Desert Solitaire: Season in the Wilderness*, by Edward Abbey, describes the author's job as a park ranger in Arches National Park in the 1950s, when the park was still a monument reached by a dirt road and locals easily outnumbered tourists in nearby Moab. Abbey shares his philosophy and passions about the desert, the mismanagement of the Southwest, and the problems of mass tourism – which he foresaw with striking clarity. This book is a classic.

An Abbey protégé is Charles Bowden, who wrote eloquent essays about Arizona in *Blue Desert* and *Frog Mountain Blues*.

The curiously named *Jack Ruby's Kitchen Sink*, by Tom Miller, is accurately subtitled *Offbeat Travels Through America's Southwest*. It's a quirky read that will satisfyingly accompany your own Southwestern odyssey. Other insightful essays on the Southwest are found in *The Telling Distance*, by Bruce Berger.

Also consider reading *Cadillac Desert: The American West and Its Disappearing Water*, by Marc Reisner, a thorough, compelling and readable account of how the exploding populations of Western states have utilized every possible drop of available water. *The Man Who Walked Through Time*, by Colin Fletcher tells the story of the author's many weeks backpacking the length of the Grand Canyon – the first account of such a trip and a seminal book on the modern 'sport' of backpacking.

## NEWSPAPERS

Of over 1500 daily newspapers published in the USA, those with the highest circulation include the *Wall Street Journal* (with an emphasis on financial and business news), *USA Today* (general US and world news), the *New York Times* and the *Los Angeles Times*, all of which are available in main cities.

Phoenix and Tucson publish daily papers. These papers are generally available in many other towns, which often have daily or weekly papers of their own.

## RADIO & TV

All rental cars have radios. In the southern parts of the state, stations broadcasting from Mexico (in Spanish) can easily be picked up. In and near major cities, you have scores of stations to choose from, with a wide variety of music and entertainment. In rural areas, be prepared for a predominance of country & western music, Christian programming, local news and 'talk radio.' National Public Radio features news, discussion, music and more. NPR stations usually broadcast on the lower end of the FM dial.

All the major TV networks have affiliated stations throughout the USA. These include ABC, CBS, NBC, FOX (all commercial stations) and PBS (noncommercial Public Broadcasting System). Cable TV offers about 45 channels, including Cable News Network (CNN). Almost all hotel rooms have TVs (most with cable), but many B&Bs do not.

## PHOTOGRAPHY & VIDEO
### Film & Equipment

Film can be damaged by excessive heat, so don't leave your camera and film in the car on a hot summer's day and avoid placing your camera on the dashboard while you are driving. Color print film is widely available, but slide and black & white film is found only in larger towns. Acceptable, fast film developing is available in many drugstores.

## Video Systems

Overseas visitors who are considering purchasing videos should remember that the USA uses the National Television System Committee (NTSC) color TV standard, which is incompatible with other standards (PAL or SECAM) used in Africa, Europe, Asia and Australasia.

## Photographing People & Places

See the boxed text 'Visitor's Etiquette in Pueblos & on Reservations' for information on taking photos without offending.

## Airport Security

All passengers have to pass their luggage through X-ray machines. Since the September 11, 2001, attacks on the World Trade Center and the Pentagon, airport security has been source of concern in the USA. Airlines suggest that all passengers allow two hours to get through security. There is, however, no consistency to how long security can take; many travelers find themselves either sitting around in airports after having breezed past security, or anxiously waiting in security lines and running to catch planes.

## TIME

Arizona is on Mountain Standard Time, which is seven hours behind Greenwich Mean Time. Arizona does not use daylight saving time, so during that period (first Sunday of April to the last Sunday in October), it is eight hours behind Greenwich Mean Time and one hour behind the rest of the Southwest. The exception is the Navajo Reservation, which, in keeping with those parts of the reservation in Utah and New Mexico, observes daylight saving time.

## ELECTRICITY

The USA uses 110V and 60 cycles and the plugs have two (flat) or three (two flat, one round) pins. Most European appliances will require voltage converters and plug adapters.

## WEIGHTS & MEASURES

Distances are in feet (ft), yards (yds) and miles (m or mi). Three feet equal 1 yard; 1760 yards or 5280 feet equal 1 mile (1.61 kilometers). In southern Arizona and New Mexico, distances are also marked in kilometers to aid Mexican drivers on trips into the USA.

Dry weights are in ounces (oz), pounds (lb) and tons (16 ounces are one pound; 2000 pounds are one ton), but liquid measures differ from dry measures. One pint equals 16 fluid ounces; 2 pints equal 1 quart, a common measure for liquids like milk, which is also sold in gallons (4 quarts). Gasoline is dispensed in US gallons, about

20% less than Imperial gallons. Pints and quarts are also 20% less than Imperial ones. There is a conversion chart on the inside back cover of this book.

## LAUNDRY

Visitors will find self-service, coin-operated laundry facilities in most towns of any size and in better campgrounds and many hotels. Washing a load costs about $1 and drying it another $1.

## TOILETS

Public toilets are normally free and found in shopping malls and parks. People often use the facilities in restaurants, gas stations or hotel lobbies when necessary. Toilets are commonly, and more politely, called 'bathrooms' or 'rest rooms.'

## HEALTH

Generally speaking, the USA is a healthy place to visit, and the country is well-served by hospitals. However, because of the high cost of health care, international travelers should take out comprehensive travel insurance (see Health Insurance in this section) before they leave.

Immunizations are rarely required unless you are arriving from a country with cholera or yellow fever outbreaks.

### Health Insurance

A travel insurance policy to cover medical problems (as well as theft or loss) is recommended. Even the most cursory visit to a doctor will cost around $50, and hospitalization for two days may cost more than your entire vacation. Get insurance! Because policies vary a great deal, be sure to talk to a travel agent and do some research before choosing a policy that suits your needs. Few policies cover emergency evacuations, body repatriation or flights home requiring two or three seats to stretch out on. This may require a separate policy.

### Health Preparations

Before leaving on a long trip, make sure your immunizations are up to date. Take spare glasses and your prescription. New spectacles are made for under $100 (except for difficult prescriptions or better frames). Take an adequate supply of necessary medications, along with prescriptions in case you lose your supply.

### Travel- & Climate-Related Problems

**Sunburn** In the desert or at high altitude you can get sunburned in an hour, even through cloud cover. Use a sunscreen (protection factor 30+) and take extra care to cover areas not normally exposed to sun.

**Heat Exhaustion** Dehydration or salt deficiency can cause heat exhaustion. Take time to acclimatize to high temperatures and make sure you get enough liquids. Salt deficiency is characterized by fatigue, lethargy, headaches, giddiness and muscle cramps. Salt tablets may help. Vomiting or diarrhea can also deplete your liquid and salt levels. Always use water bottles on long trips. A gallon per person per day is recommended if hiking. It's a good idea to carry jugs of drinking water in your car in case it should break down.

**Heatstroke** Long, continuous exposure to high temperatures can lead to this serious, sometimes fatal, condition, which occurs when the body's heat-regulating mechanism breaks down and body temperature rises to dangerous levels. Symptoms include feeling unwell, lack of perspiration and a high body temperature. Hospitalization is essential for extreme cases, but meanwhile get out of the sun, remove clothing, cover with a wet sheet or towel and fan continually.

**Hypothermia** Skiers and winter hikers will find that temperatures in the mountains or desert can quickly drop below freezing. A sudden soaking or even high winds can lower your body temperature rapidly. Travel with a partner whenever possible.

Woolen clothing and synthetics, which retain warmth even when wet, are superior to cottons. Carry a quality sleeping bag and high-energy easily digestible snacks like chocolate or dried fruit.

Get hypothermia victims out of bad weather and into dry, warm clothing. Give hot liquids (not alcohol) and high-calorie easily digestible food. In advanced stages, place victims in warm sleeping bags and get in with them. Do not rub victims.

**Fungal Infections** Fungal infections occur with greater frequency in hot weather. Minimize them by wearing loose, comfortable clothes, avoiding artificial fibers, washing frequently and drying carefully. If you are infected, wash the area daily with a disinfectant or medicated soap and water; rinse and dry well. Apply antifungal powder, air the infected area when possible, wash towels and underwear in hot water and change them often.

## Infectious Diseases

**Diarrhea** Changes in water or food can cause the runs; diarrhea from contaminated food or water (uncommon in the USA) is more serious. Use bottled water if you are susceptible, and never drink from streams or lakes.

Despite precautions you may still have a mild bout of travelers' diarrhea, but this is rarely serious. Dehydration is the main danger, particularly for children, where dehydration can occur quite quickly. Fluid replacement is important. With severe diarrhea, a rehydrating solution is necessary to replace minerals and salts. Commercially available ORS (oral rehydration salts) are useful.

Lomotil or Imodium relieve the symptoms, but do not cure the problem. Use them only if absolutely necessary – if you *must* travel.

**Giardiasis** Also called Giardia, this intestinal parasite is present in apparently pristine backcountry streams. Giardia can appear weeks after you have ingested contaminated water; symptoms may recur repeatedly, disappearing for a few days and then returning.

Symptoms are stomach cramps, nausea, bloated stomach, watery, foul-smelling diarrhea and frequent gas. Tinidazole (Fasigyn)

or metronidazole (Flagyl) are the recommended drugs; antibiotics are useless.

**HIV/AIDS** Any exposure to infected blood, blood products or bodily fluids may put an individual at risk for HIV. Infection can come from practicing unprotected sex with somebody who is infected or sharing contaminated needles. It is impossible to detect the HIV status of an otherwise healthy-looking person without a blood test.

A good resource for help and information is the US Centers for Disease Control AIDS hotline (☎ 800-342-2437).

## Cuts, Bites & Stings

Skin punctures can become infected in hot climates and may heal slowly. Treat cuts with an antiseptic such as Betadine. Where possible avoid bandages and Band-Aids, which can keep wounds wet.

Bee and wasp stings, unless you are allergic, are usually painful rather than dangerous. Calamine lotion gives relief, and ice packs reduce pain and swelling.

Some spiders have dangerous bites, and scorpion stings are very painful, but both are rarely fatal. Avoid bites by not using bare hands to turn over rocks or pieces of wood. There are no special first-aid techniques for spider or scorpion injuries. A black widow spider bite may be barely noticeable, but their venom can be dangerous. Seek medical attention if you think you've been bitten.

Bites from snakes do not cause instantaneous death, and antivenins are usually available. Seek medical help. Keep a healthy

Scorpion

distance away from snakes and watch where you step.

If you are bitten or stung, call Poison Control (☎ 800-222-1222). These are staffed 24 hours a day and advise about bites, stings and ingested poisons of all kinds. Call the listed number anywhere in the USA for the poison control nearest you.

After a snakebite, avoid slashing and sucking the wound, avoid tight tourniquets (a light constricting band above the bite can help), avoid ice, keep the affected area below the level of the heart and move it as little as possible. Don't ingest alcohol or drugs. Stay calm and get to a medical facility promptly.

If you are hiking far from help and you are bitten or stung, hike out and get help, particularly in the case of snake and spider bites. Often, reactions are delayed for up to 12 hours, and you can hike out before then. Hiking with a companion is recommended. Also see Dangers & Annoyances later in this chapter.

## WOMEN TRAVELERS
In general, exercise more vigilance in large cities than in rural areas. However, the vast expanses of Arizona can leave women traveling alone particularly vulnerable. Avoid hiking or camping alone. If staying at a motel, try to stay in one with interior corridors rather than at one where you park your car directly in front of the door to your room – ask if a motel has interior corridors when making a reservation.

In any emergency, call the police (☎ 911). In some rural areas where 911 is not active, dial ☎ 0 for the operator. Cities and larger towns have crisis centers and women's shelters that provide help and support; these are listed in the telephone directory, or the police can refer you to them.

At night avoid leaving your car to flag down help; turn on your hazard lights and wait for the police to arrive. Never open your car door to a stranger, even if he seems to be a cop, until you see proper identification through the window.

The headquarters for the National Organization for Women (NOW; ☎ 202-331-0066), 1000 16th St NW, Suite 700, Washington, DC 20036, is a good resource for any woman-related information and can refer you to state and local chapters; its website is www.now.org. Planned Parenthood (☎ 212-541-7800), 810 7th Ave, New York, NY 10019, can refer you to clinics throughout the country and offer advice on medical issues. Check the yellow pages under 'Women's Organizations & Services' for local resources.

## GAY & LESBIAN TRAVELERS
There are out gay people throughout the USA, but by far the most visible gay communities are in the major cities (in Arizona, the most active gay community is in the Phoenix area).

## Organizations & Resources
Though gay men and women will find it relatively easy to live their lives with a certain amount of openness, as you travel into the rural and often very conservative regions of Arizona it is much harder to be open. Gay travelers should be careful, *especially* in the predominantly rural areas – holding hands might get you bashed.

A couple of good national guidebooks are *Women's Traveller,* providing listings for lesbians, and *Damron's Address Book* for men, both published by the Damron Company (☎ 800-462-6654, 415-255-0404); information is available at www.damron .com. *Men's Travel* and *Women's Travel,* both published by Ferrari (☎ 602-863-2408) are international in scope, but also useful. All these guidebooks are available from good bookstores or the publishers. The Ferrari website, www.ferrariguides.com, is especially useful.

Another good resource is the Gay Yellow Pages (☎ 212-674-0120), PO Box 533, Village Station, NY 10014-0533, which has a national edition as well as regional editions.

National resource numbers include the National Gay and Lesbian Task Force (☎ 202-332-6483 in Washington, DC), and the Lambda Legal Defense Fund (☎ 212-995-995-8585 in New York City, 213-937-2728 in Los Angeles).

In Arizona, there are few gay organizations compared to coastal cities. They are listed under 'Gay & Lesbian Organizations' in the yellow pages of major cities' telephone directories.

## DISABLED TRAVELERS

Public buildings (including hotels, restaurants, theaters and museums) are now required by law to be wheelchair accessible and to have available rest room facilities. Public transportation services (buses, trains and taxis) must be made accessible to all, including those in wheelchairs, and telephone companies are required to provide relay operators for the hearing impaired.

Larger private and chain hotels have suites for disabled guests. Main car-rental agencies offer hand-controlled models at no extra charge. All major airlines, Greyhound buses and Amtrak trains allow service animals to accompany passengers and frequently sell two-for-one packages when attendants for seriously disabled passengers are required. Airlines also provide assistance for connecting, boarding and deplaning – just ask for assistance when making your reservation. (Note: Airlines must accept wheelchairs as checked baggage and have an onboard chair available, though some advance notice may be required on smaller aircraft.)

## Organizations & Resources

**Access-Able Travel Source**
(☎ 303-232-2979, fax 239-8486), PO Box 1796, Wheat Ridge, CO 80034
Access-Able has an excellent website with many links.
website: www.access-able.com

**Mobility International USA (MIUSA)**
(☎ 541-343-1284, fax 541-343-6812), PO Box 10767, Eugene, OR 97440
MIUSA primarily runs educational exchange programs, both in the USA and overseas.
website: www.miusa.org

**Moss Rehabilitation Hospital's Travel Information Service**
(☎ 215-456-9600, TTY 456-9602)

**Society for the Advancement of Travel for the Handicapped (SATH)**
(☎ 212-447-7284, fax 725-8253), 347 Fifth Ave

No 610, New York, NY 10016
email: sathtravel@aol.com

## SENIOR TRAVELERS

Though the age when the senior benefits begin varies with the attraction, travelers aged 50 years and older can expect to receive cut rates and benefits. Be sure to inquire about such rates at hotels, museums and restaurants.

The National Park Service (see Useful Organizations) issues Golden Age Passports that cut costs greatly for seniors.

## Organizations & Resources

**American Association of Retired Persons (AARP)**
(☎ 800-424-3410), 601 E St NW, Washington DC 20049
AARP is an advocacy group for Americans 50 years and older and is a good resource for travel bargains. US residents pay US$10 for annual membership (spouse included). Foreign residents should ask about membership.
website: www.aarp.org

**Elderhostel**
(☎ 617-426-8056), 75 Federal St, Boston, MA 02110-1941
This is a nonprofit organization that offers seniors the opportunity to attend academic college courses and tours throughout the USA and Canada. The programs last one to three weeks and include meals and accommodations. They are open to people 55 years and older and their companions.
website: www.elderhostel.org

**Grand Circle Travel**
(☎ 617-350-7500, 800-350-7500), 347 Congress St, Boston, MA 02210
This group offers escorted tours and travel information in a variety of formats, mainly for mature travelers.
website: www.gct.com

## TRAVEL WITH CHILDREN

Children receive discounts on anything ranging from motel stays to museum admissions. The definition of 'child' varies widely, from under 18 to under six.

Many hotels allow children to share a room with their parents for free or for a modest fee, though B&Bs rarely do and some don't allow children at all. More expensive hotels can arrange babysitting services or have 'kids' clubs' for younger children. Most buses and tours have discounted children's prices, though the discounts aren't substantial, and children under the age of two are allowed to travel free on most airlines. Car-rental companies provide infant seats for their cars on request; be sure to reserve one in advance, and to specify whether you want a rear-facing seat (for infants under 22 pounds and one year of age) or a forward-facing seat (for toddlers).

## USEFUL ORGANIZATIONS

For information on a very useful organization know as the American Automobile Association (AAA), refer to the Getting Around chapter.

### National Park Service (NPS)

The NPS, part of the Department of the Interior, administers almost all national parks, monuments and historic sites, and a few other areas. Visitors often can camp and hike in the bigger areas, but hunting and commercial activities like logging are prohibited in these protected sites. All have visitor centers with information (exhibits, films, park ranger talks, etc) explaining why that particular site has been preserved for posterity.

National parks often surround spectacular natural features and cover hundreds of square miles. National park campground and reservations information can be obtained by telephone (☎ 800-365-2267) or online at http://reservations.nps.gov. Lodges within parks, and motels and campgrounds near them, are privately owned. Details are given in the text.

Most NPS areas charge entrance fees, valid for seven days, of $6 to $20 per vehicle (usually half-price for walk-in or biking visitors). Additional fees are charged for camping and some other activities, depending on each park.

**Passes** Various passes can be obtained at the first park you visit. The National Parks Pass costs $50 annually and offers one-year entry into all national parks to the holder

and anyone in the holder's vehicle. Golden Age Passports cost $10 and allow permanent US residents aged 62 years and older unlimited free entry to all NPS sites, plus 50% discounts on camping and other fees. Golden Access Passports are free and give free admission to US residents who are legally blind or permanently disabled. Golden Eagle Passports cost $65 and are similar to National Park Passes but also allow entrance to BLM, USFS and USFWS with entrance fees.

### US Forest Service (USFS)

The USFS is part of the Department of Agriculture. National forests are less protected than parks, allowing commercial logging or privately owned recreational facilities in some areas. Forests are multiuse, with recreational activities such as hunting, fishing, snowmobiling, 4WD use and mountain biking permitted in many areas, unlike the NPS parks, where these activities are infrequently permitted. There are many forest campgrounds, which vary from simple sites with a fire ring and a pit toilet but no water to campgrounds with showers and sometimes limited RV hookups. Most sites are $6 to $14; a few without water are free.

Entrance into national forests is often free, although some of the most popular roads through the forest cost $2 to $5 (per vehicle) to drive through. Golden Eagle Passports are usually accepted.

Current information about national forests can be obtained from ranger stations, which are listed in the text. National forest campground and reservation information can be obtained by calling ☎ 800-280-2267 (☎ 800-280-CAMP).

### Bureau of Land Management (BLM)

The BLM, within the Department of the Interior, manages public use of many federal lands outside of the parks and forests. This includes grazing and mining leases as well as recreational uses. They may offer no-frills camping, often in untouched settings. Entrance fees are charged for a small number of BLM sites, and Golden Passports may be valid in some cases. Local information offices are detailed in the text.

## State Fish & Game Departments

Unlike the above organizations, fish & game departments are run by state governments. Information about seasons, licenses and other regulations is available the Arizona Fish & Game Department (☎ 602-942-3000), 2222 W Greenway Rd, Phoenix, AZ 85023-4313

## DANGERS & ANNOYANCES
### Crime

Always lock cars and put valuables out of sight, whether leaving the car for a few minutes or for longer, and whether you are in towns or backcountry. Rent a car with a lockable trunk. If your car is bumped from behind by another vehicle, keep going to a well-lit area, service station or even a police station.

Be aware of your surroundings and who may be watching you. Avoid walking dimly lit streets at night, particularly if you are alone. Avoid unnecessary displays of money or jewelry. Split up your money and credit cards to avoid losing everything and try to use ATM machines in well-trafficked areas.

In hotels, don't leave valuables lying around your room. Use safety deposit boxes or at least place valuables in a locked bag. Keep your door locked, and don't open your door to strangers – check the peephole or call the front desk if unexpected people are trying to enter.

### Weather

Flash floods and searing heat are the two most dangerous elements of Arizona weather. See the boxed text 'Flash Floods – A Deadly Danger in the Desert' and the Hiking and Backpacking Safety section in the Outdoor Activities chapter. Whether you are hiking or driving, always carry a minimum of 4 quarts of water per person a day. Furthermore, lightning during summer storms can be dangerous in Arizona. Avoid being in the open, especially on canyon rims or hilltops, or next to tall or metallic objects.

## Wildlife Big & Small

Drivers should watch for livestock on highways, especially on Indian reservations, which are generally unfenced, and in areas signed as 'Open Rangelands.' Hitting a cow (or a deer) at 65mph can total your car and kill the animal, and it might kill you as well. When camping in highlands where bears are present, follow instructions about not placing your food inside your tent.

Despite the large numbers of snakes, spiders, scorpions and other venomous creatures in Arizona, fatalities are very rare. This is partly because these animals tend to avoid humans and partly because their venom is designed to kill small animals rather than big ones like ourselves. If you are bitten or stung by one of these critters, refer to the Health section, earlier.

When hiking, watch where you are stepping, particularly on hot summer afternoons and evenings when rattlesnakes like to bask on the trail. These snakes are most easily identified by the 'rattle' of scales at the tip of the tail, which emit a rapid rattling sound when the snake is disturbed. Most rattlesnakes have roughly diamond-shaped patterns along their backs and vary in length from 2 to 6 feet. If you are bitten, you will experience rapid swelling, very severe pain and possible temporary paralysis, but rarely do victims die. Antivenin is available at hospitals.

Black widow spiders (identified by a red hourglass shape on the underside of the

Rattlesnake

abdomen) make very messy webs. Their bites are very painful but rarely fatal, except in young children. Again, antivenin is available. The large and hairy tarantulas rarely bite unless harassed; their bites are painful but not serious. Scorpions spend their days under rocks or woodpiles, so use caution when handling these. The long stinger curving up and around the back is characteristic of these animals. The stings can be very painful but are almost never fatal; again, small children are at highest risk. Centipedes bite occasionally, resulting in a painfully inflamed wound that lasts for about a day.

## EMERGENCIES

If you need any kind of emergency assistance, such as police, ambulance or firefighters, call ☎ 911. This is a free call from any phone. A few rural phones might not have this service, in which case you must dial ☎ 0 for the operator and ask for emergency assistance.

## LEGAL MATTERS

If you are stopped by the police for any reason, remember that there is no system of paying fines on the spot. Attempting to pay the fine to the officer is frowned upon at best and may lead to a charge of bribery to compound your troubles.

If you are arrested for more serious offenses, you are allowed to remain silent and are presumed innocent until proven guilty. Apart from identifying yourself, there is no legal mandate to speak to a police officer if you don't wish to. All persons who are arrested are legally allowed the right to make one phone call. If you don't have a lawyer or family member to help you, call your embassy. The police will give you the number upon request.

Driving laws vary slightly from state to state in the US, but some general rules are that you must be at least 16 years of age to drive (older in some states). In Arizona, you must be at least 18 years old (16 with parental consent) to obtain a driver's license. Speed limits are normally 55 to 75mph on interstates and freeways. Speed limits on other highways are 60mph or less, and in cities can vary from 25 to 45mph. Watch for school zones, where the speed limit can be as low as 15mph during school hours – these limits are strictly enforced.

Drivers and front-seat passengers are required to wear safety belts. Children under age five must use child restraints. You must be over 16 to obtain a motorcycle license. Motorcycle helmets are required for the rider and the passenger if under 18. The blood-alcohol concentration over which you are legally considered drunk while driving is 0.08%. You are considered guilty of a more serious drunk driving offense if your blood-alcohol concentration is over 0.15%.

For more information on other car-related topics, see the Getting Around chapter.

## BUSINESS HOURS

Generally speaking, business hours are from 9am to 5pm, but there are certainly no hard and fast rules. In large cities, a few supermarkets, restaurants and the main post office lobby are open 24 hours a day. Shops are usually open from 9 or 10am to 5 or 6pm, or until 9pm in shopping malls, except on Sunday, when hours are approximately noon to 5pm.

Post offices are open from 8am to 4 or 5:30pm Monday to Friday, and some are open from 8am to 3pm on Saturday.

Banks are usually open from either 9 or 10am to 5 or 6pm Monday to Friday. A few banks are open from 9am to 2 or 4pm on Saturday. Call individual banks for exact hours.

## PUBLIC HOLIDAYS

National public holidays are celebrated throughout the USA. Banks, schools and government offices (including post offices) are closed and ground transportation, some museums and other services are on a Sunday schedule. Air travel is especially difficult around these holidays, with Thanksgiving, Christmas, and Memorial and Labor Days being the busiest.

### January
**New Year's Day** January 1
**Martin Luther King Jr Day** Third Monday

### February
**Presidents' Day** Third Monday

### April
**Easter** A Sunday in early April, sometimes in late March

### May
**Memorial Day** Final Monday (honors the war dead; marks the unofficial beginning of the summer tourist season)

### July
**Independence Day** July 4

### September
**Labor Day** First Monday (honors working people; the unofficial end of the summer tourist season)

### October
**Columbus Day** Second Monday in October (a federal holiday, though celebrating Columbus' 'discovery' of America has become controversial)

### November
**Veterans Day** November 11
**Thanksgiving** Fourth Thursday in November

### December
**Christmas Day** December 25

## SPECIAL EVENTS
From highbrow arts festivals to down-home country fairs, from American Indian ceremonial dances to chile-cooking competitions, from duck races to hot-air balloon ascents, Arizona has literally hundreds of holidays, festivals and sporting events. As dates for these vary slightly from year to year, it's best to check local papers or chambers of commerce for precise dates.

### January
**Fiesta Bowl** January 1 – a major post-season college football game that's staged in Tempe, Arizona
**Professional Golf** – men's PGA (Professional Golfer's Association) tournaments include the Tucson Open in mid-January and the Phoenix Open in late January.

### February
**Quartzsite Gem & Mineral Show** – from late January to mid-February. Draws thousands of gem fans to this small Arizona town – be prepared to camp.

**Tucson Gem & Mineral Show** – first two weeks. One of the biggest in the country
**La Fiesta de los Vaqueros** – last Thursday to Sunday of February in Tucson. Begins with the world's largest nonmotorized parade, followed by a rodeo and other cowboy events – even the city's schools close for the last two days of what is locally called 'Rodeo Week.'

### March
**Wa:k Powwow Conference** – early March; hosted by the Tohono O'odham tribe in San Xavier del Bac Mission, near Tucson, is attended by members of many Southwestern Indian tribes; highlights include several days of dances, singing, food and other entertainment.

**Professional Golf** – women's PGA tournaments include the Tucson Open in mid-March and the Turquoise Classic, held in Phoenix in late March.

### May
**Santa Cruz Day** May 3 – dances at Cochiti and Taos Pueblos
**Cinco de Mayo** May 5 – the anniversary of Mexico's 1862 victory over the French in the Battle of Puebla, celebrated in many towns, especially those with a strong Hispanic heritage. Parades, dances, music, arts and crafts, street fairs and Mexican food are the order of the day.

### July
**Frontier Days** – first week. Prescott, Arizona, hosts one of the world's oldest professional rodeos plus other entertainment
**Independence Day** July 4 – American independence is celebrated in most Arizona towns with events including races, rodeos, arts and crafts fairs, ceremonial Indian dances, pageants, music festivals, pancake breakfasts, barbecues, picnics, country & western dancing and the obligatory parades and fireworks.

### August
**Payson Rodeo** – mid-August; another of the world's oldest rodeos is held in Payson, Arizona.

### September
**Navajo Nation Fair** – mid-September; held in Window Rock, it's the largest Indian fair in the country and offers a rodeo, parade, dances, songs, arts and crafts, food and more.

### October
**Halloween (All Hallows Eve)** October 31 – kids dress in costumes and, in safer neighborhoods, go 'trick-or-treating' for candy; some adults go to parties to act out their alter egos.

### November
**Day of the Dead** November 2 – a traditional Mexican celebration for families to honor dead relatives; often, breads and sweets are made

resembling skeletons, skulls and such, and graveyard visits are made.

**Thanksgiving** – third Thursday; this important
family gathering is celebrated with a bounty of
food (traditionally a turkey dinner with fall
harvest vegetables) and, more recently, Ameri-

can football games on TV; the following day is
considered the biggest shopping day of the year.

**December**

**Christmas** – festivities occur all month, including
Nativity pageants and festivals of lights in many
Southwestern towns.

## Visitors' Etiquette in Pueblos & on Reservations

Indian pueblos and reservations are governed by both federal and tribal law. Each tribe is independent and visitors should be aware that what is permitted on one reservation may be banned on
another. Language, customs and religious ceremonies differ from one reservation to the next.
Many Indians prefer to speak their own language and some don't speak English. Privacy is cher-
ished, both on an individual and community level. Visitors to pueblos and reservations are generally welcome, but they should behave in an appropriately courteous and respectful manner. Tribal
rules are often clearly posted at the entrance to each reservation, but here are a few guidelines.

**Photography & Other Recording** Many tribes ban all forms of recording, be it photography, video-
taping, audiotaping or drawing. Others permit these activities in certain areas only if you pay the
appropriate fee. If you wish to photograph a person, do so only after obtaining his or her permission. This also holds true for children. A posing tip is usually expected. Photographers who dis-
regard these rules can expect tribal police officers to confiscate their cameras and then escort them
off the reservation.

**Private Property** Do not walk into houses or climb onto roofs unless invited. Do not climb on ruins.
Kivas are always off-limits to visitors. Do not remove any kind of artifact. Off-road travel (foot,
horse or vehicle) is not allowed without a permit.

**Verbal Communication** It is considered polite to listen without comment, particularly when an
elder is speaking. Silent listening does not mean that the listener is ignoring the speaker; to the
contrary, intent listening is considered respectful. Be prepared for long silences in the middle of
conversations; such silences often indicate that a topic is under serious consideration.

**Ceremonials & Powwows** These are either open to the public or exclusively for tribal members.
Ceremonials are religious events. Applauding, chatting, asking questions or trying to talk to the
performers is rude. Photography and other recording are rarely permitted. While powwows also
hold spiritual significance, they are usually more informal. Many ceremonials and powwows don't
have a fixed date and are arranged a couple of weeks ahead of time. The tribal office can inform
you of upcoming events.

**Clothing** Modest dress is customary. Especially when watching ceremonials, you should dress con-
servatively. Halter or tank tops and miniskirts or short shorts are inappropriate.

**Alcohol** Most reservations ban the sale or use of alcohol. The Apache reservations are notable exceptions. Drugs are banned on all reservations.

**Eating** There are few restaurants. Especially during public ceremonials, visitors may be invited into
a house for a meal. Courteous behavior includes enjoying the food (of course!) but not lingering at
the table after your meal, because others are waiting. Tipping is not customary.

**Recreation** Activities such as backpacking, camping, fishing and hunting require tribal permits. On
Indian lands, state fishing or hunting licenses are not valid.

## WORK

Seasonal work is possible in national parks and other tourist sites; for information, contact park concessionaires or local chambers of commerce.

If you're coming from abroad and want to work in the USA, you need to apply for a work visa from the US embassy in your home country before you leave. The type of visa varies depending on how long you're staying and the kind of work you plan to do. Generally, you need either a J-1 visa, which you can obtain by joining a visitor-exchange program, or an H-2B visa, which you get when being sponsored by a US employer. The latter is not easy to obtain (since the employer has to prove that no US citizen or permanent resident is available to do the job); the former is issued mostly to students for work in summer camps.

## ACCOMMODATIONS

Arizona has a comprehensive range of accommodations, including free camping, developed campsites for tents and RVs, youth hostels, cheap and mid-range motels, B&Bs, expensive hotels, guest ranches and luxury resorts. For information on lodging taxes, see Money, earlier in this chapter.

### Camping

**Public Campgrounds** These are on public lands such as national forests, state and national parks and BLM land. The more developed areas may accept or require reservations. For USFS campground reservations, call ☎ 800-280-2267; for national parks call ☎ 800-365-2267. Credit cards are required.

Free dispersed camping (meaning you can camp almost anywhere) is permitted in many public backcountry areas in national forests and BLM lands, less so in national parks. Sometimes you can camp right from your car along a dirt road, and sometimes you can backpack your gear in. Information on where camping is permitted, and detailed maps, are available from many local ranger stations (contact details are in the text) and may be posted along the road. Sometimes a camping permit is required.

The less-developed sites are often on a first-come, first-served basis.

Camping in undeveloped areas, whether from your car or backpacking, entails basic responsibility (see Wilderness Camping in the Outdoor Activities chapter). Developed areas usually have toilets, drinking water, fire pits (or charcoal grills) and picnic benches. Some don't have drinking water. At any rate, it is always a good idea to have a few gallons of water in the vehicle if you are going to be out in the boonies. These basic campgrounds usually cost about $6 to $12 a night. More developed areas may have showers or recreational vehicle (RV) hookups. These cost more.

**Private Campgrounds** These are on private property and are usually close to or in towns. Most are designed with recreational vehicles (RVs) in mind. Fees given in the text are for two people per site. There is usually a charge of $1 to $3 per extra person, and state and city taxes apply. However, they may offer discounts for weeklong or monthlong stays. Private campgrounds often have many facilities lacking in public ones. These include hot showers, a coin laundry, a swimming pool, full RV hookups, a games area, a playground and often a convenience store. Kampgrounds of America (KOA; ☎ 406-248-7444) is a national network of private campgrounds with sites averaging $20; visit www.koa.com.

### Hostels

The US hostel network is less widespread than is in Canada, the UK, Europe and Australia, and is predominately in the coastal parts of the country. Not all hostels are affiliated with Hostelling International–American Youth Hostels (HI-AYH). Those that are offer discounts to HI-AYH members and allow nonmembers to stay for $3 more. Dormitory beds cost about $10 to $14 per person a night. Rooms are around $20 for one or two people, sometimes more. Annual membership is $25 for 18- to 54-year-olds, free for youths and $15 for seniors. Get further information from HI-AYH (☎ 202-

783-6161), 733 15th St NW, Suite 840, Washington, DC 20005. The HI-AYH website is at www.hiayh.org. There are many more independent hostels in Arizona that have comparable rates and conditions to HI-AYH hostels and may sometimes be better. The Internet Guide to Hostelling (www.hostels.com) lists hostels throughout the world.

## B&Bs

B&Bs all have breakfast included in their prices, but similarities stop there. A few establishments, with rooms for around $50, may have clean but unexciting rooms with a shared bathroom. Most B&Bs are pricier ($75 to $130, though some go over $200) and have rooms with private baths and, perhaps, amenities such as fireplaces, balconies and dining rooms with enticingly delicious breakfasts. Other places may be in historical buildings, quaint country houses or luxurious urban homes. Most B&Bs have fewer than ten rooms, and many don't accept pets or smokers.

## Motels & Hotels

The cheapest motel rooms are around $20 for a double. Prices vary tremendously from season to season. A double room for $50 in the high season may drop to $25 in the low and may raise its rates to $75 for a special event when the town is overflowing. A $290 per night luxury resort may offer special weekend packages for $89 in the low season. So be aware that the prices in this book are only an approximate guideline at best. Also, be prepared to add room tax to prices. Rates given are usually for one or two people; extra people are charged anywhere between $3 and $10 per person. A single room refers to one person, not two people in one bed.

Although high seasons and special events (when prices may rise) are indicated in the text, you never know when a convention may take over several hundred rooms and make beds temporarily hard to find. The prices advertised by hotels are called 'rack rates' and are not written in stone. If you simply ask about any specials that might apply, you can often save quite a bit of money. Members of AARP and AAA can qualify for a 'corporate' rate at several hotel chains.

Making phone calls directly from your hotel room may be expensive. Many motels allow free local calls, but fancier hotels may charge for them. Long-distance rates may be inflated 100% to 200%.

**Budget Motels** Motels with $20 rooms are found especially in small towns on major highways and in the motel strips of some larger towns. A quick drive through one of these will yield a selection of neon-lit signs such as '$19.95 for Two.' Take your pick.

Rooms are generally small, beds may be soft or saggy, but the sheets are usually clean. A minimally acceptable level of cleanliness is maintained, but expect scuffed walls, atrocious decor, old furniture and strange noises from your shower.

In smaller towns, cheap rooms may be acceptable 'mom-and-pop' type places, but in larger towns, the cheap motels may be in the least salubrious areas. Don't leave valuables out in your car, and exercise caution. Budget travelers shouldn't shun these $20-a-night cheapies, though single women may want to think twice about them.

**Motel & Hotel Chains** The many motel and hotel chains in the USA maintain a certain level of quality and style throughout the chain. It's partially true that 'If you've stayed in one, you've stayed in them all!' but, depending on location, there are certainly individual variations in both standards, amenities (some have pools) and, especially, prices. Many motels have at-the-door parking, with exterior doors. If, for safety reasons in particular, interior corridors are important to you, be sure to ask about it in advance.

The cheapest national chain is Motel 6, with small, clean, white and spartan rooms. Rooms start around $30 for a single in smaller towns, $40 to $50 in larger towns and $60 to $70 in some pricier destinations. Several motel chains, with rooms perhaps $5 to $20 more than a Motel 6, offer larger rooms, attractive decor and often little extras like a light continental breakfast, a refrigerator or a bathtub with your shower. These include Super 8 Motel, Econo Lodge, Howard Johnson and the less-common (and cheaper) Budget Host and Red Roof motels.

Stepping up to chains with rooms in the $45 to $90 range (or more, depending on location), you'll find noticeably nicer rooms; cafés, restaurants or bars may be on the premises or adjacent to them; and the swimming pool may be indoors with a Jacuzzi or exercise room also available. Days Inn properties are a good choice in this price range; Best Western motels are ubiquitous but inconsistent.

The Choice Hotel network (www.choice hotels.com) operates Sleep Inns, Comfort Inns or Suites, Quality Inns and Clarion Hotels. Rooms are spacious, and well-appointed, and continental-plus breakfasts are offered. These rooms tend to be in the $50 to $120 range, depending on season. The Holiday Inn, Howard Johnson and Ramada Inn chains now have 'Express' hotels that are comparable in price to the Choice Hotel network. Because these are new buildings, they are often the nicest chain hotel in a town, and most have interior corridors.

Other more expensive and consistently reliable hotels are less widespread in the Arizona, usually found only in large towns, and include Courtyard or Fairfield Inn by Marriott, Hampton Inn, Hilton, Holiday Inn, La Quinta, Marriott, Radisson, Ritz Carlton and Sheraton.

**Private Hotels & Cabins** There are, of course, nonchain establishments in all these price ranges. Some of them are funky historical hotels, full of turn-of-the-century furniture and artifacts. Others are privately run establishments that just don't want to be a part of a chain. In smaller towns, complexes of cabins are available – these often come complete with fireplace, kitchen and an outdoor area with trees and maybe a stream a few steps away.

Another choice is self-contained condo units, which are apartments (flats) with kitchen and laundry facilities. They often have two or more bedrooms, and are designed for longer stays for groups or families. These places don't always have hotel services such as daily maids.

**Full-Service Hotels** If you want bellhops and doormen, restaurants and bars, exercise rooms and saunas, room service and concierge, splurge when you hit the big urban areas because they are otherwise few and far between.

## Lodges

In national parks, you can either camp or stay in park lodges operated as concessions. Restaurants are on the premises, and tour services are often available. National park lodges are not cheap, with most rooms going for around $100 or more for a double during the high season, but they are your only option if you want to stay inside the park without camping. A lot of people want to do that, so many lodges are fully booked in advance. Want a room today? Call anyway – you might be lucky and hit on a cancellation. But your best bet for national park lodges, especially in the high season, is to make reservations well ahead.

## Resorts & Guest Ranches

Luxury resorts and dude ranches really require a stay of several days to be appreciated and are often destinations in themselves. Guests at a luxury resort can start the day with a round of golf, then continue with a choice of tennis, massage, horseback riding, shopping, beauty treatments, swimming, sunbathing, hot tubbing, drinking and dancing. Guest ranches are even more like 'whole vacations,' with busy schedules of horseback riding and maybe cattle roundups, rodeo lessons, cookouts and other Western activities. Ranches in the desert lowlands may close in summer, while those in the mountains may close in winter or convert into skiing centers.

## Reservations

Chain hotels take reservations days or months ahead. Normally, you have to give a credit card number to hold the room if you plan a late arrival. If you don't show and don't call to cancel, you will be charged the first night's rental. Cancellation policies vary – some let you cancel at no charge 24 hours or 72 hours in advance; others are less forgiving. Chains often have a toll-free reservation number or website, but their central reservation system might not be aware of local special discounts.

Chain hotels are listed and marked on city maps in this book for your convenience, but other details are not given. Contact them as follows:

| | |
|---|---|
| Best Western | ☎ 800-937-8376 www.bestwestern.com |
| Budget Host | ☎ 800-283-4678 www.budgethost.com |
| Clarion Hotel | ☎ 800-252-7466 www.clarionhotel.com |
| Comfort Inn | ☎ 800-228-5150 www.comfortinn.com |
| Courtyard by Marriott | ☎ 800-321-2211 www.courtyard.com |
| Days Inn | ☎ 800-329-7666 www.daysinn.com |
| Econo Lodge | ☎ 800-553-2666 www.econolodge.com |
| Fairfield Inn by Marriott | ☎ 800-228-2800 www.fairfieldinn.com |
| Hampton Inn | ☎ 800-426-7866 www.hampton-inn.com |
| Hilton | ☎ 800-445-8667 www.hilton.com |
| Holiday Inn | ☎ 800-465-4329 www.holiday-inn.com |
| Howard Johnson | ☎ 800-446-4656 www.hojo.com |
| La Quinta | ☎ 800-531-5900 www.laquinta.com |
| Marriott | ☎ 800-228-9290 www.marriott.com |
| Motel 6 | ☎ 800-466-8356 www.motel6.com |
| Quality Inn | ☎ 800-228-5151 www.qualityinn.com |
| Radisson | ☎ 800-333-3333 www.radisson.com |
| Ramada | ☎ 800-272-6232 www.ramada.com |
| Red Roof Inn | ☎ 800-843-7663 www.redroof.com |
| Ritz-Carlton | ☎ 800-241-3333 www.ritzcarlton.com |
| Sheraton | ☎ 800-325-3535 www.sheraton.com |
| Sleep Inn | ☎ 800-753-3746 www.sleepinn.com |
| Super 8 Motel | ☎ 800-800-8000 www.super8.com |
| Travel Lodge | ☎ 800-578-7878 www.travelodge.com |

## FOOD

This book's restaurant listings provide a good cross-section of possibilities for everybody, including 24-hour restaurants, funky local places where townsfolk gather for breakfast, ice cream parlors, restaurants with an interesting history, and, of course, the various ethnic, Mexican, nouvelle Southwestern and swank uptown possibilities. You can count on every town having several fast-food places, usually on the main drag, their neon-lit logos visible from many blocks away; the Denny's chain serves food 24 hours a day. Supermarkets, many open late or for 24 hours, are shown on city maps for the convenience of travelers.

Many authentic, inexpensive restaurants serve delicious Mexican fare. In small towns, your best choice is often between Mexican and American food – only in the bigger cities and resort areas will you find large varieties of ethnic dining and fine Continental cuisine.

Mexican food is often hot and spicy, but it doesn't have to be. If you don't like spicy food, go easy on the salsa and you'll find plenty to choose from (see the glossary, following). In Arizona, Mexican food is of the Sonoran type, with dishes like *carne seca* being a specialty. Meals are usually served with refried beans, rice, and flour or corn tortillas, and the chiles used are relatively mild.

And then, of course, there's *nouvelle* Southwestern cuisine, an eclectic mix of Mexican and Continental (especially French) traditions that began to flourish in the 1970s. This is your chance to sample innovative combinations such as chiles stuffed with lobster or barbecued duck tacos. But don't expect any bargains here.

Native American food is not readily available in restaurants. More often, you'll be able to sample it from food stands at state fairs, powwows, rodeos and other outdoor events in the region. The variety is quite limited. The most popular is fry bread (deep-fried cakes of flattened dough), which may be topped with honey or other delights. Navajo tacos are fry bread topped with a combination of beans, cheese, tomato, lettuce, onion or chile – and sometimes with ground beef.

## Southwestern Food Glossary

Arizona, New Mexico and Texas, each with distinct regional differences, all offer what is commonly referred to as 'southwestern food,' a general term for a variety of Mexican, Spanish and Indian influenced dishes. Below is a general description of common dishes travelers will encounter all over Arizona.

*burrito* (or *burro*) – a soft flour tortilla folded around a choice of chicken, beef, chile, bean or cheese filling. A breakfast burrito is stuffed with scrambled eggs, potatoes and ham. (A burro is a large burrito.)

*carne adobada* – pork chunks marinated in spicy chile and herb sauce, then baked.

*carne seca* – beef that has been dried in the sun before cooking.

*chile relleno* – chile stuffed with cheese and deep-fried in a light batter.

*chimichanga* – a burrito that is deep-fried to make the tortilla crisp.

*enchilada* – a rolled corn tortilla stuffed with a choice of sour cream and cheese, beans, beef or chicken, and smothered with a red (or green) chile sauce and melted cheese.

*fajitas* – marinated beef or chicken strips, grilled with onions and bell peppers, and served with tortillas, salsa, beans and guacamole.

*flauta* – similar to a burrito but smaller and tightly rolled rather than folded, and then fried.

*guacamole* – mashed avocado seasoned with lime juice and cilantro, and optionally spiced with chopped chiles and other condiments.

*huevos rancheros* – fried eggs on a soft tortilla, covered with chile sauce and melted cheese, and served with beans.

*menudo* – spicy tripe soup; a hangover remedy.

*mole* – a mildly spicy, dark sauce of chiles flavored with chocolate, usually served with chicken.

*nachos* – tortilla chips covered with melted cheese and other toppings.

*pozole* – a corn stew (similar to hominy in other states), which may be spicy and have meat.

*refried beans* – a thick paste of mashed, cooked pinto beans fried with lard.

*salsa* – a cold dip or sauce of chopped chiles, pureed tomatoes, onions and other herbs and spices.

*sopaipilla* – deep-fried puff pastry served with honey as a dessert.

*taco* – a crispy, fried tortilla, folded in half and stuffed with a combination of beans, ground beef, chiles, onions, tomatoes, lettuce, grated cheese and guacamole.

*tamale* – slightly sweet corn dough *(masa)* stuffed with a choice of pork, beef, chicken, chile or olives (or nothing) and wrapped in a corn husk before being steamed.

*tortilla* – a pancake made of unleavened wheat or corn flour. They stay soft when baked, become crisp when fried, and form the basis of most Mexican dishes. Small pieces, deep-fried, become the crispy tortilla chips served with salsa as an appetizer (often at no extra cost) in many Mexican restaurants.

*tostada* – a flat (ie, open-faced) taco.

## DRINKS
### Nonalcoholic

Restaurants provide customers with free ice water (tap water is safe to drink). All the usual flavors of soft drinks are available. Many restaurants offer milk or juices; a few have a wide variety of fruit juices. British travelers should remember that 'lemonade' is a lemon-sugar-ice water mix rather than the carbonated variety.

Coffee is served much more often than tea. Most restaurants offer several free coffee refills to customers eating a meal. Drinkers of English-style tea will be disappointed. Tea is usually a cup of hot water with a tea bag next to it – milk is not normally added but a slice of lemon often is.

Herb teas are offered in better restaurants and coffee shops.

## Alcoholic

Bland and boring 'name brand' domestic beers are available everywhere alcohol is sold. Most stores, restaurants and bars also offer much tastier but lesser known local brews, which may cost more than a Bud, but are worth it. Imported beers, especially Mexican brands, are also easily available and, although a little more expensive, offer a wider choice of flavors than do domestic brands.

Wine drinkers interested in experimenting will find little-known wineries in Arizona. A few of these offer tours and wine tasting and are mentioned in the text.

## Alcohol & Drinking Age

Persons under the age of 21 (minors) are prohibited from consuming alcohol. Carry a driver's license or passport as proof of age to enter a bar, order alcohol at a restaurant or buy alcohol. Servers have the right to ask to see your ID and may refuse service without it. Minors are not allowed in most bars and pubs, even to order nonalcoholic beverages. Unfortunately, this means that most dance clubs are also off-limits to minors, although a few clubs have solved the under-age problem with a segregated drinking area. Minors are, however, welcome in the dining areas of restaurants where alcohol is served.

Beer, wine and spirits are sold in grocery stores from 6 am to midnight except Sunday, when sales begin at 10am. Restaurants must have licenses to serve alcohol; some licenses are limited to beer and wine. Bars close at 2am and the sale of alcohol in them stops at 1am. Alcohol is prohibited on most Indian reservations.

## ENTERTAINMENT
### Cinemas

Most sizable towns have multiscreen cinemas showing a variety of first-run Hollywood flicks on two to eight screens. Only the bigger towns have one or two independent cinemas screening foreign, alternative or underground films.

## Nightlife

In small Arizona towns, a bar might be the best place in town to have a beer, meet some locals, shoot a game of pool or listen to a country & western band. Patrons usually take an interest upon hearing a foreign accent, so if you have one, this is a good opportunity to meet people. Bars in bigger towns offer anything from big TV screens showing sporting events to live music of various genres.

## Performing Arts

The main cultural centers are cited under Arts in the Facts about Arizona chapter. In addition, smaller towns may have amateur theatrical performances. These include Indian pageants, vaudeville shows with audience participation (boo the villain, cheer the hero), mystery crime weekends (where a hotel becomes the scene of a hideous 'crime' and guests are both suspects and sleuths) and standard dramatic performances.

## Gambling

The gambling laws in the state of Arizona are complicated. Casino gambling is illegal, but you can buy lottery tickets, bet on horse and dog races, and take part in bingo games organized by local church groups. Indian reservations have their own laws, and increasing numbers of tribes have been opening casinos in the past few years. Arizona state leaders are not happy with this and threaten to take the tribes to federal court if necessary. The Feds, however, seem to be leaning in favor of allowing the Indians to do what they want on the reservations, as long as they keep within federal laws. To avoid lawsuits, the tribes and the state recently agreed to permit casinos under a 10-year 'compact' in which gamblers could compete with machines or each other, but not against a dealer. Hence, games like blackjack (21) are not allowed, but poker, video keno, bingo and slot machines are.

About 20 casinos operate on reservations throughout the state, attracting good-sized crowds of locals who don't have the time or money to make it to Las Vegas. Only the two Apache casinos serve alcohol.

## SPECTATOR SPORTS

Sports in the USA developed separately from the rest of the world, and baseball, American football and basketball dominate the sports scene, both for spectators and participants. Soccer has made limited inroads, and remains a relatively minor diversion.

Arizona has a few nationally ranked teams playing the big three US professional sports. Tickets for these events are hard to get, although you might be lucky. Scalpers sell overpriced tickets outside the stadiums before a game. The Arizona Cardinals of Phoenix play National League Football, and the Arizona Diamondbacks of Phoenix are a major league baseball team. Several other major league baseball teams come from the wintry north in February and March for

## Rodeo: A Western Ritual

Rodeo, from the Spanish word meaning 'roundup,' began with the cowboys of the Old West. As they used to say, 'There was never a horse that couldn't be rode – and never a rider that couldn't be thrown.' Naturally, cowboys riding half-wild horses eventually competed to determine who was the best. The speed with which they could rope a calf also became a competitive skill.

Rodeo as we know it today began in the 1880s. The first rodeo to offer prize money was held in Texas in 1883, and the first to begin charging admission to the event was in Prescott, Arizona, in 1888. Since then, rodeo has developed into both a spectator and professional sport under the auspices of the Professional Rodeo Cowboys Association (PRCA). Despite rodeo's recognition as a professional sport, very few cowboys earn anywhere near as much as other professional athletes.

For the first-time spectator, the action is full of thrills and spills but may be a little hard to understand. Within the arena, the main participants are cowboys and cowgirls, judges (who are usually retired rodeo competitors) and clowns. Although the clowns perform amusing stunts, their function is to help out the cowboys when they get into trouble. During the bull riding, they are particularly important if a cowboy gets thrown. Then clowns immediately rush in front of the bull to distract the animal, while the winded cowboy struggles out of the arena.

While men are the main contenders in a rodeo, women also compete, mainly in barrel racing, team roping and calf roping.

Each rodeo follows the same pattern, and once you know a few pointers, it all begins to make sense. The first order of the day is the grand entry, during which all contestants, clowns and officials parade their horses around the arena, raise the US flag and sing the national anthem. The rodeo then begins and usually includes seven events, which are often in the following order:

**Bareback Bronc Riding** A rider must stay on a randomly assigned bucking bronco (a wild horse) for eight seconds. This might not seem long from a comfortable seat in the stands, but from the back of a horse it can seem like an eternity. The cowboy holds on with one hand to a handle strapped around the horse just behind its shoulders. His other hand is allowed to touch nothing but air; otherwise he's disqualified. His spurs must be up at the height of the horse's shoulders when the front hooves hit the ground on the first jump out of the chute, and he must keep spurring the horse during the ride. Two judges give up to 25 points to both the horse and the rider, for a maximum possible total of 100. A good ride is one in which the horse bucks wildly and the rider stays on with style – a score of over 70 is good.

**Calf Roping** This is a timed event. A calf races out of a chute, followed closely by a mounted cowboy with a rope loop. The cowboy ropes the calf (usually by throwing the loop over its head, although a leg catch is legal), hooks the rope to the saddle horn and dismounts, keeping the rope tight all the way to the calf. Watch the horse as the cowboy goes to the calf. A well-trained horse will stand still and hold the rope taut to make the cowboy's job less difficult. When he reaches the

training seasons in the warm climate of Phoenix (see the boxed text 'Major League Baseball's Spring Training: Cactus League' in the Phoenix chapter).

Professional basketball is well represented, with the Phoenix Suns (men) and Phoenix Mercury (women). College basketball is always popular – fans seem to enjoy watching the students as much as they do the pros. Currently, the University of Arizona Wildcats (from Tucson) are the highest-ranked Southwestern team, consistently placing among the top 25 college teams in the nation.

Rodeo is popular throughout the Southwest, and Arizona is no exception. Generally speaking, the rodeo season runs from late spring to early fall. Rodeo circuits

## Rodeo: A Western Ritual

calf, the cowboy throws the animal down, ties three of its legs together with a 6-foot-long 'piggin string' and throws up his hands to show he's done. A good roper can do the whole thing in under eight seconds.

**Saddle-Bronc Riding** This has similar rules to the bareback event and is scored the same way. In addition to starting with the spurs up above the horse's shoulders and keeping one hand in the air, the cowboy must keep both feet in the stirrups. Dismounting from the saddle of a bucking bronco is not easy – watch the two pickup men riding alongside to help the contestant off. This demands almost as much skill as the event itself.

**Steer Wrestling** In this event (also called 'bull-dogging'), a steer that may weigh as much as 700lb runs out of a chute, tripping a barrier line, which is the signal for two cowboys to pursue the animal. One cowboy – the hazer – tries to keep the steer running in a straight line, while the other cowboy – the wrestler – rides alongside the steer and jumps off his horse trying to grip the steer's head and horns – all of this happens at speeds approaching 40mph. The wrestler must then wrestle the enormous steer to the ground. The best cowboys can accomplish this feat in under five seconds.

**Barrel Racing** Three large barrels are set up in a triangle, and the rider must race around them in a cloverleaf pattern. The turns are incredibly tight, and the racer must come out of them at full speed to do well. There's a five-second penalty for tipping over a barrel. Good times are around 15 to 17 seconds.

**Team Roping** A team of two horseback ropers pursues a steer running out of the chute. The first roper must catch the steer by the head or horns and then wrap the rope around the saddle horn. The second team member then lassos the steer's two rear legs in one throw. Good times are under seven seconds.

**Bull Riding** Riding a bucking and spinning 2000lb bull is wilder and more dangerous than bronc riding, and it is often the crowd's favorite event. Using one heavily gloved hand, the cowboy holds on to a rope that is wrapped around the bull. And that's it – nothing else to hold on to, and no other rules apart from staying on for eight seconds and not touching the bull with your free hand. Scoring is the same as for bronc riding.

sponsored by the Professional Rodeo Cowboy Association (PRCA) draw competitors from many western states. You can find a thorough listing of Arizona rodeo events at www.azlife.net.

## SHOPPING

The main items of interest to travelers are Indian, Hispanic and Southwestern arts and crafts. Often, the dividing line between traditional tribal or Hispanic crafts and Southwestern art is a hazy one, with the latter often being heavily influenced by the former. Tribal crafts, too, have changed somewhat in response to what travelers want to buy.

Buying Indian crafts on reservations, directly from the makers, is often substantially cheaper than buying in off-reservation gift shops. However, the latter afford the buyer a greater selection and, in the best stores, knowledgeable sales staff who have chosen the finest quality work and can tell you about it. Buying from roadside stands in reservations can be fun, and you know that you are avoiding the middleman, but it's definitely a case of 'buyer beware' – the quality will vary tremendously.

Various tribes are especially known for particular crafts, though, again, there is much overlap between them. Just about all of them make beautiful jewelry, for example. Navajo weavings are highly sought after (see the boxed text 'Navajo Weaving' in the Northeastern Arizona chapter). The Hopis are famed for their kachina dolls (see 'Kachinas' in the Northeastern Arizona chapter). The Tohono O'odham of southern Arizona are famed for their intricate basketwork, which requires many days of labor and is therefore not cheap.

Hispanic art includes religious paintings and altarpieces called *retablos*, brightly painted handmade wooden furniture, metal work (especially tin, copper and wrought iron) and fine art such as paintings and sculptures.

Off the reservations, gift shops and trading posts in all the major and many of the smaller cities have good selections of Indian and Hispanic crafts and their spinoff, Southwestern art. This can vary from tacky to breathtaking, from utilitarian to completely decorative. Towns renowned for art galleries include Scottsdale, Sedona, Tubac and Bisbee.

 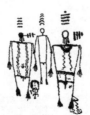

# Outdoor Activities

For many of the millions of people who visit Arizona, especially for the first time, the sheer scale and grandeur of the scenery viewed from vehicle windows and scenic overlooks is reward enough. Locals, however, know that the state offers a multitude of world-class outdoor activities.

## GENERAL BOOKS & RESOURCES

Of the thousands of books about hiking, climbing, rafting, canyoneering, bicycling and other activities in Arizona, some general ones are mentioned in relevant parts of this chapter. Books about a specific place are mentioned in the appropriate parts of the text. Most of the books have extensive bibliographies. Outdoor equipment stores, as well as bookstores, will have many of these and other books.

*Adventuring in Arizona,* by John Annerino, gives a selection of hikes, car tours, river expeditions, climbs and canyoneering adventures all around the state.

Many outdoor activities are described on the Internet. One of the most wide-ranging sites is Great Outdoors Recreation Pages at www.gorp.com. For information about activities and permits in national parks, browse the National Park Service (NPS) website at www.nps.gov (with links to every park). Other lands are managed by the US Forest Service (USFS), Bureau of Land Management (BLM) and state wildlife and fisheries departments. The Federal Government has a website (www.recreation.gov) with detailed information about federally owned public lands, including forests, BLM areas and national wildlife refuges. See Useful Organizations in the Facts for the Visitor chapter for more details.

## HIKING & BACKPACKING

If you have transportation, you can find perfect hiking and backpacking at any time of year. When highland trails are blanketed in snow, southern Arizona delights in balmy weather, and when temperatures hit the hundreds during Phoenix summers, cooler mountain trails beckon. Of course, hardy and experienced backpackers can don cross-country skis or snowshoes and head out into the mountains in winter as well.

### Planning

Perhaps the most attractive backpacking trip for many visitors is the descent into the Grand Canyon. This trip in particular requires careful advance planning because the number of backpackers is limited by the number of campsites available. Reservations are essential for most months of the year and details are given in the Grand Canyon chapter.

Visitors can also hike and backpack in many other public areas, especially in national forests, BLM lands and state parks. Addresses and phone numbers of individual state parks and USFS or BLM ranger stations are given in the text. These places are less famous than the national parks, and usually there is no problem with just showing up and going backpacking. These areas are generally less restricted for wilderness camping than the national parks.

### Books & Maps

*Arizona Day Hikes: A Guide to the Best Trails from Tucson to the Grand Canyon,* by Dave Ganci covers day hikes in Arizona. For suggestions about hiking the desert as safely and comfortably as possible, read Ganci's *Desert Hiking.* Falcon Press publishes a series of hiking guides, including *The Hiker's Guide to Arizona,* by Stewart Aitchison and Bruce Grubbs. Lonely Planet's *Hiking in the USA* covers the whole country and includes a section on major hikes in the Southwest generally and Arizona specifically. There are hundreds of books about smaller areas, covering one national park or mountain range, for example. The best are mentioned in the text.

A good map is essential for any hiking trip. NPS visitor centers and USFS ranger

## The Arizona Trail

Proposed by Flagstaff hiker and teacher Dale Shelwater in the mid-1980s, this 790-mile trail running from the Mexican border to the Utah state line is finally becoming a reality. About 600 miles of the trail have been completed and most of it is open, though some work, such as signing, remains to be done. This is a non-motorized trail, designed mainly for hikers and, in some spots, cross-country skiers or snowshoers in winter.

Meanwhile, most of the trail remains quite an adventure because no trail guide, as such, exists. Bits and pieces of the trail are described in various hiking books, but the best single source of information is the Arizona Trail Association (☎ 602-252-4794), PO Box 36736, Phoenix, AZ 85067; visit www.aztrail.org. There are 44 sections of trail, each with a trailhead that can be reached by vehicle, and the ATA has planning maps and information sheets about those sections that are open.

The trail varies from desert to pine forest and from canyon to mountain. (A side trail reaches Arizona's highest point, Humphreys Peak, at 12,633 feet.) Depending on the time of year, there is always a part of the trail where weather conditions are ideal for hiking. Parts of the trail, such as crossing the Grand Canyon via the Bright Angel and North Kaibab Trail, can be quite busy and require advance permits, and other areas are remote and lightly traveled and don't require a permit. There's something for everyone.

stations usually stock topographical maps that cost $3 to $7. Apart from these, local bookstores and outdoor equipment stores often sell maps. There are many free planning maps available from the national parks that may not be adequate for the trip itself.

Longer hikes require two types of maps: USGS quadrangles and USFS maps. To order a map index and price list, contact the US Geological Survey (☎ 888-275-8747), PO Box 25286, Denver, CO 80225. The website (www.usgs.gov) has links to map stores throughout the United States. For general information on maps, see the Facts for the Visitor chapter; for information regarding specific maps of forests, wilderness areas or national parks, see the appropriate geographic entry.

## Minimizing Your Impact

Backcountry areas are composed of fragile environments and cannot support an inundation of human activity, especially any insensitive and careless activity. A new code of backcountry ethics is evolving to deal with the growing numbers of people in the wilderness. Most conservation organizations and hikers' manuals have their own set of backcountry codes, all of which outline the same important principles: minimizing the impact on the land, leaving no trace and taking nothing but photographs and memories. To avoid erosion, be sure to stay on the main trail.

## Wilderness Camping

Camping in undeveloped areas is rewarding for its peacefulness but raises special concerns. Take care to ensure that the area you choose can comfortably support your presence, and leave the surroundings in at least as good condition as when you arrived. The following list of guidelines should help:

• Camp below timberline, since alpine areas are generally more fragile. Good campsites are found, not made. Altering a site shouldn't be necessary.

• Camp at least 200 feet (70 adult steps) away from the nearest lake, river or stream.

• Bury human waste in cat holes dug 6 to 8 inches deep, at least 200 feet from water, camp or trails. The salt and minerals in urine attract deer; use a tent-bottle (funnel attachments are available for women) if you are prone to middle-of-the-night calls by Mother Nature. Camouflage the cat hole when finished.

• Use soaps and detergents sparingly or not at all, and never allow these things to enter streams or lakes. When washing yourself (a backcountry luxury, not a necessity), lather up (with biodegradable soap) and rinse yourself with cans of water 200 feet away from your water source. Scatter dishwater after removing all food particles.

- Some folks recommend carrying a lightweight stove for cooking and using a lantern instead of a campfire.

- If a fire is allowed and appropriate, dig out the native topsoil and build a fire in the hole. Gather sticks no larger than an adult's wrist from the ground. Do not snap branches off live, dead or downed trees. Pour wastewater from meals around the perimeter of the campfire to prevent the fire from spreading, and thoroughly douse it before leaving or going to bed.

- Burn cans to remove odors, then take them from the ashes and pack them out.

- Pack out what you pack in, including all trash. Make an effort to carry out trash left by others, as well.

- In bear country, do not bring food inside your tent. Either place it in supplied bear-proof containers, or hang it at least 10 feet off the ground between two trees..

## Safety

The major forces to be reckoned with while hiking and camping are the weather (which is uncontrollable) and your own frame of mind. Be prepared for some unpredictable weather, such as heavy downpours that can cause deadly flash floods (see the boxed text 'Flash Floods – A Deadly Danger in the Desert'). In Arizona, the most frequent weather problem is the heat. People die of dehydration every year. A gallon of water per person per day is the recommended minimum in hot weather; more if you are working up a real sweat. This will have to be carried in waterless areas. Sun protection (brimmed hats, dark glasses and sunblock) are all basic parts of a desert hiker's equipment. If you are not an experienced hiker, don't head out into the wilderness for five days; stick to day hikes.

The most stringent safety measures suggest that you never hike alone, but solo travelers should not be discouraged, especially if they value solitude. The important thing is to always let someone know where you are going and how long you plan to be gone. Use sign-in boards at trailheads and ranger stations. Travelers looking for hiking companions can inquire or post notices at ranger stations, outdoors stores, campgrounds, and youth hostels.

People with little hiking or backpacking experience should not attempt to do too much too soon, or they might end up being nonhikers for the wrong reasons. Know your limitations, know the route you are planning to take and pace yourself accordingly. Remember, there is absolutely nothing wrong with turning back or not going as far as you originally had planned to hike.

Beginners should refer to one of the many books available about how to go backpacking. Chris Townsend's *The Backpacker's Handbook* is a beefy collection of tips for the trail. More candid is *A Hiker's Companion,* by Cindy Ross and Todd Gladfelter, who hiked 12,000 miles before sitting down to write.

An excellent overview is *Hiking & Backpacking: A Complete Guide,* by Karen Berger. *How to Shit in the Woods* is Kathleen Meyer's explicit, comic and useful manual on wilderness 'toilet' training for adults.

## Canyoneering

At its simplest, canyoneering is visiting canyons under your own power. A canyoneer's adventures can vary from a pleasant day hike to a multiday walking excursion stretching the length of a canyon. Longer trips may involve rock climbing with ropes, swimming across pools and down waterfalls, and camping; many experienced canyoneers bring inflatable mattresses to float their backpacks on as well as to sleep on. Some canyon areas designated as 'wilderness' are very remote, as no development is allowed. Canyoneers must reach the edges of these areas by dirt roads and then continue on foot over poor or barely existent trails to canyon bottoms.

Arizona, along with its northern neighbor Utah, provides some of the best canyoneering anywhere. The first canyoneers in the huge gashes of the Colorado Plateau were Native Americans, whose abandoned cliff dwellings and artifacts mark their passage. Adventurers and

## Flash Floods: A Deadly Danger in the Desert

A flash flood can occur when a very large amount of rain falls suddenly and quickly. This is most common in the Southwest during the 'monsoon months' of mid-July to early September, although heavy precipitation in late winter can also cause these floods. They occur with little warning and reach a raging peak in a matter of minutes. Rainfall occurring miles away is funneled into a normally dry wash or canyon from the surrounding mountains, and a wall of water several feet high can appear seemingly out of nowhere. There are few warning signs – perhaps some distant rain clouds – and if you see a flash flood coming, the only recommendation is to reach higher ground as quickly as possible.

A swiftly moving wall of water is much stronger than it appears. At only a foot high, it will easily knock over a strong adult. A 2-foot-high flood sweeps away vehicles. Floods carry a battering mixture of rocks and trees and can be extremely dangerous. August 1997 was a particularly bad month for flash floods. One event, in Antelope Canyon on the Arizona-Utah border, killed 11 hikers. Another, near Kingman, Arizona, was strong enough to derail an Amtrak passenger train. In a third, several hundred locals and visitors were evacuated by helicopter from the village of Supai in the Havasupai Indian Reservation. The following September, a Capitol Reef National Park ranger had his pickup truck swept away and completely submerged in a flood (the ranger jumped out in time). There were many other flash floods during this period.

Especially during the monsoon season, heed local warnings and weather forecasts, and avoid camping in sandy washes and canyon bottoms – the likeliest spots for flash floods. Campers and hikers are not the only victims; every year foolhardy drivers attempt to drive across flooded roads and are swept away. Flash floods usually subside fairly quickly. A road that is closed will often be passable later on the same day.

explorers in the 19th and 20th centuries sought to unravel the many secrets of the canyons. The most famous was John Wesley Powell, the one-armed geologist who led the first boat descent of the Colorado River.

Today the Grand Canyon is the most popular place for canyoneering, with thousands of hikers descending from the rim every year. Many other canyons, however, are more difficult to access and provide uncrowded and equally scenic challenges. One of the most remote and lovely areas is the rarely visited **Sycamore Canyon Wilderness**, about 16 miles due west of the heavily traveled Oak Creek Canyon near Sedona. It takes three days to hike, scramble and wade the canyon's 25-mile length; Coconino National Forest rangers in Sedona or Flagstaff can provide information. In the same forest, the **Wet Beaver Creek Wilderness** (east of Camp Verde) provides an even more challenging three-day canyoneering adventure; you'll need to swim through more than 20 ponds, so be sure to bring a flotation device; rangers will have details about these remote, difficult trips.

Then there are the slot canyons, hundreds of feet deep and only a few feet wide. These must be negotiated during the dry months, because summer monsoon rains can cause deadly flash floods that may raise the height of the river by many feet in mere minutes. Always check with the appropriate rangers for weather and safety information. The **Paria Canyon**, a tributary of the Colorado River on the Arizona-Utah border, includes the amazing Buckskin Gulch, a stretch of canyon 12 miles long, hundreds of feet deep and only 15 feet wide for most of its length. Perhaps the best-known slot canyon is Antelope Canyon (also called Corkscrew Canyon) outside Page near Lake Powell.

Adventures in these and other canyons are described in Annerino's *Adventuring in Arizona*. One of the greatest canyoneering challenges, however, is to get topo maps and set out on your own to explore side canyons of the better-known areas, or to find new canyons that aren't described in guidebooks or elsewhere.

## BICYCLING

As with hiking and backpacking, perfect cycling weather can be found at any time of year. Southern Arizona is a perfect winter destination, and Tucson is considered a bicycle-friendly city with many bike lanes and some parks with bike trails. In the summer, the higher elevations of northern Arizona lure bicyclists.

Local bike shops in major and many minor cities rent bikes and provide local maps and information. Bicycle shops are listed in the text. Most bicycle rentals automatically come with a helmet. State and city visitor information offices and chambers of commerce often have brochures about trails in their areas.

### Books

Several books detail road and trail rides in Arizona and the Southwest in general. *Bicycling America's National Parks: Arizona and New Mexico,* by Sarah Bennett Alley and Dennis Coello, is subtitled *The Best Road and Trail Rides from the Grand Canyon to Carlsbad Caverns.* Also read *The Mountain Biker's Guide to Arizona,* by Sarah L Bennett, and *Arizona Mountain Bike Trail Guide: Fat Tire Tales & Trails,* by Cosmic Ray.

### Transporting Your Bike

Bicycles can be transported by air. You *can* disassemble them and put them in a bike bag or box, but it's much easier simply to wheel your bike to the check-in desk, where it should be treated as a piece of baggage, although airlines often charge an additional fee. You may have to remove the pedals and front tire so that it takes up less space in the aircraft's hold. Check any regulations or restrictions on the transportation of bicycles

with the airline well in advance, preferably before you pay for your ticket. Bear in mind that while some airlines welcome bicycles, others consider them a nuisance and do everything possible to discourage them.

You can also take bicycles on Greyhound buses and Amtrak trains, but again, check with them in advance. For full protection, bicycles must be boxed.

Bikes are often allowed on metropolitan public transportation, but the number of buses or other types of transport able to accommodate bikes may be limited. Call the local transit authorities for information.

### Safety

On the road, bicyclists are generally treated courteously by motorists. You may, though, encounter the occasional careless one who passes too closely or too fast (or both). Helmets should always be worn to reduce the risk of head injury; in most states they are required by law. Always keep at least one hand on the handlebars. Stay close to the edge of roads and don't wear anything, such as headphones, that can reduce your ability to hear. Bicyclists should always lock their bicycles securely and be cautious about leaving bags on the bike, particularly in larger towns or more touristed locations.

Bicyclists should carry at least a gallon of water and refill bottles at every opportunity. Dehydration is a major problem in the arid Southwest.

## Laws & Regulations

Cycling has increased in popularity so much in recent years that concerns have risen over damage to the environment, especially from unchecked mountain biking. Know your environment and regulations before you ride.

Bikes are restricted from entering wilderness areas and some designated trails but may otherwise ride in NPS sites, state parks, national and state forests and BLM single-track trails. In many NPS sites, there are no bicycle trails, and cyclists are limited to paved roads only. In other areas, off-road trails are shared with other users. Trail etiquette requires that cyclists yield to horses and hikers.

Bikes aren't normally allowed on interstate highways (freeways) and are expected to use the frontage roads paralleling the freeway. On stretches where frontage roads are lacking, bicycles may be permitted on the interstates. In cities, obey traffic lights and signs and other road rules; yield to pedestrians; in downtown areas don't ride on the sidewalk unless there's a sign saying otherwise and don't ride two abreast unless in a cycle lane or path.

## RAFTING

Although it is possible to run rivers privately, most visitors who want to go rafting will take a guided tour. Many companies run the Colorado River through the Grand Canyon – they are listed in that chapter. Bear in mind that most Grand Canyon trips are fully booked a year or more in advance. However, most of these companies offer other rafting options on several other rivers in the Southwest and beyond. Not all rafting trips have to be white water; many companies run scenic float trips. Trips through the Grand Canyon and some other rivers are multiday affairs with camping on beaches. See the Grand Canyon & Lake Powell chapter.

## BOATING

Despite its desert location, Arizona has more boats per capita than any other state. The main reason for this is the region's many dams, which form huge artificial lakes providing boaters with relief from the heat.

Arizona's 'West Coast' is a series of dammed lakes on the lower Colorado River on the California-Arizona state line. These lakes are described in detail in the Western Arizona chapter. This is the lowest and hottest part of the entire Southwest, and the lakes are thronged with boaters for much of the year. You can rent canoes, fishing boats, speedboats, water-skiing boats, jet skis and windsurfers at the marinas on those lakes. On the biggest lakes, especially Lake Powell in the Glen Canyon National Recreation Area and Lakes Mead and Mojave in the Lake Mead National Recreation Area, you can also rent houseboats that will sleep from six to 12 people and allow you to explore remote areas that are hard to reach on foot. Many smaller lakes throughout the Southwest offer at least basic fishing and rowing boat rentals. Details are given in pertinent sections of the text.

In addition, the rivers suitable for rafting are also often suitable for kayaking or canoeing, and many of the companies at the Grand Canyon will arrange guided kayaking or canoeing excursions.

## Safety

The many lakes and marinas offer boat-rental opportunities to the general public, but many folks are not very knowledgeable about watercraft. Accidents, sometimes fatal, do happen. The main contributing factors to accidents include alcohol and speed – two things that don't mix. You should take the same precautions with alcohol as when you are driving a car. Have a designated sober person to pilot the boat if you are having a party. Check local regulations about speed limits – in some places you should not leave a wake. This not only limits your speed but also cuts down on erosion of the banks caused by waves. Always use lifejackets, even if you know how to swim. If you have an accident, a bump on the head can render your swimming skills useless.

A recently recognized and insidious threat is carbon monoxide, emitted by houseboat engines. This colorless, odorless and deadly gas is heavier than air and so it gathers at water level, sometimes underneath diving or swimming decks situated immediately above the engine exhausts. Several swimmers have drowned because of this in recent years.

## FISHING

The many popular boating lakes also give rise to excellent fishing. Frequent species caught in lakes include bass (striped, large-mouth and smallmouth), bluegill, catfish, crappie and walleye, while river anglers go for a variety of trout and salmon. Fish hatcheries are used to stock many lakes and rivers. Although you can eat what you catch, you should check locally about limits in number and size as well as for possible health problems in some places. Many anglers practice 'catch and release.'

Fishing is regulated by the individual states rather than by the federal government and anglers require a state license for each state that they fish in. The exception is on Indian reservations, where tribal permits are normally required. Licenses are widely available from the Fish & Game Departments of each state, as well as from numerous outdoor outfitting stores and guide services, and often in gas stations, marinas and state or national parks on or near good lakes and rivers. The cost of licenses varies from about $10 to $50 depending on how many days you want to fish (normally, licenses are available for one day, one year, and various intermediate lengths like a week or a season). Residents of Arizona get substantial discounts. In some federal areas, additional permits that cost a few dollars may be required, such as 'Habitat Improvement Stamps.'

## DOWNHILL SKIING & SNOWBOARDING

Though not particularly known for its skiing, Arizona has four ski areas, with Snowbowl near Flagstaff and Sunrise on the White Mountain Apache Reservation near Pinetop-Lakeside considered the best. There's also a small area in Williams. Mt Lemmon near Tucson is the southernmost ski area in the USA. Snow conditions in Arizona are more variable than in other states, and Arizona's ski season may be just a few weeks in some years.

Snowboarding has swept the nation's ski culture and taken on a following of its own. Many Southwestern ski areas are developing half-pipes, renting the necessary equipment in ski shops and offering introductory lessons. Most at least permit snowboarding. Snowboarders stand sideways, strapped to a board 4 or 5 feet long, to cruise down the mountains. The motion is comparable to surfing or skateboarding rather than skiing.

### Planning

The skiing season lasts from about late November to early April, depending on the area (some have shorter seasons). State tourist offices have information on resorts, and travel agents can arrange full-package tours that include transport and accommodations. If you have travel insurance, make sure that it covers you for winter sports.

Ski areas are often well equipped with accommodations, eateries, shops, entertainment venues, child-care facilities (both on and off the mountain) and transportation. Equipment rentals are available at or near even the smallest ski areas, though renting equipment in a nearby town can be cheaper if you can transport it to the slopes.

Recreational programs for handicapped people are offered by Disabled Sports USA (☎ 301-217-0960, TDD 301-217-0963), 451 Hungerford Dr, Suite 100, Rockville, MD 20850. Its website is www.dsusa.org, and it has state branches across the country. Skiers 70 years of age and over can contact the 70+ Ski Club (☎ 518-346-5505), 1633 Albany St, Schenectady, NY 12304, or email RTL70plus@aol.com.

*Ski* (www.skimag.com) and *Skiing* (www.skiingmag.com) are year-round magazines available in most newsstands, airports and sporting-goods stores. Their websites are full of useful information about snow conditions, resorts, events etc. Another useful website is www.sno country.com, detailing snow conditions, pass rates, types of runs and accommodations in resorts throughout the world.

## Ski Schools

Visitors planning on taking lessons should rent equipment on the mountain, since the price of a lesson usually includes equipment rentals, with no discount for having your own gear. Children's ski schools are popular places to stash the kids for a day, offering lessons, day-care facilities and providing lunch.

## OTHER WINTER ACTIVITIES

Both cross-country skiing and snowmobiling are popular, and often conflict with one another. Anywhere that there is substantial snowfall, you'll find groomed tracks designed for both activities, and equipment rental readily available. Snowshoeing is another activity for which equipment rental is available in higher areas with lots of snow. A useful book is *Cross-Country Ski Vacations: A Guide to the Best Resorts, Lodges, and Groomed Trails in North America,* by Jonathan Wiesel and Diana Delling.

Lakes often freeze hard in the mountains, where both ice-skating and ice fishing are possible. Ice-skating is also featured in various towns with ice-skating rinks, including, surprisingly, Tucson, where a year-round indoor ice-skating rink remains open even when summer temperatures soar above 100°F.

## BIRD WATCHING

The Southwest has a great variety of different habitats, which leads to many different species of bird. Southeastern Arizona, in particular, has great avian biodiversity, with species from Mexico flying in to add to the many birds found in the deserts, mountains, forests and riparian zones of that area. Sixteen hummingbird species have been recorded in southeastern Arizona, of which eight are quite commonly seen. This attracts avid birders from around the world. The

Tucson Audubon Society is a great resource for this area. More information can be found in the Tucson & Southern Arizona and Southeastern Arizona chapters of this book.

For general information on bird watching, log on to the Audubon Society website at www.audubon.org or call the national office at ☎ 212-979-3000.

## HORSEBACK RIDING

Cowboys and Indians, the Pony Express, stagecoaches, cattle drives and rodeo riding – horse legends are legion in the Southwest. This continues to the present day with Bob Baffert, the horse trainer from Nogales, Arizona, whose *Real Quiet* won the Kentucky Derby and Preakness Stakes of the USA's leading 'Triple Crown' horse races in 1998 and came in second (literally by a nose) in the third race, the Belmont Stakes. (This was the closest that a horse has come to winning the Triple Crown since 1978.)

OK. You probably aren't looking at winning the Derby, but horseback riding is a popular attraction in Arizona. This ranges from one-hour rides for complete beginners (or experienced riders who just want to get on a horse again) to multinight horsepacking trips with wranglers, cooks, guides and backcountry camping. Another possibility is staying at a ranch where the main activity is horseback riding on a daily basis, and the comforts of a bed and shower await at the end of the day.

Many towns have stables and offer horseback rides. In a few locations, such as on the South Rim of the Grand Canyon, only mules are available, and these must be booked months in advance. During the winter, southern Arizona has delightful weather for riding. When the weather warms up, head up to Sedona and Pinetop-Lakeside. More places are listed in the text.

If your idea of a southwestern vacation is a week in a comfortable ranch in the country, with cozy log cabins, excellent food, and well-maintained horses available for daily riding, then an excellent resource is

*Ranch Vacations,* by Gene Kilgore. Updated every two years, this book describes many ranches in detail, including some that include fly-fishing and hunting among their activities. However, most of the ranches have horseback riding as the main focus. Check out Kilgore's website at www.ranch web.com. Another useful resource is the Dude Ranchers' Association (☎ 970-223-8440), PO Box F-471 LaPorte, Colorado 80535, which lists dozens of ranches throughout the Southwest, as well as the whole country; get details at www.dude ranch.org. The commercial www.dude ranches.com is also worth a look.

## ROCK CLIMBING

There are many rock-climbing areas, some of which have become quite famous, such as Mt Lemmon near Tucson. There is also good climbing in the Sedona area – in fact almost anywhere that there are mountains. Some cities, such as Flagstaff and Tucson, have indoor rock-climbing gyms where the public is welcome to practice for a small fee.

Outdoor equipment stores sell guidebooks, some for large areas and others covering a small local area. *Rock Climbing Arizona,* by Stewart M Green, is a particularly useful source.

## HOT-AIR BALLOONING

Dozens of companies offer scenic hot-air balloon flights over many parts of the Southwest. Flights usually lift off in the calm morning air, drift for about an hour and finish with a traditional champagne brunch; costs are in the low hundreds per person. Most companies can arrange flights on a day's notice, but flights may be canceled in windy weather and in summer. Tucson, Phoenix and Sedona are particularly known for this activity.

## ROCKHOUNDING

Rockhounding – the search for semiprecious or just plain pretty rocks, minerals and crystals – is a passion for some people in the Arizona. Tucson has an annual Gem & Mineral Show in February that is one of the biggest in the world, and the area around Quartzsite is a famous gathering ground for hundreds of thousands of rock hounds and collectors during January and February. Most national parks, such as the Petrified Forest National Park, famous for its fossilized wood specimens, do not permit any collecting at all, though there are plenty of shops in nearby Holbrook that legally sell samples.

## JEEP TOURING

Taking to the backcountry in a 4WD vehicle, whether just for a half day or equipped with camping gear, water and food for several days, is a popular activity. Sedona is particularly popular for 4WD activities, and several agencies rent vehicles.

You can drive on dirt roads in many federally owned lands, such as national forests and BLM areas; however, there are some restrictions and certain roads are periodically closed.

## GOLFING

Just about every sizeable town in Arizona has a golf course, and the bigger cities have dozens of courses, a few of which are listed in the text. The Phoenix area alone has almost 200 courses. In many desert areas, golf courses are viewed as a welcome green amenity, but the greenness comes at a high price – it has to be irrigated. Conservationists decry the use of this most precious of desert resources for golf courses, but this hasn't stopped the development of this activity throughout the area.

Golf can be an expensive habit. Some courses don't allow golfers to walk from hole to hole. A round of 18 holes on the best courses, often in upscale resorts that specialize in golf vacations, can cost close to $200 (including use of a golf cart) in the balmy days of a southern Arizona winter. During the heat of summer, rates can drop to under $100 for the same resort. If you don't have that kind of money, try the public city courses where rounds are much more reasonable. Most chambers of commerce will tell you about local city courses charging $30 to $50 for 18 holes, or even less in small towns. Though some greens are marked on town and city maps, it is beyond the scope of this book to offer detailed information in the text on the hundreds of golf courses in the state.

For further information, including details on state gold associations, contact the United States Golf Association (☎ 908-234-2300), PO Box 708, Far Hills, NJ 07931. website: www.usga.org

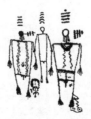

# Getting There & Away

Most travelers to Arizona arrive by air, bus or private vehicle. Train service is a little-used fourth option. The landlocked Southwest can't be reached by sea, but the lack of ports has been remedied somewhat by naming the Phoenix International Airport 'Sky Harbor.'

This chapter focuses on getting to the major transportation hubs in Arizona from the major US ports of entry and other parts of the world.

## AIR

Most travelers fly into Phoenix or Tucson and rent a car. If time is not a problem, drive – and enjoy the rest of the country.

## Airports & Airlines

Sky Harbor Airport in Phoenix is among the busiest international airports in the USA and the region's most important. The much smaller airport in Tucson has a few direct flights to Mexico, but international airport facilities are limited to customs and immigration. Many major US carriers service Tucson from several large US cities. Los Angeles, busier than any of these, is an easy day's drive from western Arizona.

Phoenix is an important hub for America West and Southwest Airlines. Many other major airlines fly into one or more of these cities.

The main domestic airlines serving the Southwest include the following:

| | |
|---|---|
| Alaska | ☎ 800-426-0333 |
| | www.alaskaair.com |
| America West | ☎ 800-235-9292 |
| | www.americawest.com |
| American | ☎ 800-433-7300 |
| | www.aa.com |
| Continental | ☎ 800-523-3273 |
| | www.continental.com |
| Delta | ☎ 800-221-1212 |
| | www.delta.com |
| Frontier | ☎ 800-432-1359 |
| | www.flyfrontier.com |
| Hawaiian | ☎ 800-367-5320 |
| | www.hawaiianair.com |
| Mesa Air | ☎ 800-637-2247 |
| | www.mesa-air.com |
| Midwest Express | ☎ 800-452-2022 |
| | www.midwestexpress.com |
| Northwest | ☎ 800-225-2525 |
| | www.nwa.com |
| Southwest | ☎ 800-435-9792 |
| | www.southwest.com |
| TWA | ☎ 800-221-2000 |
| | www.twa.com |
| United | ☎ 800-241-6522 |
| | www.ual.com |
| US Airways | ☎ 800-428-4322 |
| | www.usairways.com |

## Warning

The information in this chapter is particularly vulnerable to change: prices for international travel are volatile, routes are introduced and canceled, schedules change, special deals come and go, and rules and visa requirements are amended. Airlines and governments seem to take a perverse pleasure in making price structures and regulations as complicated as possible. You should check directly with the airline or a travel agent to make sure you understand how a fare (and any ticket you may buy) works. In addition, the travel industry is highly competitive, and there are many lurks and perks.

The upshot of this is that you should get opinions, quotes and advice from as many airlines and travel agents as possible before you part with your hard-earned cash. The details given in this chapter should be regarded as pointers and are not a substitute for your own careful, up-to-date research.

Some US carriers have different phone numbers for their international desk:

| | |
|---|---|
| Air Canada | ☎ 888-247-2262 |
| | www.aircanada.ca |

| Air France | ☎ 800-237-2747 |
| | www.airfrance.com |
| American | ☎ 800-433-7300 |
| | www.aa.com |
| British Airways | ☎ 800-247-9297 |
| | www.britishairways.com |
| Continental | ☎ 800-231-0856 |
| | www.continental.com |
| Delta | ☎ 800-221-4141 |
| | www.delta.com |
| Japan Air Lines | ☎ 800-525-3663 |
| | www.japanair.com |
| KLM | ☎ 800-374-7747 |
| | www.klm.com |
| Lufthansa | ☎ 800-645-3880 |
| | www.lufthansa.com |
| Northwest | ☎ 800-447-4747 |
| | www.nwa.com |
| Qantas Airways | ☎ 800-227-4500 |
| | www.qantas.com |
| TWA | ☎ 800-892-4141 |
| | www.twa.com |
| United | ☎ 800-538-2929 |
| | www.ual.com |
| US Airways | ☎ 800-622-1015 |
| | www.usairways.com |

## Buying Tickets

Fares within the USA are incredibly varied. An economy roundtrip ticket from Phoenix to the West Coast can cost $100 or four times as much, and these disparities occur almost wherever you fly in the USA. The cheapest flights are often (but not always) those booked 21 days or more in advance of your travel dates and with a Saturday night stopover. Nothing determines fares more than demand, and when things are slow, airlines lower their fares to fill empty seats. Competition is stiff, and at any given time any of the airlines could be offering the cheapest fare.

The most expensive fares are those booked at the last minute; cheap standby fares are not normally offered. One-way tickets usually cost as much as an economy roundtrip ticket with major airlines; smaller airlines such as America West and Southwest are the best places to look for one-way flights. Departure taxes are normally included in the cost of your ticket, and you don't have to pay any extra taxes flying from any US airport.

To avoid the problem of losing a paper ticket, ask for an electronic ticket. Remember to buy travel insurance as early as possible.

**Discount Tickets** The opportunities for discount tickets is incredible; research carefully before purchasing your plane tickets. Student travel agencies found in many countries worldwide include Council Travel (☎ 800-226-8624), www.counciltravel.com, and STA (☎ 800-781-4040), www.statravel .com. They not only provide cheap tickets to students, they often have some of the best deals for the general public as well. The Internet is a source of discounted tickets but, as always, shop around. New sites appear every month. Internet buying involves paying by credit card, and many of these sites will also provide hotel reservations, car rental and other services. Apart from the airlines' sites (some of which do offer discounted tickets occasionally), look at the following:

www.atevo.com
www.cheaptickets.com
www.discounttickets.com
www.expedia.com
www.lowestfare.com
www.orbitz.com
www.travelocity.com

**Seasons** High season in the USA is mid-June to mid-September (summer) and the days around major holidays (Thanksgiving is one of the busiest times of year, and Christmas, New Year's, Easter, and Memorial Day and Labor Day weekends are all very busy with few cheap fares). The best rates for travel to and within the USA are found November through February (except for the holidays). Prices often go up, and availability is more limited, during March, which is spring break season.

**Visit USA Passes** Most domestic carriers offer Visit USA passes to non-US citizens.

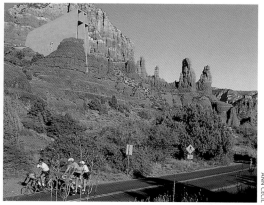

Fly, swim, hike or bike through Arizona.

RICHARD CUMMINS

Pine and juniper

DALLAS STRIBLEY

A local character

WADE EAKLE

Cholla cacti

RICHARD CUMMINS

Parry's penstemon

MICHAEL AW

Prairie dog

The passes are a book of coupons – each coupon equals a flight. Typically, the minimum number of coupons is three or four and the maximum is eight or ten, and they must be purchased in conjunction with an international airline ticket anywhere outside the USA except Canada and Mexico. Coupons cost anywhere from $100 to $160, depending on how many you buy. Airlines may require you to plan your itinerary in advance and to complete your flights within 60 days of arrival, but rules vary among individual airlines. A few airlines may allow you to use coupons on standby, in which case call the airline a day or two before the flight.

## Baggage & Other Restrictions

Many but not all airlines will allow a bicycle or other specialized oversized items as checked luggage. On some international flights the luggage allowance is based on weight, not size; check with the airline. For more information on transporting your bike, see Transporting Your Bike in the Outdoor Activities chapter.

If your luggage is delayed upon arrival, some airlines will give a cash advance to purchase necessities. If sporting equipment is misplaced, the airline may pay for rentals. If your luggage is lost, you should submit a claim. The airline doesn't have to pay the full amount of the claim; rather, it can estimate the value of your lost items. It may take the airline anywhere from six weeks to three months to process the claim and pay you.

**Smoking**  Smoking is prohibited on all domestic flights in the USA, and some international flights. Many airports in the USA also ban smoking; some allow it in designated smoking rooms only.

**Illegal Items**  Items that are illegal to take on a plane, either checked or as carry-on, include weapons, aerosols, tear gas and pepper spray, camp stoves with fuel and divers' tanks that are full. Matches should not be checked.

Items permitted in checked baggage but not on your person or in carry-on luggage

include knives and cutting instruments of any kind, anything with a folding or retractable blade, straight razors, metal scissors, metal nail files or clippers and corkscrews.

## Arriving in the USA

You must complete customs and immigration formalities at the airport where you first land, even if you are continuing immediately to another city. Choose the proper immigration line: either US citizens/residents or non-US citizens. After immigration, recover your luggage in the customs area and proceed to an officer who will ask a few questions and perhaps check your luggage. Dogs trained to detect drugs, explosives and restricted food products might sniff your bags.

If you are continuing to another city, you must recheck your baggage. Airline representatives outside the customs area will assist you.

## Canada

Travel Cuts (☎ 866-246-9762) has offices in all major cities and online at www.travel cuts.com. They have good deals for students and deal with the general public as well. The Toronto *Globe and Mail* and *Vancouver Sun* carry travel agents' ads.

Many connections between the Southwest and Canada are through Vancouver, BC. Phoenix has frequent and inexpensive flights to and from Vancouver, which is serviced by Air Canada and many domestic US airlines.

## The UK & Ireland

Discount ticket agencies ('bucket shops') generally provide the cheapest fares from London. Agencies usually advertise in the classifieds of Sunday newspapers, magazines such as *Time Out* and many free papers at newsstands everywhere. London is arguably the world's headquarters for bucket shops, which are well advertised and can usually beat published airline fares. Good, reliable agents for cheap tickets in the UK include the student agencies mentioned under discount tickets. Among the numerous others is Trailfinders (☎ 020-7938-3939), 194 Kensington High St, London, W8 7RG, at www.trailfinders.com and in many other cities. Try also Flightbookers (☎ 020-7437-7767), 177 Tottenham Court Rd, London, W1. Internet travel agencies include www.flynow.com (☎ 020-7835-2000, 0870-444-0045), www.cheapflights.co.uk, and also www.lastminute.co.uk.

A daily nonstop flight from London to Phoenix is available on British Airways, but this popular route is more expensive than connecting flights. Several carriers fly nonstop to Los Angeles.

## Continental Europe

There are no direct flights to Arizona from Europe. Flying straight to the West Coast is quicker than transferring in a city such as New York or Chicago. Nonstop flights to Los Angeles are available from Amsterdam with Northwest and KLM; from Frankfurt with Delta, United and Lufthansa; from Paris with Air France; and from Rome with Delta. For San Francisco there are nonstop flights from Paris with United and Air France and from Frankfurt with United and Lufthansa. These flights are the most convenient, but they usually cost more than flights that require stops or connections.

Council Travel has several locations in Paris, as well as in the French towns of Aixen-Provence, Lyon and Nice. The main travel office in Paris is at 22, rue des Pyramides, 75001 (☎ 01-44-55-55-44). Other Council Travel offices include the following in Germany: Düsseldorf (☎ 211-36-30-30), at Graf Adolph Strasse 18, 42112, and Munich (☎ 089-39-50-22), Adalbert Strasse 32, 80799. STA Travel is at Bergerstrasse 118, 60316 Frankfurt 1, Germany (☎ 069-43-01-91). STA is also in a dozen other German cities – call the Frankfurt office for details.

## Australia & New Zealand

Flights to Los Angeles or San Francisco leave from Sydney, Melbourne, Cairns and Auckland. STA Travel in Australia (☎ 1-300-360-960) and New Zealand (☎ 0800-874-773) has many offices in the major cities and online at www.statravel.com. Flight Centres

International is another major dealer in cheap air fares; check the travel agents' ads in the yellow pages and call around.

Depending on time of year, roundtrip flights to Los Angeles run from AUS$1300 to AUS$2100.

## Asia

Hong Kong is the discount plane ticket capital of the region, but its bucket shops can be unreliable. Ask the advice of other travelers before buying a ticket. STA Travel, which is dependable, has branches in Japan, Singapore, Thailand, and Malaysia. Council Travel, also reliable, has branches in Japan, Singapore and Thailand. Singapore and Bangkok seem to be reliable places for cheap flights, many of which go via Honolulu, Hawaii. Sometimes, a free stopover can be included. Nonstop flights to the West Coast go from several Japanese cities with various airlines.

## Mexico, Central & South America

Most flights from Central and South America to the Southwest go via Miami, New Orleans, Houston, Dallas/Fort Worth or Los Angeles. Most countries' international flag carriers or privatized airlines, as well as US airlines like United, American and Continental, serve these destinations from Latin America, with onward connections to cities in the Southwest. America West, Continental and AeroMexico have flights from Phoenix and Tucson to numerous Mexican cities.

## BUS

Greyhound (☎ 800-231-2222) is the main bus system in the USA and plays an important transportation role in Arizona and the Southwest in general. A few minor regional bus lines, detailed in the text, link minor towns with major cities. However, bus lines don't serve most national parks or some important, off-track tourist towns; these can be reached by tour buses only. Traveling by car is definitely recommended as more convenient, although bus services are described in the text if you can't drive or prefer bus travel. Long-distance buses can get you to the region, and then you could rent a car.

Meal stops, usually in inexpensive and unexciting cafes, are made on long trips; you pay for your own food. Buses have on-board lavatories and seats recline for sleeping. Smoking is not permitted aboard Greyhound buses. Long-distance bus trips are often available at bargain prices if you purchase or reserve tickets in advance. At time of writing, tickets ranging in cost from $49 for any journey under 1000 miles to $190 for any journey over about 2000 miles were sold 7 days in advance. For example, a one way ticket from New York City to Phoenix (2759 miles) cost $151. Journeys of about 100 to 250 miles cost about $20 to $40. For fare and route details, see www.greyhound.com.

Bus terminals are often in poorer or more dangerous areas of town – take a cab to your hotel if you arrive after dark.

### Bus Passes

Greyhound Discovery Passes cost between $209 for seven days and $599 for 60 days. Students and seniors receive discounts. These tickets can be bought in advance and use begins from the date of your first trip. You can get on and off at any Greyhound stop or terminal, and the pass is available at every Greyhound terminal.

Foreign tourists can buy International Discovery Passes, which are about 20% cheaper, or a four-day Monday to Thursday pass. The International Pass is usually bought abroad at a travel agency, or it can be bought in the USA through the Greyhound International depot in New York City (☎ 212-971-0492, 800-246-8572) or online, 21 days in advance. Check the website for other specials.

### TRAIN

Three Amtrak services cross the south, central and northern part of the Southwest but are unconnected with one another. Use them to reach the region, not for touring around. Sleeping cabins with private baths and hot showers are available.

The *Southwest Chief* has daily service between Chicago and Los Angeles via Kansas City. The stations in Arizona are Winslow, Flagstaff, Williams and Kingman.

The *Sunset Limited* runs thrice weekly from Los Angeles to New Orleans. Stations in Arizona are Yuma, Tucson, Benson and Lordsburg.

Tickets should be booked in advance with Amtrak (☎ 800-872-7245), online at www.amtrak.com or through a travel agent. Small stations have no facilities, and trains stop there only if you have bought a ticket in advance.

For non-US citizens, Amtrak offers various USA Rail Passes that must be purchased outside the US (check with a travel agent).

### CAR & MOTORCYCLE

Foreign motorists and motorcyclists (traveling with their own foreign vehicles) will need the vehicle's registration papers, liability insurance and an international driver's permit in addition to their domestic license. Canadian and Mexican driver's licenses are accepted.

For information on buying or renting a car, see the Getting Around chapter.

### Drive-Aways

Drive-aways are a cheap way to get to Arizon if you like long-distance driving and meet eligibility requirements. In a typical drive-away, somebody might move from Boston to Phoenix, for example, and elect to fly rather than drive; he or she would then hire a drive-away agency to get the car to Phoenix. The agency will find a driver and take care of all necessary insurance and permits. Normally, you have to pay a small refundable deposit. You pay for the gas (though sometimes a gas allowance is given). You are allowed a set number of days to deliver the car – usually based on driving eight hours a day. You are also allowed a limited number of miles, based on the best route and allowing for reasonable side trips, so you can't just zigzag all over the country. There is usually a minimum-age requirement as well.

Drive-away companies often advertise in the classified sections of newspapers under 'Travel.' They are also listed in the yellow pages of telephone books under 'Auto Transporters & Drive-away Companies.' A company that has long been providing this service and operates about 75 offices throughout the country is Auto Driveaway Co.

You need to be flexible about dates and destinations when you call. If you are going to a popular area, you may be able to leave within two days or less, or you may have to wait over a week before a car becomes available. The routes most easily available are coast to coast, although intermediate trips are certainly possible.

# Getting Around

Once you reach Arizona, traveling by car is usually the best way of getting around. A car will get you to rural areas not served by air, bus or train. However, you can use public transportation to reach towns and cities, then rent a car locally to get to places not served by public transportation. This option is usually more expensive than just renting a car and driving yourself everywhere, but it can cut down on long-distance driving trips if you don't relish them.

## AIR

Phoenix is the hub of America West Express, which serves small towns throughout Arizona, northwestern New Mexico and southwestern Colorado. These short-hop flights tend to be used mainly by local residents and businesspeople, and fares are not very cheap, but they are an option for tourists with money.

America West, Southwest and Delta are the main carriers linking Phoenix, Salt Lake City, Las Vegas, Tucson and Albuquerque. See the Getting There & Away chapter for their toll-free numbers and websites. If you are arriving from overseas or from another major airport in the USA, it is usually much cheaper to buy a through ticket to small airports as part of your fare rather than buying them separately.

Another alternative is an air pass, available from the major airlines that fly between the USA and Europe, Asia and Australia. Air passes are particularly valuable if you're flying between widely separated destinations. (See Air Passes in Getting There & Away.)

## BUS

Greyhound is the main carrier to and within Arizona (see the Getting There & Away chapter for more information). They run buses several times a day along major highways between large towns, only stopping at smaller towns that happen to be along the way. In many small towns Greyhound no longer maintains terminals but merely stops at a given location, such as a grocery store parking lot. Towns not on major routes are often served by local carriers. Greyhound usually has information about the local carriers – the name, phone number and, sometimes, fare and schedule information. Information about the many local bus companies is given in the text.

### Buying Tickets

Tickets can be bought over the phone with a credit card (MasterCard, Visa or Discover) and mailed to you if purchased 10 days in advance, or they can be picked up at the terminal with proper identification. Greyhound terminals also accept American Express, traveler's checks and cash. Reservations are made with ticket purchases only. Many bus stops are just that – a stop next to a McDonald's restaurant or a gas station. Look for the blue and red Greyhound symbol. In these unlikely terminals, boarding passengers usually pay the driver with exact change. Only larger towns have proper bus stations or terminals.

Fares vary tremendously. Sometimes you can get discounted tickets if you purchase them three, seven or 21 days in advance. It's best to call Greyhound for current details or check its website at www.greyhound.com.

## TRAIN

Amtrak's three routes through the Southwest are not convenient options for touring the region (see the Getting There & Away chapter).

Several other lines provide service using historic steam trains and are mainly for sightseeing, although the Williams to Grand Canyon run is a destination in itself.

## CAR & MOTORCYCLE

The US highway system is very extensive, and since distances are great and buses can be infrequent, traveling by automobile is worth considering despite the expense.

Officially, you must have an International or Inter-American Driving Permit to supplement your national or state driver's license, but US police are more likely to want to see your national, provincial or state driver's license.

Distances are great in Arizon, and there are long stretches of road without gas stations. Running out of gas on a hot and desolate stretch of highway can be hazardous to your health, so pay close attention to signs that caution 'Next Gas 68 Miles.' Read the Dangers & Annoyances section in the Facts for the Visitor chapter for general safety rules regarding driving and traveling in Arizona, and the Legal Matters section for information on drinking and driving laws.

## American Automobile Association

The American Automobile Association (AAA, or 'Triple A'; ☎ 800-874-7532) has hundreds of offices throughout the USA and Canada. Annual membership varies from state to state but costs about $40 (plus a one-time initiation fee of about $20) for one driver and $20 for each additional driver in the same household. Reciprocal member services for residents of one state are available in all other states. Members of many similar foreign organizations also receive reciprocal member services.

AAA provides free and detailed state and city maps and will help you plan your trip. If you're a member and break down, get a flat tire, run out of gas or have a dead battery, call their toll-free number (☎ 800-222-4357) and they will send out a reputable towing company at costs lower than if you had called the towing company yourself. They'll make minor repairs (changing a tire, jump-starting a car etc) for free or tow you to the nearest repair shop. Benefits apply when you are driving rented or borrowed cars as well. The AAA travel agency will also book car rentals, air tickets and hotel rooms at discount prices.

The main full-service offices in Arizona are in Phoenix. Maps and many other services are available at the smaller branches in Tucson, Yuma, and some other towns.

Emergency breakdown services are available 24 hours a day.
website: www.aaa.com

## Rental

Major international rental agencies have offices throughout the region. To rent a car, you must have a valid driver's license, meet minimum age requirements (25 years in many cases, or an extra fee applies) and present a major credit card (some companies will accept a large cash deposit).

Exact details vary from city to city, company to company, and depend on the time of year, so call around to find what you need. Also try calling some of the smaller, lesser known local agencies, which are more likely to allow people under 25 to rent a car with no age surcharge. Very few companies will rent cars to drivers under 21, and those that do charge significantly higher rates.

Many rental agencies have bargain rates for weekend or week-long rentals, or in conjunction with airline tickets. Prices vary greatly depending on the region, the season and the type or size of the car you'd like to rent. In the off-season, compact cars rent as cheaply as $99 a week, but rates of $129 to $250 a week are more common in the high season. Taxes are extra and average around 10% (at the Phoenix airport it is as high as 25%).

If you want to rent a car for less than a week, daily rates will be more expensive: $30 a day is a good price but closer to $45 (or as high as $90 if availability is tight!) is not unusual. You can get discounts if you are a member of AAA or another travel club. Although $150 or more a week may seem high for travelers on a tight budget, if you split the rental between two or three (or squeeze in a fourth!), it works out much cheaper than going by bus.

Rates usually include unlimited mileage, but it is important to make sure they do. If there is a mileage charge, your costs will go up quickly and disconcertingly as you drive the long distances of Arizona.

You are expected to return the car to the same place where you picked it up, but can drive from state to state with no penalty.

You can sometimes arrange to drop the car off elsewhere, but there is sometimes a large surcharge. Be aware that the person who rents the car is the only legal driver, and in the event of an accident, only the legal driver is covered. However, when you rent the car, additional drivers may be signed on as legal drivers for a fee, usually $3 per day per person.

Basic liability insurance, which will cover damage you may cause to another vehicle, is required by law and comes with the price of renting the car. Liability insurance is also called third-party coverage.

Collision insurance, also called the Collision Damage Waiver (CDW) or Loss Damage Waiver, is optional; it covers the full value of the vehicle in case of an accident, except when caused by acts of nature or fire. For a midsized car the cost for this extra coverage is around $15 per day. You don't need to buy this waiver to rent the car, though you are responsible for covering the cost of repairs in the event of a collision. It may be advisable to buy CDW unless you have some other kind of insurance.

Many credit cards will cover collision insurance if you rent for 15 days or less and charge the full cost of rental to your card. If you have collision insurance on your personal car insurance policy, this will often cover rented vehicles. The credit card will cover the large deductible. To find out if your credit card offers such a service, and the extent of the coverage, contact the credit card company.

Note that many rental agencies stipulate that damage a car suffers while being driven on unpaved roads is not covered by the insurance they offer. Check with the agent when you make your reservation. It never hurts to read the fine print when you get the contract, either.

The following companies rent cars in Arizona. The large cities have the best selection of companies, cars and rates. You can rent subcompact to luxury cars, pickup trucks, 4WDs, vans or moving trucks. Smaller cities have less selection and often charge a little more. Small companies

serving just one or two towns are not listed below.

| | |
|---|---|
| Advantage | ☎ 800-777-5500 |
| | www.arac.com |
| Alamo | ☎ 800-327-9633 |
| | www.goalamo.com |
| Avis | ☎ 800-831-2847 |
| | www.avis.com |
| Budget | ☎ 800-527-0700 |
| | www.budgetrentacar.com |
| Dollar | ☎ 800-800-4000 |
| | www.dollarcar.com |
| Enterprise | ☎ 800-325-8007 |
| | www.pickenterprise.com |
| Hertz | ☎ 800-654-3131 |
| | www.hertz.com |
| National | ☎ 800-227-7368 |
| | www.nationalcar.com |
| Payless | ☎ 800-729-5377 |
| | www.800-payless.com |
| Rent-A-Wreck | ☎ 800-944-7501 |
| | www.rent-a-wreck.com |
| Thrifty | ☎ 800-847-4389 |
| | www.thrifty.com |

## Purchase

If you're spending several months in the USA, purchasing a car is worth considering, but buying one requires some research.

It's possible to purchase a working car in the USA for about $2000, but you can't expect to go too far before you'll need some repair work that could cost several hundred dollars or more. It doesn't hurt to spend more to get a quality vehicle. It's also worth spending $75 or so to have a mechanic check it for defects (some AAA offices have diagnostic centers where they can do this on the spot for its members and those of foreign affiliates).

You have to register your car with the Department of Motor Vehicles, which will cost several hundred dollars (less for a cheap old clunker, more for a new car), and buy insurance, which will be several hundred dollars for six months. You also have to allow time at the end of your trip to sell the car. Generally, it's more hassle than it's worth unless you are spending six months or more traveling in the USA.

Inspect the title (as the ownership document is called) carefully before purchasing the car; the owner's name that appears on the title must match the identification of the person selling you the car.

## BICYCLE

Cycling is a cheap, healthy, and fun way of traveling. A note of caution: Before leaving home, go over your bike with a fine-toothed comb, and fill your repair kit with every imaginable spare part in case you break down in the back of beyond. Know how to change tires and do basic repair/maintenance. Carry and use the toughest bicycle padlock available and always carry extra water.

Bicycles can travel by air. You can take them apart and put them in a bike bag or box, but it's much easier simply to wheel your bike to the check-in desk, where it should be treated as a piece of baggage. Ask about checking bikes with airline well in advance, preferably before you pay for your ticket.

If you'd rather rent a bike when you get there, look under 'Bicycles – Rental' in the telephone directory yellow pages. There are several places to choose from in larger towns. In smaller towns, options for bicycle rentals are mentioned in the text. For a long-term rental, you might want to consider buying a new or used bike and then re-selling it. Call around bike stores in the town where you start from and explore these options.

Bicycles are generally prohibited on interstate highways if there is a frontage road. However, where a suitable frontage road or other alternative is lacking, bicyclists are permitted on some interstates. Note that some scenic areas have cycling restrictions. Also, be warned that distances between services in Arizona can be long, and vast stretches of hot desert can make bicyling particularly straining.

## HITCHHIKING

Hitching is never entirely safe in any country in the world, and we don't recommend it. Travelers who decide to hitch should understand that they are taking a small but serious risk. You may not be able to identify the local rapist/murderer before you get into the vehicle. People who do choose to hitch will be safer if they travel in pairs and let someone know where they are planning to go. Ask the driver where he or she is going rather than telling the person where you want to go.

## LOCAL TRANSPORTATION

Cities and some larger towns have local bus systems that will get you around. These generally run on very limited schedules on Sunday and at night. Telephone numbers of urban bus systems are given in the text.

Taxis will get you around, but are not cheap. Expect to pay around $2 a mile, which makes them very expensive for long distances. Check the yellow pages under 'Taxi' for phone numbers and services. Drivers expect a tip of about 10% to 15% of the fare. In most cities, you have to telephone for a taxi, as there are few to hail on the streets.

# Phoenix & Around

☎ 602, 480, 623 • pop 1,321,045;
metro area 3,251,876 • elevation 1200 feet

Phoenix, easily the largest city in the South-west and the sixth largest in the country, was surrounded by other towns before WWII, but rapid growth in the latter half of the 20th century has linked these into one huge, still-growing metropolitan area. Major towns adjoining Phoenix include Tempe (pronounced 'TEM-pee'; with 158,625 inhabitants), Scottsdale (population 202,705),

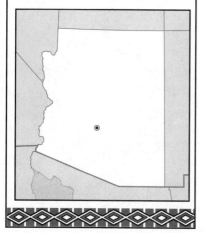

Mesa (population 396,375) and over a dozen other communities. Together, they cover almost 2000 sq miles, an area that is locally called the 'Valley of the Sun' or just 'the valley.' Sunny it certainly is; with more than 300 days of sunshine a year, it's searingly hot in summer but delightful in winter.

The climate attracts winter visitors (locally called 'snowbirds') who leave their colder northern states to spend several months soaking up the rays. Fall, winter and spring are the main cultural and tourist seasons, when places charge the highest prices. Visitors arriving during summer vacation periods will find the lowest prices in the hotels and resorts, but also daytime high temperatures above 100°F for weeks on end, commonly reaching well over 110°F in midsummer. Clothing is appropriately casual – you can wear shorts almost anywhere in summer.

Phoenix is the Southwest's most important gateway, with nonstop international flights to Europe, as well as all over the country. Major museums, superlative shopping (especially in Scottsdale, which vies with Santa Fe as an arts center), relaxing resorts, delectable dining, warm winters, spectator sports and golfing greens (where do they get that water?) are the main reasons why visitors spend some time here before moving on to the rest of the Southwest. Relaxed sophistication is a hallmark of Phoenix, where a cowboy hat and jeans are rarely out of place and where ties are seldom required.

## HISTORY

Hohokam people lived here some 2300 years ago (see the section on Pueblo Grande Museum, later) and small groups of Pima and Maricopa Indians eked out an existence along the Gila and Salt Rivers. In the mid-1860s, the US Army built Fort McDowell northeast of Phoenix. This prompted Jack Swilling to reopen Hohokam canals to produce crops for the garrison and led to the establishment of a town in 1870. Darrel Duppa, a British settler, suggested that the town had risen from the ashes of the Hohokam culture like the fabled phoenix, and the name stuck.

Phoenix established itself as an agricultural and transportation center. The railway arrived from the Pacific in 1887, and when Phoenix became the territorial capital in 1889, it had 3000 inhabitants. Settlers built Victorian houses that today stand as Phoenix's oldest historical buildings. In 1886 the Arizona Normal School, later to become Arizona State University (ASU), was established in Tempe. Other villages appeared; Mesa was founded by Mormon settlers in 1878, and Scottsdale followed a decade later, named after army chaplain Winfield Scott.

The lack of water was a major stumbling block to further growth until 1911, when the Roosevelt Dam on the Salt River was finished, the first of many large dams to be built in the state. The stage was set for growth, and grow Phoenix did.

In 1926, Phoenix's railway link became transcontinental, enabling people from the East to pour into the state in increasing numbers. Many came for recreation – to play cowboy in dude ranches or to relax at the luxurious Arizona Biltmore resort, opened in 1929 and still one of the finest in the West. Others came for their health; the dry desert air was said to cure various respiratory ailments. Many visitors stayed, including Dwight and Maie Heard, who arrived in 1895 to cure Dwight's lung complaints. They founded Phoenix's most interesting museum, the Heard. The combination of recreation and culture has been the valley's main attraction ever since.

## ORIENTATION

The greater Phoenix area is ringed by mountains that range from 2500 feet in elevation to more than 7000 feet. Because metropolitan Phoenix grew to engulf many small towns, there are several historical centers, of which Phoenix, Scottsdale and Tempe and Mesa are the most interesting. Most of this chapter is devoted to these towns.

Phoenix is the largest town and houses the state capitol, the oldest buildings, several important museums and professional sport facilities. Southeast of Phoenix lies Tempe, home of ASU and an active student population. East of Tempe, Mesa is the second largest town in the valley and is home to several museums and Arizona's main Mormon temple. Scottsdale, northeast of Phoenix and Tempe, is known for both its Western downtown area, now full of fine galleries, boutiques and crafts stores, and its many upscale resorts and restaurants.

Other towns, including Chandler to the southeast and Glendale and Peoria to the northwest, are thriving residential and manufacturing communities off the travelers' normal circuit, unless you're into antiques, in which case Glendale's downtown has dozens of antique stores. Sun City and Sun City West, in the northwest of the valley, are among the largest retirement communities in the country, with little industry or tourism but numerous quiet streets and golf courses for the dynamic older residents. Paradise Valley, nestled between the arms of Phoenix and Scottsdale, is the valley's most exclusive residential neighborhood, and Apache Junction, at the far east end of metropolitan Phoenix, is the gateway to the wild Superstition Mountains and the Apache Trail leading into east-central Arizona.

Phoenix rising

Because the valley's roads run north-south or east-west, to get from one point to another you often have to take two sides of a triangle; this, combined with large distances and slow traffic, can make getting around time-consuming.

Central Ave, running north-south in Phoenix, divides west addresses from east addresses; west of Central Ave, *avenues* are north-south bound, while east of Central Ave *streets* run north-south. Washington St, running west-east in Phoenix, divides north addresses from south addresses; thus 4100 N 16th St would be 16 blocks east of Central Ave and 41 blocks north of Washington (this is only an approximation – blocks don't always correspond exactly to 100-address increments). This numbering system continues into Scottsdale and Glendale.

Tempe and Mesa each have their own numbering systems, which means you can drive from Phoenix's 4800 E Southern Ave to Tempe's 2800 W Southern Ave just by crossing the city limits. In Tempe, Mill Ave, running north-south, divides west addresses from east addresses, while the east-west flowing Salt River divides north from south addresses. In Mesa, north-south Center St divides west from east, and west-east Main St divides north from south. Other valley towns have similar systems.

Major freeways include I-17 North (Black Canyon Hwy; this has many motels along it), I-10 West (the Papago Freeway), I-10 South (the Maricopa Freeway) and Hwy 60 East (the Superstition Freeway).

## INFORMATION

The Greater Phoenix Convention and Visitors Bureau (CVB – Map 3; ☎ 602-254-6500, 877-225-5749), 50 N 2nd St, is open 8am to 5pm Monday to Friday. This is the valley's most complete source of tourist information; visit it at www.phoenixcvb.com. Another office (☎ 602-955-1963) is at the Biltmore Fashion Park Shopping Mall, Center Lawn, 2404 E Camelback Rd, open during mall hours daily. A useful website is www.phoenix.gov, with hundreds of searchable links.

Individual towns each offer their own services. The Scottsdale CVB (☎ 480-945-8481, 800-877-1117), 7343 Scottsdale Mall, is open 8:30am to 6pm Monday to Friday, 10am to 4pm Saturday and 11am to 4pm Sunday (closed summer Sundays); its website is www.scottsdalecvb.com. The Tempe CVB (☎ 480-894-8158, 800-283-6734), 51 W 3rd, Suite 105, has a website at www.tempecvb.com; it and the Mesa CVB (☎ 480-827-4700, 800-283-6372), 120 N Center, and the Glendale Tourist Office (☎ 623-930-2957, 623-930-2957), 5850 W Glendale Ave, are all open 8am to 5pm Monday to Friday.

The Arizona Public Lands Information Center (Map 3; ☎ 602-417-9300), 222 N Central Ave, provides information about USFS, NPS, BLM and state lands and parks from 7:30am to 4:30pm Monday to Friday; look at www.publiclands.org.

Foreign exchange is available at the airport and some banks; call Bank of America (☎ 800-944-0404) or Bank One (☎ 800-366-2265) for addresses and hours of the nearest branch. The main post office is at 4949 E Van Buren (Map 2), and the main downtown post office is at 522 N Central Ave (Map 3).

The Phoenix area has three telephone area codes. These are considered local numbers when dialing from one to another, as from a hotel room, but the different area codes must be dialed.

The huge main library (Map 3; ☎ 602-262-4636) is at 1221 N Central Ave and there are many branch libraries throughout the city. The local daily is the *Arizona Republic*. The area's bookstore scene is now dominated by huge chain stores. If you're after used books, Bookman's (☎ 480-835-0505), 1056 S Country Club Dr, Mesa, is among the largest. One of the best selections of periodicals and magazines is at The Book Store (Map 2; ☎ 602-279-3910), 4230 N 7th Ave. Wide World of Maps (Map 2; ☎ 602-279-2323), 2626 W Indian School Rd, has a fine selection of maps and guidebooks.

Banner Health Arizona (☎ 602-230-2273) operates several valley hospitals and provides 24-hour doctor referral; there are also many other hospitals and clinics. For 24-hour dentist referral, call the Arizona Dental Association (☎ 602-957-4777).

The Phoenix police (Map 3; ☎ 602-262-6151) are at 620 W Washington.

## THINGS TO SEE & DO
### Central Phoenix

All museums are closed on at least some major holidays.

**Heard Museum** This museum (Map 3; ☎ 602-252-8840, 252-8848), 2301 N Central Ave, emphasizes quality rather than quantity and is one of America's best museums in which to learn Southwest Indian tribes' history, life, arts and culture. Certainly, there are thousands of exhibits, but these are well displayed in a relatively small space, making a visit here much more relaxing than the torturous slog through many major museums. The kachina-doll room is outstanding, as are the audiovisual displays, occasional live demonstrations and the superb gift shop. If you are at all interested in Native American history and culture, this museum should be at the top of your list. Combined with a visit to the nearby Phoenix Art Museum, it makes a great cultural day.

The museum is open 9:30am to 5pm daily. Admission is $7 for adults; $6 for seniors; $3 for four- to 12-year-olds; free for Native Americans. You can take a free guided tour (noon, 1:30 and 3pm) or rent a 45-minute audiotape tour for $3.
website: www.heard.org

**Phoenix Art Museum** Galleries show works from around the world, produced between the 14th and 20th centuries; don't miss the collection of clothing from the last two centuries, and be sure to check out the many fine changing exhibitions. There is a café.

The art museum (Map 3; ☎ 602-257-1880, 257-1222), 1625 N Central Ave, is open 10am to 5pm daily (till 9pm on Thursday) except Monday. Take a guided tour at 2pm or sit in on the half-hour talks given daily at noon.

Admission is $7 for adults; $5 for seniors and full-time students; $2 for six- to 17-year-olds. Admission is free to all on Thursday.
website: www.phxart.org

**Heritage Square** Eight late-19th- and early-20th-century houses are preserved in Heritage Square (Map 3; ☎ 602-262-5071), the block southeast of 6th St and Monroe. This is about as historical as it gets in Phoenix. Try to ignore the surrounding skyscrapers and imagine thudding hooves and squeaking stagecoach wheels creating clouds of dust outside the buildings.

The square is open 10am to 4pm Tuesday to Saturday and noon to 4 pm Sunday, and is closed August. Admission is free, but to visit the 1895 two-story restored **Rosson House**, the most splendid in the square, you must join a tour ($4 for adults, $3 for seniors, $1 for six- to 13-year-olds) offered every 30 minutes 10am to 3:30pm Wednesday to Saturday and noon to 3:30pm on Sunday. Also in the square, the **Arizona Doll & Toy Museum** (☎ 602-253-9337) charges $2.50, $1 for children.

Other buildings offer free admission and contain places to eat as well as arts and crafts shops.

**Arizona Science Center** This complex (Map 3; ☎ 602-716-2000), 600 E Washington, adjoining Heritage Square, is open 10am to 5pm daily, and stays open later for special events. A **museum** with 350 hands-on exhibits encourages visitors to explore and experiment with computers, bubbles, weather, physics, biology and more. Live demonstrations are held throughout the day. A five-story **giant-screen theater** features changing shows playing every hour from 11am to 4pm and a **planetarium** has star shows two or three times a day.

Museum admission is $8 for adults; $6 for seniors and three- to 12-year-olds. Tickets for the theater or planetarium are an extra $3 each per person.
website: www.azscience.org

**Phoenix Museum of History** Displays at this modern and attractive museum range

# SUBURBAN PHOENIX – MAP 1

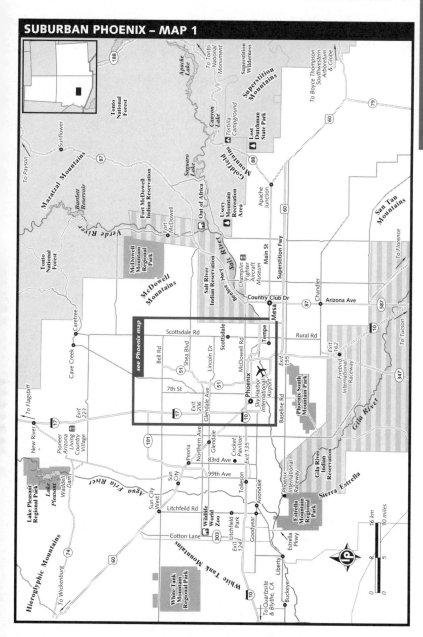

# PHOENIX – MAP 2

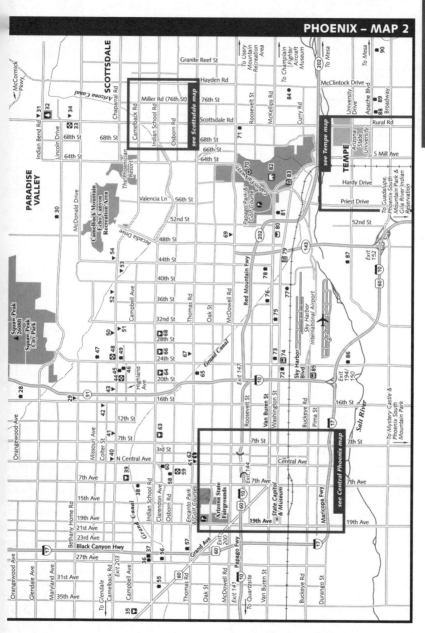

PHOENIX – MAP 2

## PHOENIX – MAP 2

**PLACES TO STAY**
2 Days Inn
5 Best Western Bell Motel;
   Motel 6; Fairfield Inn
6 Embassy Suites
12 Fairmont Scottsdale Princess
   Resort; La Hacienda
14 Motel 6
15 Pointe Hilton Tapatio Cliffs
   Resort
18 Scottsdale Fairfield Inn
19 Royal Suites
22 Motel 6; Super 8 Motel
23 Hampton Inn
26 Hyatt Regency Scottsdale at
   Gainey Ranch Resort
28 Pointe Hilton Squaw Peak
   Resort
30 Marriott's Camelback Inn
37 Motel 6
45 Courtyard by Marriott; Ruth's
   Chris Steak House
46 Phoenix Inn Suites
47 Arizona Biltmore Resort & Spa
49 Ritz-Carlton
55 Howard Johnson
56 Super 8 Motel
57 Days Inn
58 Quality Hotel
60 Lexington Hotel at City
   Square
65 Embassy Suites
71 Best Western Papago Inn &
   Resort
72 Motel 6
73 Flamingo Airporter Inn
75 Pyramid Inn; Days Inn;
   Phoenix Airport Super 8
   Motel

76 Phoenix Sunrise Motel
78 Doubletree Suites
81 Motel 6
86 Best Western Airport Inn
87 Airport Hilton; Airport
   Courtyard by Marriott
88 Comfort Suites
89 Days Inn - Tempe/ASU
90 Econo Lodge - Tempe

**PLACES TO EAT**
4 Good Egg
8 India Palace
9 Taste of India
10 Chompie's
16 The Eggery
17 Good Egg
21 Maria's When in Naples
24 El Bravo
27 The Coffee Roastery
29 Texaz Bar & Grill
31 Ruth's Chris Steak House
34 Good Egg
40 The Eggery; Orbit Restaurant
   & Jazz Club
41 Good Egg
42 5 & Diner
43 Greekfest
50 La Madeleine
51 Harris'
52 Vincent Guerithault on
   Camelback
53 Havana Cafe
54 The Eggery
61 Durant's
67 Avanti
69 India Delhi Palace

**OTHER**
1 Deer Valley Rock Art Center
3 Rawhide
7 Arizona Game & Fish Dept
11 Crackerjax
13 Fleischer Museum
20 Metrocenter Mall; Castles 'n
   Coasters
25 Cosanti Foundation
32 McCormick-Stillman Railroad
   Park
33 Borgata Shopping Mall; Café
   Terra Cotta
35 Mr Lucky's
36 Wide World of Maps
38 The Book Store
39 Char's Has the Blues
44 Town & Country Mall (Baby
   Kay's Cajun Kitchen, Tuchetti,
   Ed Debevic's)
48 Biltmore Fashion Park
   (RoxSand, Steamers)
59 Park Central Mall
62 Arizona Office of Tourism
63 Rhythm Room
64 Mason Jar
66 Warsaw Wallies
68 Ain't Nobody's Bizness
70 Desert Botanical Garden
74 White Mountain Passenger
   Lines
77 Phoenix Greyhound Park
79 Pueblo Grande Museum
80 Main Post Office
82 Phoenix Zoo
83 Hall of Flame
84 Big Surf
85 Greyhound Bus Terminal

from 2000-year-old archaeological artifacts to an exhibit about the sinking of the USS *Arizona* at Pearl Harbor in 1941. The museum (Map 3; ☎ 602-253-2734), 105 N 5th St, adjoining Heritage Square, is open 10am to 5pm Monday to Saturday, and noon to 5pm on Sunday. Admission is $5 for adults; $3.50 for seniors; $2.50 for seven- to 12-year-olds.

### Other Central Museums

The old state capitol building (Map 3; ☎ 602-542-4675), 1700 W Washington, built in 1900, is now the **Arizona State Capitol Museum** displaying documents and exhibits from late-territorial and early-state days. Admission is free; hours are 8am to 5pm Monday to Friday. The **Arizona Hall of Fame** (Map 3; ☎ 602-542-4581), housed in the 1908 Carnegie Library building at 1101 W Washington and open by appointment only, presents changing exhibits on people who have contributed to Arizona's history in memorable and not-so-memorable ways.

The **Arizona Mining & Mineral Museum** (Map 3; ☎ 602-255-3791), 1502 W Washington, also has a Rose Mofford room with

# CENTRAL PHOENIX – MAP 3

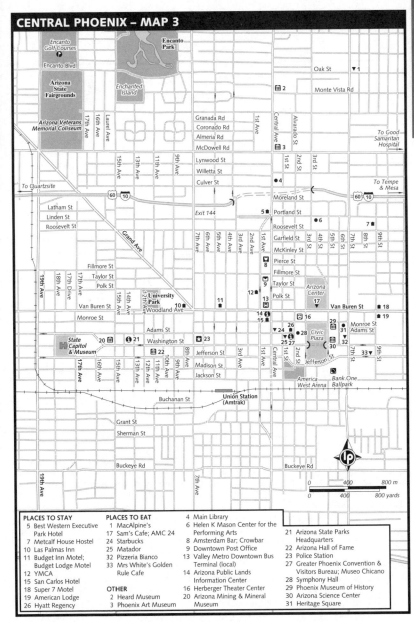

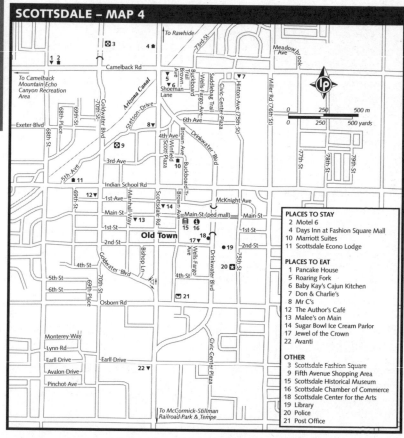

## SCOTTSDALE – MAP 4

**PLACES TO STAY**
2 Motel 6
4 Days Inn at Fashion Square Mall
10 Marriott Suites
11 Scottsdale Econo Lodge

**PLACES TO EAT**
1 Pancake House
5 Roaring Fork
6 Baby Kay's Cajun Kitchen
7 Don & Charlie's
8 Mr C's
12 The Author's Café
13 Malee's on Main
14 Sugar Bowl Ice Cream Parlor
17 Jewel of the Crown
22 Avanti

**OTHER**
3 Scottsdale Fashion Square
9 Fifth Avenue Shopping Area
15 Scottsdale Historical Museum
16 Scottsdale Chamber of Commerce
18 Scottsdale Center for the Arts
19 Library
20 Police
21 Post Office

memorabilia of Arizona's first woman governor. Hours are Monday to Friday 8am to 5pm, Saturday 11am to 4 pm; free.

The **Museo Chicano** (☎ 602-257-5536), 147 E Adams, exhibits mainly artwork by local and national Hispanic artists. Hours are 10am to 4pm Tuesday to Saturday; admission is $2, seniors and students $1.

### Outer Phoenix

**Desert Botanical Garden** This 145-acre garden in Papago Park (Map 2) exhibits thousands of species of arid-land plants from Arizona and around the world. The flowering season of March to May is the busiest and most colorful time to visit, but any month provides insight into how plants survive in the desert. The garden (☎ 480-941-1225), 1201 N Galvin Parkway, has a gift shop and café and offers occasional tours and events; it is open 8am to 8pm daily (from 7am October through May). Admission is $7.50 adults; $6.50 for seniors; $3.50 for five- to 12-year-olds.

The surrounding **Papago Park** has picnic areas, jogging, biking and equestrian trails, a city golf course and a children's fishing pond; it also houses the Phoenix Zoo.

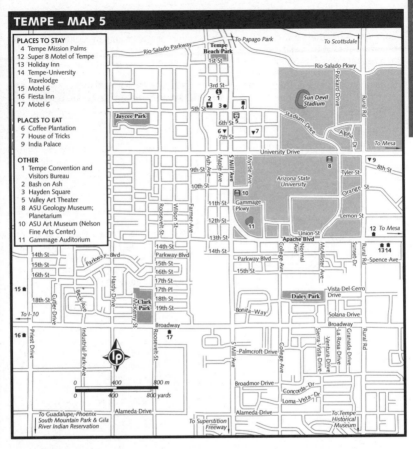

TEMPE – MAP 5

**PLACES TO STAY**
4 Tempe Mission Palms
12 Super 8 Motel of Tempe
13 Holiday Inn
14 Tempe-University
   Travelodge
15 Motel 6
16 Fiesta Inn
17 Motel 6

**PLACES TO EAT**
6 Coffee Plantation
7 House of Tricks
9 India Palace

**OTHER**
1 Tempe Convention and
  Visitors Bureau
2 Bash on Ash
3 Hayden Square
5 Valley Art Theater
8 ASU Geology Museum;
  Planetarium
10 ASU Art Museum (Nelson
   Fine Arts Center)
11 Gammage Auditorium

**Phoenix Zoo** The zoo (Map 2; ☎ 602-273-1341), 455 N Galvin Parkway, houses a wide variety of animals, including some rare ones, in natural-looking environments. There is a children's petting zoo, walk-in aviary, demonstrations and food facilities. The zoo is open 9am to 5pm September through June. Admission is $12; $9 for seniors; $5 for three- to 12-year-olds. Narrated safari train tours cost $2 and last 30 minutes. Call for shorter summer hours and discounted admissions.

**Hall of Flame** Opposite Papago Park, the Hall of Flame (Map 2; ☎ 602-275-3473), 6101 E Van Buren, exhibits more than 90 fully restored firefighting machines and related paraphernalia from 1725 onward. The hall is open 9am to 5pm Monday to Saturday, and noon to 4pm on Sunday. Admission is $6; $5 for seniors; $3 for six- to 17-year-olds.

**Pueblo Grande Museum** As early as 300 BC, the dry desert soil yielded crops for the Hohokam people, who spent centuries developing a complex system of irrigation canals only to mysteriously abandon them around AD 1450. Pueblo Grande is a

Hohokam village that has been partially excavated and then reburied for its protection. Parts of the excavation remain exposed for the visitor, and a nice little onsite museum (Map 2; ☎ 602-495-0901), 4619 E Washington, explains all that is known of the canal-building Hohokam culture. Admission is $2; $1.50 for seniors; $1 for six- to 18-year-olds; free on Sunday. Hours are 9am to 4:45pm Monday to Saturday, and 1 to 4:45pm on Sunday.
website: www.pueblogrande.com

**Mystery Castle** This 18-room fantasy was built between 1927 and 1945 by the reclusive Boyce Luther Gulley for his daughter, Mary Lou, who now gives tours of the oddly furnished property. Mystery Castle (☎ 602-268-1581), 800 E Mineral Rd (on the north border of Phoenix South Mountain Park) is open 11am to 4 pm Thursday to Sunday, October to June; admission is $5; $4 for seniors; $2 for five- to 15-year-olds.

**Deer Valley Rock Art Center** A small museum (Map 2; ☎ 623-582-8007), 3711 W Deer Valley Rd (west of I-17 exit 215A), interprets the significance and techniques involved in making the approximately 1500 prehistoric petroglyphs chipped into boulders along a quarter-mile trail outside. Hours are 9am to 5pm Tuesday to Saturday, and noon to 5pm on Sunday; call about shorter spring and summer hours. Admission is $4; $2 for students and seniors; $1 for six- to 12-year-olds.

## Scottsdale
**Old Town** Half a dozen blocks near the chamber of commerce constitute 'Old Town,' with some early-20th-century buildings and some more recent buildings styled to look like those of the Old West. One of the oldest is the 'Little Red School House,' built in 1909 and now housing the **Scottsdale Historical Museum** (Map 4; ☎ 480-945-4499), 7333 Scottsdale Mall. Hours are 10am to 5pm Wednesday to Saturday, and noon to 4pm Sunday; the museum is closed on holidays and throughout July and August. Admission is free.

Nearby, the **Scottsdale Center for the Arts** (Map 4; ☎ 480-994-2787), 7374 E 2nd St, includes the **Museum of Contemporary Art** and hosts various performing arts. The museum is open Monday to Wednesday

### The Desert as Muse

Frank Lloyd Wright (1867–1959), America's most iconoclastic well-known architect, lived, designed and taught in Scottsdale at **Taliesin West** (☎ 480-860-2700, 480-860-8810), 12621 Frank Lloyd Wright Blvd (Cactus Rd at 104th St). Set on 600 acres of desert, Taliesin West is an example of his organic architecture, which uses natural forms to shape most structures. Wright moved here in 1927 and set up a tent camp. He began building a decade later and wasn't finished until 20 years after that. Today, the natural rock, wood and canvas structures continue to be both living quarters and a teaching establishment.

Visits are limited to guided tours. One-hour tours are given daily every half hour, October to May from 10am to 4pm (call about summer hours), and cost $16. Ninety-minute tours are offered at 9am Monday to Saturday, and cost $16. Ninety-minute desert walks on the grounds are given at 11:15am and 1:15pm Monday to Saturday; $14 for all. Three-hour 'behind the scenes' tours at 9am Tuesday and Thursday are $25; call ahead for updated tour times and for reservations.

Paolo Soleri was a student of Frank Lloyd Wright who went on to develop his own form of organic architecture, which he termed 'arcology' (the combined form of architecture and ecology). Soleri's headquarters are at **Cosanti Foundation** (Map 1; ☎ 480-948-6145), 6433 Doubletree Ranch Rd, where you can see a scale model of his futuristic Arcosanti (see Around Camp Verde in the Central Arizona chapter) and various other structures, and can pick up a souvenir at the gift shop. Hours are 9am to 5pm daily, and a $1 donation is suggested.

10am to 5pm, Thursday to Saturday 10am to 8pm, and Sunday noon to 5 pm; admission is $7 and $5 for students. The whole mall area is beautifully and restfully landscaped with green areas, shade trees and fountains. Several good ethnic restaurants are near the center for the arts. West of the Scottsdale Mall, centered around Brown Ave and Main, old Western-style buildings house art galleries, restaurants and souvenir shops. The chamber of commerce offers brochures describing this popular area.

**Fleischer Museum** Very few art museums have as specific a focus as the Fleischer, dedicated to American Impressionism of the California School. The Fleischer Museum (Map 2; ☎ 480-585-3108), 17207 N Perimeter Dr, is open 10am to 4pm daily except holidays; free.

**Rawhide** About 14 miles north of downtown Scottsdale, Rawhide (Map 2; ☎ 480-502-5600), 23023 N Scottsdale Rd, is a recreated late-1800s Western town with saloons, showdowns, stagecoaches and all that stuff. Popular with tourists and fun for kids, it's open 5 to 10pm daily year-round; October to May hours are extended to 11am to 10pm on weekends, and March hours vary. Admission is free, unless there is a special event; call for details. Attractions, such as the stagecoach, burro or train rides and the Indian village (with dance performances) charge an extra $2 to $4 each. A steak house is open from 5pm daily, plus 11:30am to 3pm during winter weekends. website: www.rawhide.com

## Tempe
**Arizona State University** With some 45,000 students, this is the largest college in the Southwest. General information (☎ 480-965-9011) and a 24-hour recorded calendar of campus events during the academic year (☎ 480-965-2278) will help orient you.

The **ASU Art Museum** (Map 5; ☎ 480-965-2787), headquartered in the architecturally acclaimed Nelson Fine Arts Center at 10th St and Mill Ave, showcases a varied collection of European and American art along with changing exhibits; hours are 10am to 5 pm Wednesday to Saturday, 1 to 5pm Sunday and 10am to 9 pm Tuesday. For an experimental gallery exhibiting the work of emerging artists, visit the Matthews Center branch of the museum, about a quarter-mile northeast of the Nelson Center. Hours are 10am to 5pm Tuesday to Saturday. Admission is free to both.

The interesting and free **ASU Geology Museum** (Map 5; ☎ 480-965-7065), 250 yards west of McAllister and University Dr, exhibiting dinosaur bones, rocks, minerals and gems, is open 9am to noon Monday to Friday. The **Planetarium** (Map 5; ☎ 480-727-6234), next to the Geology Museum, has star shows from October to May for $2; call for hours. The **Gammage Auditorium** at Mill Ave and Apache Blvd (Map 5) was Frank Lloyd Wright's last major building; tour the inside between October and May, 1 to 4 pm Monday to Friday.

**Tempe Historical Museum** Permanent and changing displays, as well as interactive exhibits, showcase Tempe's prehistory and modern history at this small museum. The museum (☎ 480-350-5100), 809 E Southern Ave, is open 10am to 5 pm Monday to Thursday and Saturday, 1 to 5pm Sunday and is closed on Friday and major holidays. Admission is by donation.

## Mesa
There are quite a few museums in Mesa, including the **Arizona Museum for Youth** (see the 'Especially for Kids' boxed text).

**Mesa Southwest Museum** Animated dinosaurs, dioramas of ancient Indians, an eight-cell territorial jail, gold panning near the Dutchman's Mine and changing art shows are just a few of the many displays and interactive exhibits at this museum with a Southwestern theme.

The museum (☎ 480-644-2230), 53 N MacDonald, is open 10am to 5pm Tuesday to Saturday, 1 to 5pm on Sunday, and closed Monday and holidays. Admission is $6 for adults; $5 for seniors and students; $3 for three- to 12-year-olds.

**Mesa Historical Society Museum** Mesa's pioneer history is remembered through more than 4000 artifacts displayed at this museum (☎ 480-835-7358), 2345 N Horne. Hours are 10am to 4pm Tuesday to Saturday and 9am to 1pm in summer. Admission is free.

**Champlin Fighter Aircraft Museum** The museum (Map 1; ☎ 480-830-4540), in Falcon Field Airport at 4800 E McKellips Rd, has one of the largest collections of fighter aircraft in the world. Thirty-three flyable airplanes from WWI to the Vietnam War are on display and are explained in extensive supporting exhibits. The museum is open 8:30am to 3:30pm daily in summer and 10am to 5pm the rest of the year. Admission is $6.50 for adults; $3 for five- to 12-year-olds. Guided tours (be sure to call to reserve a spot) are given at 10:30am, 1:30 and 3pm.

### Suburban Phoenix
**Pioneer Arizona Living Country Village** About 25 authentic territorial buildings (brought here from elsewhere) and farm animals (which can be petted) form a complete village inhabited by guides/interpreters in period dress. Daily performances in a turn-of-the-19th-century opera house and various other re-enactments present a historically accurate depiction of pioneering life. The museum (Map 1; ☎ 623-465-1052), 3901 W Pioneer Rd, is at I-17 exit 225. It's open 9am to 5pm Wednesday to Sunday, and 9am to 3pm June to September. Admission to the village is $7 for adults; $5 for four- to 12-year-olds.

**Wildlife World Zoo** This zoo specializes in rare and exotic species ranging from white tigers to black jaguars. The attractions include a walk-in aviary filled with tropical birds, a parrot feeding area, a petting zoo and an aquarium with seahorses, piranhas and electric eels. The zoo (Map 1; ☎ 623-935-9453), 16501 W Northern Ave, is open 9am to 5pm daily. Admission is $14 for adults; $6 for three- to 12-year-olds.

**Out of Africa** See big cats from Africa and other continents, pet a lion cub or watch keepers swim with big cats at this wildlife park. The park presents a variety of continuous shows. Out of Africa (☎ 480-837-7779, 480-837-7677), 2 S Fort McDowell Rd (off Hwy 87 near the Fort McDowell Indian Reservation), is open 9:30am to 5pm Tuesday to Sunday from October through May. In summer, hours are 4 to 9pm Wednesday and Thursday, 9:30am to 9pm Friday and Saturday, and 5 to 9pm on Sunday. Some Monday holidays are open. Admission is $15 for adults; $14 for seniors; $7 for three- to 12-year-olds.

### Suburban Parks
Several large parks in the mountains ringing the valley provide residents with many hiking, cycling, horseback riding and picnicking areas. Some are very popular and of course get crowded; nevertheless, these parks are as wild as you can get near a major city. Outdoors, people must beware of dehydration and sunburn in summer; be sure to carry water and sun protection.

The following are some of the most important parks, going from south to north. Unless noted under Places to Stay, later, camping is not allowed.

**Phoenix South Mountain Park** Covering 25 sq miles, this is the largest city park in the USA and is part of the Phoenix Mountain Preserve system (☎ 602-495-0222). The park provides over 40 miles of multiuse trails open from dawn until dusk. There are good views and dozens of Indian petroglyph sites to admire. The park is topped by South Mountain (2690 feet) and is at 10919 S Central Ave (Map 1). Rangers can help plan your visit (8am to 5pm), and maps are available. Rangers emphasize: 'Don't leave valuables in your car'.

**Estrella Mountain Regional Park** On the southwestern outskirts of town, this 31-sq-mile county park (Map 1; ☎ 623-932-3811) is at the north end of the extremely rugged Sierra Estrella, providing 34 miles of multiuse trails, a golf course, rodeo arena and picnicking areas, mainly in the northwest corner of the park.

The park is on the Gila River Indian Reservation; reach it by driving 5 miles south of I-10 along Estrella Parkway in Goodyear. Hours are 6am to 8pm (10pm Friday and Saturday); admission is $3 per vehicle.

**Squaw Peak City Park** The 2608-foot summit of Squaw Peak affords one of Phoenix's most popular hikes (no bikes or horses are allowed), and parking is very hard to find on weekends outside of summer; get there early in the morning. The park opens at 5:30am and the parking areas along Squaw Peak Dr, northeast of Lincoln Dr between 22nd and 24th Sts, may be full by 7:30am on winter weekends. For information, call ☎ 602-262-7901.

**McDowell Mountain Regional Park** Hiking, biking, horseback riding and camping are all permitted in this 33-sq-mile county park (☎ 480-471-0173). Access is along Fountain Hills Blvd from Shea Blvd east of Scottsdale. Hours are dawn till dusk, and admission is $3 per vehicle.

## Especially for Kids

Places like the zoo, the wildlife park, the Arizona Science Center, the Hall of Flame and Rawhide will interest the whole family, but the following are especially for kids.

Art exhibits and hands-on art workshops are aimed at elementary school children at the **Arizona Museum for Youth** (☎ 480-644-2467), 35 N Robson St, Mesa. Exhibitions and workshops change every few months, so call ahead for details. Hours are 9am to 5pm Tuesday to Saturday. Admission is $2.50 for ages three and up. Preregistration for workshops is suggested. The 30-acre **McCormick-Stillman Railroad Park** (Map 1; ☎ 480-312-2312), 7301 E Indian Bend Rd, Scottsdale, has a miniature railroad at 5/12 scale. Rides, open from 10am to about 6pm, cost $1. Other attractions are model railroads, a traditional carousel and a railroad museum ($1).

Cool off in summer at **Waterworld Safari** (☎ 623-581-1947), 4243 W Pinnacle Peak Rd (2 miles west of I-17 exit 217), with a six-story-high water slide; **Big Surf Waterpark** (☎ 480-947-7873), 1500 N McClintock Dr, Tempe; and **Golfland/Sunsplash** (☎ 480-834-8319), 155 W Hampton Ave, Mesa. All offer acres of swimming pools, water slides and wave-making machines; Golfland also has tube floats, bumper boats, miniature golf and go-carts. It is open daily from Memorial Day to Labor Day, and admission is about $17.50 ($14.50 for four- to 11-year-olds).

**Castles 'n Coasters** (Map 1; ☎ 602-997-7575), 9445 E Metro Pkwy (by the Metrocenter Mall) is the area's largest amusement park, with the 2000-foot-long Desert Storm roller coaster, complete with two 360° loops, providing fun for kids of all ages with strong stomachs. Smaller coasters are suitable for younger riders and there are a dozen other attractions, including four miniature golf courses, video arcades, go-carts and carousels. Desert Storm and major rides are $4.50; smaller rides are $2 and miniature golf is $7. All-day unlimited rides are $18; $23 with unlimited miniature golf. The park is open daily. Near downtown, **Enchanted Island** (Map 2; ☎ 602-254-2020), 1202 W Encanto Blvd, has 10 rides aimed at younger kids for 75¢ each; $9 for unlimited day use. It's open Wednesday to Sunday year-round, and some Mondays and Tuesdays.

Local 'Family Fun Parks' offering miniature golf, video games, batting cages, bumper boats, go-carts, volleyball and other activities year-round include the **Crackerjax** (Map 1; ☎ 480-998-2800), 16001 N Scottsdale Rd, and **Fiddlesticks** (☎ 480-961-0800), 1155 W Elliot Rd in Tempe (a mile east of I-10 exit 157), and in Scottsdale (☎ 480-951-6060), 8800 E Indian Bend Rd. They are open daily (hours vary seasonally) and you pay for the activities you want. Multiple-activity passes may be available.

**White Tank Mountain Regional Park** This 41-sq-mile park (Map 1; ☎ 623-935-2505) offers hiking, mountain biking, horseback riding and camping. Of the many trails, one leads to the 4018-foot summit of White Tank Mountain and another goes to a waterfall (which is sometimes dry). Park hours are dawn till dusk, and admission is $3 per vehicle. To reach the park from Phoenix, drive 10 miles northwest on Grand Ave (Hwy 60), then 15 miles west on Olive Ave (the western extension of Dunlap Ave).

## ACTIVITIES

In addition to the activities listed below, look in the yellow pages for skating rinks (both ice and roller), skydiving, gliding, bicycle rentals and other activities offered in the valley.

### Golf, Tennis & Swimming

Serious golfers probably already know that the valley, despite its desert location, is a major golfing center with almost 200 greens ranging from 'pitch and putt' to PGA championship courses. Many resorts offer fine courses and package golfing or tennis vacations (see Places to Stay). American Golf Reservations (☎ 480-962-4653, 602-953-1127), 443 N Central Ave, Suite 819, Phoenix, 85032, makes local tee-time reservations up to 60 days in advance.

Phoenix Parks and Recreation (☎ 602-262-6861) runs dozens of city parks with several golf courses, many tennis courts, swimming pools and other recreational programs. City courses generally offer the cheapest golfing, often at a quarter the price of the fancier golf courses. Search www.phoenix.gov for sports listings or check with the tourist office.

The city operates 27 swimming pools (call ☎ 602-534-7946 for general pool information). Also see the 'Especially for Kids' boxed text.

### Horseback Riding

As if to emphasize the valley's Western roots, over 30 horse rental and riding outfits are listed in the Phoenix yellow pages. Short rides, often combined with a country break-fast or barbecue cookout, are popular activities, and overnight packing trips can be arranged. Rates are about $20 for an hour. Reservations are suggested from late fall through spring; and it's too darn hot to do much riding in the summer, pardner.

Some better-known outfits include Ponderosa Stables (☎ 602-268-1261), 10215 S Central Ave, which leads rides into South Mountain Park. For both short and overnight trips into the mountains east of Phoenix, contact Don Donnelly Stables (☎ 480-982-7822, 800-346-4403), 6010 S Kings Ranch Rd, Apache Junction. In Scottsdale, there's MacDonald's Ranch (☎ 480-585-0239), 26540 N Scottsdale Rd.

### Tubing

Floating down the Salt River in an inner tube is a great way to relax and cool down in summer. From 6800 E Main, Mesa, head north on Power Rd, which becomes Bush Hwy and intersects with the Salt River. Follow Bush Hwy east along the river; the road reaches Saguaro Lake after about 10 miles.

Along the Bush Hwy, Salt River Recreation (☎ 480-984-3305, 480-984-1857) gives information, rents tubes and provides van shuttles to good starting places for short or all-day floats. Costs are $10 per person for shuttle and tube; rent an extra tube for your cooler full of cold drinks (don't bring glass). Bring sunblock and shoes suitable to protect your feet from the river bottom. Tubing season is mid-April through September, and weekends draw crowds of people bent on cooling off and partying on.

### Hot-Air Ballooning

Some experienced outfits include A Aerozona Adventures (☎ 480-991-4260, 888-991-4260) and Unicorn Balloon Company (☎ 480-991-3666, 800-468-2478), but many others are just as good. Also see the Outdoor Activities chapter.

### Shooting & Archery

The Ben Avery Shooting Range (☎ 623-582-8313), northwest of I-17 on Hwy 74, is the largest public recreational shooting area in the USA, providing practice facilities and competitions for a variety of firearms as well as archery.

## ORGANIZED TOURS

Several companies offer tours in and around the Phoenix area. Gray Line (☎ 602-495-9100, 800-732-0327) has a website at www.greylinearizona.com. Vaughan's Southwest (☎ 602-971-1381, 800-513-1381) offers 4½-hour tours cost $38; they're online at www.southwesttours.com. Both these and other companies do longer tours, such as a 14-hour tour to the Grand Canyon for $100 (for people with really limited time); children under 12 get discounts.

Many companies offer 4WD tours into the surrounding desert that last anywhere from four hours to all day and stress various themes: ghost towns, cookouts, Indian petroglyphs and ruins, natural history, sunset tours and target shooting. Costs start around $60 a person. Some reputable companies include Arizona Desert Mountain Jeep Tours (☎ 480-860-1777) in Scottsdale (go to www.azdesertmountain.com); Arrowhead Desert Tours (☎ 602-942-3361), 841 E Paradise Lane, Phoenix; and Wild West Jeep Tours (☎ 480-922-0144), 7127 E Becker Lane in Scottsdale.

## SPECIAL EVENTS

Something is happening just about all the time from October to May in Phoenix, but few events occur during the searing summer. The chambers of commerce are knowledgeable about all the scheduled events and provide free calendars. Some of the most important follow.

One of the Southwest's biggest parades precedes the Fiesta Bowl college football game on New Year's Day at the ASU Sun Devil Stadium. Late January and early February see Western events in Scottsdale, such as a horse-drawn parade, a rodeo, Pony Express reenactments and an All-Arabian Horse Show. Performers dress in Renaissance garb, joust and host many other medieval events on weekends from late February through early April during the Renaissance Festival, held on Hwy 60,

9 miles southeast of Apache Junction. Admission is $16 for adults; $8 for four- to 12-year-olds.

The Heard Museum hosts the Guild Indian Fair and Market during the first weekend in March, which has been held annually since 1958. View Indian dancers, eat Native American food, and browse and buy top-quality arts and crafts.

In mid-March, watch the Phoenix Rodeo of Rodeos, held at the Veterans Memorial Coliseum, 1826 W McDowell Rd. The costumed Yaqui Indian Easter Ceremonies are held Friday afternoon during Lent and from Wednesday to Easter Sunday of Holy Week. The events occur in the main plaza of the village of Guadalupe at the south end of Tempe.

The Arizona State Fair takes place in the last two weeks of October. Simultaneously and continuing into mid-November, the Cowboy Artists of America exhibition is on display at the Phoenix Art Museum. The Thunderbird Hot-Air Balloon Classic lifts off in early November, and dance, song and arts and crafts are featured at Pueblo Grande's Annual Indian Market during the second weekend in December.

## PLACES TO STAY

From very basic motels to ritzy resorts, the valley's hundreds of accommodations have one thing in common – prices plummet in summer. January-to-April rates can be two or even three times more expensive than summer rates in the top-end places, although at the cheapest ones, the seasonal price difference is not so vast. The price drop presents bargains for summer vacationers. Winter rates are overpriced because that is when hotels make enough money to offset the low rates in the stiflingly hot summers. Always ask for discounts – AAA, senior, student, military, business, whatever you can think of. Note that special events, such as the Fiesta Bowl, command very high prices. Also, when travelers might least expect it, a major rock concert at the Sun Devil Stadium drawing tens of thousands of fans from all over Arizona can suddenly fill rooms.

Chain motels outnumber everything else in town. Many chains are represented by a dozen or more properties scattered around the valley, so if you have a favorite, check their websites for a suitable choice. Travelers watching their budget will find cheaper motels strung out along several of the main drags in and around Phoenix. Most every hotel will boast at least a swimming pool. At the other end of the scale, expensive spas and resorts are destinations in themselves. Swanky and stylish Scottsdale tends to the upper end.

One area in which the valley appears to be lacking, though, is B&Bs. Agencies are helpful in booking the upper mid-range and top end hotels and resorts.

## Camping

You can camp at several of the suburban parks and recreation areas: *McDowell Mountain Regional Park* has about 70 campsites with water and electrical hookups for $15, as well as showers. The year-round campground at *White Tank Mountain Regional Park* offers 40 sites for $8, and provides showers but no hookups. *Estrella Mountain Regional Park* has both developed and undeveloped sites for $15/8.

*Mesa/Apache Junction KOA* (☎ 480-982-4015, 1540 S Tomahawk Rd, Apache Junction) is the closest KOA to the center of things. It has a pool and hot tub and charges $21 for tents and $23 to $28 for RV sites. Check www.koa.com for others in the Phoenix area.

For those 55 or older, huge adult-only RV parks (they should call them RV cities) are found in Mesa. All have extensive recreation facilities and are popular with long-term visitors (who get substantial discounts) so reservations are suggested. *Mesa Spirit* (☎ 480-832-1770, 3020 E Main) has almost 1800 sites priced at about $36. The *Mesa Regal RV Resort* (☎ 480-830-2821, 800-845-4752, 4700 E Main) has about 2000 sites priced at $30.

About 100 more RV parks, many for adults only, are listed in the Phoenix yellow pages.

Check with the US Forest Service for information about campgrounds in the Tonto National Forest, north and east of the Phoenix area. Also see the Apache Trail in the East-Central Arizona chapter.

## Budget

Central Phoenix has the region's best selection of cheap places to stay. Many young budget travelers head over to the friendly *Metcalf House Hostel (Map 3;* ☎ *602-254-9803, 1026 N 9th St)*. This hostel will not take telephone reservations but nearly always has space in the dorms, priced at $15 per person. Just show up during office hours, from 5 to 10pm. Kitchen and laundry facilities are available. It is located four houses northwest of the empty lot on the corner of 9th and Roosevelt.

The *YMCA (Map 3;* ☎ *602-253-6181, 350 N 1st Ave)* rents single rooms with shared showers for $28 a night or $110 to US$140 a week, and doubles for not much more. It is usually full and does not take reservations – show up around 9am for the best chance at a room. The guests are primarily men, but women are welcome to stay in rooms on the women's floor and use the fitness facilities.

Most of the area's cheapest motels are along Van Buren. The downtown area is OK, but as you head east of 10th St, the neighborhood deteriorates into blocks of boarded-up buildings, used-car lots and streetwalkers' turf (police patrols periodically scout the area). The neighborhood from around 24th to about 36th Sts, north of the airport, improves and is where more cheap hotels are located, some of which are acceptable though the area remains seedy. Many places will give weekly discounts.

For decent, clean lodging for $30 to $45, try the following (all on Map 4):

*Budget Lodge Motel* (☎ 602-254-7247, 402 W Van Buren)

*Budget Inn Motel* (☎ 602-257-8331, 424 W Van Buren)

*Las Palmas Inn* (☎ 602-256-9161, 765 NW Grand Ave)

*American Lodge* (☎ 602-252-6823, 965 E Van Buren)

*Super 7 Motel* (☎ 602-258-5540, 938 E Van Buren)

The *Flamingo Airporter Inn* (Map 2; ☎ 602-275-6211, 2501 E Van Buren) charges about $40 for one or two people and is the closest cheapie to the airport. Not much farther is the *Pyramid Inn* (Map 2; ☎ 602-275-3691, 3307 E Van Buren ), also cheap, and the *Phoenix Sunrise Motel* (Map 2; ☎ 602-275-7661, 800-432-6483, 3644 E Van Buren).

In Tempe, Apache Blvd has a couple of nondescript cheap motels, as well as chains. Apache Blvd becomes Main St in Mesa, and continues for about 20 miles into and through Apache Junction. This long strip of ugly, modern Americana has a number of budget motels scattered along it – if you don't need to stay near the center, drive and see.

*Motel 6* is represented by 17(!) motels in the greater Phoenix area. Most charge in the $40s during summer and the $50s or $60s in winter for a double. The most expensive Motel 6 is in classy Scottsdale, where winter rooms in the $70s are the cheapest choice in that town.

## Mid-Range
Many of the major *chain motels and hotels* have properties close to the airport and provide a free shuttle. Other properties are scattered along most of the exits of I-17 and I-10. See the Accommodations section in the Facts for the Visitor chapter for toll-free reservation numbers and websites.

Right in downtown Phoenix, the *San Carlos Hotel* (Map 3; ☎ 602-253-4121, 866-253-4121, 202 N Central Ave) has all the character you'll want if chains aren't your thing. Built in 1927, it was downtown's swankiest hotel for decades, and although recently refurbished and comfortable, the hotel retains many of its early fixtures and atmosphere. The 130 rooms ($100 to $150 a double) are small, but there are six suites (up to $210) if you need to spread out, and facilities include an exercise room and café. website: www.hotelsancarlos.com

North of downtown Phoenix, the *Lexington Hotel at City Square* (Map 2; ☎ 602-279-9811, 100 W Clarendon Ave) charges $80 to $130 for 180 standard hotel rooms. The rates include access to 35,000 sq feet of sports club amenities that include large locker rooms, aerobics and well-equipped machine workout rooms with trainers, a dozen racquetball courts, a basketball court, spa, sauna and steam room. There's also a restaurant open 6:30am to 10pm, and a busy sports bar and nightclub. website: www.phxihc.com

The *Phoenix Inn Suites* (Map 2; ☎ 602-956-5221, 800-956-5221, 2310 E Highland Ave) has 120 spacious rooms, all with refrigerators, coffee-makers and microwaves, for $130 to $170 including continental breakfast (summer rates go down to $59). Some larger suites go up to $220. A pool, Jacuzzi, exercise room and airport transportation are offered; visit www.phoenixinnsuites .com. Farther north, the *Royal Suites* (Map 2; ☎ 602-942-1000, 800-647-5786, 10421 N 33rd Ave) offers 80 clean and modern mini-suites with kitchenettes. It charges about $110 in winter, with discounts for longer stays.

South of Tempe, the *InnSuites* (☎ 480-897-7900, 800-842-4242, 1651 W Baseline Rd), near I-10 exit 155, has pleasant rooms of various sizes for $110 to $150; all rooms include kitchenettes, and some have sitting rooms or full kitchens. Continental breakfast, evening cocktail hour and airport transportation are included. With two tennis courts and an exercise room, you can get a workout while the kids are on the playground, or you can relax in the spa.

The *Scottsdale Econo Lodge* (Map 4; ☎ 480-994-9461, 800-528-7396, 6935 5th Ave) has comfortable motel rooms priced at $110 in winter, and fashionable shopping is within walking distance.

## Top End
The 24-story *Hyatt Regency* (Map 3; ☎ 602-252-1234, 800-233-1234, 122 N 2nd) is a huge downtown convention center/hotel with the expected amenities such as a health club, restaurants, room service, a concierge and shopping. More than 700 rooms, many with balconies, go for $160 to $290 a double in winter; some suites go for more than $1000 on peak nights. This is the city's biggest hotel, and the revolving rooftop

restaurant (The Compass) has great views and excellent Southwestern food.
website: www.phoenix.hyatt.com

The ritziest hotel in Phoenix is, of course, the elegant *Ritz-Carlton* (Map 2; ☎ 602-468-0700, 800-241-3333, 2401 E Camelback Rd ), offering attractive rooms and suites from $300 to over $400 in winter. Amenities include expensive but excellent restaurants, 24-hour room service, a bar with light entertainment, a fitness center with trainers and massage therapists, a spa, sauna, tennis court and golf privileges, including transportation to the courses. Traditionally elegant, The Grill is one of the best American grills in Arizona.

The nearest 1st-class hotel to ASU is the Southwestern-styled *Tempe Mission Palms* (Map 5; ☎ 480-894-1400, 800-547-8705, 60 E 5th St) with 300 rooms and suites, and in-room coffeemakers, tennis courts, golf privileges, a sauna and exercise room. Its restaurant has pool-side and room service, and there is a popular sports bar here. The Southwestern decor tends toward wood and stone which is a pleasant change from the relentlessly bright chain hotels, but may be a bit dark for some tastes. Rates range from $150 to $200 in winter, though may go higher at peak times; visit www.mission-palms.com. Fairly similar facilities with comparable rates are offered at the 270-room *Fiesta Inn* (Map 5; ☎ 480-967-1441, 800-501-7590, 2100 S Priest Dr) also in Tempe; visit www.fiestainnresort.com.

The most elegant and expensive places to stay are the resorts, of which Phoenix has more than its share. These aren't just places to stay – they are destinations to spend an entire vacation. Summer visitors can get a room for well under $200. Expect attractively landscaped grounds suitable for strolling or jogging, spacious rooms or suites (including presidential suites priced well over $1000 a night), extensive indoor and outdoor public areas, helpful and attentive staff, a variety of dining possibilities and room service, bars and entertainment, as well as several swimming pools, whirlpools, saunas, a fully equipped exercise/health center with instructors and trainers, and (at extra cost) massage, beauty treatments, tennis, racquetball and golf. Most can provide babysitting and some have children's clubs (again, at extra cost). Gift and sundries shops should be on the premises along with a hairdresser, and various other attractions may include anything from bicycle rental to basketball courts, video rental to volleyball and horseback riding to hot-air ballooning. Some of the major resorts and their main claims to fame are listed below, and you can expect them to have most of the features mentioned above. If you plan on vacationing in a valley resort, we suggest you contact the establishment for complete details or talk to a travel agent.

Much of the design for the city's first luxury resort, the *Arizona Biltmore Resort & Spa* (Map 2; ☎ 602-955-6600, 800-950-0086 ), at 24th St and E Missouri Ave, was influenced by Frank Lloyd Wright. This beautiful and historically interesting resort (opened in 1929) underwent various renovations and additions throughout the 1990s, and now boasts over 700 units, many with private balconies and some suites. Its modern facilities include two golf courses, several swimming pools (one with a long water slide) and tennis courts, an athletic club, a health spa, a children's program and two very good restaurants. Room rates are $350 to $530 in the high season and suites start at $680.
website: www.arizonabiltmore.com

The Hilton chain runs three Phoenix resorts (☎ 800-876-4683) which have less luxurious rooms and more reasonable prices than most of the area's resorts; www.pointehilton.com has information about all three. The *Pointe Hilton Squaw Peak Resort* (Map 2; ☎ 602-997-2626, 7677 N 16th St) offers nine acres of pools, including water slides and a 'river' tubing area, as well as a popular kids' program, making this a good family choice. The *Pointe Hilton Tapatio Cliffs Resort* (Map 2; ☎ 602-866-7500, 11111 N 7th St) and the *Pointe Hilton South Mountain Resort* (☎ 602-438-9000, 7777 S Pointe Parkway) both have full resort facilities, including excellent (though expensive) golf courses. Rooms are around $250 in the high season. The South Mountain location has a children's program as well as horseback riding; it's at the northeastern corner of Phoenix South Mountain Park. All three include a complimentary evening beverage service and have good restaurants, but the chain's best is the spectacularly located Different Pointe of View, serving continental food atop Tapatio Cliffs.

The 120-acre *Marriott's Camelback Inn* *(Map 2; ☎ 480-948-1700, 800-242-2635, 5402 E Lincoln Dr)* opened in 1936 and, with many dedicated customers, is considered a world-class resort. Highlights are 36 holes of excellent golf, a full-service spa and health club, several pools and tennis courts, and the highly rated Chaparral restaurant, serving pricey continental food. Rates are in the $400s for rooms with microwaves, refrigerators and coffeemakers; suites start in the $600s.

website: www.camelbackinn.com

Yet another world-class option is the *Fairmont Scottsdale Princess Resort (Map 2; ☎ 480-585-4848, 7575 E Princess Dr )*, the home of the annual PGA Phoenix Open. With 450 beautifully landscaped acres, this is one of the valley's largest full-scale resorts. The resort's La Hacienda restaurant serves the valley's most sophisticated and pricey Mexican food, and the Marquesa is simply the best Spanish (Catalan) restaurant in Arizona. Rooms start at $470, and casitas and suites are around $600; look at www.fairmont.com. At close to these prices, an even larger property, the *Hyatt Regency Scottsdale at Gainey Ranch Resort (Map 2; ☎ 480-991-3388, 800-233-1234, 7500 E Doubletree Ranch Rd)* is popular with families. Enjoy the dozens of fountains and waterfalls, 11 pools, artificial beach, huge water slide, or playground while the kids take part in a program designed just for them. The resort's well-reviewed Golden Swan restaurant serves varied Southwestern fare; visit www.hyatt.com.

Probably the most expensive is the almost overpoweringly opulent and modern *Phoenician (☎ 480-941-8200, 800-888-8234, 6000 E Camelback Rd )*, a world-class,

super-deluxe resort with the usual amenities as well as some less usual activities such as archery, badminton and croquet. The resort's top-rated Mary Elaine's restaurant serves contemporary French cuisine and is one of the Southwest's most expensive and formal restaurants; there are several more casual eating choices as well.

website: www.thephoenician.com

## PLACES TO EAT

Phoenix has the biggest selection of restaurants in the Southwest. From fast-food to ultra fancy, it's all here. Serious foodies will find several kitchens that will lighten their wallets, if nothing else. A useful little book is *100 Best Restaurants in Arizona,* by the serendipitously named Harry and Trudy Plate. This book is updated every year or two and, despite its name, squeezes about 150 restaurants into its covers; the reviews are fun. About two-thirds of these places are in the valley, and some of the very best are in the resorts (see the top end listings in Places to Stay for excellent restaurants at resorts). You don't have to stay at the resorts to eat at the restaurants. Many of these resorts serve classy Sunday brunches that require reservations. In fact, reservations are recommended at all the fancier eateries.

Several free publications available from the chambers of commerce, visitors bureaus and newsstands around the valley have extensive restaurant listings, though they lean toward the top end. The selection below is just some of the best, including good lower-priced places. All addresses are in Phoenix, unless otherwise indicated.

### Breakfast

While the diners and coffeehouses are often good choices, die-hard egg fans can have their breakfast omeleted, creped, Benedicted, scrambled, spiced or otherwise smashed at any *Eggery* or the similar *Good Egg*; see Map 4 for locations. The Good Egg also is in the Park Central Mall *(3110 N Central Ave)* and in Scottsdale *(☎ 480-483-1090, 14046 N Scottsdale Rd)* and *(☎ 480-991-5416, 6149 N Scottsdale Rd)*. All are open 6:30am to 2:30pm daily and serve other brunch items in a bright and cheerful environment. Most breakfasts are $5 to $7.50.

Some folks prefer pancakes for breakfast; the best choice is the ***Pancake House*** *(Map 4; ☎ 480-946-4902, 6840 E Camelback Rd)* in Scottsdale. These come with a European twist – German, Dutch and apple pancakes are worth trying. Hours are 7am to 2pm.

Open wide at ***Chompie's*** *(Map 2; ☎ 602-971-8010, 3202 E Greenway Rd)* and *(☎ 480-860-0475, 9301 E Shea Blvd)* in Scottsdale, as well as *(☎ 480-557-0700, 1160 E University Dr)* in Tempe. These are genuine New York kosher delis with a wide variety of fresh bagels, giant blintzes, huge puffy omelets, bialys, knishes, the kind of sandwiches you can't get your mouth around, sweet pastries and mouthwatering treats, all made on the premises. Hours are about 6am to 9pm. There's always a line for takeout, and it's always noisily busy.

On a Sunday, you can defer breakfast into a leisurely brunch, which most of the valley's resorts serve from late morning through early afternoon. Prices are mainly in the $20s (though the ***Phoenician*** really goes to town with a $45 brunch), and though these are all-you-can-eat food fests, the many varied choices are carefully prepared and delicious. Champagne and incredible desserts are included. Call any of the resorts for details.

### Coffeehouses

Dozens of coffeehouses dot the valley, many providing entertainment in the evenings. Tempe's ***Coffee Plantation*** *(Map 5; ☎ 480-829-7878, 680 S Mill Ave)* is an espresso and cappuccino place popular with ASU students. It also serves light meals and a selection of tasty pastries, and stays open till around midnight. About 10 other Coffee Plantations have opened in the Greater Phoenix area. In downtown Phoenix, ***Starbucks*** *(Map 3; ☎ 602-340-0455, 100 N 1st St)* is one of about two dozen Starbucks in the valley.

In Scottsdale, a popular place is ***The Author's Café*** *(Map 4; ☎ 480-481-3998, 4014 N Goldwater Blvd )*, open 7am to 3pm Sunday to Thursday and 9am to 11pm Friday and Saturday. Also in Scottsdale, ***The Coffee Roastery*** *(Map 2; ☎ 480-905-0881, 8120 N Hayden)* is open on Sunday and has a wide selection of beans from all over the world.

### Steak Houses

***Ruth's Chris Steak House*** *(Map 2; ☎ 602-957-9600, 2201 E Camelback Rd)* and *(Map 2; ☎ 480-991-5988, 7001 N Scottsdale Rd )*, both part of a nationwide chain known for superb steak, serve up huge steaks priced around $25 and slathered with melted butter but nothing else; if you want vegetables or potatoes, you'll have to pay $4 or $5 more. (Perhaps they could make another buck by renting you a steak knife.) Seafood and the other meat dishes are also very good. Hours are 5 to 10pm daily.

Tough to say which is the best steak house in central Phoenix, but a definite contender is ***Harris'*** *(Map 2; ☎ 602-508-8888, 3101 E Camelback Rd )*, which also does a fine salmon dinner. Closer to downtown, the traditional place is ***Durant's*** *(Map 2; ☎ 602-264-5967, 2611 N Central Ave )*, which has been serving steaks for over half a century and retains its conservative atmosphere by banning cell phones in the dining room! Both places are expensive.

Phoenix is a major baseball spring-training center, drawing the sports fans who crowd into ***Don & Charlie's*** *(Map 4; ☎ 480-990-0900, 7501 E Camelback Rd)* in Scottsdale. Here, baseball memorabilia and photos of sports personalities cover the walls and the food is meaty, with barbecue priced in the teens and steaks heading into the $20s. Hours are 5 to 10pm daily.

***Texaz Bar & Grill*** *(Map 2; ☎ 602-248-7827, 6003 N 16th St)* is not exactly a steak house but has huge, meaty meals – they don't skimp on potatoes and gravy. You can get a bowl of chili for $2 or an 18oz T-bone steak for $15; burgers and chicken-fried steaks are also popular. This fun, down-home place has every available space filled with Texan 'stuff' and is popular with locals and visitors. It's open for lunch and dinner daily, except Sunday when hours are 4 to 10pm.

Getting into the outskirts, ***Rawhide Steakhouse*** (☎ 480-502-1880) in the Rawhide tourist attraction (see the Scottsdale section, earlier) is fun, kid-friendly, and serves decent cowboy steaks – perhaps not the best in town but a good value. Also good for cowboy steaks, the ***T-Bone Steakhouse*** (☎ 602-276-0945, 10037 S 19th Ave ), way south on the north side of Phoenix South Mountain Park, has good city views. This hospitably Western steak house has a rustic setting and is locally popular for its mesquite-grilled steaks, which run into the lower $20s. It opens for dinner only. Another similar choice is ***Pinnacle Peak Patio*** (☎ 480-585-1599, 10426 E Jomax Rd) in northern Scottsdale, which features country music and dance lessons every evening to help shake down that steak.

### Soul Food & Southern

***Mrs White's Golden Rule Cafe*** (Map 3; ☎ 602-262-9256, 808 E Jefferson) is a hole in the wall with hanging, hand-lettered menus, but a greasy spoon it ain't. The food is home-style, well prepared and tasty, though you won't find any low-calorie plates here. The Golden Rule is to remember what you ate when you pay at the register at the end of your meal, which typically runs around $8. It's open for lunch but not dinner Monday to Friday.

For Cajun catfish and crawfish, try ***Baby Kay's Cajun Kitchen*** (Map 2; ☎ 602-955-0011, 2119 E Camelback Rd) in the Town & Country Mall, or in Scottsdale (Map 4; ☎ 480-990-9080, 7216 E Shoeman Lane). Both are locally famed for delicious 'dirty rice,' a mixture of rice with sausage, onions, peppers and seasonings, and a whole bunch of other Southern specials. Dinner entrées are in the $8 to $16 range, and lunches are cheaper.

### Southwestern

After enjoying great success as a Tucson favorite, the owners of ***Café Terra Cotta*** (Map

2; ☎ 480-948-8100, 6166 N Scottsdale Rd) opened a second location in Scottsdale at the Borgata Mall. The menu has steadily become pricier, with most entrées now in the teens and low $20s, but it remains innovative, even wild-sounding at times, with a few fairly straightforward choices for the less adventurous. Be sure to leave room for one of the heavenly desserts. Also in Scottsdale, the similarly priced ***Roaring Fork*** (Map 4; ☎ 480-947-0795, 7243 E Camelback Rd) is among the valley's trendiest Southwestern eateries, and deservedly so.

The classiest Southwestern restaurant is ***Vincent Guerithault on Camelback*** (Map 2; ☎ 602-224-0225, 3930 E Camelback Rd ), serving food with the famous chef's French touch. With dinner entrées priced in the $20s, the restaurant is not outrageously expensive, considering the haute cuisine. The restaurant is open for weekday lunches and dinner daily except Sunday.

For somewhat cheaper but still classy Southwestern fare, visit ***Sam's Cafe*** (Map 3; ☎ 602-252-3545, 455 N 3rd St, No 114) downtown in the Arizona Center. Sam's is open daily from 11am to 10pm, staying open to midnight on Friday and Saturday. There are other Sam's at the Biltmore Fashion Park (☎ 602-954-7100) and at 10100 N Scottsdale Rd (☎ 480-368-2800).

### Other American Cuisine

The ***5 & Diner*** (Map 2; ☎ 602-264-5220, 5220 N 16th St) is a lot of fun, with inexpensive, 24-hour food and friendly service in a '50s setting. The menu is the predictable pre-nouvelle American cuisine – burgers, fries, tuna melts, shakes, etc. The diner's success has led to the opening of eight others in the valley, but they aren't all open 24 hours. If you like this kind of atmosphere, you'll enjoy the ever-popular ***Ed Debevic's*** (☎ 602-956-2760, 2102 E Highland Ave ), which calls itself 'Short Orders Deluxe'; it makes great burgers and shakes, and also has a salad bar. Bring change for Elvis on the jukebox. The diner is open 11am to 9pm daily, till 10pm on weekends. The oldest diner in Phoenix and perhaps Arizona is ***MacAlpine's*** (Map 3; ☎ 602-252-

*3039, 2303 N 7th St* ), which features an authentic soda fountain serving up genuine sundaes and other icy delights. It opens daily for huge breakfasts and lunches.

One of Mesa's best restaurants, the **Landmark** (☎ *480-962-4652, 809 W Main St*) has been serving good American food for about 25 years. Built as a Mormon church in the early 1900s, the restaurant is decorated with antiques and photos and has a huge salad bar. The home-style, traditional American dinner entrées priced in the range of $10 to $20 (including salad bar) draw crowds of knowing locals. It is open daily for lunch and dinner.

Scottsdale shoppers like to stop at the pink and white **Sugar Bowl Ice Cream Parlor** (*Map 4;* ☎ *480-946-0051, 4005 N Scottsdale Rd* ), which serves light meals but specializes in the cold stuff; it is open from 11am to 11pm daily. For good and inexpensive New Mexican fare, **Carlsbad Tavern** (*480-970-8164, 3313 N Hayden Rd*) in Scottsdale is popular with a younger adult crowd who enjoy outdoor dining, even in summer, when a pond and mist sprinkler system keeps temperatures bearable. Inside, a mischievous menu ('the Carlsbad Daily Guano') plays up to the batty cavernous interior.

If you're a jazz fan, **Orbit Restaurant & Jazz Club** (*Map 2;* ☎ *602-265-2354* ), in the Uptown Plaza at Camelback Rd and Central Ave, provides dinner and live jazz every night.

For seafood lovers, the fanciest fresh fins are found at **Oceana** (☎ *480-515-2277, 9800 E Pinnacle Peak Rd*) in Scottsdale's La Mirada shopping center. Many dinner entrées approach $30. For the adventurous, sea urchins, scallops and sushi are on the menu. The selection is also wide at **Steamers** (*Map 2;* ☎ *602-956-3631, 2576 E Camelback Rd*) in Biltmore Fashion Park, where entrées are in the $18 to $25 range.

In Tempe, the **House of Tricks** (*Map 5;* ☎ *480-968-1114, 114 E 7th St*) has a shady patio that is often full with enthusiastic diners enjoying reasonably priced innovative meat, chicken and fish plates. Behind the patio, two early-20th-century cottages

form a charming indoor section. Dinner entrées are in the teens – a good deal.

## French

The closest thing to French fast food is **La Madeleine**, serving French pastries, baguette sandwiches and light meals for breakfast, lunch and dinner every day. Dinner entrées are mostly under $10. La Madeleine has three locations: (*Map 2;* ☎ *602-952-0349, 3102 E Camelback Rd*); (☎ *480-483-0730, 10625 N Tatum Blvd*); and (*Map 4;* ☎ *480-945-1663, 7014 E Camelback Rd*) in Scottsdale Fashion Square.

Way at the other end of the credit card scale is **Mary Elaine's** (☎ *480-423-2530*) in the posh Phoenician resort. The only Southwestern restaurant to get five stars from the folks at Mobil, it's elegant, pricey, requests reservations and expects men to wear jackets.

## Italian

The valley probably has more noteworthy Italian restaurants than any other 'non-American' cuisine. The following is just a short selection.

For top-notch food in a sophisticated setting, dine at **Avanti** (*Map 2;* ☎ *602-956-0900, 2728 E Thomas Rd*) and (*Map 4;* ☎ *480-949-8333, 3102 N Scottsdale Rd*). Most entrées are in the $20s, though simple pasta dishes are around $15. Dinner is served daily and, in Phoenix only, lunch Monday to Friday.

Homemade pasta (you can watch it being made in the open kitchen) is the highlight at **Maria's When in Naples** (*Map 2;* ☎ *480-991-6887, 7000 E Shea Blvd*) in Scottsdale. Prices for pasta dishes are in the teens, and there are other more expensive entrées. Lunch is served Monday to Friday, and dinner 5 to 10pm daily.

Families with small children enjoy the kids' menu and the wide selection of pizza and pasta dishes (many around $10) at **Tuchetti** (☎ *602-957-0222, 2135 E Camelback Rd*) close to the Town & Country Mall. The decor is Italy à la Disney; dinner is served daily and lunch Monday to Saturday.

Second floor of the rotunda in the Arizona State Capitol Museum, Phoenix

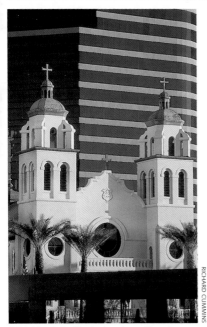

Saint Mary's Basilica in downtown Phoenix

Hayden Library, Arizona State University

RICHARD CUMMINS

Fifth St fountain in downtown Scottsdale

RICHARD CUMMINS

Tribute to the 'Navajo Code Talkers,' Phoenix

RICHARD CUMMINS

The fabled phoenix on the old city hall

After a hard day of sight-seeing, visitors to Phoenix's Heritage Square can enjoy excellent wood-oven baked pizza and healthful salads at *Pizzeria Bianco* *(Map 3;* ☎ *602-258-8300, 623 E Adams St)*. Unfortunately, they aren't open at lunch, so you'll have to wait till 5pm, Tuesday to Sunday.

## Mexican

*El Bravo* *(Map 2;* ☎ *602-943-9753, 8338 N 7th St)* serves good combination plates for just $5 and offers a choice of inexpensive à la carte Sonoran dishes as well as Navajo tacos. This simple and genuine family restaurant has received great reviews but remains uncrowded because of its noncentral location. It is open Monday to Thursday 10am to 8pm (until 9pm Friday and Saturday).

A downtown favorite, the large, modern *Matador* *(Map 3;* ☎ *602-254-7563, 125 E Adams)* is open 7am to 11pm, so you can get a Mexican breakfast and a hangover-curing menudo as well as lunch and dinner mainly in the $6 to $10 range. Choices include a few non-Mexican items as well, and lines are often out the door with office workers grabbing breakfast or lunch, but these usually move quickly.

If you want great south-of-the-border food, try *Los Dos Molinos* *(*☎ *602-243-9113, 8646 S Central Ave)* or *(*☎ *602-835-5356, 260 S Alma School Rd)* in Mesa. The food is New Mexican influenced, so it's hotter than Sonoran cuisine and delicious if you like chiles. These friendly, family-run restaurants (their slogan is 'some like it hot!') have family members working the stove and tables; ask them to hold the hot sauce if you're not a hot-chile fan. The restaurants are open Tuesday to Saturday 11am to 9pm. The Mesa location doesn't take credit cards, though with dinners around $7 or $12, you hardly need them.

Mexican dining is normally inexpensive, though an exception is the very fine *La Hacienda* *(Map 2;* ☎ *480-585-4848)* in the upscale Fairmont Scottsdale Princess Resort. You'll find beautiful surroundings, strolling mariachis and superb food and service for dinner daily. Most entrées are in the high $20s.

## Asian

Most Indian restaurants offer all-you-can-eat lunch buffets for about $5. À-la-carte dinners, while somewhat pricier ($7 to $20), are freshly prepared and are also a good value.

Among the best is the recommended *Jewel of the Crown* *(Map 4;* ☎ *602-840-2412, 7373 E Scottsdale Mall )*, one of several ethnic restaurants in Scottsdale Mall. Some other locally popular places are *Taste of India* *(*☎ *602-788-3190, 1609 E Bell Rd)*; *India Delhi Palace* *(Map 2;* ☎ *602-244-8181, 5050 E McDowell Rd)*; and two locations of *India Palace* *(Map 2;* ☎ *602-942-4224, 16842 N 7th St)* and in Tempe *(Map 5;* ☎ *480-921-2200, 933 E University Dr)*.

There are scores of Chinese restaurants. If you want opulent surroundings with your Peking duck, *Mr C's* *(Map 4;* ☎ *480-941-4460, 4302 N Scottsdale Rd)* will take care of you. The food is classic and slightly pricey Cantonese; many say it's the best in town. Mr C's is open daily for lunch and dinner.

Out in Chandler is *C-Fu Gourmet* *(*☎ *480-899-3888, 2051 W Warner Rd)*. C-Fu? That's 'sea food' and it is super fresh – you can see it swimming before it's cooked. A meal here is about $15 to $20 and selections vary from day to day depending on what's floating around; fish, crab, shrimp and other shellfish are available. This restaurant also has a recommended dim sum selection for lunch.

In Scottsdale, *Malee's on Main* *(Map 4;* ☎ *602-947-6042, 7131 E Main)* is open for lunch and dinner daily, and is perhaps the best of the many Thai restaurants in the valley. Most entrées are around $12.

## Other Eateries

Set back from the road and with only a small sign, *Greekfest* *(Map 2;* ☎ *602-265-2990, 1940 E Camelback Rd)* is an excellent bet for Greek food. Both food and ambiance are delightful, and the entrée prices, mainly in the teens and some low $20s, are reasonable. It is open for lunch and dinner daily except Sunday.

For recommended Cuban food, visit the *Havana Cafe* *(Map 2;* ☎ *602-952-1991, 4225*

*E Camelback Rd)*. The food is excellent and most dinner entrées are priced in the teens. The café is open for lunch daily except Sunday, and dinner daily, though it may close on summer Sundays.

Eclectic, adventurous, risky, creative, international and transcontinental have all been used to describe fashionable *RoxSand (Map 2; ☎ 602-381-0444, 2594 E Camelback Rd)* in the Biltmore Fashion Park. The changing menu has roamed from Jamaican jerked rabbit to African pheasant to Japanese scallops (these entrées are in the $20s) as well as some cheaper and less adventurous options (such as pizza). This is a good place to eat a complete meal or just drop in for a super dessert. They are open daily for lunch and dinner.

## ENTERTAINMENT

For what's going on, read the free alternative weekly *New Times,* published every Thursday and available at numerous boxes and other outlets around the city. On the same day, the Arizona Republic's *The Rep* also has exhaustive entertainment listings, with an emphasis on popular music and nightlife.

### Cinemas

There are dozens of cinema multiplexes throughout the valley showing the year's best and worst movies, including the huge *AMC 24 (☎ 602-244-2262)* in the Arizona Center, with armrests that fold up so you can cuddle with your date and steep seating so you don't have to peer around people's heads at the screen. There are some alternatives, including the *Valley Art Theater (Map 5; ☎ 602-222-4275 ext 027, 509 S Mill Ave)* in Tempe, with a variety of foreign and alternative flicks. The *Imax Theatre (☎ 480-897-1453)* in the Arizona Mills Mall at Priest and Baseline, shows several docu-movies on their eight-times-larger-than-normal screen.

### Nightlife

Many of the following spots are very busy on Friday and Saturday nights, but usually provide entertainment five to seven nights a week at varying cover charges.

The entertainment scene in Tempe, home of ASU, is aimed at students. Mill Ave between 3rd and 7th Sts is the off-campus nightlife center with several bars and clubs. There are plenty of cops hanging around at closing time, and their attitude is generally friendly. Places come and go, check the **Hayden Square** area (Map 5) for what sounds good.

In downtown Phoenix, the *Arizona Center* provides a number of options aimed at the younger post-work crowd, and it gets quiet early, except on Friday and Saturday when there are several bars, some with dancing, open late. If you want to make a night of it, there are a few places to eat in the center.

Go west for the best in country & western. *Mr Lucky's (Map 2; ☎ 602-246-0686, 3660 NW Grand Ave)* has live country & western and dancing, and a corral outside with bull-riding competitions on weekends (with real bulls, not the mechanical kind; there's a $5 cover). Almost every patron is dressed in Western wear. It is closed Sunday to Tuesday. More upscale country & western places are found in some of the resorts, including *Rustlers Rooste (☎ 602-431-6474)* at the Pointe Hilton on South Mountain. Popular places in Scottsdale include the *Handlebar-J (☎ 480-948-0110, 7116 E Becker St )*, which has live bands and free dance lessons some nights. The Rawhide and Pinnacle Peak Patio steak houses (see Places to Eat, earlier) also have country music.

Jazz lovers can listen to KJZZ FM (91.5). For live music, see the Orbit Restaurant & Jazz Club under Places to Eat.

For good blues, stop by the popular and crowded *Char's Has the Blues (Map 2; ☎ 602-230-0205, 4631 N 7th Ave )*, with some excellent acts most nights. *Warsaw Wallies (Map 2; ☎ 602-955-0881, 2547 E Indian School Rd)* is a small funky place but often has exceptional blues bands with low or no cover. Watch for the local band the Rocket 88s, with an outstanding harpist. Good blues is also the staple of the *Rhythm Room (Map 2; ☎ 602-265-4842, 1019 E Indian School Rd)*. For more blues information, contact the Phoenix Blues Society (☎ 602-252-0599), online at www.phoenixblues.org.

For a variety of alternative rock aimed at young people, the *Mason Jar (Map 2; ☎ 602-954-0455, E Indian School Rd)* is a good choice. They have a no-alcohol area for people under 21. In Tempe, the *Bash on Ash (Map 5; ☎ 480-966-8200, 230 W 5th St)* has good live rock bands and an 'all-ages area.'

*Ain't Nobody's Bizness (Map 2; ☎ 602-224-9977, 3031 E Indian School Rd)* is a friendly lesbian bar. Gay men dance at *Crowbar (Map 3; 702 N Central Ave)* and *Amsterdam Bar (Map 3; 718 N Central Ave)*.

## Performing Arts

The following are the most highly acclaimed places to hear and see performing arts, but not much goes on here during the summer. For sold-out events, the ticket companies listed in 'Buying Tickets' can often help.

The *Herberger Theater Center (Map 3; ☎ 602-252-8497, 222 E Monroe)* has two stages that host productions put together by the Arizona Theater Company (☎ 602-256-6995), Child's Play and others. Tickets for all but the Arizona Theater Company can be purchased at the box office.

---

### Buying Tickets

Ticketmaster (☎ 480-784-4444) sells tickets for most big sporting and cultural events. Call or buy online at www.ticketmaster.com as far in advance as possible, or if nothing is available, look in the yellow pages under 'Ticket Sales' or in newspaper classifieds for tickets (they're often overpriced). Scalpers hang out near event venues; scalping is legal as long as it is off the actual event property. You can also try Ticket City (☎ 480-507-5757, www.ticketcity.com), Western States Tickets (☎ 480-777-1111) or Tickets Unlimited (☎ 602-840-2340, 800-289-8497, www.ticketsunlimitedinc.com).

---

The *Helen K Mason Center for the Performing Arts* (Map 3; ☎ 602-258-8128, 333 E Portland) *is the home of the Black Theater Troupe and also hosts other African American performers.*

*Symphony Hall* (Map 3), at 225 E Adams, is the home of the Arizona Opera (☎ 602-266-7464), the Phoenix Symphony Orchestra (☎ 602-495-1999, 495-1117), and Ballet Arizona (☎ 602-381-1096).

The *Gammage Auditorium (☎ 480-965-3434 )*, on the ASU Campus at Mill Ave and Apache Blvd, is the university's main center for performing arts.

The *Cricket Pavillion (Map 1; ☎ 602-254-7200 )*, north of I-10 exit 135 at 83rd Ave, is a huge outdoor amphitheater hosting big-name rock bands.

## SPECTATOR SPORTS

Phoenix has some of the nation's top professional teams, but getting tickets for the best games is not always easy, as they sell out early; see the boxed text 'Buying Tickets.'

The NBA's Phoenix Suns (☎ 602-379-7800) play professional basketball at the *America West Arena (Map 3; ☎ 602-379-7867, 201 E Jefferson)* from December to April. Their website is at www.suns.com. The (women's) WNBA's Phoenix Mercury (☎ 602-252-9622) also play here in summer months. From May through August, the arena is home of the Arizona Rattlers (☎ 602-514-8383) arena football team, who were the 1994 world champions. The NHL's Phoenix Coyotes (☎ 480-473-5600) play ice hockey here from October to April. The West Coast Hockey League's Phoenix Mustangs (☎ 602-340-0001) play ice hockey at the *Arizona Veterans Memorial Coliseum (Map 3; 1826 W McDowell Rd)* in the State Fairgrounds.

The NFL's Arizona Cardinals (☎ 602-379-0102) play professional football (fall to spring) at ASU *Sun Devil Stadium (Map 5; ☎ 480-965-2381)* in Tempe, the site of the 1996 Super Bowl, the nation's most prestigious football game. ASU student teams, such as the Sun Devils, also use the stadium.

## Major League Baseball Spring Training: Cactus League

Before the start of each season, major league baseball teams spend March in Arizona and Florida auditioning new players, practicing, and playing games. For established players spring training is a chance to get back into shape, for young players it is their last chance to win a spot on the team, and for fans it is a unique opportunity to see big leaguers in smaller, more intimate parks.

Eight teams play spring training baseball in southern Arizona's Cactus League: Anaheim Angels, Chicago Cubs, Colorado Rockies, Milwaukee Brewers, Oakland Athletics, San Diego Padres, San Francisco Giants, and Seattle Mariners. The Chicago White Sox and the newly formed 2001 World Series champions, the Arizona Razorbacks, were added in 1998. The remaining teams belong to Florida's Grapefruit League. The Cleveland Indians originated the Cactus League in 1947 but eventually left for Florida in 1993; the Chicago Cubs, on the other hand, have spent spring in Arizona since 1952.

What distinguishes these games from those played during the regular season is that tickets are about half the price, and the seats are better, the lines shorter, and the games more relaxed. The baseball parks are relatively small, with attendance averaging 10,000, in contrast to the 30,000-plus crowds that may be encountered at teams' hometown stadiums. This brings players into close range. The intimacy of the parks also adds a dimension to the game – sound; fans can actually hear players sliding into home, talking to each other on the field and the umpire calling strikes and balls. Players are most accessible during team practices that begin in mid-February, which are free and open to the public.

A significant increase in the popularity of spring training has driven up ticket prices and led to the building of new, larger stadiums; tickets range from $7 to $14 for stadium seats, but open lawn seating is often available for $5. While the attendance at each game is often near capacity, you can usually get tickets at the box office before each game, and scalping, an adjunct sport, is legal more than 200 feet from the ballpark. For schedules and advance ticket information, call the Phoenix Chamber of Commerce at (800-283 6372). Game schedules are also listed online at www.mesacvb.com.cactusleague.

The Arizona Diamondbacks (☎ 602-514-8400, 888-777-4664) major-league baseball team played their first season in 1998 in the specially constructed **Bank One Ballpark** (Map 3), southwest of E Jefferson and S 7th Sts.

Professional golfers compete for a seven-figure purse at the PGA Phoenix Open, held every January at the **Tournament Players Golf Course** (☎ 480-585-3600, 17020 N Hayden Rd) in Scottsdale.

You can watch horseracing at **Turf Paradise** (☎ 602-942-1101 ), at 19th Ave and Bell, from October to May, and see greyhounds race year-round at **Phoenix Greyhound Park** (Map 2; ☎ 602-273-7181, 3801 E Washington). NASCAR car racing takes place at **Phoenix International Raceway**

(Map 1; ☎ 602-254-4622, 7602 S 115th Ave) at Baseline Rd, Avondale. Drag racing is presented at **Firebird International Raceway** (Map 1; ☎ 602-323-2000, 520-796-1010 ), off I-10 exit 162, Chandler.

## SHOPPING

The question is not so much what to buy (you can buy just about anything) but where to go. Scottsdale is the **art gallery** capital of Arizona. The **Heard Museum** has the best bookshop about Native Americans and the most reliable, excellent and expensive selection of Native American arts and crafts.

The valley has several notable shopping malls. You may not be a fan of malls, but the air-conditioning does give them a certain allure when the mercury climbs in the summer. **Shopping malls** include the Metrocenter at I-17 exit 208 and Peoria Ave (Map 2), the largest enclosed mall in Arizona; it has four department stores, standard shopping and many attractions for kids. The Park Central Mall, at Central Ave and Osborn Rd (Map 2), is the city's oldest (but still reasonably fashionable) shopping center.

For more upscale shopping, visit the Scottsdale Fashion Square at Camelback and Scottsdale Rds in Scottsdale (Map 4), or the more exclusive Biltmore Fashion Park at Camelback Rd and 24th St in Phoenix (Map 2). Both provide a good selection of cheap to expensive restaurants, and the Biltmore is home to some of the valley's best eateries. Near the Biltmore, the Town & Country Mall also has several decent restaurants.

Perhaps the fanciest selection of **boutiques and galleries** is at the Borgata, 6166 N Scottsdale Rd in Scottsdale (Map 2), a mall designed to look like a medieval town. Also very trendy is the Fifth Avenue Shopping Area (Map 4) east of Scottsdale Rd, where you'll find many galleries, boutiques and tourist-oriented shops. The Legacy Gallery, at the corner of Main west of Scottsdale Rd, is like a museum of bronze masterpieces. It anchors a couple of blocks with about 20 galleries of all kinds and of a generally high quality, with many items priced in the five figures. Look for the life-size metal horseman sculptures keeping watch on the streets. Many galleries are open from 7 to 9pm on Thursday evening 'Art Walks.'

The outdoor **Arizona Center** is revitalizing downtown at 3rd St and Van Buren, with several popular bars, restaurants and a small selection of interesting shops.

If you need **camping or outdoor gear**, REI (☎ 480-967-5494), 1405 W Southern Ave in Tempe, has one of the largest selections in the Southwest and also does mail order.

## GETTING THERE & AWAY
### Air
Phoenix's Sky Harbor International Airport (Map 2; ☎ 602-273-3300 main switchboard,

602-392-0126, 602-392-0310 airport information) is 3 miles southeast of downtown. By far the largest airport in the Southwest, its three terminals (illogically called Terminals 2, 3 and 4) contain all the standard features of any major airport. There are economy long-term parking lots ($5 or $8 a day) within a short walk or shuttle-bus ride of the terminals and pricier short-term lots ($20 a day) next to the terminals. See the Getting There & Away chapter for more information about airlines.

### Bus
Greyhound Bus Terminal (Map 2; ☎ 602-389-4200) is at 2115 E Buckeye but they can drop you at several stops throughout the Greater Phoenix area. Phoenix is at the center of a fairly extensive bus network throughout and beyond the state. White Mountain Passenger Lines (Map 2; ☎ 602-275-4245), 319 S 24th St, has a 1pm bus to Show Low ($40), and the Arizona Shuttle Service (☎ 800-888-2749) has many vans a day linking Phoenix Airport with Tucson. Other local bus companies linking Phoenix Airport with Arizona towns beyond the valley are listed in Getting There & Away sections for those towns.

## GETTING AROUND
### To/From the Airport
Valley Metro operates its Red Line every 15 to 30 minutes Monday to Friday from about 4am to 10pm, driving to Tempe and Mesa along Apache Blvd and Main, or west into downtown and then into north Phoenix. Weekend buses are less frequent.

SuperShuttle (☎ 602-244-9000) has vans providing airport-to-your-door service at any time. Fares are lower than those of taxis, which add a $1 airport surcharge in addition to their metered rates. Traveler information desks provide more details.

### Bus
Valley Metro (☎ 602-253-5000) operates buses all over the valley. Phones are answered 4am to 10pm Monday to Friday and 7am to 7pm weekends; other times there's a

recording. Some routes are limited-stop Express Services. Most routes operate from about 4am to 10pm. Fares are $1.25 (including one transfer) or $3.60 for an all-day pass. The latter can be bought at only a few locations such as the Valley Metro Downtown Bus Terminal at Central Ave and Van Buren (Map 3); call Valley Metro for other locations. A few Express Services cost $1.75. People over 65 or between six and 18 years old with a picture ID ride for half-fare. Exact fare is required. Riders can pay with Visa or MasterCard.

websites: www.valleymetro.maricopa.gov, www.bus.maricopa.gov

Valley Metro also runs free DASH buses around downtown Phoenix every six minutes 6:30am to 11pm Monday to Friday. From 11am to 2pm, DASH goes out to the State Capitol. Valley Metro's FLASH buses offer free rides every 10 minutes around the ASU area from 7am to 6pm on weekdays. FLASHLite goes from Tempe to the zoo and botanical gardens on weekends.

## Car & Motorcycle

All the main car-rental companies have airport offices and many have offices in other parts of the valley or will deliver your car. Be warned, however, that about 25% in taxes is added to car rental at the Phoenix airport. Shop around, and consider renting out of Flagstaff. Reserve a car in advance for the best rates.

Western States Motorcycle Tours (☎ 602-943-9030), 9401 N 7th Ave, rents big bikes to riders aged 21, with a motorcycle license and with two years recent riding experience. Daily rates range from $70 for an 800 cc Suzuki Intruder to $125 for an Electra-Glide Classic Harley. Weekly rates are also available.

## Taxi

There are several 24-hour cab services, but with a $3 drop fee and fares of well over $1 per mile, you can rack up a pricey ride fairly rapidly in the large valley area. Renting a car is better for most longer drives. Some of the main cab companies are Ace Taxi (☎ 602-254-1999), Checker Cab (☎ 602-257-1818) and Yellow Cab (☎ 602-252-5252).

## Bicycle

The following are a few of several bike-rental shops:

**Adventure Bicycle Co** (☎ 480-649-3394), 1110 W Southern Ave, Mesa

**Airpark Bicycle Center** (☎ 480-596-6633), 8666 E Shea Blvd, Scottsdale

**Tempe Bicycles** (☎ 480-966-6896), 330 W University Dr, Tempe

**Wheels 'n Gear** (☎ 480-945-2881), 7607 E McDowell Rd, Scottsdale

# Grand Canyon & Lake Powell

The slogan on the Arizona license plate says it all: 'Grand Canyon State.' The Grand Canyon of the Colorado River is Arizona's most famous sight – indeed, it is arguably the best known natural attraction in the entire country. This grandest of all canyons has been declared a United Nations world heritage site to be protected for all people.

At 277 miles long, roughly 10 miles wide and a mile deep, the canyon sounds big. But its sheer size is not all that makes the sight so tremendous. The incredible spectacle of differently colored rock strata, the many buttes and peaks within the canyon itself, and the meandering rims give access to fantastic views that amaze the visitor. Staring from the many rim overlooks gives you a great impression of the grandeur, but walking down into the canyon on a short hike or a multiday backpacking trip gives you a better sense of the variety in the landscape, wildlife and climate.

Although the rims are only 10 miles apart as the crow flies, it is a 215-mile, five-hour drive on narrow roads from the visitor center on the South Rim to the visitor center on the North Rim. Thus the Grand Canyon National Park is essentially two separate areas that are treated separately in this chapter. The South Rim is described first, continuing with the areas south of the park. Then comes the remote northern area known as the Arizona Strip, containing the North Rim of Grand Canyon National Park. Finally comes Page and the Glen Canyon Dam area, which is on the Colorado River just outside the northeastern corner of the park.

Scattered throughout the Grand Canyon are signs of ancient Native American inhabitants. The oldest artifacts are little twig figures of animals made by hunters and gatherers about 4000 years ago – a few of these can be seen in the Tusayan Museum, east of the Grand Canyon Village. Within the canyon are stone buildings left by

Native Americans before their unexplained departure during the 12th century.

Cerbat people began living at the western end of the canyon around AD 1300 and were the ancestors of contemporary Hualapai and Havasupai tribes. Despite attempts by Europeans to dislodge them, these two tribes continue living in reservations on the southwestern rim of the canyon. These reservations (described further in this chapter) abut Grand Canyon National Park but can't be entered from the park.

## Highlights

- Rafting the Colorado River through the Grand Canyon
- Escaping the tourist crowds of the South Rim and hiking into the Grand Canyon
- Hiking and camping at the Havasupai Indian Reservation
- Enjoying the Grand Canyon from the peaceful perspective of the North Rim, where only 10% of the canyon's visitors venture

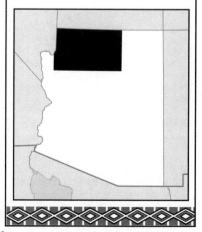

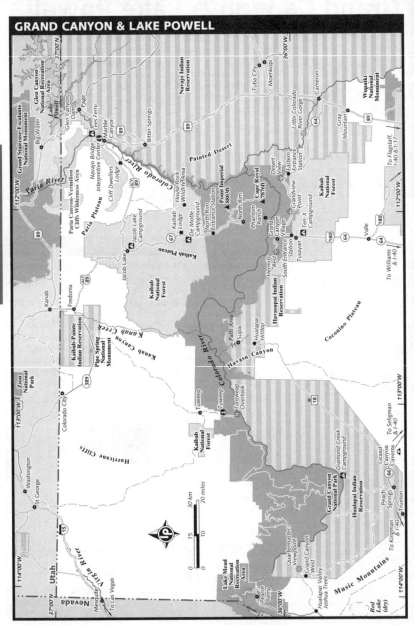

# GRAND CANYON & LAKE POWELL

The canyon's earliest European visitors were Spaniards who gazed into the depths in 1540. The canyon was difficult to reach and involved crossing large areas with little water. Because there didn't appear to be any mineral wealth and the area was generally considered magnificent but valueless, European visits were infrequent for over three centuries.

The first serious European exploration was in 1869, when John Wesley Powell, a one-armed Civil War veteran, led an expedition along the Colorado River. Using wooden boats, they ran the entire length of the Grand and other canyons – a remarkable achievement. Powell led a similar expedition in 1871–72, which resulted in detailed scientific observations and writings.

During the late 19th century, Mormons began settling the remote Arizona Strip, and prospectors and miners ventured into the canyon in search of mineral wealth but found little. One miner, John Hance, arrived in 1883 and decided that catering to tourists would be more profitable than mining. He became one of the most colorful and well-known guides into the canyon, famous for his tall tales. Some simple lodges were built for the few tourists who made it to the South Rim by stagecoach or horseback.

In 1901, the railroad arrived and tourism became big business. President Theodore Roosevelt visited the canyon in 1903, said 'You cannot improve on it' and protected the canyon, first as a national monument in 1908 and later as a park in 1919. The park has expanded since and its current size is 1892 sq miles.

# South of the Colorado River

The Colorado River has always been a major barrier for travelers in this region. If state boundaries had been made on purely geographical divisions, the river would have divided Arizona and Utah. This didn't happen.

## GRAND CANYON NATIONAL PARK – SOUTH RIM
☎ 928

The South Rim, just over 7000 feet in elevation, is lower than the North Rim and accessible year-round. Ninety percent of park visitors go to the South Rim.

The foremost attraction is the rim itself, paralleled by a 33-mile scenic drive with numerous parking areas, scenic views and trailheads. Most visitors make part of this drive or walk some of the 9 miles of trails along the rim. However, this drive can become overcrowded, so timing your visit early in the day is suggested.

Another attraction is Grand Canyon Village, with historic early-20th-century hotels and most modern amenities. Numerous hiking trails into the canyon are described below. To really get away from the traffic at the top, hike down to the canyon bottom and stay at Phantom Ranch or at one of several campgrounds, which require reservations well in advance. Other activities include mule rides, river running and backcountry backpacking, but all require advance planning.

### Information
**Climate & When to Go** On average, temperatures are 20°F cooler on the South Rim than at the bottom of the Grand Canyon. This means you could wake up on the rim to frost on the ground in April and be basking in 80°F temperatures by afternoon if you hike down into the inner gorge. The peak season ranges from about April to November, and the park is busiest from Memorial Day to Labor Day.

At the South Rim in summer, expect highs in the 80s and lows around 50°F. June is the driest month, but summer thunderstorms make July and August the wettest months. Weather is cooler and changeable in the fall, and snow and freezing overnight temperatures are likely by November. January has average overnight lows in the teens and daytime highs around 40°F. Winter weather can be beautifully clear, but be prepared for occasional storms that can cause havoc.

GRAND CANYON

GRAND CANYON

## Geology of the Grand Canyon

Approximately two billion years of geologic history are exposed in the Grand Canyon – a huge amount of time considering the earth is just 4.6 billion years old. The oldest rock in the canyon, exposed just above the Colorado River, is the **Vishnu Schist**. Deposited in the Precambrian Era as sands, silts and muds interlayered with volcanic ash, these sediments were metamorphosed (hardened by heat and pressure) about 1.7 billion years ago by a collision of tectonic plates that baked and squeezed the entire region and uplifted the Mazatzal Mountains (which have since eroded). This metamorphism continued when **Zoroaster Granite** intruded into the Vishnu as molten magma. Between 1.2 billion and 800 million years ago, the area was covered by an ocean that rose and fell more than 18 times, depositing a thick series of marine sediments and volcanic flows; these were later metamorphosed into a rock unit named the **Grand Canyon Supergroup**.

The layers making up most of the canyon walls were laid during the Paleozoic (ancient life) and Mesozoic (middle life) Eras between 570 and 65 million years ago, which is why there are so many fossils in the Grand Canyon today. During much of this time, the entire Grand Canyon region was submerged under a tropical ocean, which rose and fell repeatedly. When sea levels were high, fine-grained clays and deep-sea oozes settled to the ocean floor – sediments that would later become thinly layered shales and limestones. When sea levels fell, the area became sandy beachfront property, complete with dunes, deltas and swamps, eventually forming siltstones and sandstones. Well-known examples include the **Redwall** and **Kaibab** limestones, the **Hermit** and **Bright Angel** shales, and the **Coconino** and **Tapeats** sandstones. Around 65 million years ago, tectonic forces once again uplifted the region and the sea retreated permanently. The final rocks to be deposited in the Grand Canyon were volcanic flows that erupted into the canyon about one million years ago.

The tremendous depth and the unusually steep sides of the Grand Canyon are closely tied to the evolution of the Colorado River. The Grand Canyon lies within the **Colorado Plateau** geologic province, an area composed largely of flat-lying sedimentary and volcanic rocks. Both the Colorado Plateau and the Colorado River's source area in the Rocky Mountains has been rapidly uplifted several times since the end of the Mesozoic, with total uplift estimated as high as 10,000 feet. As its elevation increased, two separate stream systems – one flowing north and one flowing south – developed on opposite sides of the Colorado Plateau. Approximately six million years ago, a shift in the San Andreas Fault began opening the Gulf of California. Rivers that flowed south off the Colorado Plateau merged into what is now the lower Colorado River and emptied into this new sea. The headwaters of the river eroded northward through the Grand Wash Cliffs (near the present Arizona-Nevada border), connecting the river with the upper (north-flowing) Colorado River system. The upper Colorado River then changed its course from northward into Utah to southward into the Gulf of California, forming the modern Colorado River. This powerful new river cut through the hard Kaibab limestone, quickly incising the softer rocks below and forming the Grand Canyon as we see it today.

The hardness of different rocks determined many of the shapes and features of the Grand Canyon. In the upper canyon, erosion-resistant rocks formed stair-stepped cliffs and terraces such as the **Tonto Platform**, a wide, flat terrace that juts out into the canyon like a tabletop. Less resistant rocks formed slopes that are often covered in debris. The lower section of the canyon, called the Inner Gorge, is narrow and V-shaped. Composed largely of metamorphic rocks of similar hardness, each layer is eroded at about the same rate as its neighbors so none stand out farther than the others.

*– Rhawn Denniston*

The inner canyon is much drier with about eight inches of rain annually, about half that of the South Rim. During the summer, temperatures inside the canyon go above 100°F almost every day and often exceed 110°F in midsummer, which can be potentially lethal for unprepared hikers. Strong hot winds often blow in summer. Even in midwinter, freezing overnight temperatures are rare in the inner canyon, with average lows in the upper 30s and highs in the upper 50s.

**Tourist Offices & Services** Canyon View Information Plaza, at the northeast end of Grand Canyon Village, 6 miles north of the South Entrance Station, is open 8am to 6pm daily. It is reached on foot (about a quarter-mile walk) or by frequent shuttle buses – there is no parking at the information plaza. There is a small museum, an excellent bookstore and large bulletin boards with information about lodging, weather, tours, talks and a host of other things. If you can't find the information you need on the bulletin boards, rangers are available to assist you; they are often swamped by visitors, so check the posted information first.

A smaller visitor center at Desert View, near the east entrance of the park, is open daily in summer and closed in winter (depending on staff availability).

Visitors can receive assistance at ranger stations near the Grand Canyon Railway depot, Indian Garden below the South Rim, the River ranger station and Phantom Ranch at the canyon bottom, and Cottonwood Campground below the North Rim.

Telephoning the park (☎ 638-7888) gives you an automated system with recorded information on everything from weather conditions to applying for a river-running permit. You can leave your address to receive written information, or you can speak with a ranger during business hours. All park numbers are in the ☎ 928 area code; the park's website is located at www.nps.gov/grca.

A park map and a seasonal newspaper, *The Guide,* are available at no charge to all visitors. *The Guide* is the best up-to-date

source of park information available upon arrival. French, German and Spanish versions are available. Also very useful is the free *Grand Canyon Trip Planner.* You can receive information in advance from the Superintendent, Grand Canyon National Park, PO Box 129, Grand Canyon, AZ 86023.

Grand Canyon Village has most visitor services; however, prices here are substantially higher and the lines are longer than in Flagstaff, so think ahead.

Services available include hotels, restaurants, campgrounds, coin-operated laundry and showers, gift shops, pet kennels, churches and transportation services. Car towing and mechanics (☎ 638-2631) are available from 8am to 5pm and for 24-hour emergency service. A gas station is open daily; hours vary from 6am to 9:30pm in summer and 8am to 6pm in midwinter. A medical clinic (☎ 638-2551) is open 9am to 6pm Monday to Friday and 9am to 1pm Saturday.

Mather Shopping Center contains a bank (☎ 638-2437) with foreign exchange (for foreign traveler's checks only; no foreign currency is exhanged), which is open 10am to 3pm Monday to Friday and till 5pm on Friday. A 24-hour ATM accepts major credit/debit cards. A post office (☎ 638-2512) in the shopping center is open 9am to 4:30pm Monday to Friday and 11am to 3pm Saturday. Stamp machines in the lobby are accessible 5am to 10pm daily.

Canyon Village Marketplace (☎ 638-2262) sells food, clothing and camping supplies (rentals are possible) from 8am to 7pm daily.

Recycling bins are found where there are trash containers. Visitors are urged to place recyclables in the designated bins.

Near the east entrance, the Desert View Service Center has a visitor center, general store, gas station (closed in winter), campground (closed in winter), cafeteria and the Watchtower, which is the highest point on the South Rim.

**Books & Maps** The Grand Canyon Association (GCA) (☎ 638-2481), PO Box 399,

GRAND CANYON

AZ 86023, sells over 350 books, maps, trail guides and videos about the Grand Canyon. Stores are in the visitor centers, or the GCA will send you a mail-order catalog. Profits benefit the national park.
website: www.grandcanyon.org

**Fees & Permits** Entrance to the park is $20 per private vehicle or $10 for bicyclists and pedestrians. The entrance ticket is valid for seven days and can be used at any entrance point, including the North Rim. All passes are honored. Bus and train passengers either pay a lesser fee or may have the fee included in the tour.

For backcountry camping, permits are required from the Backcountry Office (see Hiking & Backpacking, following).

**Pets** Pets are allowed (when leashed) on developed sections of the rim but nowhere below the rim (except guide or service dogs). Kennels are available, but leaving pets at home is encouraged.

**Dangers & Annoyances** Each year, a few people fall to their deaths in the Grand Canyon. When visiting the rim, stay inside guardrails and on trails. When hiking below the rim, use hiking shoes or boots rather than tennis shoes or sandals. Only a few trails below the rim are maintained; use extra caution when hiking on unmaintained trails.

Some 250 hikers a year on the most popular below-the-rim trails require ranger assistance to get out safely. The main problems are too much sun and too little water. Wear a hat and sunblock, and carry at least a gallon of water per person per day in summer. Hikers can (and do) run out of water and die. Even if it turns out you don't need it, carrying extra water may save someone else's life. Before attempting long hikes, speak with backcountry rangers about where you can replenish your water bottles. (See the Hiking & Backpacking section, following.)

Feeding wildlife is detrimental to the animals and illegal. It is also dangerous – observe them from a distance. Every year

visitors are injured by wild animals. Animals that are fed by visitors become used to human food and seek it out. Frequently, rangers have the sad task of shooting deer to spare them the pain of starving to death: Their stomachs are so clogged with several pounds of indigestible food wrappers and plastic bags that they cannot feed anymore.

Other annoyances come from outside the park. Air pollution has seriously reduced visibility in the canyon in recent years. Smog from as far west as Los Angeles and sulfur emissions from the Navajo Generating Station near Glen Canyon Dam in the east are blown in. Sometimes, the far rim of the canyon is just a distant blur. Winter usually offers the clearest visibility.

The flow and characteristics of the Colorado River have changed and continue to change because of the Glen Canyon Dam. Half the species of fish in the river before the dam was built are now extinct. Anglers and river runners have had to adapt to these problems.

Hikers descending into the canyon to get away from the crowded rims hear aircraft noise from the many tourist flights over the national park.

These annoyances are being recognized and corrected to some extent, but the political ramifications are very complex.

With so many visitors, crime is also a growing problem. Lock cars and hotel rooms. Do not leave valuable objects such as cameras in view inside your car.

## Museums & Historic Buildings

In addition to the exhibits at the visitor centers, check out the following.

**Yavapai Observation Station** At Yavapai Point, at the northeast end of Grand Canyon Village, this station has a geology museum and spectacular views all the way down to Phantom Ranch at the canyon bottom. There is a bookstore and ranger-led activities. Winter hours are 8am to 5pm, extended to 6, 7 or 8pm in other seasons.

**Kolb Studio** In Grand Canyon Village, this was a photography studio opened in 1904 and run by Emery Kolb until his death in 1976. Throughout the year, a variety of changing exhibits display photographs or other items related to the canyon. Hours are the same as the Yavapai museum's, and there is a bookstore. Several other nearby historic buildings date from the same period, including the El Tovar Hotel and the gift shops of Hopi House and Verkamps Curios.

**Tusayan Museum** Located off of East Rim Drive, 23 miles east of Grand Canyon Village, this little museum has exhibits about Ancestral Puebloan life, including ancient twig figures of animals. You can visit the small Tusayan Ruin nearby; guided walks are offered several times a day in summer and less frequently in the off-peak season. Hours are 9am to 5pm in summer, with shorter winter hours. Admission is free.

**Watchtower** At Desert View near the east entrance, you can climb the stairs of the Watchtower (☎ 638-2736), which was built in 1932 and is the highest point on the South Rim. Inside, the walls are decorated with reproductions of ancient petroglyphs as well as contemporary Native American artwork. There is a 25¢ admission to the tower and coin-operated telescopes are available. Hours are 8am to 7:30pm in summer, 9am to 4:30pm in winter.

### Ranger-Led Activities

Call the park's information service (☎ 638-7888) or ask at a visitor center about free ranger-led activities. These occur year-round, though with much greater frequency in summer. Programs include talks (including slide shows) and walks (some wheelchair accessible) throughout the day and into the evening. Guided walks range from a few hundred flat yards (40 minutes) to 3 miles below the rim (three to four hours). During the summer there are Junior Ranger activities for four- to 12-year-olds.

Volunteers can join the **Habitat Restoration Team**. Projects include planting native plants or removing non-native ones, helping restore historic miners' cabins, collecting litter or doing maintenance work. A regular two-hour plant removal and restoration effort occurs at 8:30am several mornings a week (depending on season) and families are encouraged to help and learn (minimum age is five). Information about this project and longer volunteer projects is available at the main visitor center.

The **Grand Canyon Field Institute** (☎ 638-2485, fax 638-2484), PO Box 399, Grand Canyon, AZ 86023, is the educational arm of the GCA (see Books & Maps, earlier). It offers in-depth classes of one to eight days from mid-March to mid-November. Some topics include geology, biology, ecology, Native American cultures and photography. Classes are held both in classrooms and in the field, including hiking and multinight backpacking trips. Contact the field institute for a course catalog.

### Scenic Drives

Driving 51 miles north from Flagstaff on Hwy 89 to the tiny community of Cameron, and heading west on Hwy 64, entering the park from the east after driving through the Kaibab National Forest and Navajo Indian Reservation gives easier access to the Rim Drive pullouts, mostly on the north side of the road. Early morning, with the sun behind you, is suggested. It's 53 miles from Cameron to Grand Canyon Village.

Highway 64 north from Williams, through the South Entrance Station, reaches Grand Canyon Village (about 60 miles). Here, Hwy 64 turns east and becomes the Rim Drive. After exiting the national park, Hwy 64 continues east to Cameron. This way, sunlight is best in the afternoon.

### Rim Trail

The paved Rim Trail is accessible to wheelchairs and extends for over 3 miles along the rim from **Yavapai Point** to **Maricopa Point**. It extends unpaved almost 7 miles farther west past several viewpoints to Hermits Rest (see the next section). The Rim Trail is the park's most popular walk, and visitors can hike as far as they are comfortable. The rewards are beautiful views with many interpretive signs. Only foot and wheelchair traffic is allowed – no bicycles. During winter, snow or ice may temporarily cover the trail.

## Hermits Rest Route

The west rim is accessible by this road for 8 miles west of Grand Canyon Village (and by the Rim Trail described above). At the end of the drive and trail is Hermits Rest, where there is a snack bar and the Hermit trailhead down into the canyon; if you don't descend, you have to return the way you came.

Year-round you can hike the western Rim Trail or cycle along the road. Cars are not allowed along this road, but free shuttle buses operate (see Getting Around, later in the chapter). Narrated bus tours are also available (see Organized Tours, following).

## Desert View Drive

The east rim drive is longer and a little less crowded than the west rim but offers equally spectacular views. Free shuttle buses along the Kaibab Trail Route (the first section of the Desert View Drive) leave every 15 minutes as far as Yaki Point. You can also drive, bike or take a narrated bus tour.

**Tusayan**, the most accessible of the park's approximately 2000 Ancestral Puebloan sites, is along the Desert View Drive, which ends at **Desert View** about 25 miles east of Grand Canyon Village and the highest point on the South Rim. The road then leaves the national park through the Navajo Indian Reservation to Cameron. There are a couple of viewpoints into the smaller Little Colorado River canyon along the way. The Grand Canyon itself turns north at Desert View.

## Hiking & Backpacking

For backpacking, the Backcountry Office (☎ 638-7875, 1 to 5pm Monday to Friday), PO Box 129, Grand Canyon, AZ 86023, has all relevant information. The office in the Maswik Transportation Center is open 8am to noon and 1 to 5pm daily.

The easiest walks are along the Rim Trail, described earlier. Hikes below the rim into the canyon are strenuous, and some visitors prefer to use mules (see Organized Tours). Hikers meeting a mule train should stand quietly on the upper side of the trail until the animals have passed. Mule riders have the right of way.

Two important things to bear in mind when attempting any hike into the canyon: First, it's easy to stride down the trail for a few hours, but the steep uphill return during the heat of the day when you are tired is much more demanding. Allow two hours to return uphill for every hour of hiking downhill. Second, the temperatures inside the gorge are much hotter than at the rim and water is scarcely available. Carry plenty of water and protection from the sun. In summer, temperatures can exceed 110°F in the inner gorge.

The two most popular below-the-rim trails are the Bright Angel Trail and the South Kaibab Trail. These are the best-maintained trails and are both used by mule riders. Both are suitable for either day hikes or, with a permit and advance reservation, overnight backpacking trips. No permit is necessary for a day trip. Both trails are steep and strenuous. Nevertheless, they are considered the easiest rim-to-river trails in the canyon and even a short descent along part of these trails will completely alter your perspective. Day hikers should not expect to reach the river and return in one day.

**Bright Angel Trail** The trail leaves from the Rim Trail a few yards west of Bright Angel Lodge in Grand Canyon Village. From the trailhead at about 6900 feet, the trail drops to Indian Garden 4.6 miles away at about 3800 feet. Here, there is a ranger station, campground, restrooms and water. From Indian Garden, an almost flat trail goes 1½ miles to Plateau Point, with exceptional views into the inner gorge. The 12.2 miles roundtrip from the rim to Plateau Point is a strenuous all-day hike. Shorter hikes are of course possible – just walk down from the rim as far as you want. There are resthouses after 1½ miles (1130-foot elevation drop) and 3 miles (2110-foot elevation drop). The 1½-mile resthouse has restrooms; both have water in summer only.

From Indian Garden, the Bright Angel Trail continues down to the Colorado River (2450 feet elevation), which is crossed by a suspension bridge – the only bridge within the park. The Bright Angel Campground is a short way north of the bridge and 9½ miles from the South Rim. A few hundred yards beyond is Phantom Ranch. Water, food, accommodations and a ranger station are all here.

**South Kaibab Trail** This trail leaves the South Rim from near Yaki Point, about 4½ miles east of Grand Canyon Village. From the trailhead at 7262 feet, it's more than 4800 feet down to the river and Bright Angel Campground, but the distance is only 6.7 miles. Clearly, South Kaibab is a much steeper trail than Bright Angel. It follows a ridge with glorious views. The first 1½ miles drop 1300 feet to Cedar Ridge and this makes a good short half-day hike.

From the Bright Angel Campground on the north side of the river, the **North Kaibab Trail** climbs to the North Rim at 8200 feet in 14 miles (see the Grand Canyon National Park – North Rim section, later in this chapter). You can cross the canyon rim to rim. Although extremely fit hikers can descend from the South Rim to the river and return or make a rim-to-rim crossing in one long day (the record for running rim to rim is now under four hours), the NPS strongly discourages such endeavors. Certainly, during the summer the extreme temperatures make such attempts very dangerous for inexperienced hikers.

**Other Trails** Although other trails receive little or no maintenance, several are not beyond the limits of any hiker with some experience. The least difficult are the **Hermit Trail**, which leaves from Hermits Rest at the end of the West Rim Drive, and the **Grandview Trail**, which leaves from Grandview Point of the East Rim Drive, 12 miles east of Grand Canyon Village. Both of these are steep and strenuous trails, but they'll offer

popular day hikes as well as backcountry camping possibilities.

Details of the many unmaintained trails and backcountry campgrounds in the canyon are beyond the scope of this book – read a backpacking guidebook and contact the Backcountry Office for further information.

**Backpacking Itineraries** Most overnight backpacking trips go from the South Rim to the river and return because rim-to-rim trips involve a five-hour car shuttle. Typically, three days and two nights are spent below the rim, with a choice of spending two nights at either Bright Angel or Indian Garden Campground, or one night at each (normally Bright Angel on the first night). If you arrange a shuttle, you could add a night at Cottonwood Campground on the way up to the North Rim. If your time is limited, a two-day/one-night trip is also rewarding. Because the Kaibab Trail is steep, this is the usual descent route, with the longer but less steep Bright Angel Trail used for climbing out. These two trails are called the 'corridor trails' and are recommended for first-time visitors.

If you want to hike but prefer a bed to a sleeping bag, you can stay at the canyon-bottom Phantom Ranch Lodge (see Places to Stay).

**Backcountry Permits** Permits cost $10 plus $5 per person per night. Applications can be mailed or faxed to the Backcountry Office (fax 928-638-2125), PO Box 129, Grand Canyon, AZ 86023. Alternatively, use the website or deliver applications in person. Applications are accepted for the current month and the next four months *only*. In 1999 the park received 30,000 permit applications and was able to issue 14,000 permits, so your chances are pretty good if you apply early and provide alternative hiking itineraries.

If you arrive without a backcountry permit, don't despair! Immediately head over to the Backcountry Office (☎ 638-7875, 1 to 5pm Monday to Friday), by the Maswik Lodge, and get on the waiting list for cancellations, and you'll likely get a permit within one to six days depending on season and itinerary. You have a better chance of getting a permit on short notice if you are prepared to hike unmaintained trails to less developed campgrounds (ask the ranger for advice) or if you avoid the peak season.

Although it may be tempting to try backpacking without a permit, remember that backcountry rangers patrol the trails and check permits on a regular and frequent basis, so you are quite likely to get caught and fined. Backpacking without a permit is considered a serious offense by the NPS.

## Rafting

You can run the Colorado River with a tour or arrange your own private trip. But before you throw a rubber raft into the back of a pickup and head up to the Colorado River, make sure you have serious river-running experience and a permit.

Obtaining a permit is straightforward but time consuming. Call or write the national park for an application, mail it and wait about 12 years. Then throw your raft into your pickup....

Currently, well over 20,000 visitors a year run the river, almost all with commercial trips. These can be most simply divided into motorized and nonmotorized. The motorized trips are usually in huge inflatable boats that go twice as fast as the oar boats, but you have to put up with the roar of the boat's engine. Nonmotorized trips are slow, but the only roar you'll hear is the roar of the rapids, mingled with gurgled screams. Whichever way you go, expect to get very wet during the day and spend nights camping on riverside beaches. This is not as primitive as it sounds – professional river guides are legendary for their combination of white-water abilities, gastronomy and information.

Most trips run the river from Lees Ferry to Diamond Creek (in the Hualapai Indian Reservation), dropping more than 2000 feet in almost 300 miles and running scores of rapids. Passengers have the option of getting on or off at Phantom Ranch on the main rim-to-rim trail (the South and North Kaibab Trails) almost halfway into the

entire river trip. Combining these options, you can take anything from a three- or four-day motorized trip of part of the canyon to a three-week nonmotorized trip of the entire canyon.

Nonmotorized trips are varied. Many are oar trips, where the captain controls the boat with large oars and the passengers hang on. Some are paddle trips, where the passengers paddle in response to the captain's commands. All these are generally in inflatable rafts, but a couple of companies do paddle trips in wooden dories, reminiscent of those used by John Wesley Powell in 1869. In addition, experienced kayakers can join commercial trips – the gear goes in the rafts.

Commercial trips aren't cheap – expect to pay about $200 per person per day. Family discounts can be arranged, but small children are not allowed – minimum-age requirements vary from trip to trip. Sixteen companies are authorized to run the Colorado River through the national park; contact the park through phone, mail or its website for an up-to-date list. These trips fill up several months (even a year) in advance, so contact the companies early for information.

Occasionally, a cancellation will enable you to run the river on short notice, but this is unreliable. If you want to run the river on short notice, see Hualapai River Runners in the Hualapai Indian Reservation, below, for one-day white-water trips. Also see Organized Tours, following, for one-day, smooth-water raft trips.

## Bicycling

Bicycles are allowed only on roads. Mountain biking on trails is not permitted – you need to go outside the park in the Kaibab National Forest for that. In fact, no wheeled vehicles of any kind are permitted on the trails (except for wheelchairs and baby strollers on the paved Rim Trail).

The story is told of a river runner who pushed a dolly loaded with 10 cases of beer down the Bright Angel Trail to his rafting group. He received a ticket for using a wheeled vehicle on the trail and also had to push the loaded dolly all the way back to the South Rim. Bummer!

### Fishing

There is good trout fishing in the Colorado River and several of its tributaries. Licenses and tackle can be purchased at the general store in Grand Canyon Village.

Licenses are not available for purchase on the national park's North Rim – the nearest area to get a permit is Marble Canyon, where there are also guides.

### Cross-Country Skiing

The higher North Rim area offers more snow for better cross-country skiing than the South Rim area (see also the Jacob Lake Area section, later in the chapter). However, you can ski in the South Rim area in the Kaibab National Forest at the Grandview Ski Area when snow conditions permit. There are 18 miles of easy to medium difficulty, groomed and signed skiing trails near the east entrance of the park. The plowed parking area and access to the trails is on East Rim Drive, 10.1 miles north of the junction of Hwys 64 and 180, 2 miles east of Grandview Point.

About a half-mile into the access trail is an information kiosk that describes routes and distances; the longest trail is 7½ miles. One trail has a canyon-view overlook, but all trails stay in the national forest and do not go to the South Rim of the national park.

Skiers are free to tour the Kaibab National Forest regardless of trails, and there are no restrictions on camping unless you enter the park.

### Organized Tours

Once you are inside the park, most tours are run by Amfac (☎ 303-297-2757). Amfac has a transportation desk (☎ 638-2631) at the Bright Angel Lodge and information desks at the visitor center and Maswik and Yavapai Lodges.
website: www.amfac.com

See Williams, in the Central Arizona chapter, for information about train tours to the Grand Canyon.

**Bus** Narrated bus tours with several photo stops leave from lodges in the Grand Canyon Village. These include a two-hour Hermits Rest Route tour, a 3¾-hour Kaibab Trail Route tour or a combination of both. Both leave twice daily year-round and cost about $16 and $28, or $33 for combining both. Sunset and sunrise tours are $11. Children under 16 are free with an adult.

Some buses are wheelchair accessible by prior arrangement. Reservations are advised in summer but even then there are usually enough buses that you can get on a tour the next day by reserving at the transportation desk. Tax (6%) and guide tips are not included in these prices.

**Mule** A one-day trip to Plateau Point inside the canyon is offered daily. It takes about seven hours roundtrip, of which six hours are spent in the saddle. The cost is $119 plus tax and tips, including lunch.

Overnight trips to Phantom Ranch at the canyon bottom are offered daily. These take 5½ hours down and 4½ hours back up and cost about $335 for one or $600 for two persons, including meals and dormitory accommodations. During winter only, three-day/two-night trips to Phantom Ranch cost $450 or $770 for two. Rates don't include tax and tips.

Reservations are suggested, although you can get on a waiting list if you don't have one. During winter, trips can often be arranged with a day's notice; during the summer the waiting list is much longer and a wait of several days or even weeks may be necessary.

These trips are strenuous – they are supposedly easier than walking, but riders must be in good physical shape and be able to mount and dismount without assistance, weigh under 200lb (including clothing and camera), be at least 4' 7" in height, be fluent in English (so they can understand instructions) and cannot be pregnant.

Horse and mule rides are also available from the town of Tusayan (see that section, following).

You can ride your own horse into the park, but a permit is required from the

Backcountry Office (see Hiking & Backpacking, earlier). Permit procedures and costs are the same as for backpackers, with an additional fee of $5 per horse per night; there is a limit of 12 horses per group of up to six people, or five pack animals for a single mounted rider. Horse trips are allowed only on the corridor routes and only Bright Angel and Cottonwood Campgrounds have overnight horse facilities. Feed must be carried.

## Special Events

The Grand Canyon Chamber Music Festival (☎ 638-9215), PO Box 1332, Grand Canyon, AZ 86023, has been presented at the Shrine of the Ages at Grand Canyon Village in September for more than a decade. Typically, about eight concerts are performed during a two-week period in mid-September. Tickets are $18; $6 for children and students.

## Places to Stay

Reservations for all the places listed below are essential in summer and a good idea in winter. Cancellations provide a lucky few with last-minute rooms; call to check. If you can't find accommodations in the national park, see the sections on Tusayan (6 miles south of Grand Canyon Village outside the South Entrance Station), Valle (31 miles south) and Cameron (53 miles east), later in this chapter. Also see Williams (about 60 miles away) and Flagstaff (about 80 miles) in the Central Arizona chapter.

**Camping** Be prepared for freezing winter nights. In Grand Canyon Village, *Mather Campground* (☎ 301-722-1257, 800-365-2267) has 320 sites (no hookups) for $10 to $15 depending on season. Make reservations up to five months in advance. Otherwise it's first-come, first-served. Even in summer, a few sites may be available in the mornings. Coin showers and laundry are available near the campground entrance. Nearby, the Amfac *Trailer Village* has 80 RV sites with hookups for $24 year-round.

The *Desert View Campground* near the east entrance has 75 campsites on a first-

come, first-served basis from April to October. They are often full by early morning so arrive early. There is water but no showers or RV hookups and fees are $10.

**Lodges** About 1000 rooms are available on the South Rim in a variety of lodges all run by Amfac Grand Canyon National Park Lodges (☎ 638-2631 for same-day information, 303-297-2757), whose website for advance reservations is www.amfac.com. In Grand Canyon Village, there are four lodges on the canyon rim – canyon-view rooms command higher prices. Two lodges, Maswik and Yavapai, are away from the rim, while Phantom Ranch is at the bottom of the canyon near the Colorado River. Approximate prices given below are the same for single or double occupancy; add tax (about 6%) and $7 to $14 per extra person. Prices vary by room, not by season.

On the rim, the most famous and expensive is the 1905 *El Tovar Hotel*, a rustic lodge with high standards of comfort and the best dining in the area. It was renovated in 1998 but still retains its historic flavor. There are 78 small to midsized rooms from $116 to $174. About 12 mini-suites are $200 to $284 and three have private balconies with canyon views.

Budget travelers use the rustic 1935 *Bright Angel Lodge & Cabins* with more than 30 simple lodge rooms, many with shared bath, from $48 to $66. There are 42 cabins, all with bath, mostly for $73 to $121 and very popular. Some have fireplaces and canyon views. A suite with fireplace and canyon views is $220.

Between these two places are the modern *Kachina Lodge* with 49 rooms and *Thunderbird Lodge* with 55 rooms, all comfortable motel-style units with private bath, some with canyon views. Rates are about $114 to $124.

A short walk away from the rim, the *Maswik Lodge* has almost 300 rooms with private baths. Most are motel-style units, some with balconies, for $73 to $118; there are a few slightly cheaper rustic cabins with baths. Near the park headquarters, the

*Yavapai Lodge* has about 360 reasonably sized motel rooms, all with private baths and some with forest views. Rates are $88 to $102. The Yavapai Lodge and the Maswik cabins may close in winter.

*Phantom Ranch* has basic cabins sleeping four to 10 people and segregated dorms sleeping 10 people in bunk beds. Most cabins are reserved for the overnight mule tours, but hikers may make reservations (from $64 double) if space is available. There are separate shower facilities. Dorm rates are $22 per person, and bedding, soap and towels are provided. Meals are available in the dining hall by advance reservation only. Breakfast is $14.50; box lunch is $7.50; and dinner varies from $17.75 (stew) to $27.75 (steak). Meals are not fancy but are enough to feed hungry hikers. If you lack a reservation, try showing up at the Bright Angel Lodge transportation desk at 6am to snag a canceled bunk (some folks show up earlier and wait). Snacks, limited supplies, beer and wine are also sold. Postcards bought and mailed here are stamped 'Mailed by Mule from the bottom of the Canyon.'

## Places to Eat

By far the best place for quality food in an elegant setting is the historic *El Tovar Dining Room* where dinner reservations are recommended, especially in summer when they are often booked weeks ahead. Hours are 6:30am to 2pm and 5 to 10pm. Continental dinner entrées are in the $15 to $25 range and smoking is not permitted. The El Tovar has a piano bar.

More moderate prices and an American menu are available at the *Bright Angel Restaurant*, which is open 6:30am to 10 pm; an adjoining lounge is open 11am to 11pm and may have live entertainment Wednesday to Saturday. Next door to the Bright Angel Lodge, the *Arizona Steakhouse* serves steaks and seafood 4:30 to 10pm March through December. Some tables have canyon views and lines can be long – reservations are not accepted.

Self-service dining is available at the *Maswik Cafeteria* 6am to 10pm. The

Maswik Lodge has a sports bar open 5pm to midnight. The *Yavapai Cafeteria and Grill*, in the market plaza, is open 6am to 9pm. There's also a *delicatessen* in the market plaza, open 8am to 6pm.

Canyonside snacks and sandwiches are sold from 8am to 4pm at the *Bright Angel Fountain* near the Bright Angel trailhead, but it closes in bad weather and in winter. *Hermits Rest Snack Bar*, at the end of the West Rim Drive, and *Desert View Fountain* near the east entrance, are both open daily for snacks and fast food; hours vary by season.

## Getting There & Away

The majority of people drive or arrive on bus tours. The nearest airport is in Tusayan.

See Flagstaff, in the Central Arizona chapter, for the Nava-Hopi bus company, which is the only regularly scheduled bus service into the park. See Williams, in the Central Arizona chapter, for train service offered by the Grand Canyon Railway.

Canyon Airport Shuttle (☎ 638-0821) leaves the airport in Tusayan every hour on the half-hour with several stops in Tusayan en route to the Grand Canyon Village (April to October). One-way fare is $4; park entrance fees are not included. During the rest of the year you can call for taxi service; $5 per person with a $10 minimum.

## Getting Around

Free shuttles operate along three routes: around the Grand Canyon Village, west along Hermits Rest Route and east along Kaibab Trail Route. Buses run every 15 minutes during the day and every 30 minutes from one hour before sunrise till daylight and from dusk till one hour after sunset. Bus stops are clearly marked and free maps are available. Park your car and ride – it's easier.

Shuttles from rim to rim are available from May to October (when the North Rim is open), leave at 1:30pm, take five hours and cost $60 one-way or $100 roundtrip. Call Trans-Canyon Shuttle (☎ 638-2820). Other services are available on request.

## TUSAYAN

Seven miles south of Grand Canyon Village and a couple of miles south of the south entrance, the sprawling community of Tusayan offers several motels, restaurants, souvenir shops and the Grand Canyon Airport, all strung along Hwy 64.

The chamber of commerce (☎ 527-0359) has a visitor information booth in the IMAX Theater lobby, or you can find them at www.grandcanyonchamber.com. The Kaibab National Forest Tusayan Ranger Station (☎ 638-2443) is at the north end of town and is open 8am to 4:30pm Monday to Friday. The post office is opposite the theater and an ATM is inside the theater.

## IMAX Theater

Using a film format three times larger than normal 70mm movie frames, a screen up to eight times the size of conventional cinema screens and a 14-speaker stereo surround system, the IMAX Theater presents *Grand Canyon – The Hidden Secrets*. This 34-minute movie plunges you into the history and geology of the canyon through the eyes of ancient Indians, John Wesley Powell and a soaring eagle. The effects are quite splendid and are a cheaper, safer and quieter way of getting an aerial perspective than taking a flight. The theater (☎ 638-2468) is on Hwy 64, a few miles south of the park entrance. Shows are at 30 minutes past the hour from 8:30am to 9pm March through October and from 10:30am to 6:30pm the rest of the year. Admission is $10; $7 for three- to 11-year-olds. Credit cards are not accepted.

## Horseback Riding

Apache Stables (☎ 638-2891, 638-2424) at the Moqui Lodge, a half-mile south of the park entrance, has a variety of horseback rides available in both the national forest and national park from about March to November. Rides are $25 to $65 for one to four hours. Children as young as six can ride on the shorter trips.

## Other Activities

The Kaibab National Forest provides many opportunities for outdoor fun. Mountain biking on dirt roads and trails (not allowed in the Grand Canyon) is permitted throughout the national forest. About 13 miles of groomed cross-country skiing trails are found on forest lands south of the national park; these trails are accessed from a national park parking area near Grandview Point. You can enjoy hiking, backpacking and camping without the crowds and without a backcountry permit from the NPS Backcountry Office. Of course, you don't get the canyon views either.

## Places to Stay

Visit www.gcanyon.com for information on accommodations in the Grand Canyon area, as well as activities and information for your stay.

**Camping** In the Kaibab National Forest, free dispersed camping is allowed at least a quarter of a mile from paved highways. USFS roads provide access, but many are closed in winter. USFS Rd 686 heading west from Hwy 64, almost a mile south of the Ten-X turnoff, is often open year-round.

The USFS operates the *Ten-X Campground* about 3 miles south of Tusayan. It is open from May through September and has 70 sites for $10 on a first-come, first-served basis. There is water but no showers or RV hookups.

*Grand Canyon Camper Village* (☎ 638-2887) is at the north end of Tusayan, 1½ miles south of the park entrance. About 300 sites are available year-round, ranging from $15 for tents to $23 for full hookups. There are showers, a playground and mini-golf. This place often has a tent site when everywhere else is full.

**Hotels** As with the Grand Canyon, reservations are recommended, especially in summer. Summer rates are pricey for what are basically motel rooms, but if you can't get a room on the South Rim and want to stay close to the canyon, this is what you're stuck with. Winter rates (November to March) are $30 to $50 lower. All motels are along Hwy 64.

The cheapest motel is **Seven Mile Lodge** (☎ 638-2291), with 20 basic rooms for about $72 single or double. They don't take reservations – just show up. **Moqui Lodge**, which is the closest to the park entrance and operated by Amfac (see Lodges in the Grand Canyon National Park – South Rim section, above), has 140 rooms at $100, including breakfast. Rooms vary somewhat in quality though not in price. It is closed November through March. There is a tour desk and a decent restaurant and bar with inexpensive Mexican and American food. Both these hotels advertise horseback riding.

The **Rodeway Inn – Red Feather Lodge** (☎ 638-2414, 800-228-2000) has about 100 older motel rooms plus 130 newer hotel rooms. Consequently, prices vary from about $95 to $130 in summer, $60 to $90 in winter. There is a seasonal pool as well as a spa, exercise room, game room and restaurant. This is the only hotel allowing pets.
website: www.redfeatherlodge.com

The **Holiday Inn Express** (☎ 638-3000, 888-473-2269) has almost 200 rooms for about $130 in summer, including continental breakfast. Rooms are new, modern and comfortable, but the hotel lacks a restaurant and swimming pool. Some attractive suites are $160.

The **Quality Inn** (☎ 638-2673) has over 200 pleasant rooms and mini-suites for $125 to about $175 in summer. The mini-suites, of which there are about 50, each have a microwave, refrigerator and separate sitting area. Most have balconies. There is a pool, spa, restaurant and bar.
website: www.grandcanyonqualityinn.com

The **Best Western Grand Canyon Squire Inn** (☎ 638-2681, 800-622-6966) has 250 spacious rooms at $110 to $190 and a few suites for $210 to $240. There is a seasonal pool as well as a spa, sauna, tennis court, exercise room, coin laundry, gift shop and (at extra charge) a fun center with bowling, billiards and other games. A good restaurant, an inexpensive coffee shop and a bar are on the premises.

The **Grand Hotel** (☎ 638-3333, 888-634-7263) is the area's newest hotel with an indoor pool and spa, Tusayan's best restaurant and 'Native American Experience' which ranges from Indian-led workshops to dance performances. The bar also features cowboy and country singers. The 120 spacious rooms range from $120 to $150 in summer.

## Places to Eat
Apart from the hotel restaurants, there is a steak house opposite the IMAX theater, a pizza restaurant, some cafés and several fast-food places.

## Getting There & Away
The Grand Canyon Airport is at the south end of Tusayan. Flights to and from Las Vegas, Nevada, operate several times a day with Air Vegas (☎ 800-255-7474).

Many flights include an overflight of the Grand Canyon. In addition, tours in airplanes and helicopters starting from and returning to the Grand Canyon Airport are available from about $50 for the shortest flights. Contact Grand Canyon Airlines (☎ 638-2407) or Scenic Airlines (☎ 702-739-1900, 638-2436, 800-634-6801). Everybody will try and sell you one. (See the 'Grand Canyon Overflights' boxed text.)

There are shuttles from the airport to Grand Canyon Village (see Getting There & Away in the South Rim section).

## VALLE
Located about 25 miles south of the Grand Canyon National Park south entrance, Valle is the intersection of Hwy 64 to Williams and Hwy 180 to Flagstaff. There is no town here, just a couple of places to stay and eat, a gas station and an airport near the intersection.

The **Planes of Fame** (☎ 635-1000) is an aircraft museum with several classic military and civilian aircraft in flying condition, as well as models and memorabilia. It opens daily except Thanksgiving and Christmas; admission is $5; $2 for five- to 12-year-olds. The museum is in the airport, which may offer some flight services to the Grand Canyon.

**Flintstones Bedrock City** (☎ 635-2600) has 60 sites ($12.70 for tents and $17 for

GRAND CANYON

## Grand Canyon Overflights

The idea of flying over the Grand Canyon at low altitude appeals to some people. However, passengers may want to consider that there have been many complaints about aircraft noise in the park and concerns about flight safety.

It is very difficult to get away from aircraft noise anywhere in the park for more than a few minutes. The NPS has estimated that visitors have to tolerate aircraft noise during 75% of daylight hours. The natural quiet of the Grand Canyon is part of its magnificence and the current levels of aircraft noise are not acceptable in a national park.

While recent efforts to limit air pollution have met with some success, eliminating noise pollution has been a losing battle. Regulations to keep aircraft above 14,500 feet in 44% of the park and above the rim in the remaining area were a step toward limiting future increases in noise, but these regulations have not always been adhered to and the number of flights has increased. Although air-tour companies are using quieter aircraft, many visitors still find aircraft noise to be annoying.

Safety is another concern. Almost every year one or more tour aircraft crash in or near the canyon. Since the growth of air-tourism in the 1980s, more national park visitors have died in these accidents than in river-running, backpacking, hiking, mule-riding, train and car accidents combined.

## HUALAPAI INDIAN RESERVATION

This reservation borders many miles of the south side of the Colorado River northeast of Kingman. It contains the only road to the river within the Grand Canyon area. Back in the 1800s, when the area was being invaded by miners, the Hualapai fought hard to retain control of their lands. Today, most of the tribe works in ranching, logging or tourism. The reservation offers visitors a good opportunity to see some of the Grand Canyon area (outside the national park and away from the crowds) accompanied by guides from a tribe that originally inhabited the region.

### Orientation & Information

The tribal headquarters (☎ 769-2216), PO Box 179, Peach Springs, AZ 86434, are in a small community about 50 miles northeast of Kingman or almost 40 miles northwest of Seligman on Route 66. Contact the tribally operated lodge (☎ 769-2230) for information on the campground or river-running trips. For bus tours call ☎ 699-0269; online you'll find them at www.hualapaitours.com.

Entrance into the reservation for sightseeing, picnicking and hiking is $6.30 per day per person (free for children under twelve). No firearms are allowed on the reservation. Camping is available for $10 per person per night. Fishing costs $8 per day with a catch limit of eight fish. Permits can be bought in Peach Springs at the river-running office or lodge, both easy to find as you drive through on Route 66. (There is no charge for driving through on Route 66.)

Apart from Route 66, there are three roads of interest through the reservation. One is the paved road to the Havasupai Reservation (see the next section). The other two are unpaved.

From Peach Springs, 22-mile, unpaved **Diamond Creek Rd** heads north to the Colorado River. With the appropriate permit, you can drive to the Colorado River – 2WD cars with good clearance can usually make it except after heavy rains when you'll need a high-clearance 4WD. This is the only place

hookups). There are coin showers and laundry, a snack bar (Bronto Burgers and Dino Dogs) and a Flintstones recreation area complete with concretosaurs. The campground is open mid-March through November.

The *Grand Canyon Inn* (☎ 635-9203) has several sections with standard motel rooms that cost around $70 in summer. There is a restaurant, gift shop, spa and seasonal pool. Next-door you will find a gas station and a grocery store.

within the canyon that the river can be reached by road.

Three miles west of Peach Springs on Route 66 is unpaved Buck and Doe Rd, which leads about 50 miles to Grand Canyon West (see Things to See & Do). This road is entirely within the reservation. Grand Canyon West can also be reached from Kingman by heading northwest on Hwy 93 for about 26 miles, then northeast along the paved Pearce Ferry Rd (heading toward Lake Mead) for about 30 miles, and then 21 miles east along the dirt Diamond Bar Rd. (This route is 20 miles shorter than driving from Kingman to Peach Springs.)

### Things to See & Do

There's little to do in Peach Springs itself apart from seeing the **tribal powwow** held in late August. The lodge has a small cultural center.

The **Grand Canyon West** area has an airstrip and tribal office where permits, bathroom facilities and soft drinks are available. A tribally operated guided bus tour goes out to the canyon rim for $37.50 ($22 for three- to 11-year-olds) and includes a barbecue lunch on the rim and plenty of local lore and information as presented by the Hualapai guide – an interesting trip. The tour goes year-round.

A $10 permit (small children are free) allows you to drive 3 miles to the **Quartermaster Viewpoint**, which has a parking area and good views of the lower Grand Canyon but no facilities. A five-minute hike on a rough trail brings you to a small bluff with better views. You won't see many people – it's a far cry from the masses thronging the (admittedly more spectacular) South Rim of the national park.

Hualapai River Running (see Orientation & Information section, earlier) offers one-day **river running** trips along the lower reaches of the Colorado River from May through October for $250 per person. Day trips run Monday to Friday; two-day trips run on weekends and include riverside camping. This company uses motorized rafts guided by Hualapai Indians. Both white-water and floating is involved. Pack-

ages are also offered with rooms at the Hualapai Lodge before and after your trip. Children must be at least eight years old to participate.

### Places to Stay & Eat

In Peach Springs, the tribe-operated *Hualapai Lodge* (☎ 769-2230) has 60 motel rooms for $75 to $85 double in summer, and a *restaurant* open 6am to 9pm. Otherwise there are no hotels on the Hualapai Reservation.

The Hualapai tribe operates a basic *campground* near the end of Diamond Creek Rd by the Colorado River. The elevation here is 1900 feet, which makes it extremely hot in summer. There are restrooms and picnic tables but no drinking water; bring everything you'll need.

### HAVASUPAI INDIAN RESERVATION

Centered on Havasu Canyon, carved by Havasu Creek, a southern tributary of the Colorado River, this is the traditional home of the peaceful and energetic Havasupai Indians, who now offer Grand Canyon visitors a unique look at the canyon and river. Tribal headquarters are in Supai, which has been there for centuries – the only village within the Grand Canyon. The first European visitor was the Spanish priest Francisco Garcés in 1776. Just as in the old days, Supai can be accessed only by a steep 8-mile-long trail from the canyon rim. Below Supai, the trail leads past some of the prettiest waterfalls within the Grand Canyon.

Word has gotten out about this beautiful area. Although no roads directly connect Grand Canyon National Park's South Rim with the reservation, there are hundreds of daily visitors during the peak summer months. Nevertheless, it is much more tranquil than the South Rim.

### Information

Information is available from the Havasupai Tourist Enterprise (☎ 448-2141), Supai, AZ 86435. All visitors pay an entry fee of $20. The fee is valid for the length of your visit. The Supai Post Office distributes its mail by pack animals – postcards mailed from here have a special postmark to prove it. There is a small emergency clinic. Alcohol, firearms and pets aren't allowed.

Some visitors have expressed surprise that the village looks shabby, littered and unattractive. This is partly because the village is periodically flooded and partly because tribe members have a different concept of what is and isn't attractive. Come for the scenic and natural beauty and leave your urban planning ideas at home.

## Things to See & Do

The 8-mile hike down to Supai is attractive, as it follows Havasu Creek and is lined with trees, but the most memorable sections are along the 4 or 5 miles of trail below the village. Here, there are four major **waterfalls** and many minor ones.

Just over a mile beyond Supai is Navajo Falls, the first of the four big falls. Next comes the 100-foot-high Havasu Falls, with a sparkling blue pool that is popular for swimming. Beyond is the campground, and the trail then passes 200-foot-high Mooney Falls, the largest in the canyon. The falls were named after a miner who died in a terrifying climbing accident in 1880: Although Mooney was roped, he was unable to extricate himself and hung there for many hours until the rope finally broke and he was killed. A very steep trail (chains provide welcome handholds) leads to the pool at the bottom, another popular swimming spot. Finally, 2½ miles farther is Beaver Falls. From there, it is a farther 4½ miles down to the Colorado River (about 8 miles below the campground).

## Special Events

Tribal dances are held around Memorial Day and a Peach Festival is in August. Call Havasupai Tourist Enterprise (see Information, earlier) for exact dates.

## Places to Stay & Eat

In Supai, the **Havasupai Lodge** (☎ 448-2111) has 24 modern rooms, all with canyon views, two double beds, air-conditioning and private showers. There are no TVs or telephones – a plus for travelers wishing to get away from that stuff! Reservations are essential and should be made well in advance in the summer. Rates range from $75 to $96 for one to four people ($30 less in winter). Nearby, a small cultural center has tribal exhibits. Meals and snacks are served from 7am to 6pm daily at the **Village Cafe** (☎ 448-2981) near the lodge, and a general store sells food and camping fuel. Prices are high (though not prohibitive) because everything comes in by horse or helicopter.

Two miles below Supai, the **Havasupai Campground** has 400 tent sites stretching along the river between Havasu and Mooney Falls. The campground suffered disastrous flooding in 1997 and tourists were evacuated, though it was reopened soon after. There are latrines but no showers. You can swim in the river or pools, and there is a spring for drinking water, though it should be purified. Fires are not permitted, so bring a camp stove to cook. Camping fees are $10 per person and reservations (contact the lodge; see Orientation and Information) should be made because after hiking more than 10 miles in, you don't want to be turned back! The campground fills on holiday weekends and most days in summer. Don't leave gear unattended at the campground or anywhere else – thefts have occurred. There is no camping allowed elsewhere in the area.

Note that the entrance fees are in addition to the lodge or campground fees. During summer, campers outnumber villagers so don't expect much in the way of cultural interaction. To enjoy the scenery and beautiful waterfalls, a two-night trip is suggested.

## Shopping

The Havasupai are noted for basketmaking and beadwork. Their crafts are sold in the lodge's souvenir shop.

## Getting There & Away

Seven miles east of Peach Springs on Route 66, a signed turnoff indicates a 62-mile paved road to Hualapai Hilltop on the

Havasu Canyon rim in the Havasupai Reservation. There are no services.

Hualapai Hilltop has an unguarded parking area – lock in the trunk what you aren't taking to Supai. Don't leave your valuables. From the hilltop, a trail drops steeply and then flattens out, reaching Supai after about 8 miles and a 2000-foot elevation drop. The trail continues over a half mile through the village, then a farther 2 miles to the campground.

Havasupai Tourist Enterprise can arrange horses or mules by advance reservation (call a few weeks ahead). Fees per animal are $70 from hilltop to Supai, one-way. If you want to hike down and hire a mule for the climb out, you can often arrange it when you get to Supai if you are flexible with your departure time. You can bring your own horse for a $20 trail fee – you supply feed. Mountain bikes are not allowed. Most visitors walk.

A helicopter service flies from the hilltop to Supai – this is mainly for tribal use.

## CAMERON & AROUND

Cameron, a tiny community 31 miles east of the national park's eastern entrance, is on the western end of the Navajo Indian Reservation (see the Northeastern Arizona chapter). It is included here because it is on the main route from the South Rim to the North Rim of the Grand Canyon.

The historic Cameron Trading Post, opened in 1916 and still operating, sells museum-quality Navajo rugs and other crafts, some of which date from the turn of the 19th century and sell for many thousands of dollars. Even if you're not in the market for the finest-quality rugs, it's worth stopping in just to see the attractive building and the beautifully displayed pieces, including some pre-European pots and items from several other tribes. The trading post sits scenically on the south side of the Little Colorado River. Next-door is a motel, restaurant, RV park, grocery store, post office and a gift shop selling a huge variety of crafts and souvenirs at affordable prices.

About 10 miles west of Cameron on the way to the Grand Canyon is the **Little Colo-**rado River Gorge Navajo Tribal Park with a scenic overlook – it's worth a stop. Along the road are numerous stalls set up by Navajo families selling arts and crafts.

Right at the corner of Hwys 64 and 89 is the **Cameron Visitor Center**, open daily in summer and open erratically out of season. It has information about Navajo land as well as the Grand Canyon.

### Places to Stay & Eat

The *Cameron Trading Post & Motel* (☎ 679-2231, 800-338-7385) has more than 60 pleasant Southwestern-style rooms, many with balconies, for about $80 and a handful of suites with separate living quarters for $145 to $175. In summer it's difficult to get a room without a reservation and they don't take credit cards, so book ahead and mail them a check. Ask about discounts in winter. There are also *RV sites* with hookups for $16, but no tent sites or public showers. A *restaurant and café* serves decent meals and snacks but no alcohol (reservation land, remember?).

Eight miles south along Hwy 89 is the even smaller community of **Gray Mountain** where you'll find a gas station, small store and the *Anasazi Inn* (☎ 679-2214), with a restaurant and several dozen motel rooms around $70 in summer.

# The Arizona Strip

Traditionally and geographically, this area north of the Grand Canyon has closer ties with Mormon Utah than with Arizona. The Arizona Strip is wild, large, poorly roaded, a long way from Salt Lake City, and remains one of the last holdouts of the 19th-century practice of polygamy. The places described below are on the few routes from the South Rim of the Grand Canyon to the North Rim and beyond into Utah.

## MARBLE CANYON & LEES FERRY AREA

Highway 89 splits a few miles before crossing the Colorado River, with Hwy 89 heading northeast to Page and then swinging

GRAND CANYON

west to Kanab, Utah, and Hwy 89A taking a shorter route to Kanab through the Arizona Strip. Highway 89A crosses the Navajo Bridge over the Colorado at Marble Canyon. This is the only road bridge into the Arizona Strip from the south and the only one on the Colorado River between Glen Canyon Dam and Hoover Dam in Nevada. Motorists use a new bridge; the original bridge was opened in 1929 and is now closed to vehicles, though you can park your car and walk across the old bridge, staring down onto the river almost 500 feet below. The bridge marks the southwestern end of the Glen Canyon National Recreation Area (GCNRA), described later in this chapter. At the west end is the Navajo Bridge Interpretive Center, run by the GCNRA and open April through October. Almost immediately after the bridge, a side road to the right leads 6 miles to Lees Ferry, historically the only crossing point of the river for many miles and today the major put-in spot for river runners making the exciting descent through the Grand Canyon.

Lees Ferry is named after John D Lee, who established the Lonely Dell Ranch and primitive raft ferry here in 1872. Later, Lee was executed for his part in the Mountain Meadows Massacre. The ferry operated until the Navajo Bridge was opened in 1929. Some of the historic ranch buildings near Lees Ferry can still be seen. The GCNRA has a ranger station (☎ 355-2234) here, and a booklet and map describing the ranch, ferry and area's history is available. Less than a mile southwest of Lees Ferry is the mouth of the spectacular Paria River Canyon (see the boxed text, 'Paria Canyon-Vermilion Cliffs Wilderness Area').

In the smooth waters of the Colorado, below the Glen Canyon Dam, the ecosystem has changed from the tumultuous rapids of pre-dam years. The result has been favorable for fly-fishers, and the waters provide some of the country's most reliable and sought-after year-round fly-fishing serviced by several nearby fishing lodges. Approximate rates for a full guided day of fly-fishing range from about $200 (one angler, walking and wading) to $400 (three

anglers, river boat). March and April are the busiest months.

## Places to Stay & Eat

The GCNRA runs the *Lees Ferry Campground* at Lees Ferry, with 54 sites for $10. There is drinking water, toilets and a nearby boat ramp but no showers or RV hookups. Public coin showers ($2.50) are at the Marble Canyon Lodge.

*Marble Canyon Lodge* (☎ 355-2225, 800-726-1789), on Hwy 89A a half-mile west of Navajo Bridge, has 45 rooms for $60/70 single/double (one bed). Eight apartments sleeping six are $135. A restaurant is open 6am to 9pm, and there is a coin laundry, store, bar and fly shop. Guide service information (☎ 355-2245, 800-533-7339) is at www.mcg-leesferry.com.

*Lees Ferry Lodge* (☎ 355-2231, 355-2230), on Hwy 89A 3 miles west of Navajo Bridge, has 12 rooms at $54 a double. There is a restaurant and bar (with 135 types of beer), and a fishing tackle shop. Visit www.ambassadorguides.com for guide service (☎ 800-256-7596) details.

*Cliff Dwellers Lodge* (☎ 355-2228, 800-433-2543) is under the Vermilion Cliffs, 8½ miles west of the Navajo Bridge. Twenty motel rooms (no TV or phone) rent for about $60 a double in summer. There is a restaurant, bar, store and gas. For nearby angling services (☎ 355-2261, 800-962-9755) go to www.leesferry.com.

## JACOB LAKE AREA
## Orientation & Information

Highway 89A intersects with Hwy 67 at the small community of Jacob Lake, 41 miles west of Marble Canyon. Highway 67 heads south to the North Rim of Grand Canyon National Park, 44 miles away, but is closed December 1 to May 15. If a major snowstorm comes early, the road closes in November or even late October. Jacob Lake's high elevation (7921 feet) explains the long snow season. Highway 89A remains open year-round, but winter travelers should carry chains or have 4WD.

A forest service visitor center (☎ 643-7298) in Jacob Lake, on Alt Hwy 89 near the intersection, has information, displays and interpretive programs on the Kaibab National Forest. The district headquarters are in Fredonia.

## House Rock Wildlife Area

About 17 miles east of Jacob Lake along Hwy 89A, a signed turnoff to the south indicates unpaved USFS Rd 8910, which goes another 17 miles to this wildlife area on Kaibab National Forest land. House Rock Wildlife Area is known for a wild herd of buffalo, which you may be able to see with any luck. Remember, however, the wildlife area covers more than 100 sq miles so your sightings are likely to be distant. Continuing past the ranch about another 10 miles will bring you to a couple of remote viewpoints overlooking the Marble Canyon area of the Grand Canyon National Park. Condors have been sighted here. (See the boxed text

'Condors at Vermilion Cliffs.') This road is closed by snow during the long winter.

## Places to Stay & Eat

Free dispersed *camping* in the Kaibab National Forest is permitted as long as you are more than a quarter-mile from the paved highway – several unpaved forest roads give access.

*Jacob Lake Campground* (☎ 643-7395) is near the USFS visitor center on Hwy 89A. More than 50 sites are $10 on a first-come, first-served basis, with limited free camping in winter. There is water but no showers or hookups. *De Motte Campground* is about 25 miles south on Hwy 67 and has 22 similar $10 sites, open mid-May through October. Both are USFS campgrounds.

*Kaibab Lodge Camper Village* (☎ 643-7804), off Hwy 67 a mile south of Hwy 89A, has more than 100 sites from $12 (tents) to

## Condors at Vermilion Cliffs

The spectacular Vermilion Cliffs, which stretch along the north side of Hwy 89A for most of the way from Marble Canyon to Jacob Lake, were chosen as one of the first release sites for California condors, members of the vulture family. These endangered birds are magnificent – with a wingspan of 10 feet and weighing as much as 24lb, they are the largest land birds in North America. Before the arrival of Europeans, condors ranged throughout much of North America, but by the early 19th century they were found only west of the Rockies. The last confirmed sighting in Arizona was in 1924. By the 1980s, condors were extinct in the wild, but a small breeding population in the Los Angeles Zoo gave ornithologists hope that the birds could be reintroduced into the wild.

The first reintroduction was in Southern California, but this was not very successful because the release sites, though remote, were still too close to major metropolises. Condors require areas that are hundreds of miles from large cities and that provide mountain ridges or cliffs from which they can launch themselves for soaring flights. (The birds can fly as fast as 50mph under the right conditions.) The birds' preferred nesting areas are caves in inaccessible cliffs or mountains. The Vermilion Cliffs seem to meet these requirements, and six condors were initially released here in December 1996, with more releases in 1997 swelling the number to about 20. A few more have been released since then. Inevitably, some condors have not survived; one was reportedly killed by a golden eagle and another died in a clash with power lines. Others, however, appear to be thriving and there have been recent sightings from both the Grand Canyon and Lake Powell. Keep your eyes open!

Exciting news came in 2001 when a pair nested and an egg was laid in the wild. Unfortunately, the egg was damaged and the chick did not hatch, but it is an encouraging step toward the return of the condor.

$23 (hookups) open mid-May through October. There is water but no showers.

***Jacob Lake Inn*** (☎ *643-7232*) has about 50 simple motel rooms and cabins for about $90 double ($126 for family units sleeping six) in summer. At the junction of Hwy 89A and Hwy 67, it has a restaurant and store; visit www.jacoblake.com. The ***Kaibab Lodge*** (☎ *638-2389 in season,* ☎ *526-0924, 800-525-0924 year-round*), on Hwy 67, 25 miles south of Jacob Lake, is open when the road is open. Rooms with private bath in duplex cabins rent from $80 for a double to $120 for rooms that sleep five. A restaurant serves breakfast and dinner.

## GRAND CANYON NATIONAL PARK – NORTH RIM

The differences between the North and South Rims of the Grand Canyon are elevation and accessibility. The North Rim exceeds 8000 feet above sea level, with some points reaching over 8800 feet. Winters are colder, the climate wetter and the spruce-fir forest above the rim much thicker than the forests of the South Rim. There is only one road in, so visitors must backtrack more than 60 miles after their visit. Winter snows close the road to car traffic from December 1 (earlier in snowy years) until mid-May.

Because it's such a long drive from any major city or airport, only 10% of Grand Canyon visitors come to the North Rim. But the views here are spectacular. North Rim visitors are drawn by the lack of huge crowds and the desire for a more peaceful, if more spartan, experience of the canyon's majesty.

### Orientation & Information

Forty-four miles from Jacob Lake is **Bright Angel Point**, which has the main visitors' services at the North Rim. Almost 30 miles of paved roads lead to various other overlooks. The park headquarters are at the South Rim. See the South Rim section for general information, entrance fees and backcountry permits. The park's automated telephone system (☎ 638-7888) has both South and North Rim information.

The North Rim Visitor Center (☎ 638-7864) is in the Grand Canyon Lodge (the North Rim's only hotel) and is open 8am to 8pm May 15 through October 15. The usual NPS activities and information are available. The Backcountry Office (for backpackers) is in the ranger station near the campground, 1½ miles north of the visitor center/lodge. Other services available at the North Rim (in season) are a restaurant, gas station, post office, bookstore, general store, coin laundry and showers, medical clinic and tours. After October 15, all services are closed except the campground, which remains open weather permitting. After December 1, everything is closed.

Summer temperatures are about 10°F lower than on the South Rim. Winter snowfall is heaviest from late December to early March, when overnight temperatures normally fall into the teens and sometimes below 10°F, though very few people visit then.

During winter, you can ski in and, with a backcountry camping permit, camp. It takes about three days to ski in from where the road is closed, so this journey is for adventurous and highly experienced winter campers/skiers. Call the Backcountry Office for details.

### North Rim Drives

The drive on Hwy 67 through the Kaibab Plateau to Bright Angel Point takes you through thick forest. There are excellent canyon views from the point, but to reach other overlooks you need to drive north for almost 3 miles and take the signed turn east to **Point Imperial** and **Cape Royal**. It is 9 miles to Point Imperial, which is, at a lofty 8803 feet, the highest overlook in the entire park and has stunning views.

Backtrack about 4 miles from Point Imperial and then drive 15 miles south to Cape Royal where there are more great views and some short hiking trails.

With 4WD and high clearance, you can take unpaved roads to several other outlooks along the North Rim. These roads may be closed by bad weather or other factors – information is available from any ranger or the park information line. Many of these roads require leaving the park, driving through USFS or BLM lands, then reentering the park.

One of the most spectacular of these remote overlooks is the **Toroweap Overlook** at **Tuweep**, far to the west of the main park facilities. An unpaved road, usually passable to cars, leaves Hwy 389 from 9 miles west of Fredonia and heads 55 miles to the Tuweep Ranger Station, which is staffed year-round. An alternative route is a 90-mile dirt road from St George, Utah. It is five more miles from Tuweep to the Toroweap Overlook, where there is *primitive camping* but no water or other facilities – you must be totally self-sufficient.

## Hiking & Backpacking

The most popular quick hike is the paved half-mile trail from the Grand Canyon Lodge south to the extreme tip of **Bright Angel Point**, which offers great views at sunset. The 1½-mile **Transept Trail** goes north from the lodge through forest to the North Rim Campground, where there are also rim views. Other trails in the area are rugged and relatively poorly maintained. Before embarking on them, consult with a North Rim ranger.

The **North Kaibab Trail** plunges down to Phantom Ranch at the Colorado River, 5750 feet below and about 14 miles away. This is the only maintained rim-to-river trail from the North Rim and it connects with trails to the South Rim. The first 4.7 miles are the steepest, dropping well over 3000 feet to **Roaring Springs** – a popular all-day hike and mule-ride destination. Drinking water is available at Roaring Springs from May to September only. If you prefer a shorter day hike below the rim, you can walk just three-quarters of a mile down to **Coconino Overlook** or a mile to the **Supai Tunnel**, 1400 feet below the rim, to get a flavor of steep inner-canyon hiking.

Hikers wishing to continue to the river will normally camp. **Cottonwood Campground** is 7 miles and 4200 feet below the rim and is the only campground between the North Rim and the river. Here, there are

14 backcountry campsites (available by permit only), drinking water from May through September and a ranger station. About 1½ miles below the campground a short side trail leads to pretty **Ribbon Falls**, a popular bathing spot but with no camping. Phantom Ranch Lodge and the Bright Angel Campground are 7 and 7½ miles below Cottonwood (see the South Rim section).

Because it is about twice as far from the North Rim to the river as from the South Rim, rangers suggest three nights as a minimum to enjoy a rim-to-river and return hike, staying at Cottonwood on the first and third nights and Bright Angel on the second. Fit and experienced hikers could enjoy a two-night trip, staying at Cottonwood both nights and hiking down to the river and back to Cottonwood on the second day. Faster trips, while technically feasible, would be an endurance slog and not much fun.

Hiking from North to South Rim requires a shuttle to get you back (see Getting Around in the South Rim section for details).

**Backcountry Permits** In the winter, the trails of the North Rim are regarded as backcountry-use areas, and snow can accumulate to five feet at the rim. Though the North Rim Campground (see Places to Stay, below) is closed in winter, it is available for backcountry use. However, there are only two ways to get to the campground in winter – either hike from the South Rim up to the North Rim via the North Kaibab Trail or cross-country ski 52 miles from Jacob Lake, a route that takes three days.

Permits for all backcountry campgrounds must be applied for as far in advance as possible from the Backcountry Office (☎ 638-7875, 1 to 5pm Monday to Friday), PO Box 129, Grand Canyon, AZ 86023, (see the South Rim section for details). If you don't have a permit, get on the waiting list at the Backcountry Office (open 8am to noon and 1 to 5pm daily in season) in the North Rim ranger station near the campground as soon as you arrive. Your chances of getting a

GRAND CANYON

Cottonwood or Bright Angel Campground permit for the next day are slim; however, if you can wait two to four days, you'll probably get one. The ranger station can advise you of other backcountry campgrounds, most of which require a long drive on dirt roads followed by a hike.

A hikers' shuttle from the lodge to the Bright Angel trailhead is $5 for the first hiker and $2 for each additional hiker in your group. Ask at the lodge for tickets. Shuttles are available from 6am to 8pm.

### Bicycling

Mountain bikes are allowed on all paved roads and some unpaved roads on the North Rim. No wheeled vehicles are allowed on hiking trails.

### Organized Tours

In season, daily three-hour narrated tours to Point Imperial and Cape Royal leave from the lodge and cost $24 ($12 for four- to 12-year-olds). A schedule is posted in the lobby.

Trail Rides (☎ 638-9875 in season, ☎ 435-679-8665 otherwise) offers rides for $20 for an hour (minimum age is six), $45 for a half-day (minimum age is eight) and $95 for an all-day tour into the Grand Canyon, including lunch (minimum age is 12). Advance reservations are recommended, or stop by their desk (open 7am to 7pm) in the Grand Lodge to see what is available. Mule rides are not available to the Colorado River except from the South Rim.

### Places to Stay & Eat

Backcountry camping requires a permit (see Hiking & Backpacking, above).

The only other place to camp is *North Rim Campground*, 1½ miles north of the Grand Canyon Lodge, with 82 sites for $14 each. There is water, a store, snack bar and coin-operated showers and laundry, but no hookups. Make reservations (☎ 301-722-1257, 800-365-2267) up to five months in advance. Without a reservation, show up before 10am and hope for the best.

The historic *Grand Canyon Lodge* (Amfac; ☎ 303-297-2757 for reservations) is

usually full and reservations should be made as far in advance as possible. There are about 200 units: both motel rooms and a variety of rustic and modern cabins sleeping up to five people. All have private bath; only a few cabins have canyon views. Rates range from $80 to $113 double.

The lodge has a *snack bar and restaurant* open for all meals, but dinner reservations are required and breakfast reservations are advised in the attractive restaurant.

A *general store* by the campground sells food and camping supplies.

### Getting There & Away

There is no public transport. A North to South Rim shuttle (☎ 638-2820) leaves daily at 7am for $60 one-way or $100 roundtrip and takes five hours. Call for reservations.

## FREDONIA

☎ 928 • pop 1036 • elevation 4671 feet

From Jacob Lake, Hwy 89A drops 3250 feet in 30 miles to Fredonia, which is much warmer. Founded by Mormons in 1885, Fredonia is the main town in the Arizona Strip. The larger Kanab, 7 miles north in Utah, has much better developed tourist facilities, but Fredonia has information about the Kaibab National Forest.

### Information

The town offices and chamber of commerce (☎ 643-7241) are at 130 N Main (Hwy 89). Other services include the Kaibab National Forest District Headquarters (☎ 643-7395), 430 S Main; post office (☎ 643-7122), 85 N Main; and the police (☎ 643-7108), 130 N Main.

### Places to Stay & Eat

From April to October, *Blue Sage Motel* (☎ 643-7125, 330 S Main) offers basic rooms for about $35. There are a few other small places.

The *Grand Canyon Motel* (☎ 643-7646, 175 S Main) has stone cabins with kitchenettes in some units. The *Crazy Jug Motel* (☎ 643-7752, 465 S Main) charges about $50 and has a restaurant.

Two miles north of town, **Travelers Inn Restaurant & Lounge** (☎ 643-7402, 2631 N Hwy 89A) serves American dinner Monday to Saturday in summer and Friday and Saturday the rest of the year.

## AROUND FREDONIA
### Pipe Spring National Monument
Ancient Indians and Mormon pioneers knew about this permanent spring in the arid Arizona Strip. Ranching began here in 1863 and a fort named **Winsor Castle** was built in 1870 to protect the ranchers from Indian attacks. In 1923, the 40-acre ranch was bought by the NPS as a historical monument documenting pioneer and Indian life and interactions on the Western frontier.

Today, visitors can learn about frontier life by touring the well-preserved ranch buildings and fort, examining historic exhibits and attending cultural demonstrations (summer only) by rangers and volunteers. Tours of Winsor Castle are offered every half-hour (last tour at 4pm) and a short video is shown on request at the visitor center.

A visitor center (☎ 643-7105) with a bookstore is open 8am to 5pm daily except New Year's Day, Thanksgiving and Christmas. Admission is $3 for adults, or by pass. The monument is 14 miles west of Fredonia on Hwy 389. Further information is available from the superintendent, HC65, Box 5, Fredonia, AZ 86022.

### Kaibab-Paiute Indian Reservation
Fewer than 200 Paiutes live in this reservation, which completely surrounds the Pipe Spring National Monument. The tribally operated **campground** (☎ 643-7245) is a half-mile east of Pipe Spring. The remote campground offers showers, RV hookups for $10 and tent sites for $5.

### Kanab Canyon
Marked on most maps as Kanab Creek, this is actually the largest canyon leading to the Colorado River's north side. In places, Kanab Canyon is 3500 feet deep and it effectively splits the relatively developed eastern part of the Arizona Strip from the remote western part.

From Fredonia, Kanab Canyon goes south for 60 miles to the Grand Canyon. Adventurous canyoneers enjoy hiking this route, which is described in John Annerino's useful *Adventuring in Arizona.* Permits are required in some stretches. Drivers of high-clearance vehicles can drive through the Kaibab National Forest to Hack Canyon and Jumpup Canyon, both of which are popular entry points into the lower part of Kanab Canyon.

### The Northwest Corner
This is the most remote part of the state. Much of it is BLM land managed by offices in Kanab and St George, Utah. A few ranches and mines are surrounded by wilderness areas with absolutely no development, reachable by a network of dirt roads. To explore this area, a reliable high-clearance vehicle and plenty of water and food are essential. If you break down, you might not see another car for days. Consult with the BLM before you go.

The 'best' unpaved roads are the ones heading to Tuweep Ranger Station and Toroweap Overlook Campground (see North Rim Drives, earlier).

# Lake Powell Area

The next major canyon system on the Colorado River northeast of the Grand Canyon is (was) Glen Canyon. Called 'The Canyon That No One Knew,' in the 1950s it was the heart of the largest roadless area in the continental USA. A few old-time river runners and canyoneers tell of a canyon that rivaled the Grand Canyon for scenic grandeur and was full of ancestral Indian sites, but most people hadn't even heard of this remote wilderness area when work began on the Glen Canyon Dam in 1956.

Conservationists fought hard against the construction of the dam, realizing not only that the beautiful canyon would be destroyed, but also that the character of the Southwest would change dramatically.

GRAND CANYON

Seven years later, the dam was finished, and Glen Canyon slowly began filling up to become the second largest artificial reservoir in the country, helping fuel the uncurbed population growth of the desert. The reservoir is Lake Powell.

## PAGE

☎ 928 • pop 6809 • elevation 4300 feet

Dam construction in the late 1950s gave birth to this new town in the high desert. Once a drab construction town, Page is now the largest Arizonan town in the huge area north of I-40 and is a regional center for southeastern Utah as well. Tourists value Page not only as a convenient stopping place between the two states but also for the recreation opportunities afforded by Lake Powell (7 miles from the town center). The tourism industry is experiencing a boom and hotel rooms are over-priced and booked up in summer.

### Information

The chamber of commerce (☎ 645-2741, 888-261-7243), 644 N Navajo Dr, is open from 8:30am to 5pm Monday to Friday, with extended hours and weekend openings in spring, summer and fall; visit www.page-lakepowellchamber.org.

The Powell Museum (see below) has visitor information and will make motel and tour reservations. Numerous kiosks around town are stocked with useful brochures. A useful website is www.powellguide.com.

Services in town include the library (☎ 645-4270), 4795 Lake Powell Blvd; post office (☎ 645-2571), 44 6th Ave; hospital (☎ 645-2424), at Vista Ave and N Navajo Dr; and the police department ☎ 645-2463), 808 Coppermine.

### Things to See & Do

The small **Powell Museum** (☎ 645-9496, 888-5873), 6 N Lake Powell Blvd, has exhibits pertaining to Colorado River explorer John Wesley Powell, changing local art shows from April to October as well as regional information. Hours (subject to change) are 8:30am to 5:30pm Monday through Saturday; closed mid-December through mid-February. Admission is $1 or 50¢ for children five to 12.

website: www.powellmuseum.org

**Navajo Village: A Living Museum** (☎ 660-0304), 531 Haul Rd, is a collection of Navajo hogans and other buildings featuring demonstrations of the Navajo way of life – cooking, weaving, dancing, jewelry work, singing and storytelling. Guided tours of a Navajo home are offered 9am to 3pm Monday to Saturday; admission is $10, $5 for six- to 13-year olds, and $25 for a family. The Navajo Village also arranges a four-hour 'Evening with the Navajo' featuring detailed presentations of many facets of their lives, including a Navajo dinner. Rates are $50, $35 for children or $135 for families. Shorter, cheaper presentations are also offered. Tickets and reservations are available at the chamber of commerce or Powell Museum.

Several **trading posts** offer first-class Native American art, craft and jewelry. An excellent place for seeing both new and old Navajo crafts, including some exceptional old pawn jewelry and fabulous new kachina dolls for serious collectors, is Blair's Dinnebito Trading Post (☎ 645-3008), 626 N Navajo Dr. Family patriarch, Elijah Blair, has been trading on the reservation for over half a century and he and his family know all there is to know about traditional reservation crafts. Ask to see their private family collection; get more information on the Web at www.blairstradingpost.com. Also stop by the Big Lake Trading Post (☎ 645-2404), just over a mile south on Hwy 89, to see its small Diné Bikeyah Museum of ancient Native American artifacts.

The **Rimview Trail** is a municipally developed 8-mile trail that circumnavigates the town. It is open to walkers, joggers and cyclists (who must stay on the trail) and is a mix of sand, slick rock, rocky washes and other terrain. There are several access points – pick up a brochure at the chamber of commerce or museum.

### Organized Tours

The chamber of commerce and Powell Museum will make tour reservations. Most

Aerial view of the Colorado River cutting through the Grand Canyon

Tourists on mules ride down the Bright Angel Trail, Grand Canyon National Park.

Dawn at Yaki Point on the South Rim of the Grand Canyon

Bright Angel Trail passing the Colorado River

Mooney Falls, Havasupai Indian Reservation

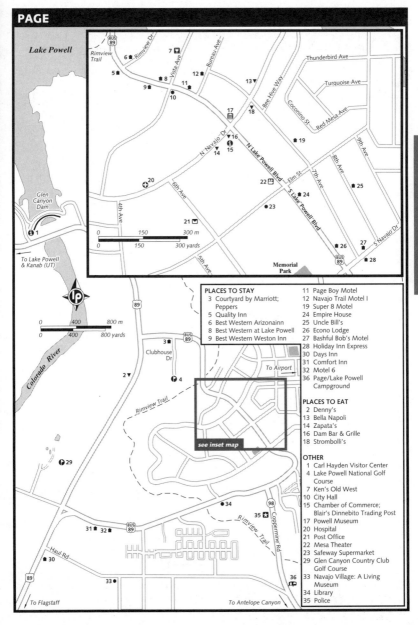

**GRAND CANYON**

**PAGE**

Lake Powell

**PLACES TO STAY**
3  Courtyard by Marriott;
   Peppers
5  Quality Inn
6  Best Western Arizonainn
8  Best Western at Lake Powell
9  Best Western Weston Inn
11 Page Boy Motel
12 Navajo Trail Motel I
19 Super 8 Motel
24 Empire House
25 Uncle Bill's
26 Econo Lodge
27 Bashful Bob's Motel
28 Holiday Inn Express
30 Days Inn
31 Comfort Inn
32 Motel 6
36 Page/Lake Powell
   Campground

**PLACES TO EAT**
2  Denny's
13 Bella Napoli
14 Zapata's
16 Dam Bar & Grille
18 Strombolli's

**OTHER**
1  Carl Hayden Visitor Center
4  Lake Powell National Golf
   Course
7  Ken's Old West
10 City Hall
15 Chamber of Commerce;
   Blair's Dinnebito Trading Post
17 Powell Museum
20 Hospital
21 Post Office
22 Mesa Theater
23 Safeway Supermarket
29 Glen Canyon Country Club
   Golf Course
33 Navajo Village: A Living
   Museum
34 Library
35 Police

see inset map

offer discounts for children or groups. Reservations are required, but often you can get on the tour of your choice with just one day's notice. The following are the best known, but there are others.

**Boat Tours** Half- or full-day boat tours to Rainbow Bridge National Monument ($80/110), cruises on Wahweap Bay for 1½ or more hours ($25 to $75) and other cruises on Lake Powell are available from Aramark at Wahweap Marina (see below). Half- or full-day float trips ($59/79) from Glen Canyon Dam to Lees Ferry along the Colorado River are also offered. No white water is involved. Children ages 3 to 12 get discounts. Tour schedules are severely curtailed in winter.

**Antelope Canyon & Land Tours** Also called Corkscrew Canyon, this spectacularly scenic narrow 'slot' canyon (much higher than it is wide) is on the Navajo Reservation a few miles east of Page. Tours are available into the upper canyon, accompanied by Navajo guides. Ask locally for current tours, which start at about $20 per person ($10 for children) plus a $5 Navajo permit. Cheaper tours will drop you off at the entrance, but not provide guiding or information service. It is over a mile from the entrance to the canyon. Most tours last 1½ hours.

Various other canyons and scenic areas can be visited. Some tours are specifically designed for photographers. Try any of the following: Antelope Canyon Adventures (☎ 645-5501); Antelope Canyon Tours (☎ 645-8579); Scenic Tours (☎ 645-5594); and Jackson Bridges Photography (☎ 645-5451). Ask at the chamber of commerce or the Powell Museum for details.

## Places to Stay

From May to October, very high summer rates apply, demand is high and reservations are strongly recommended, especially in August. Arrive by early afternoon if you don't have a reservation. The chamber of commerce and museum can help with B&B and last-minute accommodations. In winter,

some hotels charge half or less or may close. Rooms are generally clean and modern – no Route 66 motels or creaky Victorian hotels in Page. Note that there are campgrounds and a motel at Wahweap Marina, 5 miles away (see Glen Canyon National Recreation Area, later).

For camping, the **Page/Lake Powell Campground** (☎ 645-3374, 849 S Coppermine Rd) has more than 70 RV sites, with hookups ($24) and a few tent sites ($17). There are showers, a pool, spa, coin laundry and internet access.

As for budget choices, when the **Motel 6** (637 S Lake Powell Blvd) charges $76 for a double room in July and August, you know you won't find any bargains in summer. The cheapest motels, which have simple but clean doubles in the $50s or $60s in mid-summer, include **Bashful Bob's Motel** (☎ 645-3919, 750 S Navajo Dr), the **Page Boy Motel** (☎ 645-2416, 150 N Lake Powell Blvd), which has a small pool, and **Navajo Trail Motel I** (☎ 645-9508). Call ahead for all of these! Also try **Uncle Bill's** (☎ 645-1224, 115 8th Ave), which has 12 rooms with shared bathroom facilities – other budget places are also on this block.

In the mid-range category, **Empire House** (☎ 645-2406, 800-551-9005, 100 S Lake Powell Blvd) has a pool and 70 nice motel rooms for about $60 – fair value. **Chain motels** with rooms under $100 include the Econo Lodge and Super 8.

All the top end places are comfortable **chain motels** – not luxurious but not under $100 either. These include three Best Westerns, a Quality Inn and a Comfort Inn, a Days Inn, a Holiday Inn Express and a Courtyard by Marriott, considered the town's best hotel and with a golf course. All boast pools, and most have restaurants or at least breakfast areas. Some have balconies – the Best Western Arizoninn and the Quality Inn even have distant lake views.

## Places to Eat

For an early breakfast, try the hotel restaurants, which serve mainly American food. **Peppers** in the Marriott is especially good and also features Southwestern food.

*Strombolli's* (☎ 645-2605, 711 N Navajo Drive), serves pizza and other Italian specialties and is popular because of its large outdoor deck and cheap dinners, which are advertised as 'under $10.' More upscale Italian dining in a more intimate atmosphere is found at *Bella Napoli* (☎ 645-2706, 810 N Navajo Dr) with dinners only in the $8 to $18 range.

Page's 'Wild West' steak house is *Ken's Old West* (☎ 645-5160, 718 Vista Ave), open for meaty dinners priced from $10 to $20. The *Dam Bar & Grille* (☎ 645-2161, 644 N Navajo Dr) serves good steaks and Italian food in dam modern surroundings that remind you why Page is here. Lunch and dinners are served and it has sports TV and live music on weekends. *Zapata's* (☎ 645-9006, 615 N Navajo Dr) does decent Mexican meals.

## Entertainment

Movies are shown at the *Mesa Theater* (☎ 645-9565, 42 S Lake Powell Blvd).

*Ken's Old West* features both live and recorded country & western music and dancing every night except Sunday in the summer and a few times a week during other seasons.

## Getting There & Around

Air services to Page Airport may be available in summer but not year-round. Great Lakes Aviation has flown to Phoenix, Denver and Moab in the past. There are no regular bus services, though van shuttles to Flagstaff may run in summer. Contact the chamber of commerce for details.

Avis (☎ 645-2024) rents cars at the Page Airport. Rates are expensive and you can save money by renting in Flagstaff or Phoenix.

## GLEN CANYON NATIONAL RECREATION AREA

When the Glen Canyon Dam was finished in 1963, the Colorado River and its tributaries (especially the San Juan River) began backing up for 186 miles. It took until 1980 to fill the artificial Lake Powell, flooding the canyon to a depth of 560 feet at the dam

and creating almost 2000 miles of shoreline. The 1933-sq-mile Glen Canyon National Recreation Area (GCNRA) was established in 1972, primarily emphasizing activities on the lake, which accounts for 13% of the total area. The remainder is many square miles of remote backcountry, which can be explored on foot or by a few roads north of the confluence of the Colorado and San Juan Rivers.

## Information

The Carl Hayden Visitor Center (☎ 608-6404) is at the dam, 2 miles north of Page (the only town close to the GCNRA). Hours are 8am to 7pm May through September and 8am to 5pm at other times. Most of the GCNRA is in Utah, but it is treated as a whole here. Entrance to the area costs $10 per vehicle or $3 per individual and is valid for up to seven days. Boats are $10 for up to seven days or $20 a year. All passes are accepted. Up-to-date information is available in the free newspaper *Reflections*, available on arrival.

Five miles north of the visitor center is Wahweap Marina, the largest marina on Lake Powell. It offers complete visitors' services. Four more marinas are scattered along the shores of Lake Powell in Utah. All marinas have an NPS ranger station and there's a smaller visitor center at Bullfrog Marina. Details of services available in each marina are described under individual marina headings below. Aramark (☎ 602-331-5200, 800-528-6154) is the concessionaire for houseboats, tours and lodges at the lake; visit www.visitlakepowell.com.

The GCNRA also operates a ranger station at Lees Ferry and an interpretive center at Navajo Bridge on Hwy 89A (see Marble Canyon & Lees Ferry Area, earlier in this chapter).

Further information is available from the Superintendent (☎ 608-6200), GCNRA, PO Box 1507, Page, AZ 86040.

**Climate & When to Go** The area is open year-round. The water-level elevation of 3700 feet makes the GCNRA cooler than Lake Mead and other downstream recre-

GRAND CANYON

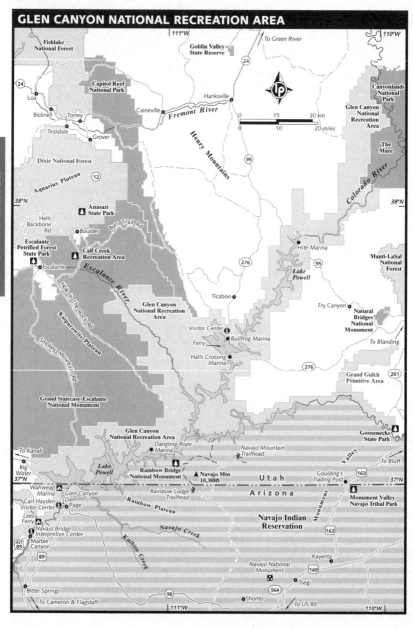

# GLEN CANYON NATIONAL RECREATION AREA

ation areas, but summer temperatures can still rise to more than 100°F on some days. Combined with reflections off the water and canyon walls, the heat can be quite stultifying until you get acclimatized. Average summer maximum temperatures are in the 90°s F, with water temperatures ranging from 70°F to 80°F from June to September. Overnight temperatures drop into the 70°s F, making sleeping comfortable. The humidity is low year-round and there is little rainfall.

Summer is the most popular season with the highest rates for boat rentals and motel rooms. The areas around the marinas are a noisy zoo of boat engines, yahoos on jet skis and inexperienced sailors, all bent on getting their money's worth after paying $200 or $300 for a day of fast boat rental. It'll take a few hours to navigate beyond this, but it makes a huge difference.

Spring can be very windy, and cold water temperatures preclude swimming or water-skiing without a wet suit – in May the water averages a brisk 64°F. Fall water temperatures average 69°F in October; the lowest average is 46°F in February.

Hikers and backpackers will find April to June and September to October the most pleasant months. In winter, overnight temperatures often fall into the 20°s F but rise into the 40°s F during the day in December and January, the coldest months.

Water levels fluctuate depending on season and water use. The highest levels are in late spring and early summer, when you can boat just a little farther into some of the side canyons.

**Books & Maps** The *Boater's Guide to Lake Powell,* by Michael R Kelsey, is for boaters interested in taking side hikes from the shore, including information about shore camping for people using small boats. *Lake Powell and Its 96 Canyons: Boating and Exploring Map* by Stan Jones is an annotated map with plenty of other useful information.

**Camping Regulations** Rising and falling water levels have caused buried human

waste to contaminate the lake and make some areas unsafe for swimming. These areas are closed and marked with yellow buoys and signs. Anyone camping within a quarter-mile of the lake must use a portable toilet. Rangers can tell you which beaches have toilets. If you camp on a beach without a toilet, you can rent portable ones from the marinas. Human waste must be disposed of in designated dump stations; sewage dumping is illegal. There are eight floating toilets on the lake.

**Dangers & Annoyances** Several people drown every year in boating, swimming or diving accidents, many of which are alcohol related. Lake Powell has no lifeguards, but the lake is patrolled by park rangers. Children under 12 are required by law to wear life jackets when on a boat, while everyone in a boat, regardless of age, is required to have a preserver immediately accessible (not stowed). Use common sense.

In recent years, several deaths have been attributed to carbon monoxide emitted by boat engines and gathering under the platforms overhanging the water from most boats. This gas is odorless and can result in swift unconsciousness of swimmers near the boat. Check with park authorities or rental agencies for information about this potentially lethal hazard.

### Glen Canyon Dam

Right next to the Carl Hayden Visitor Center, the dam can be visited on self-guided tours year-round. From April through October, free guided tours lasting 60 to 90 minutes leave hourly on the half-hour until 90 minutes before the center closes. Tours take you along the top and then deep inside the dam in elevators that drop to near the bottom. The dam is 710 feet high and required over 5 million cubic yards of concrete to build.

### Wahweap Marina

Only 7 miles from Page, Wahweap Marina & Lodge (run by Aramark; ☎ 645-2433, 800-528-6154) offers complete services – boat tours and rentals (see Water Sports and

Houseboating, below); boat and car service and fuel; laundry; showers; and a supply store. Call the marina directly for information and reservations less than seven days in advance. Otherwise, call Aramark for reservations, which are strongly recommended in summer; its website is www.visitlake powell.com.

*Wahweap Campground* has about 180 sites without hookups on a first-come, first-served basis open April through October. Sites are $15. Next door *Wahweap RV Park* has 123 year-round sites with hookups for $26, or $17 November through March (when tenting is permitted). There are showers and a playground.

*Wahweap Lodge* has 350 comfortable rooms with coffeemakers, refrigerators, balconies or patios, for about $155 to $165 in summer, dropping to $116 in winter. Suites are $225 in summer. About half the rooms have lake views, and there are two pools and a whirlpool. The lodge has room service, a moderately priced coffee shop and a good restaurant.

Aramark offers several boat tours ranging from a one-hour ride on a steam-powered paddlewheel riverboat ($14) to a seven-hour tour to Rainbow Bridge ($106). There are discounts for three- to 11-year-olds. All tours leave from Wahweap Marina. Rainbow Bridge tours also leave from Bullfrog and Halls Crossing Marinas.

### Bullfrog Marina

Bullfrog Resort & Marina (☎ 435-684-3000) is 96 miles upstream from the dam and is the lake's second largest marina. It is located on Lake Powell's north shore and the nearest town is tiny Hanksville, Utah, 72 miles north.

There is a GCNRA visitor center (open 8am to 5pm daily April to October, intermittently in November, and closed in winter); a medical clinic (summer only); post office; ranger station; laundry; showers; boat rentals (see Water Sports and Houseboating), fuel and services; auto fuel and services; and an expensive supply store. Reservations (which should be made well

in advance) for houseboats, the campground and Defiance House Lodge are provided by Aramark (see Information, earlier).

*Bullfrog RV Park and Campground* is open year-round with about 100 tent sites ($16) and 24 RV sites ($22). Ask at the ranger station about free primitive camping (no water) at several places along the shore. Note the new camping regulations (see Information, earlier).

*Defiance House Lodge* has about 60 comfortable rooms with TV, refrigerator and coffeemaker for $110 to $120 in summer, less in winter. A few housekeeping trailers, with two or three bedrooms, two bathrooms, fully equipped kitchen and electricity range from $120 a double to $160 for six people in summer, less in winter. The lodge has a restaurant open for breakfast, lunch and dinner year-round and a fast-food place open during the summer.

A ferry connects Bullfrog Marina with Halls Crossing Marina. (See the 'Lake Powell Ferry' boxed text.)

### Halls Crossing Marina

Halls Crossing Marina (☎ 435-684-7000) is on the south shore of the lake, opposite Bullfrog. The nearest town is Blanding, Utah, 75 miles to the east. Services include a ranger station; boat rentals, fuel and service; auto fuel and service; laundry; showers; a supply store; and an air strip. Services are provided by Aramark.

*Halls Crossing RV Park and Campground* has about 60 tent sites ($10) and 20 RV sites ($22). The ranger can suggest free campsites along the shore.

### Hite Marina

Hite Marina (☎ 435-684-2278) is located 139 miles upriver from Glen Canyon Dam and is the most northerly marina on the Colorado River. Hanksville, Utah, is 45 miles northwest and is the nearest small town. Services at Hite include a ranger station; boat rentals, fuel and service; auto fuel and service; and a supply shop. Aramark provides reservations.

## Lake Powell Ferry

The 150-foot-long *John Atlantic Burr* or the identical sister-ship *Charles Hall* provide a link between Bullfrog and Halls Crossing Marinas year-round. Each holds 150 passengers, 14 cars and 2 buses. The 3.2-mile crossing takes 27 minutes and can save as many as 130 miles of driving. The ferries may be delayed or canceled by bad weather. Phone Halls Crossing (☎ 435-684-7000) or Bullfrog Marina (☎ 435-684-3000) for more information.

*Fares*

| Foot Passengers | free |
|---|---|

*Vehicles*
*(including driver and passengers)*

| Bicycle | $2 |
|---|---|
| Motorcycle | $2 |
| Vehicles under 20 feet | $12 |
| Vehicles 20 to 70 feet | $15 to $40 |
| Vehicles over 70 feet | $50 |

*Schedule*

| *Departs Halls Crossing* | *Departs Bullfrog* |
|---|---|
| 8am | 9am |
| 10am | 11am |
| Noon | 1pm |
| 2pm | 3pm |

*Additional Service*
*Mid-April through May*

| 4pm | 5pm |
|---|---|

*Additional Service*
*Mid-May through September*

| 6pm | 7pm |
|---|---|

The marina has a free primitive *campground* (no water). Water is available from the boat ramp.

### Dangling Rope Marina

This marina is about 40 miles upriver from the dam and can be reached only by boat. This is the closest marina to Rainbow Bridge National Monument (see below). Services include a ranger station, boat fuel and services, and a supply store.

### Fishing

You can fish year-round. Spring and fall are considered the best times, although summer isn't bad. Bass, crappie and walleye are the main catches on the lake. Licenses are required and are available from any marina; you'll need Arizona and/or Utah licenses depending on where you fish.

### Water Sports

The public can launch boats from NPS launch ramps at the marinas. Boats ranging from 16-foot runabouts to 59-foot houseboats sleeping 12 are available for rental from Aramark. Water skis and jet skis can also be rented, but the marinas aren't geared to renting kayaks or dinghies.

Water-skiing, scuba diving, sailing and swimming are summer activities. Average water temperatures of 62°F in November and 64°F in May are too chilly except for the most dedicated enthusiasts with wet or dry suits.

Aramark rents boats: A 16-foot skiff seating six with a 25-hp motor is $75 a day in summer. Use skiffs for slow exploring and fishing. Larger boats with larger engines for towing water-skiers or getting around more quickly cost three or four times as much. Kayaks are $47 a day. Water 'toys' include jet skis for about $260 a day and water skis and other equipment packages for $25. Note that there are federal plans to limit jet-ski use in national parks as of 2002. Weekly rates usually give one free day.

All marinas except Dangling Rope rent boats.

### Houseboating

Houseboating is popular – hundreds of houseboats are available for rent and there are more every year. Despite the number of boats, the large size of the lake still allows houseboaters to get away from others. Houseboats can sleep from eight to 12 people, but accommodations are tight so

GRAND CANYON

make sure you are good friends with your fellow shipmates, or rent a boat with flexibility in sleeping arrangements. The larger boats are quite luxurious; the smaller boats are very utilitarian.

Houseboats on Lake Powell are provided by Aramark (see Information, above), which also provides small boats, tours and lodging in marinas – these can be combined into a variety of packages. Houseboats can be rented from any marina except Dangling Rope and advance reservations are required.

Summer rates range from about $1100 to $3100 for three days to $1900 to $6100 for a week in boats ranging from 36 to 59 feet in length. Four-, five- and six-day rentals are available and two-day rentals are available outside of summer. From about October to April (dates vary with boats and marinas), discounts of about 40% are offered.

Small houseboats have tiny to midsize refrigerators, simple cooking facilities, a toilet and shower, a gas barbecue grill and 150-quart ice chests.

Larger boats may have some of the following: electric generator (allowing air conditioning, microwave, toaster, coffeemaker, TV, VCR and radio), canopies, swim slides and ladders. Luxury boats have all these features upgraded and with extra space. Boats are booked up well in advance in summer.

## RAINBOW BRIDGE NATIONAL MONUMENT

On the south shore of Lake Powell, Rainbow Bridge is the largest natural bridge in the world and a site of religious importance to the Navajo. No camping or climbing on the bridge is permitted, but visitors can come by boat, horse or on foot. Primitive camping is allowed outside the monument, less than a mile from the bridge. Almost all visitors come by boat tour and then hike a short trail. Serious photographers will find that the overhead light does not lend itself to good shots; arranging dawn and dusk visits is difficult and potentially expensive.

Very few people arrive on foot. However, hikers leave from the Rainbow Lodge trailhead in Arizona (the lodge is abandoned) or Navajo Mountain trailhead (technically in Utah but approachable only from Arizona) and walk about 14 miles to the monument. The trailheads are reached by dirt roads and the trails themselves are not maintained. This hike is for experienced backpackers only; you should carry water and be self-sufficient. Both trailheads are on the Navajo Reservation and a tribal permit should be obtained from the Navajo Parks & Recreation Dept (☎ 871-6647, fax 871-6637) in Window Rock (see the Northeastern Arizona chapter). The monument is administered by the GCNRA.

# Western Arizona

Western Arizona is not only the hottest part of the state, it is often the hottest area in the nation. The low-lying towns along the Colorado River (Bullhead City, Lake Havasu City and Yuma) boast average maximum daily temperatures of more than 100°F from June to September, and temperatures exceeding 110°F are not unusual. Balmy weather during the rest of the year attracts thousands of winter visitors, many of whom end up staying – western Arizonan cities have some of the fastest growing populations in the USA.

After the Colorado River leaves the Grand Canyon, it turns south and forms the western boundary of Arizona, referred to as Arizona's 'west coast.' Several dams along it form huge artificial lakes that attract those vacationers escaping the intense summer heat – water-skiing and jet-skiing, sailing and boating, fishing, scuba diving and plain old swimming are popular activities. In addition, travelers enjoy the wild scenery, visit dams, explore wildlife refuges and ghost towns, gamble in casinos and see perhaps the most incongruous of sights in the desert Southwest, London Bridge.

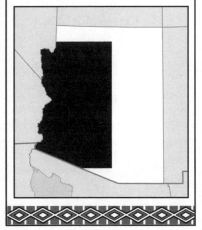

## Highlights

- Visiting the self-styled ghost town of Oatman, with its old buildings, staged gunfights and western dancing
- Boating and swimming in Lake Mead
- Trying your luck at the casinos in Laughlin
- Drinking a beer by the London Bridge (yes, *the* London Bridge) in the English Village of Lake Havasu – England in the Arizona desert?
- Joining more than 100,000 visitors and several thousand dealers at the annual Gem and Mineral Show in pint-sized Quartsite
- Camping in the rugged mountains of the Kova National Wildlife Refuge

## KINGMAN
☎ 928 • pop 20,069; metro area 38,000 • elevation 3345 feet
This area was virtually unknown to Europeans until 1857, when Edward Beale, using camel caravans, surveyed a wagon route across northern Arizona near what is now Kingman. Lewis Kingman surveyed a railway route through northern Arizona in 1880; the railroad was completed in 1883. Kingman is the most historic of the area's larger towns and several turn-of-the-19th-century buildings survive. Although attracting fewer visitors than the nearby resorts of Bullhead City and Lake Havasu City, Kingman provides an excellent base for exploring the northwestern corner of the state and offers plenty of inexpensive and mid-priced accommodations.

### Orientation & Information
Exits 48 and 53 from I-40 freeway span Kingman's main street, Andy Devine Ave. Named after a Hollywood actor who was raised here, Andy Devine Ave also forms part of historic Route 66 and most accommodations and services are found along it.

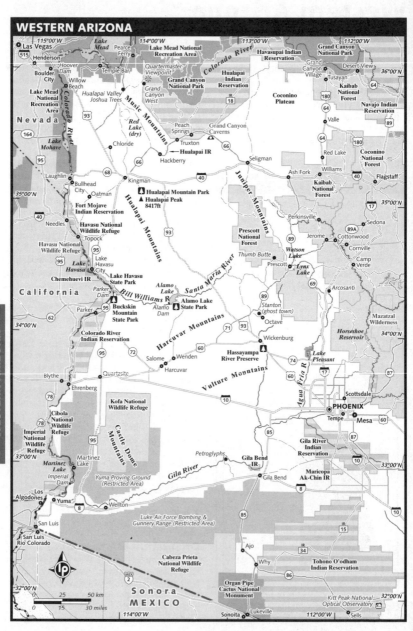

The visitor center (☎ 753-6106) at 120 W Andy Devine Ave is open daily. Its website is at www.arizonaguide.com/visitkingman.

Other services available in Kingman include the BLM (☎ 692-4400), 2475 Beverly Ave, library (☎ 692-2665), 3269 N Burbank, post office (☎ 753-2480), 1901 Johnson Ave, Medical Center (☎ 757-2101), 3269 Stockton Hill Rd, and police (☎ 753-2191), 2730 E Andy Devine Ave.

## Things to See & Do

The visitor center is inside the old Powerhouse. This building was built in 1907 and now also houses a Route 66 gift shop and diner, an art display and the **Route 66 Museum,** which follows the history of the route and has the best collection of Route 66 memorabilia west of Oklahoma. Admission is $3. The visitor center has a map detailing late-19th-century buildings that can be visited on a **Historic Walking Tour** that covers nearby streets.

The **Mohave Museum of History & Arts** (☎ 753-3195), 400 W Beale, highlights local history and homeboy Andy Devine. Hours are 9am to 5pm weekdays and 1 to 5pm on weekends, except major holidays. Admission is $3; free for children under 13. The **Bonelli House** (☎ 753-1413), N 5th and Spring, was built in 1894 by pioneers, rebuilt in 1915 after a fire and is now municipally owned and is open as an example of early Anglo architecture in Arizona. Its hours are 1 to 4pm Thursday to Monday, except major holidays. Admission is by donation.

**Hualapai Mountain Park** (☎ 757-3859) surrounds 8417-foot Hualapai Peak and offers a popular summer getaway for local residents. Fourteen miles southeast of Kingman (take Hualapai Mountain Rd from Andy Devine Ave), it features picnicking, camping, rooms and cabins, wildlife observation, and miles of maintained and undeveloped trails.

## Special Events

Route 66 Fun Run (753-5001), a vintage car rally along Route 66 between Seligman and Topock, runs over the last weekend in April or first weekend in May. Kingman has a car show followed by dancing in the evening.

There are also events in the small towns along the route.
website: www.azrt66.com

The Arts Festival during Mother's Day weekend in May includes metalworkers and woodcarvers, as well as the more usual types of artists. The Mohave County Fair is held in mid-September, and Andy Devine Days, with a parade, rodeo and other events, happens during late September.

## Places to Stay

**Camping** At *Hualapai Mountain Park*, 70 campsites are available on a first-come first-served basis for $6, most with picnic tables and grills. Eleven RV sites with hookups are $12. Water and toilets are available.

The **KOA** *(☎ 757-4397, 800-562-3991, 3820 N Roosevelt)* has mainly RV sites ($23 to $28) and a small area for tents ($18), plus a swimming pool, game room, coin laundry, and convenience store. The **Quality Stars RV Park** *(☎ 753-2277, 3131 MacDonald Ave)*, offers sites from $13 to $20 depending on whether you use the hookups. There is a coin laundry and small pool.

**Motels & Hotels** Cheap hotels are found along old Route 66. The cheapest places have basic double rooms in the $20s, including the *Arcadia Lodge (☎ 753-1925, 909 E Andy Devine Ave)* with 48 rooms, the small *Lido Motel (☎ 753-4515, 3133 E Andy Devine Ave)*, the friendly *High Desert Inn (☎ 753-2935, 2803 E Andy Devine Ave)* and the 29-room *Hilltop Motel (☎ 753-2198, 1901 E Andy Devine Ave)* which has a small pool. There are a dozen others with rooms in the $20s and $30s.

Plenty of *chain motels* are to be found. I-40 exit 53 is a good place to look for most of them (see map).

The most memorable accommodations are at the *Hotel Brunswick (☎ 718-1800, 315 E Andy Devine Ave)*, established in 1909 and recently renovated. Twelve old-fashioned cowboy/girl rooms with single beds share four bathrooms; rates are $25. Thirteen more rooms have private baths and TVs; rates range from $50 to $75. A restaurant and bar are on the premises

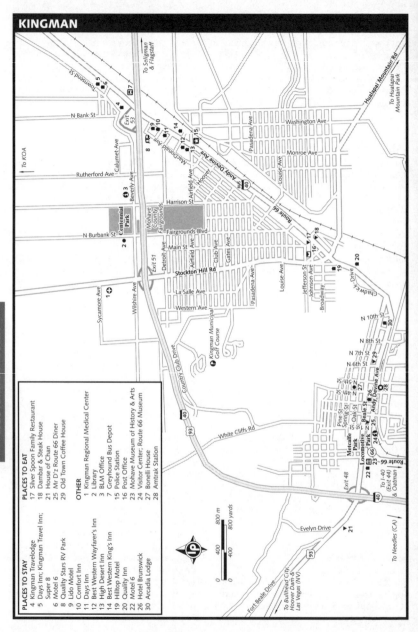

# KINGMAN

**PLACES TO STAY**
4  Kingman Travelodge
5  Days Inn; Kingman Travel Inn;
   Super 8
6  Motel 6
8  Quality Stars RV Park
9  Lido Motel
10  Comfort Inn
11  Days Inn
12  Best Western Wayfarer's Inn
13  High Desert Inn
14  Best Western King's Inn
19  Hilltop Motel
20  Quality Inn
22  Motel 6
26  Hotel Brunswick
30  Arcadia Lodge

**PLACES TO EAT**
17  Silver Spoon Family Restaurant
18  Dambar & Steak House
21  House of Chan
25  Mr D'z Route 66 Diner
29  Old Town Coffee House

**OTHER**
1  Kingman Regional Medical Center
2  Library
3  BLM Office
7  Greyhound Bus Depot
15  Police Station
16  Post Office
23  Mohave Museum of History & Arts
24  Visitor Center; Route 66 Museum
27  Bonelli House
28  Amtrak Station

To KOA

To Seligman
& Flagstaff

To Hualapai Mountain Rd

To Hualapai
Mountain Park

N Bank St

Exit 53

N Townsend St

Calumet Ave

Rutherford Ave

Beverly Ave

MacDonald Ave

Airfield Ave

Hoover

Andy Devine Ave

Washington Ave

Pasadena Ave

Monroe Ave

Louise Ave

Route 66

Harrison St

Centennial
Park

Mohave
(County)
Fairgrounds

N Burbank St

Fairgrounds Blvd

Main St

Detroit Ave

Airfield Ave

Club Ave

Gates Ave

Louise Ave

Jefferson St

Johnson Ave

Chadwick Drive

Exit 51

Stockton Hill Rd

La Salle Ave

Pasadena Ave

Broadway

N 10th St

Sycamore Ave

Wilshire Ave

Western Ave

Kingman Municipal
Golf Course

N 8th St

N 7th St

N 6th St

N 5th St

N 4th St

Pine St

Spring St

Andy Devine Ave

Oak St

Beale St

Park

Metcalfe
Park

Locomotive
Park

Country Club Drive

White Cliffs Rd

Route 66

To I-40
(Exit 44)
& Oatman

Exit 48

Evelyn Drive

To Needles (CA)

Fort Beale Drive

To Bullhead City,
Hoover Dam &
Las Vegas (NV)

0    400    800 m
0    400    800 yards

and the price of breakfast is included in the room rate.

website: www.hotel-brunswick.com

## Places to Eat

The popular and cheap **Silver Spoon Family Restaurant** (☎ 753-4030, 2011 E Andy Devine Ave) is open 5am to 9pm.

The well-recommended **House of Chan** (☎ 753-3232, 960 W Beale) is 11am to 9:30pm and is closed on Sundays. The service is good, and prime rib, steak and seafood are featured in addition to Chinese food. Dinners are in the $7 to $20 range.

The popular **Dambar & Steak House** (☎ 753-3523, 1960 E Andy Devine Ave) specializes in large steaks ($10 to $20) for dinner. Grab a burger or blue plate special at the '50s style **Mr D'z Route 66 Diner** (☎ 718-0066, 105 E Andy Devine Ave). Light snacks and international coffees are served at the **Old Town Coffee House** (☎ 753-2244, 616 E Beale).

## Getting There & Away

Kingman Airport (☎ 757-2134) is 6 miles northeast of town off Route 66. America West flies between Kingman and Phoenix, stopping at Prescott, twice a day on weekdays.

The Greyhound Bus Depot (☎ 757-8400), 3264 E Andy Devine Ave, is behind McDonald's. Buses go to Phoenix, Tucson, Las Vegas, Salt Lake City, Flagstaff, Los Angeles and other cities.

## ROUTE 66

Historic Route 66, once the main highway from Chicago to Los Angeles, has been largely forgotten in favor of the interstate freeway system (see the boxed text 'Kickin' Down Route 66'). Several cities have vestiges of the old route, but the longest remaining stretch of what was once called the 'Main Street of America' stretches 160 miles from Seligman to Topock on the Arizona-California border. Other than Kingman, Route 66 winds through mostly empty and lesser-traveled northwestern Arizonan countryside. Every year, this desolate stretch is transformed into its bustling

former self with the annual Route 66 Fun Run (see Special Events in Kingman). All places below are ☎ 928.

**Seligman** has half a dozen basic motels, including the popular **Historic Route 66 Motel** (☎ 422-3204), with rooms in the $50s, and several cheaper places like the the **Supai Motel** (☎ 422-3663). For a traditional '50s-style malt or milkshake, stop by **Delgadillo's Snow Cap** (☎ 422-3291).

**Grand Canyon Caverns**, 23 miles west of Seligman, are 210 feet underground. Early tourists were lowered on a rope, and the caverns became a popular roadside attraction during Route 66's heyday. Today, an elevator takes people below ground, where a three-quarter-mile trail winds by geological formations, including stalagmites and stalactites. Admission, including a 45-minute guided tour, costs $9.50 for adults and $6.75 for four- to 12-year-olds. Hours are 8am to 6pm in summer and 10am to 5pm in winter. The **Grand Canyon Caverns Motel** (☎ 422-3223/4) has a restaurant and charges about $45 to $65 for one to five people in summer and substantially less in winter. The caverns are a mile behind the motel.

**Peach Springs**, 12 miles west of the Grand Canyon Caverns, contains the Hualapai Indian Reservation tribal offices and tourist lodge (see the Grand Canyon & Lake Powell chapter). During the Route 66 Fun Run, the tribe prepares a barbecue for passing motorists. Nine miles farther west, the blink-and-you'll-miss-it town of **Truxton** has the basic and inexpensive (though prices rise dramatically during the Route 66 Fun Run) **Frontier Motel & Café** (☎ 769-2238) and an RV park. There is entertainment here during the Fun Run. Tiny Hackberry, 15 miles west and 25 miles from Kingman, features the eccentric **Old Route 66 Visitor Center and Hackberry General Store** (☎ 769-2605), built in 1934. The current owners are restoring it to its original condition.

The gold-mining town of **Oatman**, in the rugged Black Mountains about 25 miles southwest of Kingman, was founded in 1906. Two million ounces of gold were extracted before the last mine closed in 1942,

## Kickin' Down Route 66

Fenders! Huge, unwieldy, voluptuous fenders, pulling back the hot desert air just outside Tucum-cari, New Mexico. It's 1949, and the occupants of this fat Hudson (looking like something out of a sci-fi serial from the '40s) have pointed it west, down Route 66 to the orange groves of Southern California. Maybe it's Kerouac's Sal Paradise on his endless ramble to find America.

That's the quintessential image that innumerable would-be bohemians have of the country's possibilities. Few highways have entered American history and folklore in the way that Route 66 has. In 1926 the road linking Chicago with Los Angeles became officially designated US Route 66 for its entire 2448-mile length. During the Depression, Route 66 was the main thoroughfare to California for migrant families escaping the dust bowl of the Midwest, some only to be turned back by state immigration at the California-Arizona border. This trip was immortalized in John Stein-beck's *The Grapes of Wrath*, which won the 1940 Pulitzer Prize. In 1938, Route 66 became the first cross-country highway to be completely paved.

After WWII, Americans began buying automobiles in earnest and sought to weld themselves to their vehicles on driving vacations. Along the way, Route 66 became the most popular drive of all.

By the end of the 1950s, the growing love affair with the automobile was overwhelming the system of narrow roads linking the country's towns. Construction of the interstate highway system began, crossing the country with fast, limited-access, two-lane highways that bypassed town centers. Most of the parts of Route 66 that ran through northern Arizona and New Mexico were replaced by I-40. By 1984, the modern, efficient, soulless I-40 finally supplanted the last bit of Route 66, and the USA suddenly became a whole lot wider and the possibilities no longer so infinite. Williams was the last town on Route 66 to be bypassed by the freeway.

and the population of thousands plummeted to hundreds. Today, 500,000 visitors annually come through this self-styled 'ghost town' to see the old buildings, browse the gift shops, enjoy the weekend shenanigans (gunfights at high noon and Western dancing at night) and feed the wild burros. The ***Oatman Hotel*** (☎ 768-4408) is on the National Register of Historic Places, and the simple rooms are almost unchanged since Hollywood legends Clark Gable and Carole Lombard honeymooned here in the 1930s. Rooms with shared bathroom are $35 to $55. Nonguests can go upstairs to see the Gable-Lombard room or grab a bite alongside the grizzled miners in the ***Saloon &***

***Restaurant*** downstairs (the bar is wallpapered with $1 bills).

This stretch of Route 66 ends in tiny **Topock**, where travelers continue on I-40.

## CHLORIDE
☎ 928 • pop 250 • elevation 4200 feet

Founded in 1862 by silver miners, Chloride is the oldest mining town in Arizona and home to the oldest continuously operating post office in the state (since 1871). The semi–ghost town, 20 miles northwest of Kingman, is quieter and more low-key than crowded Oatman and Jerome. There are antique and art stores; old buildings; the original jail, with two tiny, grimly barred

## Kickin' Down Route 66

Many sections of old Route 66 fell into disuse and disrepair, but some sections, for example, Bill Williams Ave and Santa Fe Ave in Flagstaff, have been revived for nostalgic and historic reasons. The longest remaining sections of Route 66 are in western Arizona between Seligman and Kingman and between Kingman and Topock.

Today, Route 66 inspires a strange blend of patriotism, nostalgia and melancholy in most Americans. Emblematic of the enduring restless nature of the country, it has become America's Silk Road – exotic.

So exotic, in fact, that the road was the basis for the 1960s *Route 66* TV series and has appeared in many films, including *Bagdad Café*, released in 1988. (Bagdad is in California, near Siberia.) In 1946, a song by Bobby Troup reached the airwaves, and by the 1990s more than 20 musicians had recorded '(Get Your Kicks on) Route 66,' including Perry Como, Bob Dylan, Buckwheat Zydeco, Asleep at the Wheel, Depeche Mode, the Rolling Stones, and – the most famous version of all – Nat King Cole.

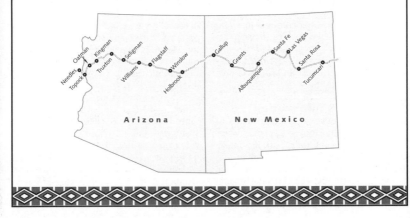

cells flanking the woodstove-heated guard's room; a visitor center (☎ 565-2204) and occasional melodramas, usually held on the first and third Saturdays of summer months. A signed dirt road goes 1.3 miles to a rocky hillside with huge murals painted by artist Roy Purcell. For more about the town, see www.chloridearizona.com.

On Old Miners Day, the last Saturday in June, locals dress in turn-of-the-19th-century garb and there's a parade and old-time music and dancing. Watch out for gunfights and showdowns!

There is a small *RV park* (☎ 565-4492). *Sheps Miners Inn B&B* (☎ 565-4251, 877-565-4251) rents 12 rooms for $35 to $65.

There are three homey cafés and a couple of Western saloons.

## LAKE MEAD NATIONAL RECREATION AREA

Hoover Dam (at the time the world's largest) was built between 1931 and 1936 in this hot, arid and desolate area. It backed up the Colorado River, flooding canyons, archaeological sites, wilderness areas and communities and producing Lake Mead, one of the world's largest artificial lakes. In 1953, the smaller Davis Dam was completed, forming Lake Mohave. The dams were built for flood control, irrigation, hydroelectricity and as a water supply to the burgeoning population of the Southwest and southern California.

When the dams were built, people decried the flooding as a destructive waste of archaeological, historical, natural and scenic resources. Today the two lakes, surrounded by wild desert scenery, attract millions of annual visitors, ranging from curious day-trippers looking at the dams to vacationing families spending a week boating on the lakes. Barely an hour's drive from Las Vegas, the area certainly doesn't suffer from a shortage of visitors.

The 2337-sq-mile recreation area encompasses two major lakes with over 280 sq surface miles of water, almost 1000 miles of shoreline, and many square miles of desert in both Arizona and Nevada. Motels, developed campgrounds, restaurants, marinas, grocery stores and gas stations are available in lakeside areas in Arizona and Nevada. There are also several undeveloped backcountry campgrounds and boat-launch areas.

## Orientation & Information

Highway 93 (between Kingman and Las Vegas) crosses the Hoover Dam and passes the main visitor center and park headquarters. Highway 68 (between Kingman and Bullhead City) goes near the Davis Dam. Both dams straddle the Arizona/Nevada state line, as does most of the recreation area. Minor roads provide access to marinas and other areas.

The Alan Bible Visitor Center (☎ 702-293-8990) in Nevada, 5 miles west of Hoover Dam, is open 8:30am to 4:30pm (Pacific time) daily except Thanksgiving, Christmas and New Year's Day. The center has maps, books, information, exhibits, films and a small desert botanical garden. The smaller Katherine Landing Visitor Center (☎ 928-754-3272) in Arizona, 3 miles north of Davis Dam, is open 8am to 4pm. There are also ranger stations throughout the area. Get advance information from the Superintendent, Lake Mead NRA, 601 Nevada Hwy, Boulder City, NV 89005.

Every year, people die here in boating, swimming or diving accidents, many of which are alcohol related. In an emergency, contact a ranger or call the 24-hour emergency number (☎ 702-293-8932, 800-680-5851).

Summer temperatures rise over 100°F most days (best for water activities), but winter highs are in the 50s and 60s (best for hiking and backpacking). Long hikes are not recommended in summer, when heat exhaustion is a real problem.

Admission is $5 per vehicle, $3 each for bikers and hikers and $10 for a boat. Admission is valid for five days. All passes are honored. Driving through on the main highways is free.

## Hoover Dam

At 726 feet high, Hoover Dam remains one of the tallest dams in the world and is an impressive feat of engineering and architecture. There is an exhibit center, and guided tours leave from here at frequent intervals throughout the day between 8:30am and 5:45pm.

The standard tours leave every 10 minutes and take up to 80 people. These tours descend into the dam by elevator, last 40 minutes, and are followed by a 25-minute video presentation. The cost is $8 ($7 for those over 62; $2 for six- to 16-year-olds). One-hour 'behind the scenes' hardhat tours are limited to 20 people paying $25 each; minimum age is seven. No bags, including camera bags, are allowed on tours, which leave several times a day.

Parking on the Arizona side is limited to several lots along Hwy 93; free shuttle buses take visitors to the dam. On the Nevada side, there is a parking area ($2) just past the exhibit center.

Highway 93 crosses the Colorado River as a two-lane road over the dam. The narrow, steep and winding road down to the dam gets backed up for miles on busy days, so prepare for delays.

## Fishing

The lakes are said to have some of the best sport fishing in the country. Striped bass (up to 50lb) are one attraction; rainbow trout, largemouth bass, channel catfish, black crappie and bluegill are also likely catches. November to February is the best time for trout and crappie; March to May is OK for trout, catfish, crappie and bass; June to August is best for catfish, bass and bluegill; September to mid-October continues to be OK for bass and, as the water cools, for crappie. Check with a visitor center or ranger station for current fishing tips.

You can fish year-round with a license, available at the boating marinas (which also have fishing supplies and charters).

## Boating

Because of the many powerboats and the huge area of the lakes, small vessels such as canoes and rafts are not encouraged, except at parts of Boulder Beach (near Hoover Dam and Lake Mead Marina). Larger boats can be rented from the marinas.

**Boat Tours** Lake Mead Cruises (☎ 702-293-6180) has several narrated cruises a day from Lake Mead Marina to Hoover Dam (1½ hours roundtrip). The boat is an air-conditioned, three-decked, Mississippi-style paddle wheeler. Fares are $19/9 for adults/children two to 12. Also available are two-hour weekend breakfast buffet cruises ($29/15), dinner cruises from Sunday to Thursday ($40/21) and dinner/dance cruises on Friday and Saturday ($45, adults only). Departure times vary with season, and reservations for meal cruises are recommended.
website: www.lakemeadcruises.com

The more adventurous can do a raft float (no white water) from below the Hoover Dam, down the Black Canyon of the Colorado River to Willow Beach Resort. The motorized rafts hold 40 passengers and the tour is $70 for adults, $40 for children under 12 and free for children under five. Lunch is included, and a bus returns you to your starting point at Black Canyon River Raft Tours (☎ 702-293-3776, 800-696-7238) in Boulder City near Hoover Dam. Tours are from February to November, and the roundtrip takes 5½ hours (three hours of boating). During the summer months, you may see desert bighorn sheep, especially in the early hours of the day.
website: www.rafts.com

**Boat Rentals** Fishing, ski, patio and houseboats are available, as well as jet skis (though these may be banned in the future). Two NPS-authorized concessionaires provide most of the boats available, ranging from small fishing boats at $70 a day to luxurious houseboats sleeping 10 for $5000 a week. Houseboat rentals for three or four nights are also possible, and rates drop outside of the summer high season. The cheaper, less crowded shoulder-seasons are recommended. Houseboats are very popular and reservations should be made months in advance for the high season. Seven Crown Resorts (☎ 800-752-9669) operates from several marinas on both lakes and has houseboat rentals sleeping four, six, eight, 10 and 14 people, as well as small boats. Forever Resorts (☎ 480- 998-1981, fax 480-998-7399) has more luxurious and expensive houseboats sleeping up to 10. In addition to boat rentals, these concessionaires provide motel rooms and restaurants, grocery stores, gas stations, and fishing bait, tackle and license facilities. You can browse options from the two agencies online at www.sevencrown.com and www.forever resorts.com.

Two things to consider when renting a boat: bring binoculars (they help to read buoy numbers) and make sure you are good friends with your shipmates – a boat sleeping 10 will be very cramped for 10 adults.

## Places to Stay & Eat

The National Park Service operates eight *campgrounds* for tents and RVs (no hookups) for $10. These are mainly on the Nevada side. Several of the marinas have RV campgrounds for $20 a night with hookups.

Seven Crown Resorts and Forever Resorts (see Boat Rentals, earlier) operate motels and restaurants at several marinas. The ***Temple Bar Resort*** (☎ 928-767-3211) is 47 miles by paved road east of the Hoover Dam. Rates range from $55 to $105 for fishing cabins (restrooms are in a separate cabin), double rooms with patios and kitchen suites sleeping four. Rooms are comfortable enough and this is one of the more remote spots on Lake Mead, which makes it fun. Rates go down in the winter. The *Lake Mohave Resort* (☎ 928-754-3245) at Katherine Landing near Bullhead City charges $70 to $120 for doubles, some with kitchenettes. Both of these have nearby RV sites, restaurant, groceries and small boat rentals.

Seven Crown Resorts (☎ 800-752-9669) also has similarly priced motels at *Lake Mead Resort* and *Echo Bay Resort*. Forever Resorts' *Cottonwood Cove Motel* (☎ 702-297-1464) on the Nevada shore charges $90 for doubles from May to October and holidays, and $60 the rest of the year.

## BULLHEAD CITY & LAUGHLIN
☎ 928 • pop 33,769 • elevation 540 feet
Bullhead City, or 'Bull' as some locals call it, is just south of the south end of Lake Mohave and was established in the 1940s for the builders of Davis Dam. It's a popular destination for Arizonans, who visit Lake Mohave or cross the bridge over the Colorado River to Laughlin, Nevada, which has the closest casinos to Arizona. Gambling here is the main attraction, though river tours are offered daily. The casinos also provide nightlife, entertainment, cinemas and ten-pin bowling.

The small free **Colorado River Museum** (☎ 754-3399), 355 Hwy 95, is open on changing days and hours dependent on season and describes city history.

In Bullhead City, canoes and kayaks can be rented or guided trips taken with Desert River Outfitters (☎ 763-3033), 9649 Hwy 95. Review the various packages offered at www.desertriveroutfitters.com.

## Information
The Bullhead Area Chamber of Commerce (☎ 754-4121) is at 1251 Hwy 95. Other services include a post office (☎ 758-5711), 990 Hwy 95, medical center (☎ 763-2273), 2735 Silver Creek Rd, and police (☎ 298-2450), 1255 Marina Blvd.

The Laughlin Visitors Center (☎ 702-298-3321, 800-452-8445), at 1555 S Casino Dr, is open weekdays.
website: www.visitlaughlin.com.

Nevada time is one hour behind Arizona in the winter but is the same in summer (because Arizona doesn't change to daylight saving time).

## Places to Stay
**Camping** RV parks are near Hwy 95 south of Bullhead City. Free camping (no facilities) is available at *Katherine Landing* (☎ 754-3245, 800-752-9669) on the shore of Lake Mohave, 3 miles north of Davis Dam (see Lake Mead NRA earlier; you must pay park fees). In Laughlin, RVs can park overnight in the casino parking lots. There are no hookups, but restaurants and gambling are right on your doorstep. The *Riverside Resort* has full hookups for $17 a night.

**Hotels** From Sunday to Thursday, the Laughlin casinos are fantastic values with spacious modern double rooms in the teens or low $20s. These are the Southwest's best lodging bargains, if you limit your gambling to what you can afford. The Laughlin Visitors Center has a free phone that connects to the casinos so you can call to see which has the best deal. Weekend and holiday rates jump to $50 or more.

Bullhead City has some *chain hotels* including a Super 8 and a Best Western. Cheaper choices ($25 and up midweek) include the *La Plaza Inn* (☎ 763-8080, 1978 Hwy 95) and the *Hilltop House Motel* (☎ 753-2198, 2037 Hwy 95). The pleasant *Lodge on the River* (☎ 758-8080, 1717 Hwy 95) features kitchenettes in some rooms and charges in the $40s midweek for a double. It has a pool.

**Casinos** The casinos, all with hotels, are along Laughlin's Casino Drive. Casino restaurants have 24-hour service and very cheap, good meals, but lines can be long.

**Colorado Belle** (☎ 702-298-4000, 800-477-4837)
website: www.coloradobelle.com

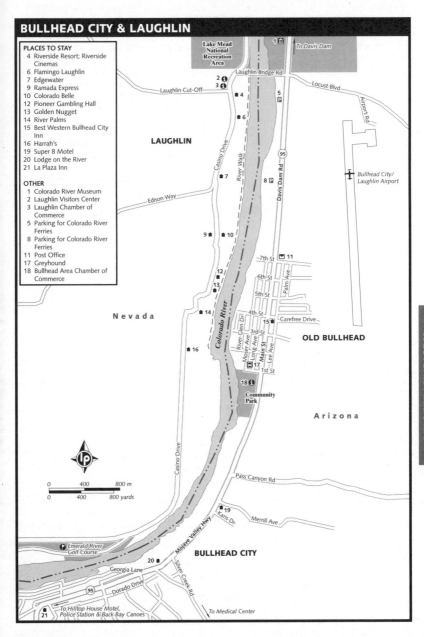

# BULLHEAD CITY & LAUGHLIN

**PLACES TO STAY**
4 Riverside Resort; Riverside Cinemas
6 Flamingo Laughlin
7 Edgewater
9 Ramada Express
10 Colorado Belle
12 Pioneer Gambling Hall
13 Golden Nugget
14 River Palms
15 Best Western Bullhead City Inn
16 Harrah's
19 Super 8 Motel
20 Lodge on the River
21 La Plaza Inn

**OTHER**
1 Colorado River Museum
2 Laughlin Visitors Center
3 Laughlin Chamber of Commerce
5 Parking for Colorado River Ferries
8 Parking for Colorado River Ferries
11 Post Office
17 Greyhound
18 Bullhead Area Chamber of Commerce

Lake Mead National Recreation Area

To Davis Dam

Laughlin Bridge Rd

Laughlin Cut-Off

Locust Blvd

Airport Rd

**LAUGHLIN**

Casino Drive

River Walk

Edison Way

Davis Dam Rd

95

Bullhead City/ Laughlin Airport

Colorado River

7th St

11

6th St

Palm Ave

5th St

4th St

Carefree Drive

**OLD BULLHEAD**

River Glen Dr

Moser Ave

3rd St

Long Ave

Main St

Lee Ave

1st St

17

18

Community Park

**Arizona**

**N**evada

**LP**

0        400        800 m
0        400        800 yards

Pass Canyon Rd

19

Karis Dr

Merrill Ave

Emerald River Golf Course

20

**BULLHEAD CITY**

Mojave Valley Hwy

Silver Creek Rd

Georgia Lane

95

Dorado Drive

21

To Hilltop House Motel, Police Station & Back-Bay Canoes

To Medical Center

**Edgewater** (☎ 702-298-2453, 800-677-4837)
website: www.edgewater-casino.com

**Flamingo Laughlin** (☎ 702-298-5111, 800-352-6464)
website: www.laughlinflamingo.com

**Golden Nugget** (☎ 702-298-7111, 800-237-1739)
website: www.gnlaughlin.com

**Harrah's** (☎ 702-298-4600, 800-447-8700)
website: www.harrahs.com

**Pioneer Gambling Hall** (☎ 702-298-2442, 800-634-3469)
website: www.pioneerlaughlin.com

**Ramada Express** (☎ 702-298-4200, 800-272-6232)
website: www.ramadaexpress.com

**River Palms** (☎ 702-298-2242, 800-835-7903)
website: www.rvrpalm.com

**Riverside Resort** (☎ 702-298-2535, 800-227-3849)
website: www.riversideresort.com

## Getting There & Away

The airport (☎ 754-2134) is at 600 Hwy 95. Sun Country (☎ 866-797-2537, 800-359-8786) flies to Minneapolis, Minnesota; Denver, Colorado; San Antonio, Texas; and Seattle, Washington.

Greyhound Bus (☎ 754-5586), 125 Long Ave, has buses to Kingman and on to Flagstaff, Phoenix or Albuquerque. There are also buses to Las Vegas and Los Angeles.

Tri-State Super Shuttle (☎ 704-9000, 800-801-8687) has buses between Bullhead City and the Las Vegas airport. It picks up at major hotels.

## HAVASU NATIONAL WILDLIFE REFUGE

This is one of a string of wildlife refuges and other protected areas along the lower Colorado River. Habitats include marshes, sand dunes, desert and the river itself. Overwintering birds – geese, ducks and cranes – are found here in profusion. After the migrants' departure, herons and egrets nest in large numbers.

The section of the reserve north of I-40 is the Topock Marsh. South of I-40, the Colorado flows through Topock Gorge. The southern boundary of the reserve abuts the northern boundary of Lake Havasu State Park, 3 miles north of London Bridge.

The refuge headquarters (☎ 760-326-3853), 317 Mesquite Ave, Needles, California, has maps, bird lists and information.

The Jerkwater Canoe Company (☎ 768-7753), PO Box 800, Topock, AZ 86436, offers canoe rentals and guided day trips through the gorge as well as a variety of overnight excursions along the river.

## LAKE HAVASU CITY

☎ 928 • pop 41,938 • elevation 575 feet

Developer Robert McCulloch planned Lake Havasu City as a center for water sports and light industry/business. The city received a huge infusion of publicity when McCulloch bought London Bridge for $2,460,000, disassembled it into 10,276 granite slabs and reassembled it here. The bridge, opened in London, England in 1831, was rededicated in 1971 and has become the focus of the city's English Village – a touristy complex of restaurants, hotels and shops built in pseudo-English style. Students flock to town during spring break in March, when hotels get busy and live bands entertain.

## Information

The tourism bureau (☎ 453-3444, 800-242-8278), 314 London Bridge Rd, is open Monday to Friday and is online at www.golakehavasu.com. A visitor information center at the English Village is open daily. Other services include the library (☎ 453-0718), 1770 McCulloch Blvd; post office (☎ 855-2361), 1750 McCulloch Blvd; hospital (☎ 855-8185), 101 Civic Center Blvd; and police (☎ 855-4111), 2360 McCulloch Blvd.

## Activities

Once you've walked over London Bridge, you'll find that most of your options are water-related. Plenty of companies provide boat tours and rentals, and the visitor center has numerous brochures. One-hour, narrated, day and sunset tours are offered by boats at English Village and cost about $13 ($7 for four- to 12-year olds). Longer tours (2½ hours) are $25/15 or more, depending on the boat and destination. Just show up

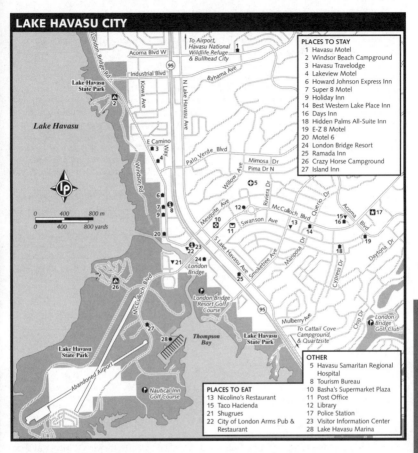

**LAKE HAVASU CITY**

**PLACES TO STAY**
1 Havasu Motel
2 Windsor Beach Campground
3 Havasu Travelodge
4 Lakeview Motel
6 Howard Johnson Express Inn
7 Super 8 Motel
9 Holiday Inn
14 Best Western Lake Place Inn
16 Days Inn
18 Hidden Palms All-Suite Inn
19 E-Z 8 Motel
20 Motel 6
24 London Bridge Resort
25 Ramada Inn
26 Crazy Horse Campground
27 Island Inn

**PLACES TO EAT**
13 Nicolino's Restaurant
15 Taco Hacienda
21 Shugrues
22 City of London Arms Pub & Restaurant

**OTHER**
5 Havasu Samaritan Regional Hospital
8 Tourism Bureau
10 Basha's Supermarket Plaza
11 Post Office
12 Library
17 Police Station
23 Visitor Information Center
28 Lake Havasu Marina

**WESTERN ARIZONA**

and you can usually reserve a tour leaving within an hour or two; many boats are air-conditioned.

Fishing, rowing, water-skiing and sight-seeing boats can be rented from Lake Havasu Marina (☎ 855-2159) and Blue Water Rentals (☎ 453-9613) in the English Village. Canoes and kayaks are rented (from $25 a day), sold and guided at Western Arizona Canoe & Kayak Outfitter (WACKO; ☎ 855-6414, 680-9719).

The best months for fishing are April to July and October and November for large-mouth bass, May to July for striped bass,

June to September for catfish, March to May for crappie and May to September for bluegill. Licenses, gear and information are available from the boat rental places and many other stores.

Outback Off-Road Adventures (☎ 680-6151) has 4WD desert tours for $65 a half day, $130 a full day with lunch. Groups of four or more and children get discounts.

## Places to Stay
**Camping** Two miles north of town on London Bridge Rd is ***Windsor Beach Campground*** (☎ 855-2784) and 15 miles

south on Hwy 95 is *Cattail Cove* (☎ 855-1223); both are state park campgrounds with showers, boat launch and tent/RV camping (no hookups) for $12 per day. Cattail Cove also has 40 RV sites with hookups for $15. Day use is $7 per vehicle. The *Crazy Horse Campground* (☎ 855-4033, 1534 Beachcomber Blvd), has several hundred RV sites with full or partial hookups for $24 and 200 tent sites for $13. Showers, a laundry room and a grocery store are available.

**Hotels**   Rates vary tremendously from summer weekends to winter weekdays. The cheapest places, offering doubles for around $30 in winter but about $50 or more during summer (weekly discounts are often available), include the following: the *E-Z 8 Motel* (☎ 855-4023, 41 Acoma Blvd,) with a pool and whirlpool, the *Havasu Motel* (☎ 855-2311, 2035 Acoma Blvd) and the basic *Lakeview Motel* (☎ 855-3605, 440 London Bridge Rd).

For more upscale lodging, try *Hidden Palms All-Suite Inn* (☎ 855-7144, 2100 Swanson Ave), which has a pool and units with kitchenettes for $60 to $120. The *Island Inn* (☎ 680-0606, 800-243-9955, 1300 McCulloch Blvd) has a pool, spa and many rooms with balconies and lake views for $65 to $120. It also has pricier suites.

The *London Bridge Resort* (☎ 855-0888, 888-503-9148, 1477 Queens Bay Rd) has three pools, hot tub, exercise room, golf, tennis, shops and views of London Bridge. Several restaurants, bars and nightclubs offer a range of dining, drinking and dancing options that attracts folks looking for a playful resort rather than restful luxury. Over 120 units feature either one or two bedrooms and come with kitchenette, some with whirlpool bathtubs and dining areas. Rates range from $100 to $300 depending on the room, the date and the time of week (weekends are higher).
website: www.londonbridgeresort.com

Several *chain motels* are represented here, including Motel 6, Days Inn, Super 8, Travelodge, Howard Johnson, Best Western, Ramada Inn and Holiday Inn.

## Places to Eat

Several restaurants are on or near the half mile of McCulloch Blvd between Smoketree Ave and Acoma Blvd.

*Shugrues* (☎ 453-1400, 1425 McCulloch Blvd), advertises several dozen entrées featuring fresh seafood, steak, chicken and pastas. Dinner entrées include soup or salad and range from about $10 to over $30, most in the mid-teens. Lunches are cheaper, and many tables have some sort of bridge view. At about half this price, the *City of London Arms Pub & Restaurant* (☎ 855-8782) at the English Village has decent pub food and imported British brews.

For Mexican lunches and dinners, head over to *Taco Hacienda* (☎ 855-8932, 2200 Mesquite Ave). This locally popular place has been here for two decades (eons by Lake Havasu City standards!). Italian-food lovers can try *Nicolino's Restaurant* (☎ 855-3545, 86 S Smoketree Ave); it's closed on Sundays.

## Getting There & Away

Lake Havasu City Airport (☎ 764-3330), 5600 N Hwy 95, is 7 miles north of town. America West has several daily flights to and from Phoenix.

Greyhound buses (☎ 764-4010) leave from the Busy 'B' Service Station (☎ 764-2440), 3201 N Hwy 95, 4 miles north of town.

## PARKER

☎ 928 • pop 3140 • elevation 417 feet

Parker, about 30 miles south of Lake Havasu on Hwy 95, thrives on local tourism. The stretch of road between Parker and the Parker Dam, known as the Parker Strip, has many campgrounds, boat-launch areas and marinas. The SCORE 400 in late January is an off-road, 4WD jeep and pickup truck race that covers more than 300 miles and attracts 100,000 visitors. The chamber of commerce lists several other wild events.

Greyhound buses stop at the Hole-in-the-Wall restaurant.

## Orientation & Information

Almost all of the town's major businesses are on or near California Ave (Hwy 95/62).

or Riverside Drive (Hwy 95) and are easy to find.

The chamber of commerce (☎ 669-2174) is at 1217 California Ave, and its useful website is at www.coloradoriverinfo.com/parker. Other services include the library (☎ 669-2622), 1001 Navajo Ave; post office (☎ 669-8179), at Joshua Ave and 14th; hospital (☎ 669-9201), 1200 Mohave Rd; and police (☎ 669-2265), 1314 11th.

## Things to See & Do
Members of four tribes live on the surrounding Colorado River Indian Reservation: Mohave, Chemehuevi, Navajo and Hopi. Their stories are presented in the **Colorado River Indian Tribes Museum** (☎ 669-9211) at Mohave Rd and 2nd Ave, southwest of town. Hours are 8am to noon and 1 to 5pm Monday to Friday.

Eight miles north of Parker, **La Paz County Park** (☎ 667-2069) has a tennis court, horseshoe pits, a playground, beach, boat ramp, swimming and tent/RV sites for $10/15. Three miles farther north, **Buckskin Mountain State Park** (☎ 667-3231) offers tent and RV camping, a boat ramp, beach, swimming, picnicking, a playground, recreation room, laundry, grocery store and ranger-led activities on weekends. A mile north is the River Island Unit (☎ 667-3386), with more camping spaces in a scenic desert setting. Rates are $6 for day use and $12 to $20 for camping.

**Parker Dam**, 15 miles north of Parker, looks small, but 70% of its structural height is buried beneath the riverbed, making it the world's deepest dam.

Locals go **boating** here and launching areas are located along the Parker Strip. Launching is free or subject to nominal fees. Fishing, water-skiing, jet skiing and inner tubing are also popular. Some rental services are available at the many places along the strip.

## Places to Stay & Eat
Apart from the parks listed above, dozens of other places along the Parker Strip and just across the river in California offer both tent and RV camping. These often cost more than the parks, with the exception of BLM campgrounds, several of which can be found on the California side of the river up to 15 miles north of Parker.

The **El Rancho Parker Motel** (☎ 669-2231, 709 California Ave), has a pool, complimentary coffee and rates beginning at $37. The pleasant **Kofa Inn** (☎ 669-2101, 1700 California Ave) has a pool and is adjacent to **Coffee Ern's** (☎ 669-8145), a decent 24-hour family restaurant. Rates start at $45.

The **Stardust Motel** (☎ 669-2278, 800-786-7827, 700 California Ave), has a pool and rooms for similar rates as well as slightly more expensive rooms with kitchenettes. **Chain motels** include a Motel 6 and a Best Western.

The finely named **Hole-in-the-Wall** (☎ 669-9755, 612 California Ave) is good for home-style breakfasts. There are Mexican and fast-food places as well.

In addition, there are several restaurants and motels along the Parker Strip, most with boat docks and launching areas, handy for boaters.

## QUARTZSITE
☎ 928 • pop 3354 • elevation 879 feet

Quartzsite's population explodes to hundreds of thousands of people during the early January to mid-February gem and mineral shows. Several thousand dealers and more than a million visitors buy, sell, trade and admire their wares. These folks can't quite squeeze into the town's four tiny motels, so as the chamber of commerce puts it, the desert around Quartzsite turns into a 'sea of aluminum.' Thousands upon thousands of RVs stretch out as far as the eye can see – a strange sight, indeed.

The chamber of commerce (☎ 927-5600) is on the north side of I-10 exit 17. Hours are 9am to 4pm daily in January and February, cutting back to 10am to 3pm on Tuesday, Wednesday and Thursday from April to October. Call the chamber for recorded information when it's closed.

During the January/February gem and mineral shows there are stagecoach rides, balloon and helicopter rides, camel and ostrich races, cookouts, dances and other

Western events. In the prostrating heat of summer, though, the population dwindles, and the town looks like a semi-abandoned junkyard.

Quartzite's most curious and beloved monument is a small stone pyramid topped by a metal camel. The memorial is to Haiji Ali, a Syrian camel driver who arrived in 1856 to help with US army experiments using camels in the desert. After the trials failed, Ali, nicknamed Hi Jolly, became a prospector and died here around 1902. Hi Jolly 'Daze,' with a parade and other festivities, occurs in early January to welcome back winter visitors.

Petroglyphs, ghost towns, ruins, wildlife and desert scenery surround Quartzsite, but visits require long, energetic exploration on poor trails. The chamber of commerce sells a map with over 40 points of interest. Also see below for nearby places that can be visited by car.

The RV camps surrounding town have hookups for RVs and charge up to $20 a night. The farther you park from the center, or the fewer facilities you need, the less you pay. The BLM (☎ 317-3200 in Yuma) runs the *La Posa Long Term Visitor Area* at the south end of town on Hwy 95. For $125, you can camp here (tent or RV) for as long as you want between September 15 and April 15. Permits for one day cost $5. Facilities include toilets, water (no showers) and dump stations. South of La Posa at mile marker 99, and north of town at mile marker 112, are areas where you can camp for free anytime (14 day limit) but there are no services.

## YUMA
☎ 928 • pop 77,515 • elevation 200 feet

Arizona's sunniest, driest and third-largest metropolitan area, Yuma blazes with sun for 93% of its daylight hours and receives just three inches of rain annually. Winter temperatures in the 70°s F attract many thousands of visitors, who spend the entire winter in scores of trailer parks around the city.

Local Quechan, Cocopah and Mohave Indians, collectively known as the Yumas, knew this was the easiest place to cross the Colorado River for hundreds of miles. Some 30,000 people crossed the Colorado here during the 1849 California gold rush. Steamships once reached Yuma Crossing from the Gulf of Mexico, but dams have changed the site to a shadow of the port it was.

The town was founded in 1854, first named Colorado City, then Arizona City – grandiose names considering that the 'city' population was only 85 in 1860, growing to 1100 by 1870. In 1873, Arizona City was renamed Yuma. Three years later, Arizona's Territorial Prison (now a local attraction) was opened – a notorious hellhole that operated for 33 years until a new prison was built in Florence.

### Information
The Convention & Visitors Bureau (☎ 783-0071), 377 S Main St, is open 9am to 6pm weekdays, with shortened winter hours. Check its website at www.visityuma.com. Other services include the Kofa NWR headquarters (☎ 783-7861), 356 W 1st St; BLM (☎ 317-3200), 2555 E Gila Ridge Rd; AAA of Arizona (☎ 783-3339), 1045 S 4th Ave; library (☎ 782-1871), 350 3rd St; post office (☎ 783-2124), 2222 4th Ave; Medical Center (☎ 344-2000), 2400 Ave A; police (☎ 783-4421), 1500 1st Ave.

### Yuma Territorial Prison State Historic Park
Between 1876 and 1909, the prison housed 3069 prisoners, including 29 women – Arizona's most feared criminals. Some buildings still exist, notably the guard tower and the rock-wall cells fronted by gloomy iron-grille doors, giving an idea of what inmates' lives were like. Despite the grim conditions, this was considered a model prison at the time. The jail is complemented by a small museum of interesting artifacts. The whole place is slightly gruesome, mildly historical, definitely offbeat and suitable for the whole family. The prison (☎ 783-4771) is open 8am to 5pm daily except Christmas. Admission is $3 for adults, $2 for seven- to 13-year-olds and free for kids under seven. Guided tours are offered.

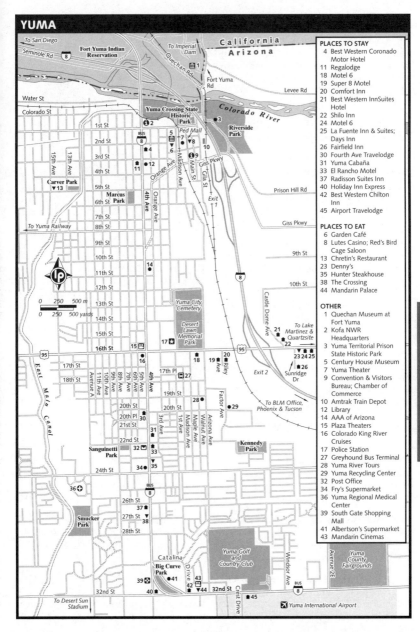

# YUMA

**WESTERN ARIZONA**

## Yuma Crossing
## State Historic Park

US Army supply buildings predate the prison by a decade or more, and parts of them still exist here. Other buildings have been restored, and there is a museum and guided tours of what was once the hub of southwestern Arizona. The depot (☎ 783-4771), 180 1st St, is open 10am to 5pm, closed Christmas and Tuesday and Wednesday from May to October. Admission is the same price as the prison.

## Century House Museum

Sponsored by the Arizona Historical Society, this museum (☎ 782-1841), 240 S Madison Ave, is in one of the oldest houses (built 1891) in Arizona's southwestern corner. There are exhibits of local historical interest and a garden full of exotic plants and birds. Hours are 10am to 4pm Tuesday to Saturday. Admission is free (donations encouraged).

## Quechan Museum at Fort Yuma

Across the river in California on Indian Hill Rd (off Picacho Rd), Fort Yuma was built in the 1850s. The building now houses a small museum (☎ 760-572-0661) of photographs and historical artifacts operated by the Quechan tribe. Tribal offices are nearby. Museum hours are 8am to noon and 1 to 5pm Monday to Friday. Admission is $1 for those over 12. Get there by taking the first California exit on I-8 and heading north.

## Agricultural Attractions

During winter (about October through March) several farms offer tours (call for reservations) and sell products. Though they don't grow the peanuts here, the the **Peanut Patch** (☎ 726-6292), 4322 E County 13th St, gives tours of the roasting and candy-making processes. Call to see what they're making, as it varies by day. You can pick citrus and other fruits at the **Farm** (☎ 627-3631), Ave A1/2 and County 17 near Somerton. **Imperial Date Gardens** (☎ 760-572-0277), 1517 York Rd, is across the state line in Bard.

## Organized Tours

Yuma River Tours (☎ 783-4400), 1920 Arizona Ave, has jet-boat tours to Imperial NWR, Imperial Dam and historic sites (petroglyphs, mining camps etc). Tour guides provide chatty explanations of local history and Indian lore. Five-hour tours are $52 ($25 for children three to 12) and include lunch. Sunset cruises and custom charters are available. Departures are from Fisher's Landing (see Imperial NWR later in this chapter) and run almost daily in winter, less frequently in the hot months.
website: www.yumarivertours.com

The Yuma Railway (☎ 783-3456) leaves from the west end of 8th St, 6 miles west of downtown. The vintage train makes two-hour runs along the Arizona-Sonora border. Departures are at 1pm on Saturday and Sunday from November to March, Sunday only in October, April and May. Fares are $13 for adults, $12 for those over 55 and $7 for those four to 16. Call ahead for hours and prices for family picnic runs and steak dinner runs.

The *Colorado King I* is a small, two-deck paddleboat offering narrated, three-hour Colorado River cruises from Fisher's Landing (see Imperial NWR). Departure times vary seasonally; contact the Colorado

King River Cruises office (☎ 782-2412, 1636 S 4th Ave) for information. Costs are about $30 with discounts for children 12 and under.

## Special Events

The annual Silver Spur Rodeo in early February has been held for more than half a century and features Yuma's biggest parade, arts and crafts shows and various other events along with the rodeo. The Yuma County Fair is held at the beginning of April. Several times a year there are Main Street Block Parties with free street entertainment.

## Places to Stay

Winter rates (usually January to April) can be up to $30 higher than summer rates, especially on weekends. In addition, hotels are booked in advance and charge their highest prices during the opening days of dove-hunting season (Labor Day weekend). Rates vary substantially according to demand and those given in the following sections are only approximate.

**Camping** There are over 70 campgrounds, mainly geared to RVs on a long-term basis during the winter. Most have age restrictions (no children, sometimes only for people over 50) and prohibit tents. People planning a long RV stay should contact the visitor's bureau for lists.

**Budget** All Yuma motels listed have swimming pools (some very small). Many budget hotels charge mid-range prices in winter and the opening of dove-hunting season. They include the simple *El Rancho Motel* (☎ 783-4481, 2201 4th Ave), with doubles for $30 in summer and $40 in winter; this is among the cheapest of them. The well recommended and well maintained *Yuma Cabaña* (☎ 783-8311, 800-874-0811, fax 783-1126, 2151 4th Ave) has a large pool and good rooms with interior entrances. A few rooms have kitchenettes. Rates run from about $40 to $70, depending on rooms and season. Continental breakfast is included. Many other budget places are found in this area of 4th Ave. The *Regalodge* (☎ 782-4571, 344 S 4th Ave) is one of the better cheap motels near downtown and has rooms with refrigerators and some kitchenettes. Summer rates are in the $30s, going up to the $40s in winter and more in dove season.

**Mid-Range & Top End** Most of the *chain motels* are found near I-8, exit 2. They include two Motel 6s, a good Super 8, a Days Inn, a well-appointed Comfort Inn and an upscale Fairfield Inn with interior corridors. Two Travelodges, a Holiday Inn Express and a Radisson Suites are found away from the freeway.

Of the three Best Westerns, the nicest is the *Best Western Coronado Motor Hotel* (☎ 783-4453, 233 4th Ave), the most attractive hotel close to downtown. It features two pools, a whirlpool, gift shop, continental breakfast and a decent mid-priced adjoining restaurant. Rooms have refrigerators; some have a microwave and/or spa. Some units have two bedrooms, and there are several suites. Summer rates start in the $50s, winter rates in the $80s, with larger units going up to $100.

The *La Fuente Inn & Suites* (☎ 329-1814, 800-841-1814, fax 343-2671, 1513 E 16th St) is a modern, Spanish-colonial-style building surrounding a landscaped garden and pool. There is a hot tub and exercise room for guest use. Rooms are mainly one- or two-room suites, many including microwaves and refrigerators. Rates, which include continental breakfast and evening cocktail hour, are $80 in summer and $100 and up in winter.

The *Shilo Inn* (☎ 782-9511, 800-222-2244, fax 783-1538, 1550 Castle Dome Ave) is the fanciest place in town. Amenities include an exercise room, spa, sauna and steam bath, and the pool is said to be the town's largest. There is a good restaurant and lounge, room service and an airport shuttle. Some rooms have kitchenettes; others feature a balcony or open onto the courtyard. All have refrigerators and interior corridors. Rates range from $100 to $160; the kitchenette suites can go to $225.

## Places to Eat

Restaurants can be fairly dead midweek in summer but bustling during the busy winter season. *Lutes Casino* (☎ 782-2192, *221 Main St*) is a locally popular hamburger joint. Eclectically decorated and with a bar, pool tables, dominoes and arcade games, it claims to be Arizona's oldest pool hall. Read about its history on the souvenir menu. Kids are welcome.

For more elegant breakfasts and lunches, the *Garden Café* (☎ 783-1491, *250 Madison Ave*) is popular. It serves good breakfasts, coffees, sandwiches, salads and desserts in a pleasant outdoor patio; there's also an indoor dining room. Hours are 9am to 2:30pm, closed Monday. For lunches and dinners, *The Crossing* (☎ 726-5551, *2690 4th Ave*) specializes in prime rib, catfish and ribs and also has Italian dishes. Dinner entrées are in the $7 to $17 range.

Yuma has many Mexican restaurants. *Chretin's* (☎ 782-1291, *485 15th Ave*) is a locally popular place tucked away inconspicuously on a residential street. It is closed Sunday. For Chinese food, the *Mandarin Palace* (☎ 344-2805, *350 E 32nd St*) is both elegant and excellent. The *Hunter Steakhouse* (☎ 782-3637, *2355 4th Ave*) open Monday to Friday for lunch and daily for dinner, does good steaks and prime rib.

By far the fanciest place in Yuma is *Julieanna's Patio Cafe* (☎ 317-1961, *1951 W 5th)* (call for directions), which features excellent beef, seafood and veal entrées averaging $20. Open for lunch on weekdays, but a better bet is dinner (Monday to Saturday) when the place glows romantically.

## Entertainment

Professional baseball teams do their spring training in sunny Yuma at the 7000-seat *Desert Sun Stadium* (☎ 344-3800), south of town off Avenue A. Call ☎ 343-1715 for a schedule (most games are in February) and tickets.

For information on performances by the local chamber orchestra, community theater and both classical and Mexican folkloric ballet companies, call ☎ 376-6107. Renovations at *Yuma Theater*, which presents musical reviews, should be completed by the end of 2003.

Choose movies from the multiscreened *Plaza Theaters* (☎ 782-9292, *1560 4th Ave*) or *Mandarin Cinemas* (☎ 782-7409, *3142 S Arizona Ave*).

For pool, dominoes and other games during the day, see Lutes Casino under Places to Eat. Next door is *Red's Bird Cage Saloon* (☎ 783-1050, *231 Main St*), for pool, darts and drinking after Lutes closes. It sometimes has live entertainment.

## Getting There & Away

The airport (south of 32nd St) is served by Skywest Airlines, America West Express and United Express. Many flights serve Phoenix, and some go to Los Angeles. Avis, Budget, Hertz and Enterprise rent cars at the airport.

The Greyhound Bus Terminal (☎ 783-4403), 170 E 17 Place, has buses to Phoenix; Tucson; Lordsburg, New Mexico; El Paso, Texas; and San Diego, California.

San Luis-Yuma Transit (☎ 627-1130), at the Greyhound terminal, has several daily departures to San Luis on the Mexican border. American Shuttle Express (☎ 726-0906, 888-749-9862) has vans from Yuma to Phoenix Airport ($50).

# WILDLIFE REFUGES NEAR YUMA
## Imperial National Wildlife Refuge

Thousands of overwintering waterfowl make mid-December through February the best time to visit this refuge, 36 miles north of Yuma, for birding. The small **Martinez Lake** has some water-skiing and boating activity in summer. Refuge headquarters (☎ 783-3371), on Martinez Lake, is open 7:30am to 4pm Monday to Friday. An observation tower nearby gives views, and a dirt road reaches several observation points and a 1-mile interpretive trail. There is no camping.

*Martinez Lake Resort* (☎ 783-0253, 783-9589, 800-876-7004) and the smaller *Fisher's Landing* (☎ 783-6513, 783-5357) both offer boating, RV camping, a grocery store and lounge. Martinez Lake Resort also has boat rental, motel and restaurant; Fisher's Landing has tent camping. These places are reserved weeks in advance for national holidays in summer.

## Cibola National Wildlife Refuge

This is an important overwintering site for Canada geese (up to 25,000 in midwinter), about 1000 greater sandhill cranes and many other waterfowl – a good place to watch for migrants from mid-November to late February. Some 237 species have been recorded, including the endangered Yuma clapper rail. Information is available from Cibola NWR (☎ 857-3253). There is no camping.

Hours are from 8am to 4:30pm Monday to Friday. From the headquarters, the Canada Geese Drive auto tour road is open daily during daylight hours.

## Kofa National Wildlife Refuge

Three rugged mountain ranges, the Kofa, the Castle Dome and the Tank Mountains, meet together in a splendidly wild tangle. The refuge covers just over 1000 sq miles, most of which is designated wilderness with vehicular access limited to a few dirt roads. Off-road driving is prohibited. Other visitor facilities are nonexistent. Bighorn sheep roam the area, but are hard to spot.

Most visitors drive into the refuge from the west on Hwy 95 to the entrance to Palm Canyon, about 29 miles south of Quartzsite, or 51 miles northeast of Yuma. A passable 7.2-mile dirt road leads to a parking area from where a steep, rocky, half-mile trail climbs to views of Palm Canyon: a sheer-walled crack to the north within which a stand of California palms *(Washingtonia filifera)* can be seen – the only place in Arizona where they grow naturally. Best views are around midday; at other times the palms are in shadow. There are several other access points and poor dirt roads through the refuge. Obtain information from Kofa NWR (☎ 783-7861), 356 W 1st St, Yuma. Camping is allowed any time, anywhere (except within a quarter mile of water holes), with a 14-day limit.

# Central Arizona

North of Phoenix there is nowhere to go but up. In summer, droves of southern Arizonans head north to camp, fish, sightsee, shop and find cool relief. During the winter, many of the same folks make the trip in search of snow and skiing. But central Arizona isn't just the province of canny locals; this area, with the important town of Flagstaff, is the gateway to the Grand Canyon.

Apart from the outdoor activities, visitors will find several national monuments sprinkled throughout the area, some protecting Indian sites. Old mining towns either lie forgotten or flourish with a new lease on life as artists' communities. Prescott, the first territorial capital, preserves architecture from its Wild West days. Sedona, a modern town amid splendid red-rock scenery, draws tourists seeking relaxation as well as New Agers looking for spiritual and psychic insights at the area's many vortexes. And Flagstaff provides museums, cultural events, nightlife and a laid-back atmosphere fueled by students, skiers and international visitors.

From Phoenix to Flagstaff takes under three hours along I-17, or you can spend a few days wandering through the intriguing small towns that dot the countryside along and around Hwys 89 and 89A, the route described in this chapter.

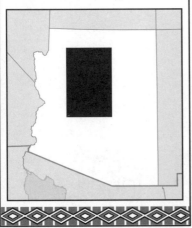

## WICKENBURG
☎ 928 • pop 5082 • elevation 2093 feet

In the 1860s Wickenburg was a thriving community surrounded by gold mines. Today Wickenburg, an hour northwest of Phoenix, has several ranches offering cowboy-style vacations in fall, winter and spring. Casual visitors stop to see the Western buildings constructed between the 1860s and the 1920s (ask the chamber of commerce for a walking map). The 1863 **Trinidad House** is said to be Arizona's oldest home. Locals will point out the 19th-century 'jail' – a tree to which outlaws were chained.

There is no bus service. Highway 93 to Kingman is dubbed Joshua Tree Parkway for the many stands of those plants lining the highway.

### Information
The chamber of commerce (☎ 684-5479, 800-942-5242), 216 N Frontier, is open daily

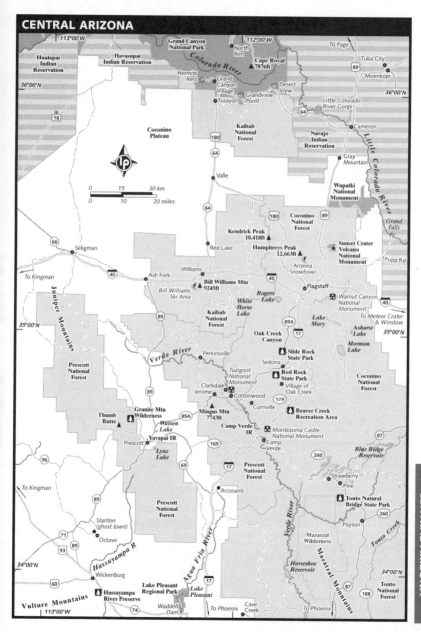

# CENTRAL ARIZONA

113°00'W

112°00'W

To Page

Tuba City

Hualapai Indian Reservation

Havasupai Indian Reservation

Grand Canyon National Park

North Rim

Cape Royal
▲7876ft

89

Moenkopi

36°00'N

Colorado River

Hermits Rest

Grand Canyon Village

Desert View

36°00'N

IR 18

Coconino Plateau

Tusayan

Grandview Point

Little Colorado River Gorge

Cameron

Kaibab National Forest

180

64

Navajo Indian Reservation

Gray Mountain

Little Colorado River

Wupatki National Monument

66

Seligman

Valle

64

180

Coconino National Forest

89

Grand Falls

Leupp Rd

Kendrick Peak 10,418ft ▲

Humphreys Peak 12,663ft ▲

Sunset Crater Volcano National Monument

40

To Kingman

Ash Fork

Red Lake

Williams

Arizona Snowbowl

Bill Williams Mtn 9245ft ▲

40

Flagstaff

Walnut Canyon National Monument

40

Bill Williams Ski Area

White Horse Lake

Rogers Lake

To Meteor Crater & Winslow

Juniper Mountains

89

Kaibab National Forest

89A

Lake Mary

Ashurst Lake

35°00'N

35°00'N

Oak Creek Canyon

17

Mormon Lake

Prescott National Forest

Verde River

Perkinsville

Tuzigoot National Monument

Slide Rock State Park

Sedona

Red Rock State Park

Coconino National Forest

Clarkdale

Jerome

Cottonwood

Village of Oak Creek

89

Cornville

179

Beaver Creek Recreation Area

Thumb Butte

Granite Mtn Wilderness

89A

Watson Lake

Mingus Mtn 7743ft ▲

Montezuma Castle National Monument

Blue Ridge Reservoir

87

96

Prescott

Yavapai IR

Lynx Lake

Camp Verde IR

169

Camp Verde

260

Strawberry

89

69

Pine

17

Prescott National Forest

To Kingman

Arcosanti

Tonto Natural Bridge State Park

260

89

Stanton (ghost town)

Prescott National Forest

Verde River

Payson

71

Octave

Mazatzal Wilderness

Tonto Creek

93

89

34°00'N

Hassayampa R

Wickenburg

Agua Fria River

Horseshoe Reservoir

Mazatzal Mountains

34°00'N

60

Vulture Mountains

113°00'W

Hassayampa River Preserve

Lake Pleasant Regional Park

Lake Pleasant

17

Tonto National Forest

87

188

74

Waddell Dam

To Phoenix

Cave Creek

To Phoenix

0    15    30 km
0   10   20 miles

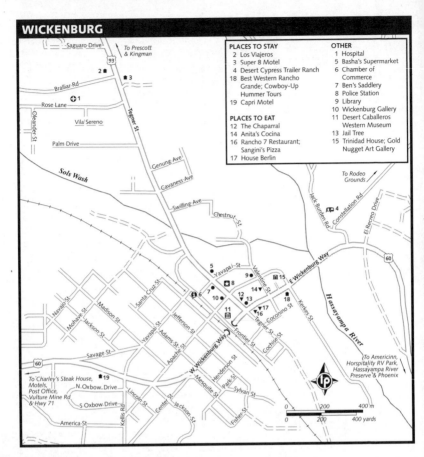

**WICKENBURG**

| PLACES TO STAY | OTHER |
|---|---|
| 2 Los Viajeros | 1 Hospital |
| 3 Super 8 Motel | 5 Basha's Supermarket |
| 4 Desert Cypress Trailer Ranch | 6 Chamber of |
| 18 Best Western Rancho | Commerce |
| Grande; Cowboy-Up | 7 Ben's Saddlery |
| Hummer Tours | 8 Police Station |
| 19 Capri Motel | 9 Library |
| | 10 Wickenburg Gallery |
| PLACES TO EAT | 11 Desert Caballeros |
| 12 The Chaparral | Western Museum |
| 14 Anita's Cocina | 13 Jail Tree |
| 16 Rancho 7 Restaurant; | 15 Trinidad House; Gold |
| Sangini's Pizza | Nugget Art Gallery |
| 17 House Berlin | |

and offers information on the Web at www .wickenburgchamber.com. Services include the library (☎ 684-2665), 164 E Apache; post office (☎ 684-2138), 2030 W Wickenburg Way; hospital (☎ 684-5421), 520 Rose Lane; and police (☎ 684-5411), 155 N Tegner.

## Things to See & Do

The **Desert Caballeros Western Museum** (☎ 684-2272), 21 N Frontier, features a fine collection of Indian arts and canvases and bronzes by famous Western artists such as Frederic Remington. There are changing shows and a gift shop. Hours are 10am to

5pm daily except noon to 4pm on Sundays, and closed on major holidays. Admission is $5 for adults, $4 for seniors and $1 for six- to 18-year-olds.

website: www.westernmuseum.org

The **Hassayampa River Preserve**, on the west side of Hwy 60, 3 miles south of town, is operated by the Nature Conservancy and protects one of the few riparian habitats remaining in Arizona. A visitor center (☎ 684-2772) provides information about 2 miles of trails. Hours are 8am to 5pm Friday to Sunday in summer and Wednesday to Sunday the rest of the year. A $5

DALLAS STRIBLEY

Elderly Navajo couple wearing traditional turquoise and silver jewelry

IZZET KERIBAR

Sand dunes at Monument Valley

Ancestral Puebloan cliff dwellings built between AD 1100 and 1300, Canyon de Chelly

Monument Valley seen through Teardrop Arch

Rock art in Monument Valley

donation to the Nature Conservancy is suggested.

The **Vulture Mine** (☎ 602-859-2743), where Henry Wickenburg found gold nuggets lying on the ground in 1863, can be visited for $5; $4 for six- to 12-year-olds. Rent a gold pan for another $4 – you just might strike it rich! Hours are 9am to 4pm daily from fall to spring. The mine is 12 miles south along Vulture Mine Rd, which is 3 miles west of downtown.

**Robson's Mining World** (☎ 685-2609), about 30 miles west of town on Hwy 71, has two dozen restored buildings, a huge collection of early mining equipment, a restaurant (offering lunch daily and dinner) and a B&B. Hiking trails lead to Indian pictographs. Hours are 10am to 4pm on weekdays and 8am to 6pm weekends, from October through April. Admission is $5; free for B&B guests and children ages 10 and under.

Cowboy-Up Hummer Tours (☎ 684-4970), 295 E Wickenburg Way, and BC Jeep Tours (☎ 684-7901) drive you into the backcountry. Rincon Ranch Lodge (☎ 684-2328, rideaz@primenet.com) offers horse rides from $45 (two hours) to $100 (all day).

Wickenburg celebrates its Western heritage during Gold Rush Days, held the second Friday to Sunday in February since the 1940s. Rodeo action, parades, gold panning and shootouts headline the events. The chamber of commerce lists numerous other events throughout the year.

### Places to Stay

**Camping** *Horspitality RV Park* (☎ 684-2519), 2 miles southeast on Hwy 60, has hookups, showers and horse stables. Rates are $15/25 for tent/RV sites, and winter reservations are suggested. Similar facilities, plus a pool, are found at the adult-only *Desert Cypress Trailer Ranch* (☎ 684-2153, 610 Jack Burden Rd).

**Hotels** Rates drop during the hot summer months and rise during winter weekends or special events. Basic cheapies include the *Capri Motel* (☎ 684-7232, 521-A W Wickenburg Way) and *Circle JR Motel* (☎ 684-

*2661, 741 W Wickenburg Way)*, with simple rooms around $40. The well-run *Americinn* (☎/fax 684-5461, 800-634-3444, 850 E Wickenburg Way) has a pool, whirlpool and restaurant serving breakfast, lunch and dinner. Some rooms have balconies. Rates range from $50 to $80. Spacious rooms with patios or balconies are featured at *Los Viajeros* (☎ 684-7099, 1000 N Tegner), with a pool and whirlpool. Rates are $85/95, single/double. The *Best Western Rancho Grande* (☎ 684-5445, 5293 E Wickenburg Way) has a pool and tennis court and some rooms with kitchenettes at rates from $70 to $100. Both this and the cheaper *Super 8* (☎ 684-0808, 925 N Tegner) have attractive Western motifs.

**Guest Ranches** Ranches usually close in summer. During the cooler months, they offer all-inclusive packages including horseback riding, meals and other activities such as shuffleboard, mountain biking, tennis, golf etc. Daily rates range from $100 to over $300 depending on dates, rooms and activities chosen. Contact the following to compare what's offered (all addresses are in Wickenburg): *Flying E Ranch* (☎ 684-2690/2173, 2801 W Wickenburg Way, AZ 85390-1087)*, www.flyingeranch.com; *Kay El Bar Ranch* (☎ 684-7593, 800-684-7583, PO Box 2480, AZ 85358)*, www.kayel bar.com; *Rancho de los Caballeros* (☎ 684-5484, 1551 S Vulture Mine Rd, AZ 85390)*, www.sunc.com; and *Rancho Casitas* (☎ 684-2628, 56550 Rancho Casitas Rd, AZ 85390).

### Places to Eat

Locally popular for decades, *Rancho 7 Restaurant* (☎ 684-2492) features home-style American and Mexican cooking from 11am to 9pm daily. Play darts, pool and shuffleboard in the adjoining bar. *Charley's Steak House* (☎ 684-2413, 1181 W Wickenburg Way)*, the town's best steak house, is open 5 to 9pm Tuesday to Saturday. The *House Berlin* (☎ 684-5044) offers haute German cuisine for lunch and dinner daily except Monday. Dinner entrées are $10 to $14.

*Sangini's Pizza* (☎ 684-7828) serves lunch and dinner daily. They deliver. Try

**CENTRAL ARIZONA**

*Anita's Cocina* (☎ 684-5777) for Mexican lunch and dinners. *The Chaparral* (☎ 684-3252) serves homemade ice cream, pastries and snacks.

## Shopping

The chamber of commerce can give you a list of art galleries and antique shops downtown. The Gold Nugget Art Gallery (☎ 684-5849), in the historic Trinidad House, and the Wickenburg Gallery (☎ 684-7047), 10 W Apache, are among the best. For a real whiff of the Old West, mosey into Ben's Saddlery (☎ 684-2683), 184 N Tegner; even if you aren't in the market for a saddle, the leathery smell makes it the most memorable shop in town.

## PRESCOTT

☎ 928 • pop 33,938 • elevation 5346 feet

Founded in 1864 by gold prospectors, Prescott, 60 miles north of Wickenburg, became Arizona's first territorial capital. President Abraham Lincoln preferred the progressive mining town over conservative Tucson, considered to have Confederate leanings. Vestiges of early territorial life remain in Prescott's many early buildings, including the first governor's mansion. Prescott's historic character, outdoor recreation in surrounding national forest, the adjacent Yavapai Indian Reservation with legal gambling, two colleges, a small artists' community and galleries give the town a bohemian air.

Frontier Days, held around the Fourth of July, features the world's oldest rodeo. Hotels are booked well in advance and rates rise.

## Information

The chamber of commerce (☎ 445-2000, 800-266-7534), 117 W Goodwin, is open 9am to 5pm Monday to Friday, 9am to 3pm Saturday and 10am to 2pm Sunday. Call them for a list of the many special events held in summer.

website: www.prescott.org

Other services include Prescott National Forest Supervisor's Office (☎ 771-4700), 344 S Cortez; the library (☎ 445-8110), 215 E Goodwin; main post office (☎ 778-1890), 442 Miller Valley Rd; the downtown branch at Goodwin and Cortez; medical center (☎ 445-2700), 1003 Willow Creek Rd; and police (☎ 778-1444), 222 S Marina.

## Historic Buildings

Montezuma St west of Courthouse Plaza was once the infamous 'Whiskey Row,' with 40 drinking establishments serving cowboys and miners who attempted to have a drink in each. A devastating 1900 fire destroyed 25 saloons, five hotels and the red-light district, but many early buildings remain so you can still have a drink on colorful Whiskey Row. The County Courthouse in the center of the shady and relaxing plaza dates from 1918.

Buildings east and south of the plaza escaped the 1900 fire and date from the late 19th century. Some were built by East Coast settlers who built wooden Victorian houses in New England style, markedly different from adobe Southwestern buildings.

## Museums

The **Sharlot Hall Museum** (☎ 445-3122), 415 W Gurley, covering two city blocks, is Prescott's most important museum. You can stroll by the two-story log building that was the first governor's mansion and view many other buildings from the 1860s and '70s surrounded by flowery gardens. The Museum Center displays historical artifacts and old photographs. Hours are 10am to 5pm Monday to Saturday (till 4pm in winter) and 1 to 5pm on Sunday. Admission is a suggested $4 donation per adult or $5 per family.

website: www.sharlot.org

Six miles north of town, the **Phippen Museum of Western Art** (☎ 778-1385), 4701 N Hwy 89, named after cowboy artist George Phippen and displaying some of his works, has a good collection of Western paintings, bronzes and photographs, as well as changing exhibits. Hours are 10am to 4pm daily except Sunday (1 to 4pm) and Tuesday (closed). Admission is $3 for adults, $2 for seniors and children 12 and over.

website: www.phippenmuseum.org

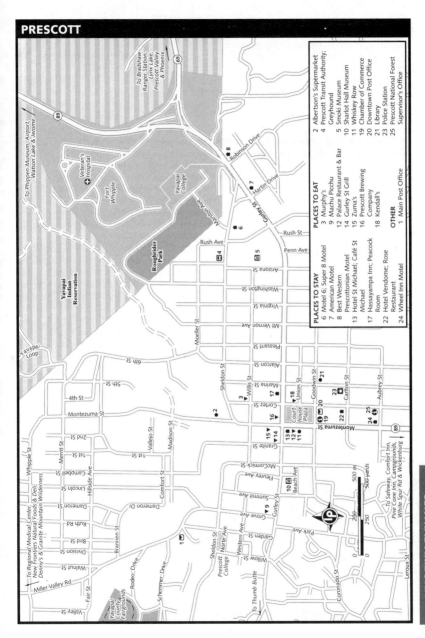

# PRESCOTT

**PLACES TO STAY**
6  Motel 6; Super 8 Motel
7  American Motel
8  Best Western
   Prescottonian Motel
13 Hotel St Michael; Café St
   Michael
17 Hassayampa Inn; Peacock
   Room
22 Hotel Vendome; Rose
   Restaurant
24 Wheel Inn Motel

**PLACES TO EAT**
3  Murphy's
9  Machu Picchu
12 Palace Restaurant & Bar
14 Gurley St Grill
15 Zuma's
16 Prescott Brewing
   Company
18 Kendall's

**OTHER**
1  Main Post Office
2  Albertson's Supermarket
4  Prescott Transit Authority;
   Greyhound
5  Smoki Museum
10 Sharlot Hall Museum
11 Whiskey Row
19 Chamber of Commerce
20 Downtown Post Office
21 Library
23 Police Station
25 Prescott National Forest
   Supervisor's Office

CENTRAL ARIZONA

Built to resemble an Indian pueblo, the **Smoki Museum** (☎ 445-1230), 147 N Arizona, displays Southwestern Indian artifacts dating from prehistoric times to the present. Hours from April 15 through October are 10am to 4pm Monday to Saturday, 1 to 4pm Sunday. Admission is a $2 donation for adults.

website: www.smoki.com

---

### Sharlot Hall

Twelve-year-old Sharlot Mabrith Hall arrived in Prescott in February 1882, after an arduous horseback trip all the way from Kansas with her family. During the journey, she was thrown by her horse, causing a back injury that plagued her for the rest of her life.

While helping run her family's ranch, she became fascinated with life on the frontier. Largely self-schooled, she began describing the gold miners, Indians and ranchers around her in a series of stories and poems that soon gained local admiration. In 1909 she was appointed territorial historian, the first woman to hold a political office in Arizona.

In 1924 she traveled to Washington, DC, to represent Arizona in the electoral college. She caused a stir in the capital with her outfit that included a copper mesh coat provided by a local mine. There was no mistaking that Arizona was 'The Copper State.' During her visit to the east, she toured several museums; these inspired her to found a museum of Arizona history.

On her return to Prescott, Hall leased the first territorial capitol building and restored the governor's mansion. In 1928, she moved her extensive personal collection of historical artifacts into the mansion and opened it as a museum. She lived on the property, expanding and adding to the collection until her death in 1943. The museum bearing her name has continued to flourish since then. In 1981, Sharlot Hall was elected to the Arizona Women's Hall of Fame.

---

## Activities

The Prescott National Forest office can suggest hikes, climbs, picnic areas, campgrounds and fishing holes. Local lakes are stocked with trout, bluegill, bass and catfish. Popular nearby areas are Thumb Butte, Lynx Lake and the Granite Mountain Wilderness.

Looming over the west side of town, **Thumb Butte** is reached by driving 3 miles along Gurley and Thumb Butte Rd. A 1.2-mile trail makes it almost to the summit, 1000 feet above town. The last 200 feet are the province of rock climbers.

To reach **Lynx Lake**, drive 4 miles east on Hwy 69, then 3 miles south on Walker Rd. Here you'll find fishing, hiking, camping, a store, a small-boat rental (summer only), a small Indian site and bird watching.

The **Granite Mountain Wilderness** has a fishing lake, campgrounds and hiking trails, and is popular with rock climbers. Head north on Grove Ave from downtown, which becomes Miller Valley Rd, bear left on Iron Springs Rd, and about 4 miles from Prescott, turn right on unpaved USFS Rd 347 and continue for another 4 miles.

Try picnicking, fishing and camping at **Watson Lake**, about 4 miles north on Hwy 89. Just beyond are the **Granite Dells**, a landscape of 100-foot-high, rounded red-rock outcrops that you can hike through or climb.

Buy camping and climbing equipment at Granite Mountain Outfitters (☎ 776-4949), 320 W Gurley. Rent mountain bikes from Ironclad Bicycles (☎ 776-1755), 710 White Spar Rd. For horseback riding, try Granite Mountain Stables (☎ 771-9551), about 10 miles northwest of town. Mile High Adventures (☎ 776-0399) does guided hikes, bike and jeep rides.

## Places to Stay

Summer weekend rates are often much higher than weekdays. Prescott Valley, 8 miles east along Hwy 69, has several other motels (mainly chains).

**Camping** *Point of Rocks RV Park* (☎ 445-9018, 3025 N Hwy 89) has 100 RV-only sites

for $19 with hookups. *Willow Lake RV Park* (☎ 445-6311), 4 miles north on Hwy 89 then west on Willow Lake Rd, has about 170 RV sites with hookups for $20 and 30 tent sites for $14 as well as a pool, showers, a playground and a coin laundry.

The USFS (☎ 771-4700) operates many simple campgrounds with picnic tables, grills, toilets, and water but no showers. Rates vary from $6 (no drinking water) to $10 (drinking water available).

**Hotels** It's difficult to find a motel room under $40 in the summer. The *American Motel* (☎ 778- 4322, 1211 E Gurley) is one of several satisfactory budget hotels in that area. *Wheel Inn Motel* (☎ 778-7346, 800-717-0902, 333 S Montezuma) and some others on Montezuma are also $40 and up.

The popular *Hotel St Michael* (☎ 776-1999, 800-678-3757, 205 W Gurley) is an old Whiskey Row hotel rebuilt in 1900. It has 72 older but clean rooms with baths for $42 to $59 ($20 more on weekends); a few family units and 'suites' are $80 to $100. There's a restaurant, and rates include continental breakfast.

The historic *Hotel Vendome* (☎ 776-0900, 888-463-3583, 230 S Cortez) has charm dating to 1917 in 17 rooms for $80 to $120 double, all with modern private bath, and four suites for $120 and up, depending on season. Rates include continental breakfast. The lobby with a cozy wooden bar is an attractive place for a drink.

website: www.vendomehotel.com

The *Hassayampa Inn* (☎ 778-9434, 800-322-1927, 122 E Gurley) was one of Arizona's most elegant hotels when it opened in 1927. Restored in 1985, the hotel has a vintage hand-operated elevator, many of its original furnishings, hand-painted wall decorations and a lovely dining room. The 68 rooms vary (standard, choice, suite, suite with spa) and run $100 to $200 including full breakfast and an evening cocktail.

website: www.hassayampainn.com

Several *chain motels* provide satisfactory lodging, including Motel 6, Super 8, Comfort Inn, Days Inn, Best Western, Holiday Inn Express and Hampton Inn.

**B&Bs** Some old houses have been attractively restored as B&Bs, and it's hard to choose the nicest. None allow smoking indoors and many offer multi-day discounts. Rates start around $100. For a listing of over a dozen Prescottian B&Bs, check out www.prescott-bed-breakfast.org.

## Places to Eat

On the plaza, *Café St Michael*, underneath the Hotel St Michael, serves reasonably priced breakfasts, espressos and light meals throughout the day.

*Kendall's* (☎ 778-3658, 113 S Cortez) is a 1950s-style place that doesn't believe in small portions. It's open 11am to 8pm daily (6pm on Sunday); look for the sign promising 'Famous Burgers & Ice Cream.' The popular *Gurley St Grill* (☎ 445-3388, 230 W Gurley) has burgers, sandwiches, pastas, pizzas and grilled chicken lunches and dinners at moderate prices. Good microbrews and English- and American-style pub food are featured at the *Prescott Brewing Company* (☎ 771-2795, 130 Gurley St), a large but usually crowded place. Bring the whole family. The old-fashioned (check out their pressed-tin ceilings and tiled bathrooms) *Palace Restaurant & Bar* (☎ 541-1996, 120 S Montezuma) has tasty lunches and dinners (entreés $12 to $24) served by waitstaff in late-19th-century clothing. Definitely worth a bite.

*Murphy's* (☎ 445-4044, 201 N Cortez) was a general store in the 1890s. Much of the old charm remains, and the American food is good and fairly priced in the $12 to $19 range for dinner, much less at lunch. The *Peacock Room* (☎ 778-9434), in the Hassayampa Inn, serving a wide range of breakfasts, lunches and dinners, is another highly recommended and elegant dining spot. The tiny *Rose Restaurant* (☎ 777-8308, 235 S Cortez) features Prescott's most celebrated chef and is as gourmet as it comes; dinners only from Wednesday to Sunday and reservations recommended.

*Zuma's* (☎ 541-1400, 124 N Montezuma) has wood-fired pizzas, decent Italian food (entrées up to $18), an above-average selection of libations and a slightly alternative atmosphere. *Machu Picchu (☎ 717-8242, 111 Grove Ave)* has a Peruvian chef and serves authentic ceviches and all things Peruvian. Call for hours; prices are around $10.

The *Pine Cone Inn (☎ 445-2970, 1245 White Spar Rd)* serves dinner from 4pm Tuesday to Saturday; Prescottians drive out from town for a change of pace and to enjoy the frequent live music and dancing. On Sunday, it serves breakfast from 8am and closes at 9pm.

### Getting There & Away
America West Express flies daily to Phoenix from Prescott Airport, 9 miles north on Hwy 89.

Prescott Transit Authority/Greyhound (☎ 445-5470, 800-445-7978), 820 E Sheldon, has 13 buses a day to Phoenix ($24). Shuttle U (☎ 800-304-6114), or www.shuttleu.com, runs several vans a day to Phoenix Airport. Coconino/Yavapai Shuttle (☎ 775-8929) has two buses a day to Flagstaff ($22).

## JEROME
☎ 928 • pop 329 • elevation 5400 feet
Rich in copper, gold and silver, this area was mined by Indians before the arrival of Europeans. Jerome had 15,000 inhabitants in the 1920s, but the 1929 stock market crash shut down many of the mines. The last closed in 1953 and Jerome looked as if it would become another ghost town.

In the late 1960s, Jerome's spectacular location and empty houses were discovered by hippies, artists and retirees, and slowly Jerome became what it is today, a collection of late-19th- and early-20th-century buildings housing art galleries, souvenir shops, restaurants, saloons and a few B&Bs, all precariously perched on a steep hillside. Highway 89A slowly wends through town 34 miles northeast of Prescott (not recommended for large trailers, allow 90 minutes), and the 15mph speed limit makes this a tourist trap in more ways than one. However, many of the antique shops and art galleries feature high quality pieces – the shopping can be definitely upscale.

The **Mine Museum** (☎ 634-5477), 200 Main, displays old photos, documents, tools

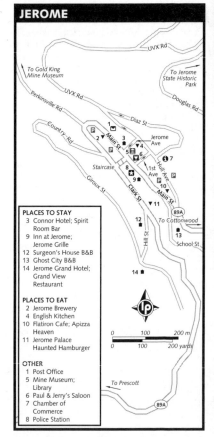

**JEROME**

**PLACES TO STAY**
3  Connor Hotel; Spirit Room Bar
9  Inn at Jerome; Jerome Grille
12 Surgeon's House B&B
13 Ghost City B&B
14 Jerome Grand Hotel; Grand View Restaurant

**PLACES TO EAT**
2  Jerome Brewery
4  English Kitchen
10 Flatiron Cafe; Apizza Heaven
11 Jerome Palace Haunted Hamburger

**OTHER**
1  Post Office
5  Mine Museum; Library
6  Paul & Jerry's Saloon
7  Chamber of Commerce
8  Police Station

and other memorabilia explaining Jerome's history. Hours are 9am to 4:30pm, and admission is $1 for people 13 and over. A mile north of town, the **Gold King Mine Museum** (☎ 634-0053) is a miniature ghost town with demonstrations of antique mining equipment, a walk-in mine, a gift shop and a few animals for children to pet. Hours are 9am to 5pm daily; admission is $4, $3 for seniors and $2 for six- to 12-year-olds.

The **Jerome State Historic Park** (☎ 634-5381), 2 miles beyond Jerome en route to Cottonwood, surrounds the 1916 mansion of colorful mining mogul 'Rawhide' Jimmy

Douglas and gives a thorough understanding of the town's mining history. View models, exhibits, a video presentation inside the mansion and old mining equipment outside. Admission is $2.50; $1 for seven- to 13-year-olds. Hours are 8am to 5pm daily except Christmas.

### Information

The chamber of commerce (☎ 634-2900), on Hull Ave, is open 11am to 3pm and is online at www.Jeromechamber.com. Other services include the library (☎ 639-0574), 111 Jerome Ave and post office (☎ 634-8241), 120 Main. The police station (☎ 634-8992) is in the town hall building on Main St.

Parking can be tight during the summer, though several parking lots generally provide enough space.

### Places to Stay

Most accommodations are pricey but fun, with antique flourishes and quaint decor. The *Inn at Jerome* (☎ 634-5094, 800-634-5094, 309 Main) has six clean Victorian rooms with shared baths ($55 to $75) and two with a private bath ($75 to $85), including breakfast. All rooms have sinks and TVs, and a guest parlor is available. The 1898 *Connor Hotel* (☎ 634-5006, 800-523-3554, 164 Main) has 10 restored bedrooms with period furniture and private baths ranging from $75 to $125. The hotel is over the popular Spirit Room Bar with occasional live music; rooms one to four get the worst (or best) of the bar noise. The *Jerome Grand Hotel* (☎ 634-8200, 200 Hill St) was built as a hospital in 1926 and renovated into a hotel in 1996. Perched above town, many of its 30 simple rooms have balconies and excellent views. Rates are $85 to $110, and some suites are available for $190.

*Ghost City B&B* (☎ 634-4678, 888-634-4678, 541 Main), in an 1898 building, has a verandah with great views and a hot tub. Rooms and suites, some with shared bath, cost $85 to $125, including breakfast and afternoon tea. The *Surgeon's House B&B* (☎ 639-1452, 800-639-1452, 101 Hill St), built in 1917 at the top of the town, has three suites with great views (one has a huge

picture window) at $100 to $150, including full breakfast. Check the chamber of commerce for details of these and several other small B&Bs.

### Places to Eat

The *English Kitchen* (☎ 634-2132, 119 Jerome Ave), serving meals since 1899, claims to be Arizona's oldest restaurant. Eat standard inexpensive breakfasts and lunches inside or on the outside deck from Tuesday to Sunday. It's often busy with daytrippers.

The *Flatiron Cafe* (☎ 634-2733, 416 Main) has a great selection of coffee and baked goods and also serves trendy light meals. Next door, *Apizza Heaven* (☎ 649-1834) sereves up good pizzas daily except Tuesday. *Jerome Brewery* (☎ 639-8477, 111 Main) has the best sandwiches in town and serves microbrews. The *Jerome Palace Haunted Hamburger* (☎ 634-0554, 410 Clark) features a tasty selection of burgers, steaks, salads and pasta; they have a full-service bar.

The *Jerome Grille*, in the Inn at Jerome, serves reasonably priced American and Southwestern breakfast, lunch and dinner daily. The *Grand View Restaurant*, in the Jerome Grand Hotel, has varied but mainly American cuisine.

### Entertainment

A good place to get drinks is *Paul & Jerry's Saloon* (☎ 634-2603, 206 Main), originally called the Senate Saloon when it first opened in 1899. On weekends they feature live blue grass music. The *Spirit Room Bar*, under the Hotel Connor, is the town's liveliest watering hole.

## COTTONWOOD

☎ 928 • pop 9179 • elevation 3320 feet

Named after the trees growing along the Verde River, Cottonwood was first settled in the 1870s but is essentially a modern town and a good base for exploring the area. Main St north of the police station is 'Old Town.' The **Clemenceau Heritage Museum** (☎ 634-2868), 1 N Willard, illustrates local history and has a superb and realistic model railroad exhibit of the area. Hours are 9am to noon Wednesday and 11am to 3pm Friday to Sunday; admission is by donation.

The Sedona-Phoenix Shuttle (☎ 282-2066) stops in Cottonwood.

## Information

The chamber of commerce (☎ 634-7593), 1010 S Main, open 9am to 5pm, has limited information; see its website at www .chamber.verdevalley.com. Other services include the library (☎ 634-7559),100 S 6th; post office (☎ 634-9526), 700 E Mingus Ave; medical center (☎ 634-2251), 269 S Candy Lane; and police (☎ 634-4246), 816 N Main.

## Tuzigoot National Monument

Tuzigoot (☎ 634-5564) features a two-story Sinaguan pueblo (1125 to 1425 AD) that once housed 200 people; the remnants can be visited on a short, steep trail (no wheelchairs) and are memorable for their ridgetop location affording fine views of the Verde River Valley. Don't miss the visitor center's exhibit of Sinaguan artifacts. Hours are 8am to 7pm from Memorial Day to Labor Day and 8am to 5pm the rest of the year. Admission is $2 for adults; all passes are honored. Tuzigoot is 2 miles north of Cottonwood – follow signs from Hwy 89A.

## Verde Canyon Railroad

Vintage FP7 engines pull coaches on four-hour guided roundtrips into splendid countryside north of Cottonwood Pass, traveling through roadless areas with views of red rock cliffs, riparian areas, Indian sites, wildlife and, from December to April, bald eagles. The midpoint is Perkinsville, a remote ranch where parts of *How the West Was Won* were filmed; the train returns the way it came, over bridges and trestles. Views far surpass that of the Grand Canyon Railway. Year-round departures from Clarkdale (2½ miles north of Cottonwood) leave at varying times depending on the season; it is closed on Tuesday year-round. Moonlight rides leave at 5:30pm on Saturday nights in summer. First-class car-

riages feature plush seating, complimentary hors d'oeuvres and cash bar service; coach class is comfortable but more crowded and has a cash snack bar. All first-class tickets cost $60. Coach-class tickets are $40; seniors pay $35 and kids under 12 pay $25. Reservations are required. Carriages are climate controlled and all passengers have access to open-air viewing cars. The Clarkdale depot has a café and small museum. For schedule and reservations call ☎ 639-0010 or ☎ 800-293-7245.

website: www.verdecanyonrr.com

## Places to Stay

For camping, the ***Dead Horse Ranch State Park*** *(☎ 634-5283)*, on the north side of Cottonwood, has showers and 45 basic sites for $10, as well as some with hookups for $15. The park also offers picnicking, fishing, nature trails and a playground ($4 for day-use).

***Rio Verde RV Park*** *(☎ 634-5990, 3420 Hwy 89A)* has showers and a coin laundry and charges $11 for tents or $21 with hookups. The ***Turquoise Triangle RV Park*** *(☎ 634-5294, 2501 E Hwy 89A)* is RV-only for $22.

The funky older ***Sundial Motel*** *(☎ 634-8031, 1034 N Main)* charges $40 a double. The ***View Motel*** *(☎ 634-7581, 818 S Main)* has a pool, whirlpool and hilltop location. Rates start at $40 and go over $60 with kitchenettes. The ***Willow Tree Inn*** *(☎ 634-3678, 1089 S Hwy 260)* lacks a pool but is clean and about $55.

Cottonwood's three ***chain motels***, the Super 8, Quality Inn and Best Western, all with pools, whirlpools and free continental breakfasts, provide rooms for $60 to $90.

## Places to Eat

***Rosalie's Bluewater Inn*** *(☎ 634-8702, 517 N 12th)* features good and inexpensive home-style breakfast, lunch and dinner. A handful of hole-in-the-wall eateries in Old Town yield surprisingly good cheap food, especially ***Old Town Café*** *(☎ 634-5980, 1025 N Main)* for sandwiches and salads and ***Gas Works Mexican Restaurant*** *(☎ 634-7426, 1033 N Main)*.

*Blazin' M Ranch* (☎ 634-0334, 800-937-8643, *oldwest@blazinm.com*), next to Dead Horse Ranch State Park, has filling chuckwagon suppers with rootin' tootin' cowboy entertainment for $20 ($10 for kids 10 and under). It is open Wednesday to Saturday and is closed January and August.

## AROUND CAMP VERDE

On I-17, 85 miles north of Phoenix, Camp Verde (elevation 3133 feet) is on the way to Jerome, Sedona and Flagstaff for travelers taking the quicker freeway rather than the long trip through Wickenburg and Prescott. Several places along the interstate north and south of Camp Verde are worth a look. Near exit 287, stay at the *Microtel Inn* (☎ 567-3700, 888-567-8483), for $50 to $80, or at the *Super 8 Motel* or *Comfort Inn*.

### Fort Verde State Historic Park

Four original fort buildings have been restored, which together with the original parade grounds and some foundations, give the visitor an idea of what life was like here in the 1880s. Visit the museum (☎ 567-3275) for self-guided tour brochures describing the area. Volunteers in period costumes give interpretive demonstrations periodically. Fort Verde Day, on the second Saturday of October, has several historical reenactments. Hours are 8am to 4:30pm daily except Christmas. Admission is $2 for adults; $1 for seven- to 14-year-olds.

### Montezuma Castle National Monument

Like nearby Tuzigoot, Montezuma Castle is an Ancestral Puebloan site built and occupied between the 12th and 14th centuries. The name refers to the splendid castle-like location high on a cliff; early explorers thought the five-story-high pueblo was Aztec and hence dubbed it Montezuma. A museum (☎ 567-3322) interprets the archaeology of this well-preserved site, visible from a self-guiding, wheelchair-accessible trail. Entrance into the 'castle' itself is prohibited. Access the monument from I-17 exit 289, then follow signs for 2 miles.

Montezuma Well, 10 miles northeast of the castle, is also part of the monument. It's a natural limestone sinkhole, 470 feet across and surrounded by remnants of Sinaguan and Hohokam dwellings. Water from the sinkhole was used for irrigation by the Indians as it is today. Access is from exit 293.

Both areas have picnic sites and are open 8am to 5pm; from Memorial Day to Labor Day, they are open to 7pm. Admission to the castle is $3 for adults; the well is free. All passes are honored.

### Arcosanti

Two miles east of I-17 exit 262, a short unpaved road leads to this architectural experiment in urban living. Designed by architect Paolo Soleri, Arcosanti will be home to 6000 people who want to live in a futuristic, aesthetic, relaxing and environmentally sound development. The space-age project has been under construction for decades, and rivals the Biosphere and London Bridge as one of Arizona's most unexpected tourist attractions. Tours leave hourly from 10am to 4pm and cost $8. A gift shop sells the famous ceramic and cast bronze Soleri windbells, and a café is on site. Overnight accommodations, week- and month-long seminars and other events are offered. For

Ancestral Puebloan vase

information contact Arcosanti (☎ 632-7135), HC 74, PO Box 4136, Mayer, AZ 86333.
website: www.arcosanti.org

## SEDONA

☎ 928 • pop 10,195; metro area 16,500 • elevation 4500 feet

Sedona, seated among splendid crimson sandstone formations at the south end of lovely Oak Creek Canyon, is one of the prettiest locations in Arizona. For decades, Sedona was a quiet farming community but in the 1940s and '50s, Hollywood began using Sedona as a movie location. In the 1960s and '70s the beauty of the surroundings started attracting retirees, artists and tourists in large numbers and the town experienced much growth. Around 1980, New Agers began finding vortexes (see the boxed text 'In Search of the New Age').

Rapid, poorly controlled growth took the area somewhat by surprise, and the strip malls look out of place among the red-rock scenery, although the town is making efforts to blend in with its surroundings. (The Sedona McDonald's lacks the famous golden arches; instead, pastel green arcs are

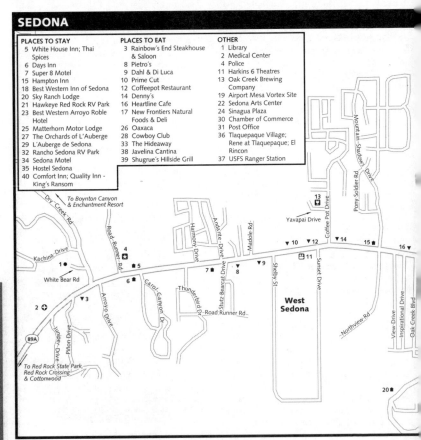

**SEDONA**

| PLACES TO STAY | PLACES TO EAT | OTHER |
|---|---|---|
| 5 White House Inn; Thai Spices | 3 Rainbow's End Steakhouse & Saloon | 1 Library |
| 6 Days Inn | 8 Pietro's | 2 Medical Center |
| 7 Super 8 Motel | 9 Dahl & Di Luca | 4 Police |
| 15 Hampton Inn | 10 Prime Cut | 11 Harkins 6 Theatres |
| 18 Best Western Inn of Sedona | 12 Coffeepot Restaurant | 13 Oak Creek Brewing Company |
| 20 Sky Ranch Lodge | 14 Denny's | 19 Airport Mesa Vortex Site |
| 21 Hawkeye Red Rock RV Park | 16 Heartline Cafe | 22 Sedona Arts Center |
| 23 Best Western Arroyo Roble Hotel | 17 New Frontiers Natural Foods & Deli | 24 Sinagua Plaza |
| 25 Matterhorn Motor Lodge | 26 Oaxaca | 30 Chamber of Commerce |
| 27 The Orchards of L'Auberge | 28 Cowboy Club | 31 Post Office |
| 29 L'Auberge de Sedona | 33 The Hideaway | 36 Tlaquepaque Village; Rene at Tlaquepaque; El Rincon |
| 32 Rancho Sedona RV Park | 38 Javelina Cantina | |
| 34 Sedona Motel | 39 Shugrue's Hillside Grill | 37 USFS Ranger Station |
| 35 Hostel Sedona | | |
| 40 Comfort Inn; Quality Inn - King's Ransom | | |

To Boynton Canyon & Enchantment Resort

Dry Creek Rd

Kachina Drive

White Bear Rd

Road Runner Rd

Harmony Drive

Andante Drive

Madole Rd

Yavapai Drive

Coffee Pot Drive

Pony Soldier Drive

Mountain Shadows Drive

West Sedona

Shelby St.

Sunset Drive

Northview Rd.

View Rd.

Inspirational Drive

Oak Creek Blvd

Thunderbird Dr.

Carol Canyon Dr.

Stutz Bearcat Drive

Arroyo Drive

Piñon Drive

Juniper Drive

89A

Road Runner Rd.

To Red Rock State Park, Red Rock Crossing & Cottonwood

painted on a pink stuccoed wall.) Tourist development has tended toward the high-end curiously blended with the psychic. The town is home to several fine resorts, some of Arizona's best restaurants, fine art galleries and boutiques, and numerous New Age businesses, but no cheap motels.

Despite the bustle of four million annual visitors, it's possible to get away from the crowds and enjoy the beautiful scenery on a 4WD tour, bike ride or hike. It's the environs that make Sedona an attractive, if pricey, destination. It is about 110 miles north of Phoenix, if you are driving directly from there, 20 miles northeast of Cottonwood, if you're coming up Hwy 89A, or 25 miles south of Flagstaff (later in this chapter).

## Information

The chamber of commerce (☎ 282-7722, 800-288-7336,), Forest Rd at Hwy 89A, has oodles of information. It's open from 8:30am to 5pm daily (till 3pm on Sunday), and check the website at www.Visit Sedona.com. Other services include USFS Ranger Station (☎ 282-4119), 250 Brewer Rd, AZ 86339; the library (☎ 282-7714),

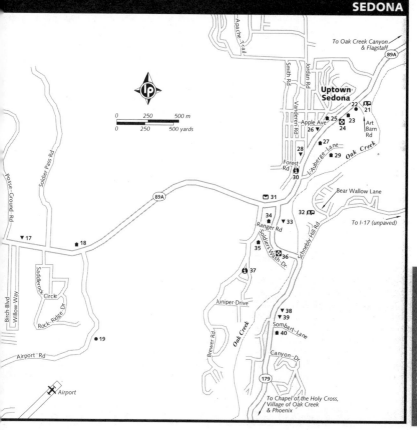

SEDONA

3250 White Bear Rd; post office (☎ 282-3511) on Hwy 89A at Hwy 179; medical center (☎ 204-3000), 3700 W Hwy 89A; police (☎ 282-3100), 100 Road Runner Dr. Note that the intersection of Hwy 89A with Hwy 179 is called 'the Y.'

Much of the surrounding land is national forest and a Red Rock Pass parking pass is required ($5 per day, $15 per week, $20 per year). Buy it at the chamber of commerce or various local businesses.

## Chapel of the Holy Cross

Spectacularly located between red-rock towers 3 miles south of town, this nondenominational chapel (☎ 282-4069) is open

### In Search of the New Age

Sedona is the foremost New Age center in the Southwest and one of the most important anywhere. The term 'New Age' loosely refers to a trend toward seeking alternative explanations or interpretations of what constitutes health, religion, the psyche and enlightenment. Drawing upon new and old factual and mystical traditions from around the world, 'New Agers' often seek to transform themselves psychologically and spiritually in the hope that such personal efforts will eventually transform the world at large.

You can't miss the New Age stores in town – many of them have the word 'crystal' in their names. They sell books, crystals and various New Age paraphernalia, distribute free maps showing vortex sites, provide information, and may arrange various spiritual or healing events. The Center for the New Age (☎ 928-282-2085), 341 Hwy 179, is open daily and is a good place to start or visit online at www.SedonaNewAge.com. Sedona's offerings include mainstream services such as massages, nutrition counseling, acupressure, meditation, and yoga and tai chi classes, all the way through increasingly esoteric practices such as herbology, psychic channeling, aura photography, astrology, palmistry, tarot card and runes reading, aromatherapy, past-life regressions, crystal healing, shamanism, drumming workshops, reflexology, hypnotherapy and more…

The four best known vortexes, or high-energy sites where the earth's power is said to be strongly felt, are in the Sedona's local red rock mountains. These include Bell Rock near Village of Oak Creek east of Hwy 179, Cathedral Rock near Red Rock Crossing, Airport Mesa along the Airport Rd, and Boynton Canyon. Local maps show these four main sites, though some individuals claim that others exist.

Several people lead guided tours of vortexes and other important New Age sites. These tours differ from many of the standard vortex tours in that the guides believe in what they tell you, as opposed to simply showing you the place. Try the following (there are others):

Sedona Nature Excursions/Mystic Tours by Rahelio
1405 W Hwy 89A, PO Box 1171, Sedona, AZ 86339 (☎ 928-282-6735)

Spirit Steps Tours
PO Box 3151, West Sedona, AZ 86340 (☎ 928-282-4562, 800-728-4562)

Vortex Tours/Medicine Wheel Journeys
PO Box 535, Sedona, AZ 86339 (☎ 928-282-2733, 800-943-3266)

New Agers (for want of a better term) are generally gentle folk, but some have been criticized for performing rituals, such as chantings or offerings, in scenic areas. Chanting in a public scenic area can be as irritating as a loud radio, revving motorcycle or droning aircraft, and leaving offerings of crystals or food is tantamount to littering. If you want to participate in such public rituals, please keep your vocal interactions with the planet to a peacefully personal level, pick up your offerings when you're through, and leave nothing but your love, energy and blessings.

9am to 5pm daily. Head south on Hwy 179 and turn left on Chapel Rd.

## Sedona Arts Center

The center (☎ 282-3809, 888-954-4442), at the corner of Hwy 89A and Art Barn Rd, has changing exhibits, a gift shop, classes in performing and visual arts, and a variety of cultural events during the September to May season. Hours are 10am to 5pm. website: www.sedonaartscenter.com

## Red Rock State Park

This park has an environmental education center, visitor center (☎ 282-6907), picnic areas and six short hiking trails in a riparian habitat amid gorgeous scenery. Ranger-led activities include nature walks, bird walks and full-moon hikes during the warmer months. Hours are 8am to 5pm, to 6pm in summer. Admission is $5 per vehicle (four passengers) and $1 for extra passengers or pedestrians/cyclists. The park is 5½ miles west of the Y along Hwy 89A, then 3 miles left on Lower Red Rock Loop Rd.

## Oak Creek Canyon

The section of Oak Creek northeast of Sedona along Hwy 89A is where the canyon is at its narrowest, and the red, orange and white cliffs are the most dramatic. Forests of pine and juniper clothe the canyon, providing a scenic backdrop for trout fishing in the creek.

The USFS maintains six campgrounds in the canyon as well as picnic areas. It also maintains the **Oak Creek Scenic Viewpoint**, 16 miles north of Sedona at the top of a particularly steep and winding section of N Hwy 89A.

Seven miles northeast of Sedona along N Hwy 89A, **Slide Rock State Park** (☎ 282-3034) is a very popular spot for swimming, picnicking and bird watching. Oak Creek sweeps swimmers (especially kids) through the natural rock chute from which the park derives its name. Hours are 8am to 6pm (5pm in winter), and admission is $7 per car or $1 for pedestrians/cyclists. Another popular swimming hole is **Grasshopper**

**Point**, just over 2 miles north of town on the right side of N Hwy 89A.

Southwest of Sedona is **Red Rock Crossing**, best reached via Upper Red Rock Loop Rd, off Hwy 89A. The area is managed by the USFS, which provides picnicking areas and parking on either side of this section of Oak Creek. The creek can be waded (usually with little difficulty), but there is no bridge. The highlights are the splendid views of Cathedral Rock above a pretty stretch of Oak Creek.

Note that Village of Oak Creek, 7 miles south on Hwy 179, has places to stay and eat, but is not part of the canyon.

## Backcountry Drives

Aside from the scenic drives around Oak Creek Canyon and the Chapel of the Holy Cross (see those sections), the following offer good views. The short drive up paved **Airport Rd** is one good option, especially at sunset. **Dry Creek Rd**, at the west end of town, leads to scenic Boynton Canyon, where you can hike as well. View the photogenic Cathedral Rock along the roads of Lower and Upper **Red Rock Loop** (which you can take without entering the park). A rough unpaved road is the scenic 12-mile **Schnebly Hill Rd**, which turns off Hwy 179 near Oak Creek and ends up at I-17 exit 320. This road is closed in winter.

## Hiking & Mountain Biking

There are easy scenic trails in Red Rock State Park and more difficult ones in the national forest. Hiking is possible year-round, though some higher trails may close in winter. The USFS ranger station sells hiking maps.

There are plenty of good biking trails; ask at any of the bike rental places, including Mountain Bike Heaven (☎ 282-1312), 1695 W Hwy 89A; Sedona Sports (☎ 282-1317), 251 Hwy 179; and Bike & Bean (☎ 284-0210), 6020 Hwy 179.

## Organized Tours & Activities

Sedona Trolley (☎ 282-5400) departs on the hour from its bus stop near the chamber of commerce. Narrated tours lasting 55 minutes cover Tlaquepaque, a shopping and art-gallery center, and the Chapel of the Holy Cross leaving at 10am, noon, 2 and 4pm; tours to West Sedona and Boynton Canyon leave at 11am and 1, 3 and 5pm. Tours are $8 each, or $12 for both; kids 12 and under pay $3.

Many companies offer 4WD 'Jeep Tours' of Sedona's backcountry and surrounding areas. These run from two hours to all day at costs ranging from $25 to $130 per person. Choose tours to see or photograph scenery, experience energy vortexes, look at archaeological sites or visit the Grand Canyon or Hopi Indian Reservation. The following list gives information about several established tour companies, but there are many more. Most expect a minimum of four passengers and charge more per person for smaller groups. Many also offer overnight tours. For New Age tours, see the boxed text 'In Search of the New Age.'

**Crossing Worlds** (☎ 649-3060, 800-350-2693) Hopi, Navajo and other Indian cultures. Vortexes.
website: www.crossingworlds.com

**Earth Wisdom Tours** (☎ 282-4714, 800-482-4714), 293 N Hwy 89A Vortexes, Indian lore.

**Northern Light Balloon Expeditions** (☎ 282-2274, 800-230-6222) Daily sunrise flights. Hotel pickup.
website: www.sedona.net/fun/balloon

**Pink Jeep Tours** (☎ 282-5000, 800-873-3662) Backcountry scenery.
website: www.pinkjeep.com

**Pink Jeep Tours-Ancient Expeditions** (☎ 282-2137, 800-999-2137), 276 N Hwy 89A, PO Box 1447, Sedona, AZ 86339 Indian sites.

**Red Rock Balloon Adventures** (☎ 284-0040, 800-258-3754) Daily morning flights. Hotel pickup.
website: www.redrockballoons.com

**Sedona Adventures** (☎ 282-3500, 800-888-9494), 273 N Hwy 89A Jeep tours, vortexes, petroglyphs and scenery.
website: www.sedonaadventures.com

**Sedona Red Rock Jeep Tours** (☎ 282-6826, 800-848-7728), 270 N Hwy 89A Backcountry scenery, vortexes, archaeology, horseback rides.
website: www.redrockjeep.com

**Trail Horse Adventures** (☎ 282-7252, 800-723-3538), Lower Red Rock Loop Rd One-hour to six-day horseback rides; must be at least six years old.
website: www.trailhorseadventures.com

## Special Events
The chamber of commerce has information about the many events throughout the year; most are oriented toward the arts. The annual all-day Jazz on the Rocks (☎ 282-1985) features big-name musicians on the last Saturday in September. The concert usually sells out, so buy tickets in advance. Other noteworthy events include the Sedona Arts Festival during the third weekend in October and the lighting of the luminarias at Tlaquepaque during the second weekend in December. Both Tlaquepaque and the neighboring Los Abrigados Resort are fantastically lit up over the Christmas period.

## Places to Stay
**Camping** The USFS (☎ 282-4119) runs the following campgrounds, none with hookups or showers, in Oak Creek Canyon along N Hwy 89A: *Manzanita*, 6 miles north of town (19 sites); *Banjo Bill*, 8 miles (eight sites); *Bootlegger*, 8½ miles (10 sites); *Cave Springs*, 11½ miles (78 sites); and *Pine Flat*, 12½ miles (58 sites). Sites cost $12. The season is May through September, but some campgrounds may open longer. Be sure to arrive early: Sites are on a first-come, first-served basis, and campgrounds are often full on Friday morning for the weekend.

*Rancho Sedona RV Park* (☎ 282-7255, 888-641-4261, 135 Bear Wallow Lane) has a laundry, showers and 30 RV sites, most with full hookups, for $33 to $52. *Hawkeye Red Rock RV Park* (☎ 282-2222, 40 Art Barn Rd) offers coin showers that are available to the public and has both tent and RV sites for $19 to $31.

**Hostels** *Hostel Sedona* (☎ 282-2772, 5 Soldiers Wash Drive), behind the Burger King, offers basic accommodations in two small, single-gender dormitories, each with eight bunks and a bathroom. Rates are $15 to $18 per person. There are two rooms for couples ($30 and $40). Free tea, coffee and simple kitchen facilities are provided.

**Hotels – Budget & Mid-Range** The following are $50 to $80 for a double, which is considered budget during Sedona's lengthy (mid-February to mid-November) high season. Most also have rooms sleeping up to four or five.

The *White House Inn* (☎ 282-6680, 2986 W Hwy 89A) has 22 motel rooms, some with kitchenettes. The *Sedona Motel* (☎ 282-7187), on Hwy 179 near 89A, has 16 pleasant rooms with refrigerators and is often full. Down in Village of Oak Creek, the *Village Lodge* (☎ 284-3626, 800-890-0521, 78 Bell Rock Blvd) has rooms with refrigerators, some with fireplaces. Check their website at www.sedonalodge.com.

In the $80 to $130 range, the *Sky Ranch Lodge* (☎ 282-6400, 888-708-6400) on Airport Rd is a good value by Sedona standards; its 94 rooms, pool and hot tub are in a nicely landscaped setting above town. Some pricier and larger units have kitchenettes, fireplaces and good views; see their website at www.skyranchlodge .com. The 23 rooms at the *Matterhorn Motor Lodge* (☎ 282-7176, fax 282-0727, 230 Apple Ave) all have balconies or patios overlooking uptown Sedona and Oak Creek. Amenities include in-room coffeemakers and refrigerators, a pool and a whirlpool. There are several *chain motels*, including a Super 8, Days Inn, two Best Westerns, Comfort Inn, Quality Inn, Hampton Inn and, down in Village of Oak Creek, a Holiday Inn Express. Most have interior corridors, swimming pool and continental breakfast.

**Hotels – Top End** The *Briar Patch Inn* (☎ 282-2342, 888-809-3030, 3190 N Hwy 89A), 3 miles north of town, has 17 rustic traditional cottages (frequently renovated), some with kitchenettes or fireplaces, attractively located on eight wooded acres right next to Oak Creek, making it convenient for swimming and fishing. Most cabins are for two; a few hold four people. Rates are $159 to $325 for a double, including breakfast. There are no TVs, but classical music performances may accompany breakfast, and occasional workshops and seminars keeps guests entertained.
website: www.briarpatchinn.com

The *Junipine Resort* (☎ 282-3375, 800-742-7463, 8351 N Hwy 89A), in woodland 8 miles north of Sedona, provides easy access to hiking, swimming and fishing in Oak Creek. The 50 one- and two-bedroom townhouses (called 'creek houses'), all with kitchens, living/dining rooms, fireplaces and decks and some with lofts, range from $170 to $280. Try the excellent restaurant if you're not in the mood to cook.
website: www.junipine.com

*L'Auberge de Sedona* (☎ 282-1661, 800-272-6777, 301 L'Auberge Lane) is a 'country French inn' next to Oak Creek in uptown Sedona. Although there is a pool and whirlpool, the emphasis is on romantic relaxation and eating fancy French food (this is one of the few places in Arizona where a jacket is required for men). The highlight is the 34 romantic one- and two-bedroom cottages scattered in the gardens and along the creek. With fireplaces and no TVs, these run about $300 to $450 in the high season, while spacious rooms in the attractive lodge overlooking the cottages are $210 to $300. *The Orchards of L'Auberge*, under the same management but up the hill on Hwy 89A, overlooks the L'Auberge complex and affords the best views. The two are linked by a short aerial tram. Rooms here are more American style and run $170 to $250; most have private balconies and some have fireplaces.
website: www.lauberge.com

Of several resorts, the full-service, world-class *Enchantment Resort* (☎ 282-2900, 800-826-4180, 525 Boynton Canyon Rd) is the most spectacularly located, tucked in a canyon northwest of Sedona. Over 200 rooms, casitas and suites have private balconies and great views; trails take you high above or far into the canyon. You'll also get plenty of on-site exercise with several pools and whirlpools, seven tennis courts (lessons are available), saunas, a croquet field and a fitness center, and can recover with one of 10 kinds of massages or dozens of other treatments in their Mii amo spa. A children's program provides activities for four- to 12-year-olds. Their fine innovative restaurant and bar has Sedona's best dining views.

High-season rates are from about $350 for a spacious, amenities-filled room to over $1000 for the largest two-bedroom, three-bathroom casita suite with kitchen, living room, fireplace, deck with grill and several balconies.

website: www.enchantmentresort.com

**B&Bs** With over two dozen B&Bs, Sedona may be the B&B capital of Arizona. Most strive for a rural elegance to accompany the beauty of the surroundings, usually require advance reservations, and tend to the $125 to $250 range, with a few exceptions. Rooms with lovely views, fireplaces and spas are often featured, and fancy breakfasts are de rigeur. Often, the owners live on site and provide a personal touch. Many B&Bs don't accept young children and most are non-smoking. A good place to start looking for a place is the Sedona Bed & Breakfast Guild, which features 19 B&Bs on its website at www.bbsedona.net.

## Places to Eat

Sedona has plenty of upscale restaurants but also a good selection of budget places serving decent food. Even the pricier places are often a reasonable value, providing high-quality, innovative dishes and agreeable surroundings, especially if you take advantage of early bird specials. In fact, some visitors consider the cuisine to be as much of an attraction as the scenery. Reputable chefs are drawn to the town, rewarded both by the lovely setting and by an appreciative and (sometimes) discerning audience of food-loving travelers. Reservations are a good idea.

If you prefer to fix your own healthy meal, stop by **New Frontiers Natural Foods & Deli** (☎ 282-6311, 1420 W Hwy 89A), open 8am to 8pm daily. They also serve sandwiches to eat in or take out.

For breakfast and lunch, the **Coffeepot Restaurant** (☎ 282-6626, 2050 W Hwy 89A) has been the place to go for decades. It's always busy and service can be slow, but meals are inexpensive and the selection is huge – it has more types of omelets than most restaurants have menu items (it claims 101).

**Oaxaca** (☎ 282-4179, 321 N Hwy 89A) serves authentic Mexican fare from 8am to 9pm daily; dinners range from $10 to $15, but daily specials for about $7.50 are recommended as well. Their outdoor deck provides quiet creek views. The bustling and popular **Javelina Cantina** (☎ 203-9514, 671 Hwy 179) does a slightly more Americanized version of Mexican food for lunch and dinner. Make dinner reservations or prepare for an hour's wait. **El Rincon** (☎ 282-4648) in Tlaquepaque serves very good Sonoran Mexican lunches and dinners; closed on Mondays. Prices are somewhat higher than most Mexican places but still moderate. Out in Village of Oak Creek, the **Wild Toucan Restaurant and Cantina** (☎ 284-1604, 6376 Hwy 179) serves large portions of Mexican and American food inside or out on the patio and has a kids' menu. Dinner entrées start at around $9.

For Italian dining, the **Hideaway** (☎ 282-4204, 251 Hwy 179) serves tasty, good-value lunches and dinners (about $10) on a patio overlooking the steep and wooded walls of Oak Creek. The more expensive **Pietro's** (☎ 282-2525, 2445 W Hwy 89A) vies with **Dahl & Di Luca** (☎ 282-5219, 2321 W Hwy 89A) for the title of the best Italian food in the region. Pietro's is busier and more fun; Dahl & Di Luca is slightly quieter and more romantic. Reservations are suggested for both.

**Thai Spices** (☎ 282-0599, 2986 W Hwy 89A), despite its unpretentious exterior, serves good, spicy and inexpensive Thai food, including a wonderful coconut soup and some macrobiotic dishes. There's dinner daily and lunch on weekdays. For authentic Japanese food prepared by a chef from Tokyo (via Chicago and New York, no less) **Sasaki** (284-1757), on Hwy 179 in Village of Oak Creek at Bell Rock Blvd, is definitely recommended. Dinners run $15 to $25 served in a modern, elegant restaurant with a sushi bar and tatami room.

The **Heartline Cafe** (☎ 282-0785, 1610 W Hwy 89A) serves imaginative and tasty continental cuisine with a Southwestern twist. (The restaurant's name refers to a Zuni

Indian symbol for good health and long life rather than low-cal cooking.) It's a pretty place filled with flowers and has a patio for summer dining. Dinners, priced in the teens and $20s, are a fair value, and lunches, most under $10, are also very good. If you prefer a good old-fashioned steak, head over to *Prime Cut* (☎ 282-2943, 2250 W Hwy 89A) where top-notch cuts are in the $20s.

The *Cowboy Club* (☎ 282-4200, 241 Hwy 89A) looks like a saloon from the outside but is a large and determinedly Southwestern restaurant. The Grille Room has a good and interesting selection of snacks (rattlesnake if you must try a bite!) and meals at moderate to high prices. Pricier fine dining is offered in the Silver Saddle Room. The *Rainbow's End Steakhouse & Saloon* (☎ 282-1593, 3235 W Hwy 89A) serves excellent burgers and steaks in its restaurant, and has country & western bands and dancing on weekends.

*Shugrue's Hillside Grill* (☎ 282-5300, 671 Hwy 179) affords memorably panoramic red-rock views and both indoor and outdoor lunch and dinner, as well as jazz entertainment on weekends. The specialty is seafood, but the beef and lamb menu is just as good, though prices are at the high end. Reservations are recommended.

*Rene at Tlaquepaque* (☎ 282-9225), long considered one of Sedona's best, is a nonsmoking restaurant with upscale continental cuisine (lamb is a specialty) and some unusual meats (pronghorn antelope, ostrich) and plenty of art on the walls. Though food, service and surroundings are top notch, diners dress neatly but casually for lunch and dinner. Entrées at dinner are in the high teens and $20s. Reservations are recommended.

All Sedona's resorts have good restaurants. The most famous is *L'Auberge de Sedona* (☎ 282-1667). It's beautiful, elegant, romantic and very French. The high prices, small portions and formal dining are irresistible to many visitors; reservations and dinner jackets are required. The best value is the prix-fixe dinner menu, which changes daily and runs at about $60 for six courses. Otherwise, dinner entrées are around $30 and include French delicacies such as frog legs, pheasant, veal and escargot. The Enchantment Resort's *Yavapai Dining Room* (☎ 282-2900) serves superb food in a jaw-dropping setting (make a reservation). The Southwestern cuisine has all sorts of interesting twists and the menu changes regularly. Seafood, meat and pasta dinner entrées range from $15 to $25, a fair value for the food and a bargain considering the location. The restaurant also puts together a good champagne Sunday brunch ($28.50).

## Entertainment

Read the monthly *Red Rock Review* for local events. Nightlife is fairly quiet, with mainly lounge entertainment at the resorts. Exceptions include the *Oak Creek Brewing Company* (☎ 204-1300, 2050 Yavapai Drive), which serves hand-crafted beers and has an outdoor patio and live music (rock, blues, reggae) on most evenings. The *Rainbow's End* (see Places to Eat) also has music and dancing.

The *Sedona Cultural Park* (☎ 282-0747, 800-780-2787), at the far west end of town, opened for its first full season in 2001. From Shakespeare to the symphony, film festivals to jazz; this is where highbrow events happen amid great scenery. For details see www.sedonaculturalpark.org. Also check the *Sedona Arts Center* (see earlier in this chapter) for cultural events.

The *Harkins 6 Theatres* (☎ 282-0222, 2081 W Hwy 89A) shows movies.

## Shopping

Sedona is a prime shopping destination. The uptown area along Hwy 89A is the place to get souvenirs. The Book Loft (☎ 282-5173), 175 Hwy 179, has new and used books.

Tlaquepaque Village (☎ 282-4838) has dozens of high-quality art galleries that are also high priced, but they are a good place to start for comparison shopping. Almost opposite is the Crystal Castle (☎ 282-5910), one of several stores selling New Age books and gifts. Continuing south, Garland's Navajo Rugs (☎ 282-4070), 411 Hwy 179, has the area's best selection of rugs as well as other Indian crafts. Village of Oak Creek has Oak Creek Factory Outlets (☎ 284-2150), 6601 Hwy 179, with about 30 outlets providing name brands at discounted prices.

## Getting There & Away

The Sedona-Phoenix Shuttle (☎ 282-2066, 800-448-7988) leaves Phoenix Airport eight times a day for $35 one-way or $60 roundtrip.

## FLAGSTAFF

☎ 928 • pop 52,894; metro area 61,000 • elevation 6900 feet

Flagstaff was first settled in early 1876 by shepherd Thomas Forsyth McMillan. On the Fourth of July of that year, a pine tree was stripped of its branches and a US flag hung from it to celebrate the country's centennial, hence the town's name. The arrival of the railroad in 1882 really put Flagstaff on the map. Cattle and sheep ranching became economic mainstays, and the surrounding forests formed the basis of a small logging industry. The Lowell Observatory was founded in 1894, the still-functioning Hotel Weatherford was built in 1897, and the school that later became Northern Arizona University (NAU) was established in 1899. In the early 1900s, the Riordan Mansion and several other historic buildings were erected.

Today, tourism is Flagstaff's major industry. The cool summer temperatures attract Arizonans; it's 141 freeway miles north of Phoenix, 25 slow rural highway miles north of Sedona. From Flagstaff it's under a two-hour drive to the Grand Canyon, with the Navajo and Hopi Indian Reservations longer day trips. In winter, there's Alpine and cross-country skiing.

Although 'Flag,' as locals dub it, is a great base for travel, it is also a destination in its own right, with museums, a historical downtown, cultural attractions and northern Arizona's best nightlife. Flagstaff is Arizona's fourth largest urban area, and the largest between Phoenix and Salt Lake City.

## Information

The visitor center (☎ 774-9541, 800-842-7293), 1 E Route 66 (also called Santa Fe Ave), is in the historic Amtrak railway station. The center is open daily; the station is open from 6:15am to 11:25pm daily, when free maps and brochures are available. Two blocks north and east from the visitor center, many late-19th- and early-20th-century buildings comprise 'historic downtown.'

website: www.flagstaff.az.us or www.flagstaff arizona.org

Other services include the Coconino National Forest Supervisor's Office (☎ 527-3600), 2323 Greenlaw Ln; USFS Peaks Ranger Station (☎ 526-0866), 5075 N Hwy 89; Mormon Lake Ranger Station (☎ 774-1147), 4373 S Lake Mary Rd; Arizona Game & Fish (☎ 774-5045), 3500 S Lake Mary Rd; the library (☎ 774-4000); 300 W Aspen Ave; main post office (☎ 714-9302), 2400 Postal Blvd and the downtown branch (☎ 779-3589), 104 N Agassiz; medical center (☎ 779-3366), 1200 N Beaver; police (☎ 556-2316, 774-1414), southeast corner of Butler and Lone Tree.

## Museum of Northern Arizona

In an attractive stone building set in a pine grove, this small but thorough museum (☎ 774-5211), 3001 N Fort Valley Rd, is Flagstaff's most important and worth visiting. Galleries feature exhibits on local Indian archaeology, history and customs as well as geology, biology and the arts. Call for information about its excellent changing exhibits. The museum sponsors workshops and tours, ranging from half-day to multi-day trips exploring the surrounding country. For a program call the museum's education department (☎ 774-5213).

You can also browse the gift and bookstore, examine the exhibits and sales of Navajo, Hopi and Zuni art, and stretch your legs on the short nature trail. Museum hours are 9am to 5pm daily except major holidays. Admission is $5, seniors $4, students $3 and children aged 7 to 17 $2.

website: www.musnaz.org

## Lowell Observatory

Named after its founder, Percival Lowell, this observatory continues to be a working astronomical research center. Of many important observations made here, the discovery of the planet Pluto in 1930 is the most famous. Eight telescopes are in use, including the historic 24-inch Clark refractor (which visitors can try).

The visitor center (☎ 774-2096, 1400 W Mars Hill Rd) has exhibits and various activities, including several daily tours. Hours are 9am to 5pm in summer and vary at other times. Admission is $4 for adults; $2 for children and seniors. Frequent night programs, including lectures and stargazing through telescopes, are held year-round; call for hours.

website: www.lowell.edu

### Riordan State Historic Park

Brothers Michael and Timothy Riordan made a fortune from their Arizona Lumber Company and, in 1904, built a 13,000-sq-foot mansion to house their two families. The park preserves this building with its original furnishings, which were of the then-fashionable and luxurious Craftsman style. The building, made of stone fronted by log slabs, gives the false appearance of a palatial log cabin. The park is at 1300 Riordan Ranch St, surrounded by NAU.

Stop by the visitor center to see exhibits and a slide program. Visitors are welcome to walk the grounds and picnic, but entrance to the house is by guided tour only. Tours are worthwhile but limited to 20 people and reservations (☎ 779-4395) are recommended. Park hours are 8am to 5pm from mid-May to mid-September and 10:30am to 5pm in other months; closed December 24-25. Tours leave hourly from 9am to 4pm in summer and from 11am to 4pm the rest of the year. For a spooky tour, reserve in advance for an evening preceding Halloween. Admission is $6; $2.50 for 12- to 17-year-olds.

### Pioneer Museum & Arts Centers

Housed in the old 1908 county hospital, the Pioneer Museum (☎ 774-6272), 2340 N Fort Valley Rd, preserves Flagstaff's early history in photographs and memorabilia that ranges from vintage farm equipment to early medical instruments. Frequent special events highlight the area's past. Hours are 9am to 5pm Monday to Saturday except major holidays. Admission is by donation.

Near the museum, the Coconino Center for the Arts (☎ 779-2300), 2300 N Fort Valley Rd, exhibits a wide scope of works by local artists and presents various performances and programs. There's always something going on. A gift shop features local fine art. Hours vary. The Art Barn (☎ 774-0822), 2320 N Fort Valley Rd, has been displaying and selling both local and Reservation artists' work for three decades. Hours are 9am to 5pm daily.

### The Arboretum

The Arboretum (☎ 774-1442), 4001 S Woody Mountain Rd, has 200 acres of grounds and greenhouses dedicated to horticultural research and display. At 7150 feet on the southwest side of Flagstaff, this is the country's highest research arboretum. Locals come to discover what to grow in their backyards, and plant-loving visitors can learn about alpine flora. Hours are 9am to 5pm daily from April to December 15; closed in winter. Free guided tours are given at 11am and 1pm. Admission is $4 for adults and $1 for six- to 12-year-olds.

website: www.thearb.org

### Activities

The mountains and forests around Flagstaff offer scores of **hiking** and **mountain biking** trails – far too many to describe here. A useful resource is *Flagstaff Hikes and Mountain Bike Rides* by R & S Mangum. The USFS ranger stations have maps and advice, and bookstores have trail guides. The closest hiking is on Mt Elden; the trailhead is just past the ranger station on Hwy 89, and it's a steep 3-mile (one-way) climb to the Elden Lookout, 2300 feet above Flagstaff. Shorter and longer loops are possible – ask at the ranger station or just go to the trailhead; it's well signed.

Arizona's highest mountain, the 12,663-foot Humphreys Peak north of Flagstaff in the San Francisco Mountains, is a reasonably straightforward though strenuous hike

# FLAGSTAFF

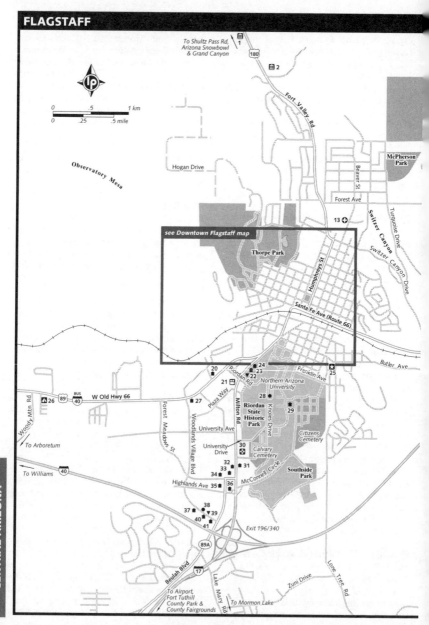

To Shultz Pass Rd,
Arizona Snowbowl
& Grand Canyon

1
180
2

Fort Valley Rd

McPherson
Park

Observatory Mesa

Hogan Drive

Beaver St

Forest Ave

Turquoise Drive

13

Switzer Canyon Drive

see Downtown Flagstaff map

Thorpe Park

S Humphreys St

Switzer Canyon Drive

Santa Fe Ave (Route 66)

Butler Ave

20
21
24
23
22

Franklin Ave

25

26

89

BUS
40

W Old Hwy 66

Forest Meadows St

Plaza Way

27

Riordan Rd

Milton Rd

Northern Arizona
University

28

29

Woody Mtn Rd

To Arboretum

University Ave

University Drive

Woodlands Village Blvd

Knoles Drive

Riordan
State Historic
Park

30

Calvary
Cemetery

Citizens
Cemetery

40

To Williams

32
33
34

31

Highlands Ave 35

36

McConnell Circle

Southside
Park

37

38
39
40
41

Exit 196/340

89A

Beulah Blvd

17

Lake Mary Rd

Zuni Drive

Lone Tree Rd

To Airport,
Fort Tuthill
County Park &
County Fairgrounds

To Mormon Lake

CENTRAL ARIZONA

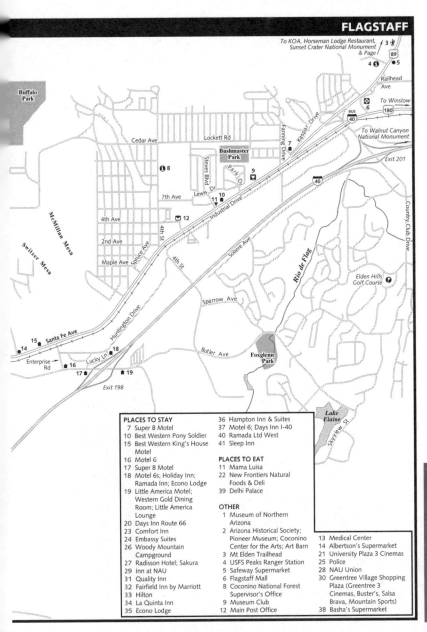

**FLAGSTAFF**

To KOA, Horseman Lodge Restaurant,
Sunset Crater National Monument
& Page

Railhead Ave

To Winslow

To Walnut Canyon
National Monument

Exit 201

Buffalo Park

Cedar Ave

Lockett Rd

Bushmaster Park

7th Ave

4th Ave

2nd Ave

Maple Ave

McMillan Mesa

Swizer Mesa

Santa Fe Ave

Enterprise Rd

Lucky Ln

Exit 198

Rio de Flag

Elden Hills
Golf Course

Country Club Drive

Sparrow Ave

Butler Ave

Foxglenn Park

Lake Elaine

Skyview St

Industrial Drive

Soliere Ave

Huntington Drive

Fanning Drive

Kaspar Drive

Park Dr

Steves Blvd

Lewis Dr

Spruce Ave

4th St

| PLACES TO STAY | |
|---|---|
| 7 | Super 8 Motel |
| 10 | Best Western Pony Soldier |
| 15 | Best Western King's House Motel |
| 16 | Motel 6 |
| 17 | Super 8 Motel |
| 18 | Motel 6s; Holiday Inn; Ramada Inn; Econo Lodge |
| 19 | Little America Motel; Western Gold Dining Room; Little America Lounge |
| 20 | Days Inn Route 66 |
| 23 | Comfort Inn |
| 24 | Embassy Suites |
| 26 | Woody Mountain Campground |
| 27 | Radisson Hotel; Sakura |
| 29 | Inn at NAU |
| 31 | Quality Inn |
| 32 | Fairfield Inn by Marriott |
| 33 | Hilton |
| 34 | La Quinta Inn |
| 35 | Econo Lodge |

| | |
|---|---|
| 36 | Hampton Inn & Suites |
| 37 | Motel 6; Days Inn I-40 |
| 40 | Ramada Ltd West |
| 41 | Sleep Inn |

**PLACES TO EAT**
| | |
|---|---|
| 11 | Mama Luisa |
| 22 | New Frontiers Natural Foods & Deli |
| 39 | Delhi Palace |

**OTHER**
| | |
|---|---|
| 1 | Museum of Northern Arizona |
| 2 | Arizona Historical Society; Pioneer Museum; Coconino Center for the Arts; Art Barn |
| 3 | Mt Elden Trailhead |
| 4 | USFS Peaks Ranger Station |
| 5 | Safeway Supermarket |
| 6 | Flagstaff Mall |
| 8 | Coconino National Forest Supervisor's Office |
| 9 | Museum Club |
| 12 | Main Post Office |

| | |
|---|---|
| 13 | Medical Center |
| 14 | Albertson's Supermarket |
| 21 | University Plaza 3 Cinemas |
| 25 | Police |
| 28 | NAU Union |
| 30 | Greentree Village Shopping Plaza (Greentree 3 Cinemas, Buster's, Salsa Brava, Mountain Sports) |
| 38 | Basha's Supermarket |

**CENTRAL ARIZONA**

in summer. Trails begin from the Arizona Snowbowl and wend through forest, eventually coming out above timberline. It is windy and cold up high, so hike prepared. The last mile of the trail is over crumbly and loose volcanic rock, so you'll need decent boots, and you must stay on the trails to protect the delicate alpine tundra. No camping or fires are allowed. The elevation, steepness and loose footing make for a breathless ascent, but the views make the work worthwhile. The total distance is 4½ miles one-way; allow six to eight hours roundtrip if you are in average shape.

**Downhill skiing** and **snowboarding** at the Arizona Snowbowl (☎ 779-1951, snow report 779-4577) is popular with Arizonans. It's small but high, with four lifts servicing 30 runs between 9200 and 11,500 feet; beginners to experts. Day lodges offer rentals, lessons and meals, but no accommodations. The season is mid-December to mid-April if the snowfall is good. In summer, you can take the longest lift (climbing to 11,500 feet) for **sightseeing** tours from 10am to 4pm. The trip takes almost half an hour, provides fine views and costs $9 for adults, with discounts for seniors and kids. Arizona Snowbowl is 7 miles northwest of Flagstaff along Hwy 180, then another 7 miles on Snowbowl Rd; chains or 4WD may be required but ski buses for a few dollars are available. website: www.arizonasnowbowl.com

**Cross-country skiing** is good at the Flagstaff Nordic Center (☎ 779-1951), 15 miles northwest of Flagstaff on Hwy 180, with 30 miles of groomed trails, skiing lessons, rentals and food. Trail passes cost $10. Past the Nordic Center on Hwy 180, there are plenty of USFS cross-country skiing pullouts where you can park and ski for free (no facilities or rentals are provided). The season is short, so call for conditions.

Sports stores that have maps, books, gear or rental equipment include Peace Surplus (☎ 779-4521), 14 W Route 66; Babbitt's (☎ 774-4775), 12 E Aspen Ave; Mountain Sports (☎ 779-5156, 800-286-5156), 1800 S Milton Rd; Aspen Sports (☎ 779-1935), 15 N San Francisco; and Absolute Bikes (☎ 779-

5969), 18 N San Francisco. These are all good information sources.

Vertical Relief Rock Climbing (☎ 556-9909), 205 S San Francisco, has 6000 sq ft of artificial indoor walls to practice **rock climbing**. Routes range from beginner level to the most difficult grades. Hours are 10am to 11pm Monday to Friday and noon to 8pm on weekends. They also have classes on real rock surrounding Flagstaff.
website: www.verticalrelief.com

Hitchin' Post Stables (☎ 774-1719, 774-7131), 448 S Lake Mary Rd, has day-long **horseback riding** trips to Walnut Canyon and other destinations on request; in the winter, horse-drawn sleigh rides are offered.

## Special Events

Flagstaff is busy throughout the summer with many events, often held simultaneously. The visitor center has details. From late June to mid-August, in the Coconino Center for the Arts, there is a Festival of Native American Arts with performances and art exhibits. The Museum of Northern Arizona hosts Indian arts exhibits throughout the summer with some weekends highlighting the work of specific tribes, including

the Zuni, Hopi and Navajo. The Flagstaff Winter Festival throughout February is also a big highlight, with sled dog races, skiing excursions and races, and other snowy events.

## Places to Stay

Flagstaff provides the best cheap and moderate lodging in this region for most of the year. Summer is the high season and hotel prices rise accordingly – a room that costs $20 in April can be $50 on an August weekend. Avoid summer weekends if possible.

Flagstaff Central Reservations (☎ 527-8333, 800-527-8388) makes reservations for the better motels and B&Bs in northern Arizona; call or get information online at www.flagstaffrooms.com.

**Camping** Campgrounds can fill in summer, so make reservations where possible. *Fort Tuthill County Park* (☎ 774-3464), near I-17 exit 337, has 100 tent sites for $9 and 14 sites with hookups for $13. There are no showers. The campground is open from May to September. *Woody Mountain Campground* (☎ 774-7727, 2727 W Route 66), offers 146 sites for tents and RVs for $16 to $22, as well as a pool, playground and coin laundry. It is open from April through October. *Flagstaff KOA* (☎ 526-9926, 800-562-3524, 5803 N Hwy 89) has over 200 year-round sites, many with full RV hookups, ranging in price from $20 (tents) to $27 (full hookups).

**Budget** Cheap and basic motels line Route 66, especially the 3-mile stretch east of downtown and near NAU southwest of downtown. Route 66 parallels the railway and the cheap places don't have soundproof rooms. Almost any time from September to May you can cruise along here and find 15 motels advertising rooms for about $20, or even less; prices rise dramatically during busy summer weekends. Check the room before you pay, though – some are worse than others. They are perfectly satisfactory if you are paying $20 off-season, not if you are paying more.

Flagstaff attracts international budget travelers, many of whom stay downtown in two independent youth hostels, both owned by the same folks. Look for the huge neon 'Downtowner' sign to find them. The *Grand Canyon International Hostel* (☎ 779-9421, 19 S San Francisco) sleeps 62 people and *Dubeau International Hostel* (☎ 774-6731, 19 W Phoenix Ave) handles another 58. They each charge $14 to $16 per person in dorm rooms (four people maximum at the Grand Canyon) and have some private doubles (shared bathroom) for $28 to $35. Breakfast is included and guests have use of a kitchen, BBQ area, laundry and TV/video room. Internet access is available as well. The hostels offer pickup from the Greyhound station and arrange reasonably priced tours to the Grand Canyon and other local attractions.
website: www.grandcanyonhostel.com

The *Weatherford Hotel* (☎ 779-1919, weathtel@infomagic.com, 23 N Leroux) dates back to 1898 and was then northern Arizona's finest hotel and is now Flagstaff's most historic. Eight rooms with a turn-of-the-19th-century feel (no TV or telephone) rent for $50 to $60. The popular Charly's (restaurant and pub) is downstairs, and the Zane Grey ballroom is an attractive and authentic-looking old-fashioned place for a drink. The entertainment might mean some noise in the rooms on weekends.

There are plenty of *chain motels* including four Motel 6s, all of which have pools (in summer) and singles ranging from the high $20s to $50s depending on season. Most other chains are represented, often with two or more hotels (see map). A good area to look for the cheaper ones is I-40, exit 198. The clean *Budget Host Saga Motel* (☎ 779-3631, 820 W Route 66) has a pool and charges $50 to $60 in summer. The *Canyon Inn* (☎ 774-7301, 888-822-6966, 500 S Milton) has rooms for $36 to $65.

**Mid-Range** Scenes of the movie *Casablanca* were filmed at the 1927 *Monte Vista Hotel* (☎ 779-6971, 800-545-3068, 100 N San Francisco), where many of the 50 rooms and suites are named after the film stars who slept in them. Rooms are comfortable and old-fashioned, but they are not

# DOWNTOWN FLAGSTAFF

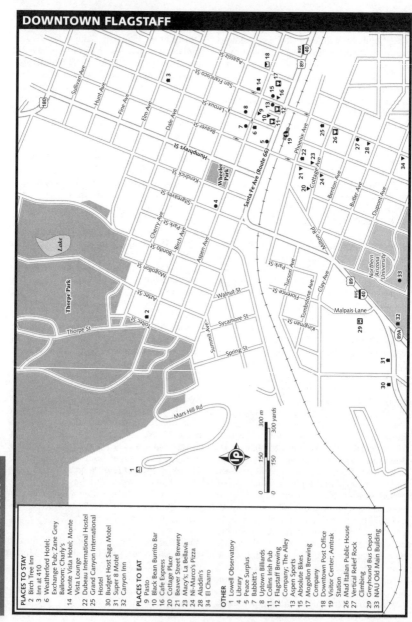

luxurious (John Wayne and Humphrey Bogart handled it just fine), though TV and telephone are included. Rates are $60 to $120 in summer. The popular basement bar is deep enough not to disturb the peace.
website: www.hotelmontevista.com

Many of the standard *chain motels* are priced in the high middle range, especially in summer. A good place to look for the better ones, most with interior corridors, pools, whirlpools and continental breakfasts, and some with in-room coffeemakers and other facilities, is north of I-40 exit 196 where it intersects with I-17 exit 340 (see map).

The *Inn at NAU* (☎ 523-1616), on the east side of the campus, is used as a training facility for NAU's School of Hotel & Restaurant Management. The inn's 19 non-smoking rooms are spacious and well maintained, and the student staff is well-trained and eager to please. Rates range from $60 in winter to $100 in summer, including a hot breakfast buffet, and are a a good value. A restaurant and lounge serves lunch and dinner on some days.
website: www.nau.edu/~hrm

**Top End** Of several hotels charging over $100 for a double in summer, the *Little America Motel* (☎ 779-7900, 800-865-1401, 2515 E Butler Ave) is one of the better ones, set amid acres of lawns and pine trees. The 250 spacious rooms have balconies, refrigerators and large TVs with Nintendo, and there is a pool, spa, and exercise room as well as a 24-hour coffee shop, a good restaurant and a lounge providing occasional entertainment. Rates are a a good value at about $110 to $120; a few suites with fireplaces or saunas go up to about $200.
website: www.littleamerica.com

The *Radisson Hotel* (☎ 773-8888, 1175 W Route 66) is the best chain hotel near downtown. The ambience is trans-Pacific, with a Japanese restaurant and Southwestern coffee shop, severely square chandeliers and tightly clipped plants in the lobby, and contemporary desert colors in the guest rooms. Facilities include a pool, spa, sauna, steamroom and exercise equipment.

Almost 200 large and attractive rooms are priced at $100 to $170 in summer; there are a few pricier suites. Room service is available and the restaurants are both very good.

*Comfi Cottages* (☎ 774-0731, 888-774-0731) offers six quaint 'cottages,' each with a kitchen stocked with your choice of breakfast items – cook your own whenever you feel like it. Cottages range from one bedroom/one bathroom at $120 a night to four bedrooms/two bathrooms at $260 a night. All are less than a mile from downtown, and have yards or gardens with barbecue grills and bicycles available for use. Some have fireplaces.
website: www.comficottages.com

If you prefer a B&B, the *Birch Tree Inn* (☎ 774-1042, 888-774-1042, 824 W Birch Ave) is a 1917 house with a wraparound verandah, a game room with billiards and an outdoor hot tub. Two rooms with shared bath are $69 and three more with private bath are $99 to $119, including a big breakfast and afternoon tea and snacks.
website: www.birchtreeinn.com

The *Inn at 410* (☎ 774-0088, 800-774-2008, 410 N Leroux), an elegant and fully renovated 1907 house, offers nine spacious and unique bedrooms, each with private bath, coffeemaker and refrigerator, and most with a fireplace or whirlpool bath. This popular place charges $135 to $190 a double, including full gourmet breakfast and afternoon snacks. Two units have adjoining rooms suitable for two children.
website: www.inn410.com

### Places to Eat
Local laws prohibit smoking in all city restaurants (but not restaurant/bars).

**Breakfast** A long-time favorite coffee shop, *Macy's* (☎ 774-2243, 14 S Beaver) also serves good pastries and eclectic light meals. Students, outdoorsy types and coffee lovers crowd this place, which is open from 6am daily. Neighboring *La Bellavia* (☎ 774-8301, 18 S Beaver) is equally casual, has just as much caffeine in its espressos and cappuccinos and serves breakfast and lunch.

CENTRAL ARIZONA

In the heart of downtown, *Cafe Express* (☎ 774-0541, 16 N San Francisco) has something for almost everyone except dedicated carnivores, including various coffees, vegetarian and natural-food meals and salads, juices, beer, wine, and pastries, which you can consume on the outdoor deck. Daily hours are 7am to 10pm.

**American** For one of Flag's best fresh seafood selections, including an oyster bar, try *Buster's* (☎ 774-5155, 1800 S Milton Rd), which also offers steaks and prime rib. While most dinner entrées are in the teens, you can eat cheaper 'sunset dinners' between 6:30 and 7:30pm. Inexpensive lunches include good salads, sandwiches and burgers. The bar selection is excellent and Buster's is popular (and often noisy) with locals and tourists.

The *Western Gold Dining Room* (☎ 779-2741), in the Little America Hotel, has a lunchtime buffet and one of the best American dinner menus in town.

For big old-fashioned steaks, *Horseman Lodge Restaurant* (☎ 526-2655, 8500 N Hwy 89) is a fine choice and is locally popular. It also has a wide selection of other American food.

*New Frontiers Natural Foods & Deli* (☎ 774-5747, 1000 S Milton Rd) has natural-food sandwiches, salads, soups, juices etc to go, or you can eat in the inexpensive deli.

**Mexican** Of the dozen or so Mexican restaurants in town, *Salsa Brava* (☎ 774-1083, 1800 S Milton Rd) with Guadalajaran rather than Sonoran food, is a good popular choice. For cheaper Mexican food, *El Charro* (☎ 779-0552, 409 S San Francisco) is good and may have mariachis playing on weekends. The cheap *Black Bean Burrito Bar* (☎ 779-9905, 12 E Route 66), in a little alley/plaza, is a simple diner with big burritos and a great variety of fillings. You can eat in (no comfort here, but there's a good people-watching window) or take out.

**Italian** Flag's best Italian restaurant is traditionally *Mama Luisa* (☎ 526-6809, 2710 E N Steves Blvd). Open for dinner only, Mama Luisa serves a wide range of Italian food for $9 to $18 in an appropriately cozy, red-checked-tablecloth setting. Popular *Pasto* (☎ 779-1937, 19 E Aspen) has a courtyard and vies with Mama Luisa for 'best Italian' honors. Again, dinner only. *Ni-Marco's Pizza* (☎ 779-2691, 101 S Beaver) is open for lunch and dinner and is popular with the student crowd.

**Asian** The recommended Japanese *Sakura* (☎ 773-9118), in the Radisson Hotel, has fresh seafood served either as sushi or grilled right in front of you. Steak and other food is also available sliced, diced and flamed tableside. Most entrées are in the teens.

At the other end of both the price range and the Asian continent is *Aladdin's* (☎ 213-0033, 211 S San Francisco), which serves inexpensive Middle Eastern and Greek food to dine in, outside or take-away. For Indian food, try the *Delhi Palace* (☎ 556-0019, 2700 S Woodlands Village Blvd), offering all-you-can-eat lunch buffets ($5.95) as well as à la carte dinners.

**Continental** The *Cottage Place* (☎ 774-8431, 126 W Cottage Ave) has several intimate and attractive rooms in an early-20th-century house. The varied continental menu has entrées (including several vegetarian plates) ranging in price from $16 to $26. The inviting and delicious appetizers pose a minor dilemma in that the entrées already include both soup and salad; it's best to come hungry and with a reservation. Dinners are served daily except Monday. Beer and wine are the only alcoholic beverages served.

**Pub Grub** *Beaver Street Brewery* (☎ 779-0079, 11 S Beaver) is very popular for its microbrewery (five handmade ales are usually on tap) and well-prepared gourmet pizzas as well as other food. It opens at 11:30am and has a beer garden in the summer. *Charly's* (☎ 779-1919, 23 N Leroux), on the ground floor of the historic Weatherford Hotel, offers soups, salads and sandwiches for $4 to $8 as well as a small selection of steak, chicken and pasta dinners in the $11 to $16 range.

## Entertainment

During the summer there are many cultural performances (see Special Events, earlier in this chapter) and skiers, students and passers-through seem to fuel a lively nightlife year-round. Read the Sundial (the Friday entertainment supplement to Flag's *Arizona Daily Sun*) and the free *Flagstaff Live* (published on the first and third Thursday of the month) to find out what's happening around town.

Several cinemas and multiplexes scattered around town show movies.

Flagstaff has plenty of bars, especially downtown, where you can relax to live music (usually on weekends and, sometimes with a small cover). Wander around a few blocks and make your choice. The *Exchange Pub* in the Weatherford Hotel has varied live music, ranging from bluegrass to blues, folk to fusion, jazz to jive. On the hotel's top floor, the fancy *Zane Grey Ballroom* is worth checking out for… who knows? Jazz? Tango? Poetry? The *Monte Vista Lounge* (☎ 774-2403), in the Monte Vista Hotel, has alternative music. The *Flagstaff Brewing Co* (☎ 773-1442, 16 E Route 66) and *The Alley* (☎ 774-7929, 22 E Hwy 89), nearby, both have handcrafted beers and a variety of live music, as does the *Mogollon Brewing Company* (☎ 773-8950, 15 N Agassiz). *Collins Irish Pub*, Leroux at Route 66, is somewhat more upscale.

More sedate live music can be heard on weekends at the *Little America Lounge* (☎ 779-2741) in the Little America Hotel. For a livelier time, try the far-from-sedate country & western music, both live and recorded, at the *Museum Club* (☎ 526-9434, 3404 E Route 66). This popular barnlike place dates from the 1920s and '30s, and used to house a taxidermy museum, which may account for its local nickname, 'The Zoo.' For pure spectacle, The Zoo, with its open and friendly cowboy spirit and spacious dance floor (which the locals unsuccessfully try to hide with their huge Stetsons) is not to be missed. Check out the entrance, which is made from a single, forked trunk of a large ponderosa pine. The Zoo provides free taxi service home (☎ 774-2934), if you're planning on making a hard-drinkin' night of it.

*Uptown Billiards* (☎ 773-0551, 114 N Leroux) has plenty of pool tables and a good beer selection in a nonsmoking environment. The *Mad Italian Public House* (☎ 779-1820, 101 S San Francisco) is a decent pub with pool tables.

## Getting There & Away

Pulliam Airport is 3 miles south of town on I-17. America West Express has several flights a day to and from Phoenix.

Greyhound (☎ 774-4573), 399 S Malpais Lane, sends buses between Flagstaff and Albuquerque along I-40; to Las Vegas (via Kingman and Bullhead City); to Los Angeles (via Kingman); and to Phoenix.

Open Roads (☎ 800-766-7117) and Grand Canyon (☎ 866-746-8439) offer shuttles to the Grand Canyon for $20 one-way, plus the national park entrance fee.

There are no buses north to Page. Ask the hostels about shuttles.

## Getting Around

Pine Country Transit (☎ 779-6624) has three local bus routes running Monday to Saturday during the daytime. There is no service on Sunday.

Flagstaff Airport has offices of the following car-rental agencies: Avis, Budget, Enterprise, Hertz, National and Sears.

A Friendly Cab (☎ 774-4444), Sun Taxi (☎ 774-7400, 800-483-4488), Alternative Taxi (☎ 213-1111) and Arizona Taxi & Tours (☎ 779-1111) provide local and long-distance taxi service.

## AROUND FLAGSTAFF

The places described here are within an hour's drive of Flagstaff.

## Sunset Crater Volcano National Monument

Sunset Crater (elevation 8029 feet) was formed in AD 1064–65 by volcanic eruptions that covered large areas with lava and

## Grand Falls of the Little Colorado

The Grand Falls give an insight into Southwestern hydrography. The Little Colorado River is a minor tributary of the Colorado, and like many Arizonan rivers, it is nearly dry for much of the year. During spring runoff, however, the river swells, and the Grand Falls come into being. The 185-foot drop is impressive, with muddy-brown spray giving the falls their local nickname of 'Chocolate Falls.' The best time for viewing is March and April, although earlier in the year can be good if there has been enough winter precipitation. Occasional summer storms will also fill the falls.

The falls are on the Navajo Reservation. Drive 14 miles east of Flagstaff along I-40 to the Winona exit, then backtrack northwest about 2 miles to Leupp Rd. Head northeast on Leupp Rd for 13 miles to the signed turn for Grand Falls. An unpaved road, passable by car, leads 10 miles to the river and a quarter-mile trail goes to a falls overlook. The Navajo tribe allows free access to the falls, where there are basic picnic facilities.

ash. Minor eruptions continued for over 200 years, but none are currently predicted. Today, Loop Rd goes through the Bonito Lava Flow and skirts the Kana-a Lava Flow. Overlooks and a mile-long interpretive trail enable visitors to get a good look at volcanic features, although walking on the unstable cinders of the crater itself is prohibited.

The visitor center (☎ 526-0502), 2 miles from Hwy 89, houses a seismograph and other exhibits pertaining to volcanology and the region. Rangers give interpretive programs in summer. Hours are 8am to 6pm in summer, 9am to 5pm in winter. Admission is $3 for those over 16 (all passes honored) and includes the Wupatki National Monument (see the following section). The 1-mile interpretive Lava Flow Nature Trail, with a quarter-mile wheelchair accessible, is a mile beyond the center.

Combine your trip to Sunset Crater with a side trip to neighboring Wupatki National Monument for an excellent day-long excursion from Flagstaff, covering 80 miles roundtrip.

### Wupatki National Monument

This monument is off Hwy 89 about 30 miles north of Flagstaff, or can be reached by continuing along the Loop Rd from Sunset Crater. Wupatki has Ancestral Puebloan sites that differ from most others

because they are freestanding rather than built into a cliff or cave. They have a distinct southern influence, indicating trading links with people from the south. The pueblos date mainly from the 1100s and early 1200s, and some of today's Hopi Indians are descended from the ancient inhabitants of Wupatki; the Hopi call their ancestors the Hisatsinom.

**Information** The narrow Loop Rd passes the visitor center and continues on past pullouts or short side roads that lead to the pueblos. Five pueblos are easily visited, and Crack-in-Rock requires an overnight backpacking trip. A brochure describing them in detail is available upon admission. Other pullouts along Loop Rd offer scenic views.

At the visitor center (☎ 679-2365), 18 miles beyond Sunset Crater, there is a museum, gift and bookshop, and vending machines. In summer, rangers may give talks or lead walks. Hours are 8am to 5pm (to 6pm in summer, open at 9am in winter) daily except Christmas. See Sunset Crater for admission information.

**Crack-in-Rock Pueblo** can be visited only on a ranger-led 16-mile roundtrip weekend backpacking tour offered in April and October; call for fees. You must supply all equipment, food and water. Each trip is limited to 15 participants, and these are chosen by lottery; apply two months in advance. For further information, call the visitor center or write to Wupatki National Monument, Attention CIR Reservations, HC33, Box 444A, NO.14, Flagstaff, AZ 86004.

## Walnut Canyon National Monument

The Sinagua buildings at Walnut Canyon are not as immediately impressive as those at other nearby sites, but their spectacular setting makes this a worthwhile visit. The buildings are set in shallow caves in the near-vertical walls of a small limestone butte set like an island in the middle of the heavily pine-forested canyon.

The mile-long **Island Trail** steeply descends 185 feet (with more than 200 stairs) and then encircles the 'island,' passing 25 cliff-dwelling rooms; many more can be seen in the distance. A shorter, wheelchair-accessible **Rim Trail** affords several views of the rooms from a distance.

A visitor center (☎ 526-3367) is near the beginning of both trails and has a museum, bookstore and overlook. Rangers may give talks during the summer; the museum is open 8am to 5pm (until 6pm in summer, from 9am in winter) daily except Christmas. The Island Trail closes one hour before the visitor center. Admission is $3 per person over 16; all passes are honored. No food or overnight facilities are available.

## Meteor Crater

A huge meteor crashing into our planet almost 50,000 years ago produced this crater, 570 feet deep and almost a mile across. It was used as a training ground for some of the Apollo astronauts; the on-site museum has exhibits about meteors and space missions. Descending into the crater isn't allowed, but you can walk the 3½-mile Rim Trail. However, apart from a big hole in the ground, there's not much to see, and several readers suggest that it is an over-priced attraction.

The crater (☎ 289-2362, 800-289-5898) is privately owned and operated, and national park passes aren't accepted. Hours are 6am to 6pm mid-May to mid-September and

8am to 5pm the rest of the year. Admission is $12, $5 for six- to 17-year-olds.

*Meteor Crater RV Park* (☎ 289-4002) has 80 RV sites with hookups for $20 and a few tent sites for $19. Showers, coin laundry, a playground, coffee shop and groceries are available.

## WILLIAMS

☎ 928 • pop 2842 • elevation 6762 feet

Mountain man Bill Williams passed through here several times before he died in 1849, and settlers in 1874 named the town after him. In 1901, the railway to the Grand Canyon opened, making Williams a tourist center. Easy road and car access closed the railway in 1969, only to return in 1989 as a popular historic steam train. The visitor center has a Route 66 display that relates that Williams had the last traffic light on that famous highway. The town is the closest to the Grand Canyon with moderately priced accommodations.

## Information

The visitor's center (☎ 635-4061, 800-863-0546), 200 W Railroad Ave, is open 8am to 5pm daily (till 6:30 in summer) and is operated by both the chamber of commerce and the USFS. Pick up a walking tour brochure here if the turn-of-the-19th-century buildings downtown spark your interest. Check the website (williamschamber.com) for more information. Other services include the library (☎ 635-2263), 113 S 1st; post office (☎ 635-4572) 120 S 1st; and police (☎ 635-4461), 501 W Rt 66.

## Things to See & Do

The **Grand Canyon Railway** uses turn-of-the-19th-century steam locomotives from late May through September and 1950s diesels the rest of the year. The trip is 2¼ hours to the Grand Canyon, with characters in period costume offering historical and regional narration or strolling around playing a banjo and answering questions. Often, the train is held up by train robbers, but the sheriff usually takes care of them. Roundtrips allow about 3 hours at the canyon. Trains leave at 10am daily except

December 24 and 25, returning to Williams by 5:45pm.

The fare was $3.95 when the railway opened in 1901. Today, passengers travel coach class ($55 roundtrip, $25 for two- to 16-year-olds) in a 1923 car, or in four other classes (up to $140/110). Tax is an extra 9.4% and national park admission is $8 extra for adults. It's a short walk from the Grand Canyon train depot to the rim, but narrated bus tours of various lengths and prices are also offered, as are various overnight packages with accommodations at either Williams or the Grand Canyon (hotel reservations essential). Contact the railway (☎ 773-1976, 800-843-8724) for information or reservations.
website: www.thetrain.com

The **Grand Canyon Deer Farm** (☎ 635-4073, 800-926-3337), located near I-40 exit 171, 8 miles east of town, is a petting and feeding zoo with several deer species, llamas, peacocks and other animals. Fawning season (May to July) is an especially nice time to go with kids. The farm is open daily and admission is $6 for adults, $5 for seniors and $3.50 for three- to 13-year-olds.

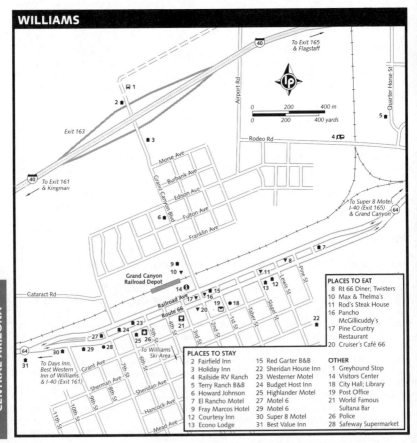

**WILLIAMS**

**PLACES TO STAY**
2 Fairfield Inn
3 Holiday Inn
4 Railside RV Ranch
5 Terry Ranch B&B
6 Howard Johnson
7 El Rancho Motel
9 Fray Marcos Hotel
12 Courtesy Inn
13 Econo Lodge
15 Red Garter B&B
22 Sheridan House Inn
23 Westerner Motel
24 Budget Host Inn
25 Highlander Motel
27 Motel 6
29 Motel 6
30 Super 8 Motel
31 Best Value Inn

**PLACES TO EAT**
8 Rt 66 Diner; Twisters
10 Max & Thelma's
11 Rod's Steak House
16 Pancho McGillicuddy's
17 Pine Country Restaurant
20 Cruiser's Café 66

**OTHER**
1 Greyhound Stop
14 Visitors Center
18 City Hall; Library
19 Post Office
21 World Famous Sultana Bar
26 Police
28 Safeway Supermarket

CENTRAL ARIZONA

The small **Williams Ski Area** (☎ 635-9330), 4 miles south of town along 4th St, has a poma lift that climbs from 7500 to 8150 feet and serves runs for beginner, intermediate and advanced skiers. The season depends on the snowfall.

## Places to Stay
Rates from mid-May to mid-September (given below) can halve in winter, or rise during special events and holidays. Summer reservations are advised unless you arrive by early afternoon.

**Camping** *Railside RV Ranch* (☎ 635-4077, 888-635-4077, railside@thegrandcanyon .com, 877 Rodeo Rd) is the closest campground to the center, with 100 RV sites with hookups for $20; four sites allow tents. There are showers, a game room and laundry.

*Red Lake Campground & Hostel* (☎ 635-5321, 800-581-4753, redlake@az access.com), on Hwy 64 eight miles north of I-40 exit 165, has 14 RV and eight year-round sites. Tenting costs $12, RVs with hookups cost $18, and there are coin showers and a grocery store. Summer reservations are recommended.

The *Circle Pines KOA* (☎ 635-4545, 800-732-0537), half a mile north of I-40 exit 167, has about 150 year-round sites ranging in price from $18 for tents to $27 for RVs with full hookups, and six Kamping Kabins available for $37. There are hot showers, a coin laundry, an indoor pool and spa, a playground and stables offering horseback rides in summer. *Grand Canyon KOA* (☎ 635-2307), on Hwy 64 five miles north of I-40 exit 165, has 100 sites open from March through October at about the same price and with similar facilities (no stables).

The Kaibab National Forest south of Williams operates several *campgrounds* open on a first-come, first-served basis from May to October, with drinking water but no showers or RV hookups. Fishing and boating is possible.

**Budget** There are 32 hostel beds in rooms sleeping up to four people at *Red Lake*

*Campground & Hostel* (see Camping). Rates are $14 per person (more for private rooms) with winter discounts.

In Williams itself, you'll see a number of motels offering rooms in the $20s in winter, but for $40 to $55 in summer when they fill up early. The most reliable of these include the 12-room *Highlander Motel* (☎ 635-2541, 800-653-0609, 533 W Route 66); the 26-room *Budget Host Inn* (☎ 635-4415, 800-745-4415, 620 W Route 66); the 24-room *Courtesy Inn* (☎ 635-2619, 800-235-7029, 344 E Route 66), which serves coffee and doughnuts for breakfast; and the 24-room *Westerner Motel* (☎ 635-4312, 800-385-8608, 530 W Route 66).

**Mid-Range** Among the *chain motels* in town are two Motel 6s, two Super 8s and an Econo Lodge. Shortly north of town at I-40, exit 163, are a Holiday Inn and Fairfield Inn, a bit closer is a Howard Johnson, and west of town near exit 161 you'll find a Days Inn and Best Western.

The pleasant *El Rancho Motel* (☎ 635-2552, 800-228-2370, ranchol@frontier net.com, 617 E Route 66), has 25 rooms with coffeemakers (some with microwaves and refrigerators) and a pool in summer. Summer rates are in the $60s. The *Best Value Inn* (☎ 635-2202, 888-315-2378, norris motel@thegrandcanyon.com, 1001 W Route 66) has a pool and whirlpool, and refrigerators in its 33 rooms which are in the $60s in summer. A few suites are about $100.

**Top End** The *Fray Marcos Hotel* (☎ 635-4010, 235 N Grand Canyon Blvd), next to the Williams Grand Canyon Railway depot, is managed by the railway, which uses the hotel for its overnight packages. Although new, the hotel was built in the style of the original railroad hotel, part of which now forms a museum. About 200 spacious modern rooms rent for $120 a double in summer, $80 in winter with discounts if you buy a railway package. The hotel features interior corridors, indoor pool and whirlpool, and an exercise room.

Downtown, the *Red Garter B&B* (☎ 635-1484, 800-328-1484, 137 W Railroad Ave) has four rooms with private baths in a re-stored 1890s bordello. Rates of $75 to $110 include a continental breakfast in the downstairs bakery.

website: www.redgarter.com

The smoke- and alcohol-free *Terry Ranch B&B* (☎ *635-4171, 800-210-5908, 701 Quarter Horse Rd*), has four rooms with turn-of-the-19th-century furnishings, all with fireplaces and TV/VCRs, and one with a two-person jetted tub. A wrap-around verandah makes a nice place to relax. Rates are $115 to $155 with a full breakfast; see the website at www.terryranchbnb.com.

The ten-room *Sheridan House Inn* (☎ *635-9441, 888-635-9345, 460 E Sheridan*) is owned by a chef who prepares great breakfasts and provides a complimentary buffet dinner and drinks in the inn bar every evening. The smoke-free inn features a fitness room, whirlpool, entertainment room, a video and CD library (and all the rooms have TV/VCRs and CD players). Summer rates range from $135 to $195; check the website at www.thegrand canyonbbinn.com for information.

## Places to Eat

Note that restaurant hours may be short-ened in winter.

If you're looking for simple family restaurants serving reasonably priced standard American food all day, try the *Rt 66 Diner* (☎ *635-9955, 425 E Route 66*) and *Pine Country Restaurant* (☎ *635-9718, 107 N Grand Canyon Blvd*).

*Twisters* (☎ *635-0266, 417 E Route 66*) is a '50s-style soda fountain with ice cream treats, hot dogs, burgers etc. Route 66 fans

will also want to check the memorabilia in *Cruiser's Café 66* (☎ *635-2445, 233 W Route 66*) with a widely varied menu in the $6 to $15 range.

For a more upscale eatery there is *Max & Thelma's* (☎ *635-8970*) at the Grand Canyon Railroad complex, named after the railroad owners. Breakfast, lunch and dinner buffets are inexpensive and crowded, but dinner in the dining room is a more sedate and pricey affair, with entrées in the teens and $20s.

*Pancho McGillicuddy's* (☎ *635-4150, 141 W Railroad Ave*) is a 'Mexican cantina' popular with tourists; it also serves gringo food and has a patio outside. The restaurant is housed in one of the town's oldest buildings – constructed of stone in 1895, the building survived several fires that burned down other buildings in this block. This was once known as 'Saloon Row,' with many bars, brothels and opium dens along here. If only walls could talk… Since they don't, you'll have to wet your whistle with a brew at the quirky *World Famous Sultana Bar* (*301 W Route 66*).

*Rod's Steak House* (☎ *635-2671, 301 E Route 66*) has been here half a century and is among the best in town. Apart from good steaks priced in the teens and $20s, there are cheaper chicken and fish dinners and a kids' menu.

## Getting There & Away

Greyhound (☎ *635-0870*) stops at Williams Chevron gas station at 1050 N Grand Canyon Blvd.

Amtrak stops on the outskirts of town, not at the Grand Canyon Railway depot.

# Northeastern Arizona

Some of Arizona's most beautiful and photogenic landscapes lie in the northeastern corner of the state. Between the fabulous buttes of Monument Valley on the Utah state border and the fossilized logs of the Petrified Forest National Park at the southern edge of the area lie lands that are locked into ancient history. Here is the Navajo National Monument, with ancient, deserted pueblos, and Canyon de Chelly, with equally ancient pueblos adjacent to contemporary farms. Here are mesas topped by some of the oldest continuously inhabited villages on the continent. Traditional and modernized Navajo hogans dot the landscape, and Hopi kivas nestle into it. Native Americans have inhabited this land for centuries; it is known today as the Navajo and Hopi Indian Reservations.

Tribal laws take precedence over state laws, although both tribes accept federal laws and are fiercely proud and patriotic citizens. The Navajo Indian Reservation is the country's biggest and spills over into the neighboring states of Utah, Colorado and New Mexico. It completely surrounds the Hopi Indian Reservation. It's the biggest reservation partly because its harsh landscape didn't seem to offer much when reservations were doled out.

The Navajo and Hopi are recent neighbors. The Hopi are the descendants of people who left more westerly pueblos in the 12th and early 13th centuries, while the Navajos are descendants of Athapaskan Indians who arrived from the north between the 14th and 16th centuries. The two peoples speak different languages and have different religions and customs. Today, they live side by side in an uneasy alliance, disagreeing, often bitterly, on their reservation borders, a dispute exacerbated by tribal population growth.

## Highlights

- Standing in a 225-million-year-old conifer forest at Petrified Forest National Park
- Watching the sun set over the Painted Desert
- Attending the Annual Navajo Nation Fair, the world's biggest Indian event
- Horseback riding at beautiful Canyon de Chelly
- Spending the night in a Navajo hogan
- Hiking in the Ancestral Puebloan sites at Navajo National Monument
- Visiting the Hopi village of Old Oraibi, which has been continuously inhabited since the early 12th century

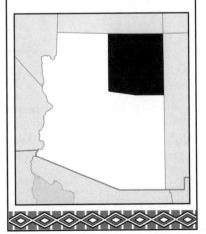

# I-40 Corridor

The southern boundary of the Navajo Reservation is roughly paralleled by I-40.

### WINSLOW
☎ 928 • pop 9520 • elevation 4880 feet
Established as a railroad town in 1882, Winslow soon became a ranching center and remains an important shipping center.

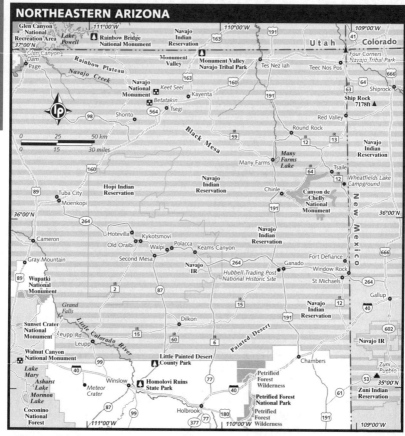

NORTHEASTERN ARIZONA

Some 60 miles south of the Hopi mesas, Winslow provides the closest off-reservation accommodations. The high school at Oak and Berry is shaped like a hogan.

Greyhound (☎ 289-2171) stops at the Pilot Truck Stop, on N Park Dr next to Walmart.

## Information

The chamber of commerce (☎ 289-2434) is by I-40 exit 253, next to one of Peter Toth's famous wooden Indian carvings. Its website is www.winslowarizona.org. The library

(☎ 289-4982), 420 W Gilmore, has Internet access. Other services available include the post office (☎ 289-2131), 223 Williamson; hospital (☎ 289-4691), 1501 Williamson; and police (☎ 289-2431), 115 E 2nd.

## Things to See & Do

The memorable lyrics 'I'm standing on the corner in Winslow, Arizona, such a fine sight to see,' from the '70s song 'Take It Easy' by the Eagles, have given rise to a small plaza on Route 66 at Kinsley Ave and 2nd, in the heart of old downtown. A life-sized bronze statue of a hitchhiker backed by a trompe

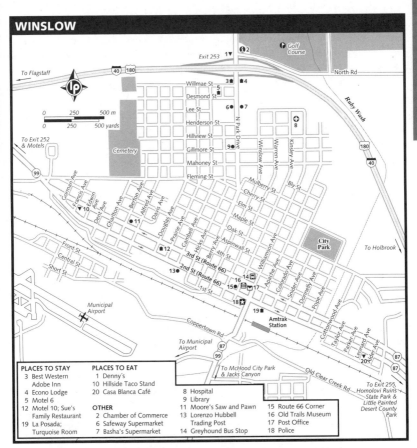

## WINSLOW

Exit 253

To Flagstaff

North Rd

Ruby Wash

0   250   500 m
0   250   500 yards

To Exit 252
& Motels

Cemetery

Willmae St
Desmond St
Lee St
Henderson St
Hillview St
Gillmore St
Mahoney St
Fleming St

Mulberry St
Cherry St
Elm St
Maple St
Oak St.
Berry St
4th St
3rd St (Route 66)
2nd St (Route 66)
1st St

Coppertown Rd

To Municipal
Airport

Municipal
Airport

To McHood City Park
& Jacks Canyon

City
Park

To Holbrook

Amtrak
Station

Old Clear Creek Rd

To Exit 255,
Homolovi Ruins
State Park &
Little Painted
Desert County
Park

| PLACES TO STAY | PLACES TO EAT |  |
|---|---|---|
| 3  Best Western | 1  Denny's |  |
|     Adobe Inn | 10 Hillside Taco Stand |  |
| 4  Econo Lodge | 20 Casa Blanca Café | 8  Hospital |
| 5  Motel 6 |  | 9  Library |
| 12 Motel 10; Sue's | OTHER | 11 Moore's Saw and Pawn | 15 Route 66 Corner |
|     Family Restaurant | 2  Chamber of Commerce | 13 Lorenzo Hubbell | 16 Old Trails Museum |
| 19 La Posada; | 6  Safeway Supermarket |     Trading Post | 17 Post Office |
|     Turquoise Room | 7  Basha's Supermarket | 14 Greyhound Bus Stop | 18 Police |

l'oeil wall mural of the girl in a flatbed Ford always attracts a posse of photographers.

Winslow's past is not forgotten in the **Old Trails Museum** (☎ 289-5861), 212 Kinsley Ave. It's open 1 to 5pm Tuesday to Saturday from April to October and Tuesday, Thursday and Saturday during other months; free admission. More history is found at La Posada Hotel (see Places to Stay) and at the **Lorenzo Hubbell Trading Post**, 523 W 2nd, where the Arizona Indian Arts Cooperative (☎ 289-3986) demonstrates silversmithing and has a small display of contemporary Indian crafts. Ask them to show you around

the trading post. Hours are 9am to 5pm weekdays and some Saturdays. Also check out **Moore's Saw and Pawn**, 1020 W 3rd, which repairs chainsaws; sells saddles, guns and old and new Navajo jewelry; and is a step back in time.

**Homolovi Ruins State Park** (☎ 289-4106), a mile north from exit 257 off Hwy 87, features petroglyphs, hundreds of small dwellings and four larger Pueblo sites, most eroded and under investigation. A visitor center is open daily. Day use is $4 per vehicle. **Little Painted Desert County Park** (☎ 524-4251) 13 miles north from exit 257 on Hwy 87, offers picnic facilities, walking trails and colorful views.

Locally popular **McHood City Park** (☎ 289-1300), 4 miles along Hwy 99, offers fishing, boating, swimming, picnicking and camping. There may be a day-use fee.

International rock climbers head 30 miles south along Hwy 87 to **Jacks Canyon**, where there is free camping and over 200 routes on French limestone ranging from 5.5 to 5.13 in difficulty.

### Places to Stay

*Homolovi Ruins State Park* has 52 sites at $10 for tents and $15 with hookups (including park entrance fee). There are showers. Another camping option is *McHood City Park*, with a few inexpensive sites open April through October on a first-come, first-served basis (subject to change).

About a dozen old motels, some run-down, are found along Route 66. Rates range from $20 in winter to $40 in summer. Several *chain motels* provide clean lodging, with relatively low summer rates. Motel 6, Super 8, Econo Lodge, Travelodge, Days Inn, Best Western and Holiday Inn Express are represented, mainly near I-40 exits 252 and 253.

The historic and recently renovated *La Posada* (☎ 289-4366, 303 E 2nd) is the best choice for many miles around. Opened in 1930, La Posada was one of a chain of grand Fred Harvey hotels along the Santa Fe Railroad line. The grand hacienda-style hotel was the finest in northern Arizona and numbered Harry Truman and Howard Hughes among its guests, but closed in 1959 as more people used cars rather than trains to get around. Restoration began in the mid '90s and care, passion and a sense of history are evident in the newly reopened hotel. The public can visit on self-guided tours 8am to 8pm daily, and travelers can bed down in one of 28 (expanding to 38 in 2003) rooms equipped with period furnishings (OK, a TV and air-conditioner are added, but no phones) and named after Western dignitaries and desperadoes. It's a fabulous value at $79, with a few suites at $99.
website: www.laposada.org

### Places to Eat

*Casa Blanca Café* (☎ 289-4191, 1201 E 2nd St) has served Mexican lunches and dinners for half a century, or stop by the *Hillside Taco Stand* in a bright yellow hut at the west end of 2nd St for authentic tacos in no-frills surroundings. *Sue's Family Restaurant* (☎ 289-1234, 723 W 3rd) is your basic diner where the locals go for home cooking. Best in town is the *Turquoise Room* in La Posada, with an eclectic menu reflecting the hotel's historical and geographical heritage. It's closed on Monday.

## HOLBROOK

☎ 928 • pop 4917 • elevation 5080 feet

Named after a railroad engineer, Holbrook was established in 1881 when the railroad reached this point. The town soon became an important ranching center and the Navajo County seat. The proximity of the Petrified Forest National Park has added tourism to the town's economic profile. Native American dancers perform for free (tips are appreciated) outside the 1898 county courthouse at 7pm during summer. Photography is permitted.

Seventeen miles from town, **Rock Art Canyon Ranch** (☎ 288-3260, 288-3527) is a working ranch with tours of Chevelin Canyon, brimming with petroglyphs. Horseback riding and other activities are offered at reasonable prices. Call for directions.

At the intersection of Hwys 180 and 77, about 2 miles south of town, **Jim Gray's Petrified Wood Company** (☎ 524-1842) has the largest commercial collection of petrified wood in the area, as well as a museum. Pieces ranging from $1 to $10,000 are for sale.

### Information

The chamber of commerce (☎ 524-6558, 800-524-2459) is in the county courthouse at 100 E Arizona. The courthouse retains the old city jail and records the area's history, which was wild and bloodthirsty in the 19th century. The library (☎ 524-3732), 451 1st Ave, has Internet access. Other services in town include the post office (☎ 524-3311), 100 W Erie; a medical center (☎ 524-3913),

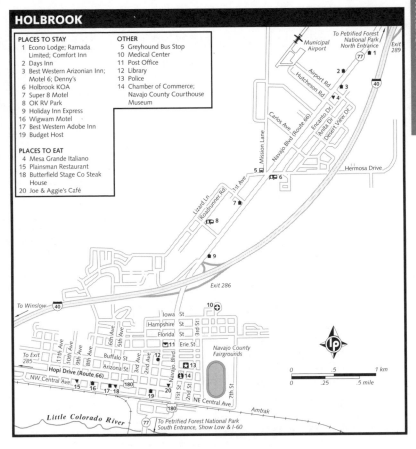

## HOLBROOK

**PLACES TO STAY**
1 Econo Lodge; Ramada
   Limited; Comfort Inn
2 Days Inn
3 Best Western Arizonian Inn;
   Motel 6; Denny's
6 Holbrook KOA
7 Super 8 Motel
8 OK RV Park
9 Holiday Inn Express
16 Wigwam Motel
17 Best Western Adobe Inn
19 Budget Host

**PLACES TO EAT**
4 Mesa Grande Italiano
15 Plainsman Restaurant
18 Butterfield Stage Co Steak
   House
20 Joe & Aggie's Café

**OTHER**
5 Greyhound Bus Stop
10 Medical Center
11 Post Office
12 Library
13 Police
14 Chamber of Commerce;
   Navajo County Courthouse
   Museum

500 E Iowa; and police (☎ 524-3991), 100 E
Buffalo.

Greyhound (☎ 524-3832) stops at the
Circle K, 101 Mission Lane.

## Places to Stay

The **Holbrook KOA** (☎ 524-6689), northwest of I-40 between exits 286 and 289,
has over 100 tent and RV sites, showers, a
pool, recreation room, playground and
coin laundry. Rates are $20 to $25, and
Kamping Kabins are $35. Summer reser-
vations are suggested. The **OK RV Park**
(☎ 524-3226, 1576 Roadrunner Rd) has

showers and more than 100 tent and RV
sites from $20.

Most motels and hotels line Hopi Dr
(east of I-40, exit 285) or Navajo Blvd, north
of Hopi Dr intersecting with I-40, exits 286
and 289. Holbrook has a surplus of hotels,
so finding reasonably priced rooms is rarely
a problem; note Hopi Dr parallels the
railway and suffers from late-night train
noise.

Most of the cheapest places are along
Hopi Dr and the downtown blocks of
Navajo Blvd. Among the best is **Budget
Host** (☎ 524-3809, 235 W Hopi Dr), which

## Not Quite FedEx

The Hashknife Posse, named after the area's biggest early cattle company, has an official contract with the US Postal Service to carry mail from Holbrook to Scottsdale via pony express. They don't have daily or even weekly service. In fact, delivery is only once a year, usually in late January or early February, and the arrival in Scottsdale is an important part of that city's Western Week. The ride takes three days. Letters with normal postage marked 'Via Pony Express' in the lower left will receive special postmarks and be delivered by the Hashknife Posse if left at the Holbrook post office during the first two weeks in January. Or put your stamped and marked letter in another envelope and send it to the Postmaster, Pony Express Ride, Holbrook, AZ 86025. After letters reach Scottsdale, they continue via normal mail. This tradition dates back to 1959.

charges in the $20s and has free coffee; email them at holbrook_inn@hotmail.com. A dozen similarly priced or cheaper places are nearby.

Devotees of historic Route 66 schlockabilia won't want to miss the **Wigwam Motel** (☎ 524-3048, 811 W Hopi Dr). This motor court has a village of 15 concrete wigwams doubling as simple rooms, each with restored 1950s-era furniture. Quite a sight! Rates are $36/42 for singles/doubles; email for information at clewis97@cybertrails.com. The office is open 4 to 9pm only.

Most of the nine **chain motels** are between I-40 exits 286 and 289 on Navajo Blvd and have seasonal pools. **Motel 6** (2514 Navajo Blvd), with 124 rooms going for $30/34, is Holbrook's biggest motel. **Holiday Inn Express** (1308 Navajo Blvd) is the priciest and the only one with interior corridors. Rates start at $60.

### Places to Eat

There are many cheap and unremarkable places to eat, mostly serving American food. The **Plainsman Restaurant** (☎ 524-3345, 1001 W Hopi Dr) serves inexpensive breakfast, lunch and dinner. **Joe & Aggie's Café** (☎ 524-6540, 120 W Hopi Dr) is a locally popular Mexican restaurant.

The **Butterfield Stage Co Steak House** (☎ 524-3447, 609 W Hopi Drive) is open for lunch and dinner in summer, dinner only in winter. Full of western memorabilia, this place delivers the region's best steaks at reasonable prices. Also recommended is the **Mesa Grande Italiano** (☎ 524-6696, 2318 Navajo Blvd), with the best Italian food for miles around.

### PETRIFIED FOREST NATIONAL PARK

Children may have the naive impression that trees here are still standing in little glades, eerily frozen in time. Parents might avoid major disappointment by explaining that the 'forest' is actually a bunch of broken, horizontal fossilized logs, scattered over a large area. Nevertheless, they are impressive: Some are 6 feet in diameter, and at least one spans a ravine, forming a fossilized bridge.

The trees are conifers from the Triassic period (225 million years ago) and pre-date the dinosaurs. Washed by floods into this area, logs were buried by sediment faster than they could decompose. Groundwater dissolved silica and other elements and carried them through the logs, which crystallized as colorful quartzes. Recently, the area was uplifted, causing the logs to break. Erosion then exposed the logs.

Thousands of tons of petrified wood were taken by souvenir seekers and entrepreneurs until 1906, when the area became a national monument and later a park. All collecting is prohibited (punishable by fines and imprisonment), but pieces gathered outside the park are sold in Holbrook and at the south park entrance.

Apart from petrified logs, visitors can see small ancient Indian sites (including one building made entirely from blocks of fossilized wood), petroglyphs and the picturesque scenery of the Painted Desert – lands that change colors as the sun plays tricks with the minerals in the earth.

### Orientation

The park straddles I-40 at exit 311, 25 miles east of Holbrook. From this exit, a 28-mile paved park road offers a splendid **scenic drive**, going briefly north and then heading south, over the freeway, to emerge at Hwy 180, 19 miles southeast of Holbrook. Unless making the complete loop from Holbrook, it is more convenient to begin at the north end if you are driving west and the south end if you are driving east.

### Information

The Painted Desert Visitor Center near the north entrance, and the Rainbow Forest Museum near the south entrance, have bookstores, park exhibits, and rangers on duty. At Painted Desert Visitor Center, a 20-minute film describes how the logs were fossilized, and at Rainbow Forest there are giant reptile skeletons. Between the two, the park road passes over 20 pullouts with interpretive signs and some short trails.

Hours are 8am to 5pm; from Memorial Day to Labor Day, hours are 7am to 7pm if staff is available (closed on December 25). Entrance is $10 per vehicle, $5 per bus passenger or bike rider. The usual passes are accepted. Visitors receive a (free) park map showing pullouts along the road. Further information is available from the superintendent (☎ 524-6228), Petrified Forest National Park, AZ 86028.

### Hiking & Backpacking

Apart from short trails at some of the pullouts, there are no trails into the park. Hikers can walk cross-country, but should speak with a ranger first to discuss their plans, as there are no maintained trails, campsites or water sources; all water must be carried. Backpackers can camp in the backcountry after obtaining a free permit from a ranger; camps must be at least a mile from paved roads, and no fires, firearms, pets or collecting are allowed. Some areas are closed to camping.

### Places to Stay & Eat

The park has no accommodations. Snacks can be purchased by the Rainbow Forest Museum and meals by the Painted Desert Visitor Center. There are two picnic areas. In **Chambers**, 22 miles east of the park on I-40, the **Best Western Chieftain Inn** has rooms ($60) and a restaurant. Otherwise, stay in Holbrook (listed earlier).

# Navajo Indian Reservation

The Navajo Indian Reservation, or the Navajo Nation as the Navajos themselves call it, covers 27,000 sq miles; it's the largest reservation in the USA. It is mainly in northeastern Arizona, but also includes parts of neighboring Utah and New Mexico. About 75% is high desert, and the remainder is high forest. The scenery is, in places, some of the most spectacular in North America, particularly in Monument Valley. Equally impressive are the beautiful (but uninhabited) ancient pueblos amid splendid settings in the Canyon de Chelly and Navajo National Monuments.

### History

Anthropological research indicates that in the 14th and 15th centuries, bands of Athabaskan-speaking people migrated from Canada into the Southwest. By 1500 these people had established themselves, and they became the ancestors of both the Navajo and the Apache Indians. In those days, they were a hunting and gathering people, occasionally raiding neighboring

NORTHEASTERN ARIZONA

## The Navajo Language

Navajo belongs to the Athapaskan language family, a group of languages that also includes Apache. Other tribes that speak Athapaskan languages live in Alaska, northwestern Canada, and coastal Oregon and California. The distribution of these tribes is considered evidence of migration patterns across the continent.

Some Navajo, especially the elders, speak only the Navajo language, but most speak both Navajo and English. All members of the tribe have a deep respect for the Navajo language whether they are fluent or not.

Navajo and English have very different sentence structures, and Navajo is not an easy language for outsiders to learn. During WWII, the Navajo Code Talkers spoke a code based on Navajo for US military radio transmissions. The code was never broken. The Code Talkers are now famous for their wartime contribution and the remaining members of this unit are frequently honored at tribal functions.

tribes. Influenced by the more sedentary and agricultural Pueblo tribes, the Navajos eventually began farming and making arts and crafts, but never built large stone villages such as the Pueblo Indians did.

The Navajo call themselves *Diné* (the People) and explain their arrival in the Southwest quite differently. According to their oral legends, Diné passed through three different worlds in various human, animal, spiritual and natural forms before finally emerging into the fourth world, called the Glittering World. Today's Diné maintain close links with their past worlds and believe that their lives should be in harmony with all the elements of the present and the earlier worlds. Dozens of ceremonies and rituals, learned with painstaking care from tribal elders and medicine men, are done for various reasons to enable the people to live in harmony with the rest of the universe.

Contact with the Spaniards in the 16th, 17th and 18th centuries was surprisingly limited, considering the Spaniards' involvement with the Pueblo and Hopi peoples. The best-documented Navajo-Spanish interaction was the massacre of more than 100 Indians at Canyon de Chelly in 1805 in response to years of Navajo raids.

When the Anglos arrived in the 19th century, they tended to follow the better-known routes in New Mexico and southern Arizona. By the middle of the 1800s, the US Army was defeating tribes, including the Navajo, along the Western frontier and 'buying' the land from the Indians in exchange for peace. (This may have made sense to the Anglos, but it didn't to the Indians, who didn't value the European concept of land ownership.) Once their land had been purchased, the surviving tribes were often 'relocated' onto distant reservations.

During the winter of 1863–64, US Cavalry troops led by Colonel Kit Carson destroyed fields and property, killed anyone they found and drove the Indians up into Canyon de Chelly until starvation forced their surrender. Thousands of Indians were rounded up and forced to march to Fort Sumner in the plains of eastern New Mexico in an episode remembered in tribal history as 'The Long Walk.'

Hundreds of Navajos died on the march or on the inhospitable new reservation. Despite this, the Navajo were one of the luckier tribes. A treaty in 1868 gave them a reservation of about 5500 sq miles in the heart of their ancient lands, and 8000 inhabitants of Fort Sumner along with about another 8000 scattered Navajos were allowed to settle on this new reservation. This grew over the years to its present size, and today over half of the approximately 175,000 members of the Navajo Nation live on the reservation. About one in seven Native Americans in the USA is a Navajo, making it the country's largest tribe.

### Information

The best information about the reservation is found at Window Rock. Other good information sources are the *Navajo Times* newspaper (www.navajotimes.com) and KTNN AM 660/KWRK 96.1 FM radio station. This broadcasts out of Window Rock with mainly Navajo-language programming in the morning and English in the afternoon and evening. The music varies between country & western and traditional and recent Navajo music, much of which involves drums and singing or flutes.

Banking facilities on the reservation are available at banks in Window Rock, Tuba City, Chinle and Kayenta. The Navajo Reservation, unlike Arizona, does observe Mountain daylight saving time. Thus during the summer, the reservation is *one hour ahead* of Arizona; on the same time as Utah and New Mexico.

Photography is permitted almost anywhere. Taking photographs of people, however, is not appropriate unless you ask for and receive permission from the individual involved. A tip is expected. Alcohol and drugs are strictly prohibited. The few hotels and restaurants in Navajoland provide clean accommodations and tasty food, but no alcohol. It is a violation of federal, state and Navajo tribal laws to disturb, destroy, injure, deface or remove any natural feature or prehistoric object.

Beware of farm animals on the roads because most of the land is not fenced. Hitting one can do as much damage to you as to the animal. Be careful of the occasional drunk driver. Despite the ban on alcohol, there are problems with drunk driving.

The reservation's phone system occasionally goes dead for short or sometimes long periods, particularly in remote locations and during severe weather.

### Special Events
The world's biggest Indian event is the Annual Navajo Nation Fair, held for several days soon after Labor Day in Window Rock. The fair has been taking place since 1946. Most visitors stay in Gallup, New Mexico, and travel to Window Rock for the intertribal powwow, Indian rodeo, tradi-

tional song and dance displays and competitions, a barbecue with Navajo food and many other events.

The oldest and most traditional Indian fair, held in nearby Shiprock, New Mexico, is held in late September or early October. The Navajo Tourism Office (see Window Rock, later) has the exact dates of smaller rodeos and powwows that are held in many smaller towns on the reservation.

### Places to Stay
Some tribally operated campgrounds are found at or near Monument Valley, the Navajo National Monument, Chinle, Tsaile and Window Rock. RV facilities are very limited.

The few motels on the reservation are found at Window Rock, Chinle, Kayenta, Tuba City, Cameron (see Cameron & Around in the Grand Canyon & Lake Powell chapter), Goulding's Trading Post in Utah and Teec Nos Pos. These are often full in summer; reservations are a good idea.

Navajo guides can arrange stays with local families or in a traditional hogan (a sleeping bag is a good idea) with primitive bathroom facilities (most hogans lack plumbing). Rates are about $90 including a Navajo breakfast; add $10 per extra person. Hiking and backpacking tours can be arranged. The Navajo Tourism Office can supply a list of approved guides.

### Shopping
The Anglo towns on the perimeter of the reservation have galleries and pawn shops where Navajo rugs, silverwork, jewelry and other arts can be purchased. On the reservation itself, you can buy from trading posts, gift shops, museums, and roadside stands.

Buying items at 'official' stores is no guarantee of their quality; high- and low-quality wares appear on the trading-post shelves just as they do at roadside stalls. When you buy direct, you may find that you pay less and have more luck negotiating the price down; the sellers may still make more from the transaction than if they had sold their wares to a trading post. In addition,

## Navajo Weaving

The Navajo are the best-known rug-weavers of the Native American tribes. A Navajo rug requires many months of labor and can involve several family members. Children tend the sheep, and various people participate in shearing, washing, carding, spinning and dyeing the wool before it even touches the loom. All is done by hand. The loom is a simple upright wooden frame, and the designs and colors are passed down from generation to generation, usually to the women. Legend has it that Spider Woman taught the women how to weave. You can watch weavers at work at some museums and trading posts; the Hubbell Trading Post near Ganado is a good place for this.

Navajo weavings were originally heavy blankets used in winter. When Anglos became interested in the work as a folk craft, they found that the origin of the rug could be recognized by the various designs and colors used in the rug. For instance, a Ganado Red was a rug with a red background coming from the settlement of Ganado. Rugs with geometrical designs in earth colors bordered by black were from the Two Grey Hills region from the eastern part of Navajo lands. And the Shiprock area was known for Yei rugs, depicting supernatural beings revered by the Navajo. Several other regional styles can easily be detected with a little experience.

Today, weavers from any part of the reservation can produce designs that were once specific to a particular area. While traditionally the designs have been geometric, some weavers currently use figurative designs. Such rugs are technically as valuable as the traditional ones.

**Tips on Buying a Rug** Whether used as a floor covering or displayed on a wall, a good quality rug can last a lifetime. Given the cost of purchasing a good quality rug, buying one is not for the average souvenir-seeker. It can take months of research, or can be bought on a whim if you see one you really love. If you're a more cautious shopper, visit museums, trading posts and crafts stores in Indian country. Talk to weavers, exhibitors and traders to learn about the various designs. Don't just look at the rugs – feel them. A good rug will be tightly woven and even in width. Prices of rugs vary from the low hundreds to thousands of dollars. This reflects the size of the rug, the weeks of work involved, the skill of the weaver and whether the yarn is store-bought or handspun.

Be aware that cheap imitation rugs are available. These may look nice, but they aren't handmade by Navajos. Some are mass-produced in Mexico using Navajo designs. The staff at a reputable store can show you the difference.

you may be able to talk directly to the artisan.

### Getting There & Away

The Navajo Transit System (☎ 729-4002, 729-4110) provides the only public transportation on the reservation using modern buses. Call for times.

From Gallup, New Mexico, the Navajo Transit System has buses to Window Rock and Fort Defiance six times a day. The ride takes an hour. There is no weekend service. Several daily buses connect Window Rock and Fort Defiance on weekdays; three do so on Saturday.

On weekdays, there is one daily bus from Window Rock to Tuba City along Hwy 264 via the Hopi Reservation. Another bus leaves on weekdays from Fort Defiance (a few miles north of Window Rock) for Kayenta via Tsaile, Chinle and other small villages. A third goes to Shiprock, New Mexico.

### WINDOW ROCK
☎ 928 • pop 3500 • elevation 6900 feet
The tribal capital is at Window Rock, at the intersection of Hwys 264 and 12. The town is named after a natural arch at the north end of town more than a mile north of the intersection.

## Orientation & Information

Information about the whole reservation is available from Navajo Tourism Office (☎ 871-6436, 871-7371, fax 871-7381), PO Box 663, Window Rock, AZ 86515. The tribal website is www.discovernavajo.com.

The main area of tourist interest is at the east end of town on Hwy 264 just east of Hwy 12. Here you'll find the FedMart shopping plaza (where the Navajo Transit System bus leaves from and where there is a cinema), bank, arts and crafts stores, the Navajo Nation Inn, the museum, post office and parks office all within a few hundred yards of one another.

Backpacking and other backcountry use anywhere on the reservation requires a permit from the Navajo Parks & Recreation Dept (☎ 871-6647, fax 871-6637). The office is next to the Zoo & Botanical Park on the east side of Window Rock. (Note that the campgrounds mentioned in this chapter are not considered 'backcountry' and don't require a tribal permit beyond the camping fee.) Hunting (very limited), fishing, and boating require tribal (not state) licenses obtainable from Navajo Fish & Wildlife (☎ 871-6451/2); details are available at www.navajofishandwildlife.org.

## Navajo Nation Museum & Library

This museum (☎ 871-7941) features permanent collections, changing shows and the tribal library. A gift shop has an excellent selection of books about the Navajo and other tribes as well as other items. Hours are 8am to 5pm Monday to Saturday, to 8pm on Wednesday; admission free.

In keeping with the traditional Navajo hogan, the museum's door faces east and is not immediately obvious from the highway. It's on Hwy 264 at Post Office Loop Rd at the east end of Window Rock. Next door is the Zoo & Botanical Park.

## Navajo Nation Council Chambers

The chambers (☎ 871-6417) are below the Window Rock Arch north of town. During tribal council sessions, you can hear the 88 elected council delegates representing the 110 Navajo chapters (communities) discussing issues in the Navajo language. Full council sessions are held at least four times a year, usually on the third Monday of January, April, July and October. At other times visitors can tour the chambers' colorful murals.

Nearby is the Window Rock Tribal Park with picnic areas and the Navajo Veterans Memorial. Camping is not allowed. The arch is important in Navajo ceremonies and is off-limits during some ceremonies.

## St Michael's Mission Museum

Housed in an 1898 Franciscan mission, 3 miles west of Window Rock just off Hwy 264, this museum (☎ 871-4171) describes the missionary work of the Franciscans in Navajoland. Hours are 9am to 4pm Monday to Friday from Memorial Day to Labor Day. Call for an appointment at other times.

## Places to Stay & Eat

There are no developed campgrounds, though you can park your RV next to the Zoo & Botanical Park. A $2 per person fee may be charged.

The *Navajo Nation Inn (☎ 871-4108, 800-662-6189)* is on Hwy 264 east of Hwy 12. There are 56 aging rooms with Southwestern motifs. Rates are about $55. A reasonably priced restaurant serves Navajo and American breakfast, lunch and dinner. There are several fast-food restaurants nearby.

Located half a mile west of St Michael's Mission on Hwy 264 is a *Days Inn (☎ 871-5690)* with indoor pool, sauna and exercise room.

## Shopping

Window Rock is the headquarters of the Navajo Arts and Crafts Enterprise (NACE), which runs a jewelry and crafts store (☎ 871-4090) next to the Navajo Nation Inn. The NACE was established in 1941 and is wholly Navajo operated. It guarantees the authenticity and quality of its products.

## HUBBELL TRADING POST NATIONAL HISTORIC SITE

John Lorenzo Hubbell established this trading post at **Ganado** (30 miles west of Window Rock) in 1878 and worked here until his death in 1930. He was widely respected by Indians and non-Indians alike for his honesty and passion for excellence. Today, his trading post is operated by the National Park Service and looks much as it would have a century ago. Indian artists still trade here.

Next to the trading post is a visitor center where respected Navajo women often give weaving demonstrations, and men might demonstrate silversmithing. Helpful interpretive signs explain what is being woven, and rangers can help with questions.

Tours of Hubbell's house (with a superb collection of early Navajo rugs and period furniture) are given several times a day. The trading post continues to sell local crafts, specializing in top-quality Navajo weavings worth thousands of dollars. If you can't quite scrape the money together, buy a postcard or a candy bar instead!

Hours are 8am to 6pm May through September, 8am to 5pm otherwise, and it's closed major holidays. Admission is free. There's a picnic area but nowhere to stay. Further information is available from the superintendent (☎ 755-3475), PO Box 150, Ganado, AZ 86505.

## CANYON DE CHELLY NATIONAL MONUMENT

Pronounced 'd-SHAY,' this many-fingered canyon contains several beautiful Ancestral Puebloan sites that are important in Navajo history. Ancient Basketmaker people inhabited the canyon almost 2000 years ago and left some pit dwellings dated to AD 350. These inhabitants evolved into the Pueblo people who built large cliff dwellings in the canyon walls between AD 1100 and 1300. Droughts and other unknown conditions forced them to leave the canyon after 1300 and it is supposed that they were the ancestors of some of today's Pueblo or Hopi Indians.

The Navajo began farming the canyon bottom around 1700 and used the canyon as a stronghold and retreat for their raids on other nearby Indian groups and Spanish settlers. In 1805, the Spaniards retaliated and killed over 100 Navajos in what is now called Massacre Cave in the Canyon del Muerto. The Spaniards claimed that the dead were almost all warriors, but the Navajo say that it was mostly women and children. In 1864, the US Army drove thousands of Navajos into the canyon and starved them until they surrendered over the winter, then relocated them in eastern New Mexico after 'The Long Walk.' Four years later, the Navajos were allowed to return. Today, many families have hogans and farms on the canyon bottom. Most families live on the canyon rims in winter, and move to the canyon bottom in the spring and summer. The whole canyon is private Navajo property administered by the NPS. Please don't enter hogans unless with a guide and don't photograph people without their permission.

The canyon begins at its west end near the village of **Chinle**. Here, the canyon walls are only a few feet high but soon become higher until they top out at about 1000 feet in the depths of the canyon. Two main arms divide early on in the canyon and several side canyons connect with them. A paved road follows the southernmost and northernmost rims of the canyon complex, affording excellent views into the splendid scenery of the canyon and distant views of uninhabited pueblos in the canyon walls; this is a worthy **scenic drive**. Most of the bottom of the canyon is off-limits to visitors unless they enter with a guide. The exception is a trail to the White House.

### Information

The visitor center, just east of Chinle, features exhibits about the canyon, a bookstore, information about guides and tours and a free newspaper guide. Inexpensive booklets with descriptions of the sights on South and North Rim Drives are available.

Outside is a traditional Navajo hogan that you can enter (it's empty). Hours are 8am to 5pm daily, extended to 6pm May through September. Admission is free as long as you stick to the visitor center, paved rim roads and White House Trail. Further information is available from the superintendent (☎ 674-5500), PO Box 588, Chinle, AZ 86503.

For information not sponsored by the National Park Service, take a look at the Unofficial Canyon de Chelly and Navajo website at www.navajocentral.org.

## White House Trail

The trailhead is about 6 miles east of the visitor center on South Rim Drive, and the steep trail is about 1¼ miles one-way; carry water. The pueblo dates to about AD 1040 to 1284 and is one of the largest in the monument.

## Rim Drives

Both drives afford several scenic overlooks into the canyon. Lock your car and don't leave valuables in sight when taking the short walks at each scenic point.

South Rim Drive is 16 miles long and passes six viewpoints before ending at the spectacular Spider Rock Overlook, with views down onto the 800-foot-high sheer-walled tower atop of which lives Spider Woman. The Navajos say that she carries off children who don't listen to their parents! This is a dead-end drive so return the way you came.

North Rim Drive has four overlooks and ends at the Massacre Cave overlook, 15 miles from the visitor center. The paved road continues to Tsaile, 13 miles further east, from which Hwy 12 heads to Window Rock or into the northern reaches of the reservation.

The lighting for photography on the north rim is best in early morning and on the south rim in late afternoon.

## Organized Tours

Ask at the visitor center about all tours. Guides belong to the Canyon de Chelly Guide Association and are usually local Navajos who know the area well and liven up tours with witty commentary.

**Hiking & Backpacking** The Guide Association offers guided hikes into the canyon. A four-hour, 4½-mile hike is offered twice daily May to September for $15 per person (five to 15 people). Other hikes may be available. Definitely bring insect repellent in spring and summer.

For more difficult hikes or to visit more remote areas, guides charge $15 an hour (three hours minimum, 15 people per guide maximum). Overnight hikes with camping in the canyon can be arranged at the visitor center (allow at least a day to organize).

During the summer, park rangers may lead free hikes. Inquire and register in advance at the visitor center.

**Horseback Riding** Justin Tso's Horseback Tours (☎ 674-5678), near the visitor center, has horses available year-round for $10 per person per hour plus $10 an hour for the guide. Tohtsonii Ranch (☎ 755-6209), at the end of South Rim Drive, charges similar prices. The ranch offers four-hour roundtrip rides to Spider Rock. Overnight trips can be arranged.

**Four-Wheel Drive** Only rough tracks enter the canyon, so you need 4WD. With your own vehicle you can hire a guide for $15 an hour (one guide can accompany up to five vehicles; three-hour minimum). Heavy rain may make the roads impassable.

Navajo-owned Unimog Tours (☎ 674-1044, 674-5433) leave from the Holiday Inn for three-hour tours at 9am and 1pm. Rates are $40 ($25 for children under 13). They rent 4WD vehicles for $125 for three hours plus $30 for each additional hour. Thunderbird Tours (☎ 674-5841), at the Thunderbird Lodge, use heavy-duty, army-style 6WD vehicles that can cross through streams that would stop a 4WD. Some Navajos refer to these as the 'shake-n-bake' tours. Half-day trips leave at 9am and 2pm and cost $42 ($32 for children). Seasonal full-day tours are $65 and include a picnic lunch.

## Places to Stay & Eat

*Cottonwood Campground*, near the visitor center, has 96 sites on a first-come, first-served basis. There is water but no hookups or showers. Camping is free and popular, so in summer get there early. During the summer, rangers may give talks. Group campgrounds are available by reservation. From November to March, water may be shut off. The remote, Navajo-run *Spider Rock Campground* (☎ 674-8261), 10 miles east of the visitor center along South Rim Drive, is surrounded by piñon and juniper trees and gets away from the activity of the visitor center. Sites cost $10. There is no water or electricity, but the owner has bottled water and lanterns available.

The attractive *Thunderbird Lodge* (☎ 674-5841/2, 800-679-2473), half a mile from the visitor center, is the only lodge with the monument. Over 70 comfortable rooms vary in size; some are in the old lodge (which dates from the late 1800s) but all have private baths, air-conditioning, TVs and telephones. Rates are about $105 a double; there are discounts mid-October through March. An inexpensive cafeteria offers tasty American and Navajo food from 6:30am to 9pm, with shorter winter hours.
website: www.tbirdlodge.com.

A half-mile west of the visitor center is the *Holiday Inn* (☎ 674-5000). They have an outdoor pool and the area's most upscale restaurant (though still not very fancy), open from 6:30am to 10pm. Parts of the public areas incorporate an old trading post, but the 108 rooms are modern and have coffee makers. Rates range from $100 to $120 in summer; email them at holidayinn-ncdc@cybertrails.com.

In Chinle, just east of Hwy 191 and 3 miles west of the visitor center, is the *Best Western Canyon de Chelly Inn* (☎ 674-5875), with 100 pleasant motel rooms, all with coffee makers, for $100 to $130 from May to October dropping to $60 to $80 in winter. They have an indoor pool and an inexpensive dining room open from 6:30am to 9pm (10pm in summer).

Seventeen miles north of Chinle, near the intersection of Hwys 191 and 59, the high school at Many Farms operates the *Many Farms Inn* (☎ 781-6362/6226) where Navajo students train in hotel management. Rooms have two single beds and bathrooms are shared. There is a TV room and a game room. Rates are $30 per person.

Apart from the hotel restaurants, there are some fast-food restaurants and Chinle's *Basha's*, the only supermarket for at least 50 miles. Alcohol is not available (reservation law).

## Shopping

The Navajo Arts & Crafts Enterprise (see Window Rock, earlier in this chapter) has a store in Chinle (☎ 674-5338) at the intersection of Hwys 191 and 7. The Thunderbird Lodge gift shop also sells a good range of crafts and T-shirts. The Thunderbird cafeteria walls are hung with high-quality Navajo rugs and paintings, which are for sale.

## TSAILE

A small town at the northeast end of Canyon de Chelly, Tsaile (pronounced 'say-LEE') is the home of Diné College (☎ 724-6600), a Navajo-owned community college. On campus, the modern six-story glass **Ned A Hatathli Center** (☎ 724-6650) has its entrance facing east, just like a traditional hogan. The center features a museum with exhibits about Indian history, culture and arts and crafts, a variety of which are offered for sale in the gift shop. Hours are 8:30am to 4:30pm Monday to Friday; admission is by donation. The college bookstore has a superb selection of books about the Navajo.

South of the college and 2 miles off of Hwy 12 is the small *Tsaile Lake Campground* accessible by dirt road. RVs aren't recommended, and there is no drinking water or facilities. Ten miles south of Tsaile on Hwy 12 is the larger and more attractive *Wheatfields Lake Campground* (☎ 871-6645, 871-7307) with nice lake views. There are pit toilets but no water. RV and tent sites are inexpensive. A nearby store sells food and fishing permits. Both lakes are stocked with rainbow and cutthroat trout and offer some of Navajoland's best fishing.

Will B Tsosie of *Coyote Pass Hospitality* (☎ 724-3383, 787-2295) can arrange off the beaten path tours and overnight stays in hogans; visit their website at www.navajo central.org/cppage.htm for information.

## FOUR CORNERS NAVAJO TRIBAL PARK

Make a fool of yourself as you put a foot into Arizona, another into New Mexico, a hand into Utah and another into Colorado. Wiggle your butt for the camera. Everyone does! The site is marked with a slab and state flags, and is surrounded by booths selling Indian souvenirs, crafts and food. This is the only place in the USA where four states come together at one point. Hours are 7am to 8pm May to August, and 8am to 5pm at other times. Admission is a steep $2.50 per person (though it might not be collected in winter). Seniors pay $1 and children under eight are free.

## KAYENTA & AROUND

☎ 928 • pop 4500 • elevation 5641 feet

Established in 1908 as a trading post, Kayenta has in recent decades developed strong (if controversial) uranium and coal mining industries. It provides lodging for Monument Valley, 24 miles away.

The visitor center (☎ 697-3572) provides information, has a small museum and sells local crafts and books. Vehicle tours to Monument Valley are provided by Roland's Navajoland Tours (☎ 697-3524, fax 697-2382) and Crawley's Tours (☎ 697-3463, 697-3734, crawley@crawleytours.com).

Halfway between Four Corners and Kayenta, the village of Teec Nos Pos is home to the small *Navajo Trails Motel* (☎ 674-3618), with basic double rooms for $49 in summer – the cheapest motel in Navajoland.

Pricey chain motels are your main choice. The Navajo-operated *Best Western Wetherill Inn* (☎ 697-3231) is 1½ miles north of Hwy 160 on Hwy 163. It has an indoor pool and 54 standard motel rooms with coffeemakers at almost $100 May to October, about $50 to $70 otherwise. The *Hampton Inn* (☎ 697-3170) features an outdoor pool and complimentary continental breakfast. Summer rates for the 73 spacious, modern rooms are in the low $100s.

The *Holiday Inn* (☎ 697-3221), at the junction of Hwys 160 and 163, is the reservation's largest hotel, with 160 rooms and a few suites. Rates are about $150 for a double July to October, dropping to about $80 in midwinter. There is an outdoor pool, a kids' pool, and a decent restaurant open all day.

The *Golden Sands Cafe* (☎ 697-3684) serves American and Navajo food near the Wetherill Inn, and the *Amigo Cafe* (☎ 697-8448), on Hwy 163 a short way north of Hwy 160, serves Mexican food. Both are open for breakfast, lunch and dinner. The

## The High Cost of Coal

In satellite photos taken from 567 miles above the Navajo and Hopi Indian Reservations, the Peabody Coal Company's mine to the west of Kayenta looks like a blackhead. The fact that it appears at all is testimony to its size and to the size of the controversies surrounding the mine at Black Mesa. One of the main issues that arises is the use of groundwater. Coal mines use exorbitant amounts of water to transport the coal to smelters, depleting a vast supply of rainwater that has accumulated over centuries.

Take into account that this land is desert and water is a precious resource for the Navajo and Hopi. Without the water, their ability to raise livestock and grow crops – the basis of their lifestyle – is threatened. Historically, treaties about tribal land have only defined the land, not the water under the surface. Bureaucracy takes over and the Indians find themselves fighting not only the federal bureaucracy, but also each other over disputed borders and use of land and resources. The issue is further complicated by the fact that Peabody is one of the primary employers on the reservation.

*Burger King* has an interesting exhibit on the Navajo Code Talkers, which makes it the Southwest's most unique chain fast-food place. There's also a *Basha's* super-market for picnic shopping.

About 10 miles west on Hwy 160 at the village of **Tsegi** is the *Anasazi Inn (☎ 697-3793)*, with 60 simple motel rooms (many with good views) for about $65 in summer, less in winter; find them on the web at anasaziinn.com. It has a 24-hour *restaurant* April to September.

## MONUMENT VALLEY NAVAJO TRIBAL PARK

Some people have a feeling of déjà vu here: This is the landscape seen in famous Westerns like the classic 1939 production of *Stagecoach,* directed by John Ford, or *How the West Was Won* (1962). The landscape is stupendous.

Great views of Monument Valley are had from the **scenic drive** along Hwy 163, but to really get up close you need to visit the Monument Valley Navajo Tribal Park (☎ 435-727-3353). Most of the park is in Arizona, but the area code is for Utah. A 4-mile paved road leads to a visitor center with information, exhibits, restaurant and tour companies.

From the visitor center, a rough unpaved loop road covers 17 miles of stunning valley views. You can drive it in your own vehicle (ordinary cars can just get by) or take a tour. Self-driven visitors pay $3 ($1 for seniors, free for kids under eight). Tour companies at the visitor center offer 2½-hour trips for about $30 a person (two minimum). Horseback rides are around $30. Note that tours enter areas that cannot be visited by private vehicle. Tours leave frequently in summer but are infrequent in winter. Outfitters in Kayenta and at Goulding's in Utah also offer tours. The road is open 7am to 7pm May through September, and 8am to 4:30pm the rest of the year, except Christmas. Bad weather may close the road.

The tribally operated *Mitten View Campground* has some coin-operated hot showers but no RV hookups. About 100 sites are $10 each on a first-come, first-served basis and may fill in summer. The showers are closed in winter, when the sites cost $5 and can be cold, windy and snowy.

Camping and motel facilities can be found at nearby Goulding's Trading Post (☎ 435-727-3231) in Utah.

## NAVAJO NATIONAL MONUMENT

This monument protects three Ancestral Puebloan sites, of which Betatakin and Keet Seel pueblos are exceptionally well preserved, extensive and impressive, and are open to the public. Well worth a visit, they are difficult to reach so part of their charm comes from your sense of achievement getting there. Visits are only in summer.

The visitor center (☎ 672-2700), 9 miles north of Hwy 160 along Hwy 564, offers audio-visual shows, a small museum and a well-stocked gift shop. Information, ranger-led programs, camping and picnicking are available.

### Betatakin

This pueblo is distantly visible from the Sandal Trail, open year-round, and an easy 1-mile loop from the visitor center.

From mid-May through September, rangers lead 5-mile, five-hour (roundtrip) hikes to Betatakin at 9am daily. Hikers must obtain *their own* free tickets for the hike at the visitor center. The hike is limited to 25 persons and, occasionally, 25 people are waiting in line before the visitor center opens. The elevation (7300 feet at the visitor center, 6600 at Betatakin) means the return hike can be strenuous, so carry plenty of water and sun protection. Unguided hikes aren't allowed.

### Keet Seel

This is one of the largest and best-preserved ancient pueblos in the Southwest and can be reached by foot only. Keet Seel is 8½ miles (one-way) from the visitor center, but the destination is worth the challenging hike involving a steep 1000-foot descent and then a 400-foot gentle climb. The trail is loose and sandy and may necessitate wading through a shallow streambed.

Although the 17-mile roundtrip can be done in a day, most visitors backpack in and stay at the primitive campsite below Keet Seel. There's no drinking water, so carry your own. Camping is limited to one night. At the site, visitors must register at a small ranger station. The pueblo may be visited only with the ranger, and visitation is limited to 20 people a day and five people at a time, so you may need to wait. The last visit is at 3:30pm. Entrance requires using a very long ladder, so it's not for people afraid of heights.

Keet Seel is open daily from Memorial Day to Labor Day. The 20 daily permits are free and often taken early, so call ahead to reserve one. No fires are allowed so bring a stove or cold food.

### Places to Stay

The *campground* at the visitor center is open May through September and has 31 sites with water, but no showers or RV hookups. Camping is free on a first-come, first-served basis. Two large group sites are available by reservation. During other months, the campground remains open but the water is turned off.

### TUBA CITY

☎ 928 • pop 7300 • elevation 4936 feet

Originally settled by Mormons in 1875 and named after a Hopi leader, Tuba City, a mile north of the intersection of Hwys 160 and 264, is the major town in the western half of the Navajo Reservation.

The **Tuba Trading Post** (☎ 283-4545) dates back to the 1880s and sells authentic Indian arts and crafts as well as food. A motel and restaurant are next door. The trading post has information about upcoming public dances and events on the Hopi and Navajo Reservations. **Dinosaur tracks** are seen 5 miles west along Hwy 160 on the north side of the road. Look for a small sign and a few Navajo crafts stalls at the turnoff. Children will guide you for $2.

The *Grey Hills Inn* (☎ 283-6271, 283-4450) is in the Grey Hills High School, a

half-mile east along Hwy 160 from the intersection with Hwy 264. Students operate a simple motel with private rooms with shared baths at $42 to $58 for one to four people from May to October, less in winter.

Navajo-run *Diné Inn Motel* (☎ 283-6107), on Hwy 160 at Peshlakai Ave, has 15 clean, modern rooms with TV and telephone in the $70s in summer, $50s the rest of the year. More rooms are planned.

The 80-room *Quality Inn* (☎ 283-4545, 800-644-8383) is part of the Tuba Trading Post complex. Rooms are $70 to $130 for a double. The *Hogan Restaurant* (☎ 283-5260) is on the premises, open daily 6am to 9pm.

See the Navajo Indian Reservation section, earlier in this chapter, for details on getting to and from Tuba City by bus.

# Hopi Indian Reservation

The Hopi are the oldest and most traditional tribe in Arizona, if not the entire continent. Their earliest villages were contemporary with the ancestral cliff dwellings seen in several of the Southwest's national parks. Unlike the residents of those dwellings, however, who abandoned them about AD 1300, the Hopi have continuously inhabited three mesas in the high deserts of northeastern Arizona for centuries. Old Oraibi, for example, has been continuously inhabited since the early 1100s and vies with Acoma Pueblo in New Mexico for the title of oldest continuously inhabited town in North America. It is thought that the ancestors of some of today's Hopi were also the people who migrated from other cliff dwellings 700 years ago.

The Hopi are a deeply religious people. They are also private people and would just as soon be left alone to celebrate their cycle of life on the mesa tops. Because of their isolated location, they have received less outside influence than most other tribes, and they have limited facilities for tourism.

When the Spaniards arrived, they stuck mainly to the Rio Grande valley and rarely struck out into the high deserts where the Hopi lived. Spanish explorers Pedro de Tovar and García López de Cárdenas, members of Coronado's expedition, were the first Europeans to visit the Hopi mesas in 1540, and Hopi guides led Cárdenas to see the Grand Canyon. In 1592, a Spanish mission was established at Awatovi and the zealous friars attempted to close down kivas and stop the religious dance cycle that is an integral part of the Hopi way of life. Because of this, the Hopi joined the Pueblo Revolt of 1680, drove out Spanish missionaries and destroyed the church. When the Spaniards returned to New Mexico in 1692, their attempts at reviving this mission failed. Although unsuccessful in establishing their religion among the Hopi, the Europeans were, unfortunately, successful importers of disease: Smallpox wiped out 70% of the tribe in the 1800s.

Meanwhile, the Hopi were forced to deal with raids by Navajo and other groups. When the Navajo were rounded up for the Long Walk, the Hopi, perceived as peaceful and less of a threat to US expansion, were left on their mesa tops. After the Navajo were allowed to return from their forced exile, they came back to the lands surrounding the Hopi mesas. Historically, the Hopi have distrusted the Navajo, and it is ironic, therefore, that the Hopi Reservation is completely surrounded by the Navajo Reservation.

Today, about 11,000 Hopi live on the 2410-sq-mile reservation, of which more than 1400 square miles are partitioned lands used by the Navajo. A US Senate bill officially resolved a complicated century-old legal conflict between the two tribes about

## Kachinas

Kachinas are several hundred sacred spirits that live in the San Francisco Mountains north of Flagstaff. At prescribed intervals during the year they come to the Hopi Reservation and dance in a precise and ritualized fashion. These dances maintain harmony among all living things and are especially important for rainfall and fertility.

Some Hopi who carefully and respectfully perform these dances prepare for the events over many days. They are important figures in the religion of the tribe, and it can be said that the dancers are the kachinas that they represent. This is why the dances have such a sacred significance to the Hopi and why the tribe is reluctant to trivialize their importance by turning a religious ceremony into a tourist spectacle. The masks and costumes used by each kachina are often quite spectacular.

One of the biggest Kachina Dances is the Powamuya, or 'Bean Dance,' held in February. During this time, young Hopi girls are presented with kachina dolls that incorporate the girls into the religious cycle of the tribe. The dolls are traditionally carved from the dried root of a cottonwood tree, a tree that is an indicator of moisture. Over time, these dolls have become popular collectors' items and Hopi craftsmen produce them for the general public as an art form. Not all kachinas are carved for the tourist trade: Some are considered too sacred. Other tribes, notably the Navajo, have copied kachina dolls from the Hopi.

In March 1992, Marvel Comics, the well-known comic-book publisher, issued an NHL Superpro comic book in which there was a story about kachinas trying to violently capture a Hopi ice-skating champion who was not living a traditional lifestyle. The Hopi people considered this an inaccurate and blasphemous portrayal of the sacred nature of the kachina's role in Hopi life. It was also the last straw in many years of inappropriate actions regarding Hopi religious practices, and most Kachina Dances are now closed to tourists.

the boundaries of the reservations in 1996, but there are still disagreements between the two tribes.

## Orientation

The reservation is crossed by Hwy 264, which passes the three mesas that form the heart of the reservation. These are pragmatically named, from east to west, First Mesa, Second Mesa and Third Mesa. In addition, paved Hwys 87, 77 and 2 enter the reservation from the south, giving access from the I-40 corridor. Travel on paved highways is freely allowed, but you can't drive or hike off the main highways without a permit.

## Information

A tribal government coordinates activities among the 12 main Hopi villages and between the tribe and the outside world. Information is available from the tribe's Office of Public Relations (☎ 734-3283), PO Box 123, Kykotsmovi, AZ 86039. Tribal office hours are 8am to 5pm Monday to Friday. Each village has its own leader, who often plays an important role in the religious practices of the village. Rules about visiting villages vary from place to place and you should contact each village (telephone numbers given below) to learn about their particular rules. These rules can change at any time. The village with the best tourism infrastructure is Walpi on First Mesa.

Outside each village and in prominent places on the highways are signs informing visitors about the villages' individual policies. All villages strictly prohibit any form of recording, be it camera, video- or audiotape or sketching. Students of anthropology and related disciplines require tribal permits, not easily obtained because the Hopi are not interested in having their culture dissected by outsiders. Alcohol and drug use is prohibited throughout the reservation. Visitors are allowed to attend some ceremonial dances, but most are closed to the public.

As with the rest of Arizona (and different from the surrounding Navajo Reservation) the Hopi Reservation does not observe daylight saving time in summer.

There are no banks, although ATMs are found in the Circle M Store in Polacca, the Secakuku Store at the junction of Hwy 264 and 87 and at the Hopi Cultural Center. Cash is preferred for most transactions. An ambulatory health care center can be reached at 738-0911 in emergencies. For other emergencies, call the BIA police (☎ 738-2233).

## Special Events

Most of the many annual ceremonial dances were closed in 1992 to the non-Indian public. This was because the religious nature of the Hopi dances was being threatened by visitors, and also because their remote mesa-top locations did not have the infrastructure (bathrooms, water, food, emergency services and space) to deal with scores of visitors.

Each individual village determines the attendance of non-Indian visitors at dances. The Kachina Dances, held frequently from January to July, are mostly closed to the non-Indian public, as are the famous Snake or Flute Dances held in August. Social Dances and Butterfly Dances, held late August through November, are often open to public viewing. All dances are very important to the Hopi people, who attend them in large numbers.

The dances are part of the Hopi ceremonial cycle and are performed in order to create harmony with nature. A particularly important aspect of this is ensuring rainfall for the benefit of all living things. The dances are expressions of prayer that require a traditional and responsible performance. The precise dates are not known until a few weeks in advance. Village officials can tell you about dance dates close to when they happen and advise you whether they will be open to the public.

The best bet for tourists is to try and see a Social Dance or Butterfly Dance in the fall. These normally occur on weekends and go intermittently from dawn to dusk. See the boxed text 'Visitors' Etiquette in Pueblos & on Reservations' in the Facts for the Visitor chapter for information on visiting pueblos.

## Shopping

Apart from kachina dolls, the Hopi are known for fine pottery, basketware and, more recently, jewelry and paintings. These can be purchased from individuals or from stores on the reservation at prices below what you'd pay elsewhere. Hopi religious paraphernalia, however, is not offered for sale. Some reputable stores are mentioned under individual villages.

### FIRST MESA

At the bottom of the mesa, **Polacca** is a nontraditional village. A steep road climbs to the mesa top, but large RVs will not make it; leave them in Polacca. The first village on the mesa is **Hano**, inhabited by Tewa-speaking Pueblo Indians who arrived in 1696 after fleeing from the Spaniards. They have been integrated into the Hopi tribe. Hano merges into the Hopi village of **Sichomovi** (you can't tell the difference), which is an 'overflow' of Walpi. The mesa is closed to visitors during Kachina Dances.

At the end of First Mesa is the tiny village of **Walpi**, built around AD 1200 in a spectacular setting on a finger-mesa jutting out into space. It is the most dramatic of the Hopi villages. The mesa is so narrow at this point that you can't drive in; cars must be left in a parking area near the entrance to the village. There is no water or electricity available, so the handful of year-round residents has to walk into Sichomovi to get water.

A tourist office (☎ 737-2262) at the parking area has Hopi guides for a 45-minute Walpi walking tour (9:30am to 4pm). Fees are $8 for adults; $5 for five- to 17-year-olds; free for those under five. The guides speak excellent English and the tour is a highlight of a visit to Hopiland.

Artisans living on First Mesa sell pots, kachina dolls and other crafts at fair prices. There are always several in front of the tourist office, and they'll give you detailed verbal explanations of the work they sell. Cameras and recorders are not allowed on the tours. Leave them locked in your car.

### SECOND MESA

Called 'the center of the universe' by the tribe, Second Mesa is 10 miles west of First Mesa. The **Hopi Cultural Center** is here, with a small but informative museum (☎ 734-6650) – no photography or note-taking allowed. Admission is $3 ($1 for children 12 and under) and hours are 8am to 5pm Monday to Friday; hours are shorter on summer weekends. It may close on major holidays.

Next door is the ***Hopi Cultural Center Restaurant & Inn*** (☎ *734-2401, fax 734-6651*), with 33 modern nonsmoking rooms for $90/95 in summer, less in winter. It is often fully booked in summer, so call as far ahead as possible. The restaurant is open 6am to 9pm in summer, 7am to 8pm in winter and serves American meals and a few Hopi foods. Nearby is a free ***RV area*** with no facilities.

Crafts are sold in the cultural center complex; in the nearby Hopi Arts and Crafts Guild (☎ 734-2463), which has good silverwork, and at Takurshovi, 1½ miles east of the cultural center, which has both high-quality arts (including baskets) and cheap 'Don't Worry, Be Hopi' souvenirs.

Also on Second Mesa are three Hopi villages that often have dances, a few of which may be open to public viewing. Call between 8am and 5pm Monday to Friday for information or ask at the Hopi Cultural Center. **Shungopavi** (☎ 734-7135) is the oldest village on the mesa and is famous for its Snake Dances, where dancers carry live rattlesnakes in their mouths. These are religious events, not circus acts, and tourists have been banned since 1984. Kachina Dances held here are off-limits too, but Social and Butterfly Dances may be open for public viewing. The other villages are **Mishongnovi** (☎ 737-2520) and **Sipaulovi** (☎ 737-2570), both of which may have some dances open to the public.

### THIRD MESA

Ten miles west of Second Mesa, this area includes both villages on the mesa and others to the west of it. The first is **Kykotsmovi** (☎ 734-2474), founded in the late 1800s and now the tribal capital.

On top of the mesa is **Old Oraibi**, which Hopis say has been continuously inhabited since the early 12th century. Oraibi is a couple of miles west of Kykotsmovi. The roads are unpaved and dusty so park next to crafts shops near the village entrance and visit on foot, to avoid stirring up clouds of dust.

Many residents left in 1906, after a disagreement over educational philosophies led to a 'pushing contest.' One faction wanted US-funded schools for their children while the other preferred a more traditional approach. The traditionalists lost and left to establish the new town of **Hotevilla** (☎ 734-2420) and, soon after, **Bacavi** (☎ 734-9360) where inhabitants remain very traditional.

There are picnic areas off Hwy 264 just east of Oraibi and just east of Kykotsmovi on Oraibi Wash. On the highway leading to Oraibi is the Monongya Gallery (☎ 734-2344) and in Oraibi itself is Old Oraibi Crafts, both with good crafts selections.

# East-Central Arizona

This region features forests lining the Mogollon Rim, a 1000- to 2000-foot-high geological break between the high desert of northeastern Arizona and the low desert of southeastern Arizona. The forested lands belong mainly to the USFS and the Fort Apache, San Carlos and Tonto Apache Indian Reservations. These highland forests offer cool respite for the citizens of Phoenix who dominate tourism in the area.

## PAYSON & AROUND

☎ 928 • pop 13,620 • elevation 5000 feet

Founded by gold miners in 1882, the town became a ranching and logging center but is now mainly a tourism and retirement center for Phoenix citizens, although ranching remains important in surrounding areas. The main drags are a curious but unappealing mix of strip malls and many **antique shops**. Check with the Forest Ranger Station about fishing and camping, which is the best reason to be here.

Learn more about the region's history at the **Rim Country Museum** (☎ 474-3483) on Main at Green Valley Pkwy, a mile west of the chamber of commerce. Hours are noon to 4pm Wednesday through Sunday; admission is $3. The town of Strawberry, 20 miles north of Payson, has Arizona's **oldest schoolhouse** built in 1885.

In the summer, **horseback riders** can get information and rent horses from OK Corral (☎ 476-4303) in Pine.

### Information

Highway 87 is known as Beeline Hwy through Payson. The chamber of commerce (☎ 474-4515, 800-672-9766), 100 W Main at Hwy 87, is open 8am to 5pm weekdays and 10am to 2pm weekends.

Other available services include the Tonto National Forest Payson Ranger Station (☎ 474-7900), 1009 E Hwy 260; library (☎ 474-5242), 510 W Main; post office (☎ 474-2972), 100 W Frontier; hospital (☎ 474-3222), 807 S Ponderosa; and police (☎ 474-5177), 303 N Beeline Hwy.

### Tonto Natural Bridge State Park

Spanning a 150-foot-wide canyon and measuring over 400 feet wide itself, the Tonto Natural Bridge was formed from calcium

## Highlights

- Cross-country skiing and hiking in the White Mountains
- Escaping the summer heat in the tiny mountain town of Greer
- Fly-fishing in the streams of the Apache-Sitgreaves National Forest
- Driving the Coronado Trail Scenic Road, particularly in September and October when fall colors are at their peak
- Enjoying the outdoor recreation opportunities at the San Carlos Apache Indian Reservation, with its 2900 sq miles of lakes, rivers, forests and desert
- Rafting on the Salt River
- Winding your way down the 75-mile Apache Trail, one of the more spectacular drives in the area

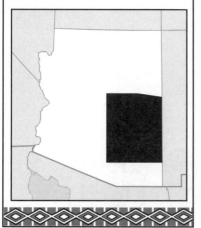

carbonate deposited over the years by mineral-laden spring waters. This is the largest travertine bridge in the world. You can go under it, walk over it or see it from several viewpoints along the short but steep trail. A guest lodge was built here in the early 1900s (everything had to be lowered into the canyon). It's been renovated, and tours are available on weekends, but the lodge is currently not in operation.

The park (☎ 476-4202) is 11 miles north of Payson on Hwy 87, then 3 miles west on a 14%-grade road (perhaps the steepest paved road in Arizona). The park is open May through September from 8am to 6pm and October through April 9am to 5pm. Admission is $5 per vehicle (up to four passengers).

## Special Events

Payson has over 50 annual events ranging from dog shows to doll sales, the most famous of which is the annual Oldest Continuous Rodeo, held every August since 1884. The state's Old Time Fiddlers Contest is in late September.

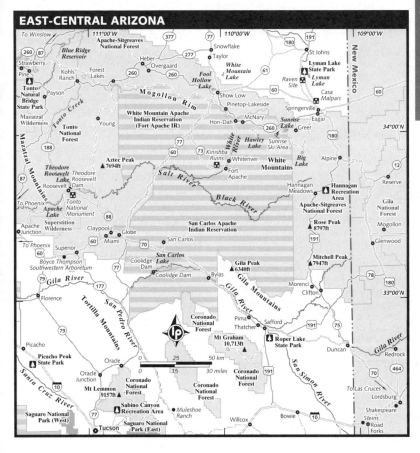

EAST-CENTRAL ARIZONA

## Places to Stay

**Camping** Free camping is allowed in the national forest, as long as you are a quarter-mile from a paved road.

Several developed USFS campsites sit along Hwy 260 east of Payson. They have drinking water but no showers. *Tonto Creek* ($8) is 17 miles east on Hwy 260, then a short drive north on USFS Rd 289. *Ponderosa*, 15 miles east, and *Christopher Creek*, 21 miles east and a short way south on USFS Rd 159, both charge $12. Other primitive campgrounds are scattered along dirt roads in the forest.

The USFS operates *Houston Mesa Campground*, a mile north of town along Hwy 87, with sites for tents, RVs and horses from $12 and up. There are showers. *Oxbow Estates RV Park* (☎ 474-2042), about 4 miles south of Payson off Hwy 87, offers tent and RV sites with hookups year-round and has showers, a coin laundry and a recreation room. Sites are $18.75 and summer reservations are recommended.

**Motels & Hotels** Rates vary depending on demand; double rooms start in the $60s during summer weekends, and in the $80s during holiday weekends. However, midweek in winter, the same room could be $40. There are no budget-priced places.

Some of the cheaper places include the basic *Best Value Inn* (☎ 474-2283, 800-474-2283, 811 S Beeline Hwy) and the nicer *Rim Country Inn* (☎ 474-4526, 101 W Phoenix) at the south end of town.

Nicer places in town charging $70 to $130 in summer include the *Majestic Mountain Inn* (☎ 474-0185, 800-408-2442, 602 E Hwy 260), set in landscaped pines and lawns with a seasonal pool, 50 rooms, all with refrigerators and coffeemakers, and many larger units with wet bars and patios, fireplaces or whirlpool baths.
website: www.majesticmountaininn.com

All the 99 rooms at the *Best Western Payson Inn* (☎ 474-3241, 800-247-9477, 801 N Beeline Hwy) have balconies or patios, coffeemakers and refrigerators; three have fireplaces, and some have microves and refrigerators. The hotel has a pool and whirlpool, and includes continental breakfast; visit their website at www.innof payson.com. *Chain motels* include a Days Inn and a Holiday Inn Express.

## Places to Eat

For Mexican food, dine at *El Rancho* (☎ 474-3111, 200 S Beeline Hwy).

## Entertainment

*Sawmill Theatres* (☎ 468-7535, 201 W Main) has six screens. *Mazatzal Casino*, run by the Tonto Apaches at the south end of town, is open 24 hours.

# SHOW LOW

☎ 928 • pop 7695 • elevation 6331 feet

Named after the 1876 card game in which the winner won a ranch by showing the lowest card (it was the deuce of clubs, which is now the name of the main street), Show Low is the gateway to the White Mountains, a region of forests and mountains popular with Arizonans. Along with neighboring Pinetop-Lakeside, it's a center for outdoor activities, including winter skiing. Though popular with lowland Arizonans escaping the heat, out-of-state visitors find it less interesting than more northerly and central parts of Arizona.

White Mountain Passenger Lines (☎ 537-4539) has a bus to Phoenix airport daily except Sunday.

## Orientation & Information

Most businesses are along Hwy 60/77, Deuce of Clubs. The chamber of commerce (☎ 537-2326) is on the web at showlow-chamberofcommerce.com. At the time of press, they don't know what their location will be by the end of 2002. Other services include the library (☎ 532-4070), 20 N 6th; post office (☎ 537-4588), 191 W Deuce of Clubs; hospital (☎ 537-4375), on Hwy 260 between Show Low and Pinetop-Lakeside; and the police (☎ 537-5091), 150 N 6th.

## Things to See & Do

A small historical museum (☎ 532-7115), 542 E Deuce of Clubs, is open from 1 to 5pm Tuesday to Friday and from 10am to

2pm Saturday from May through October. **Thunder Raceway** (☎ 537-1111), at the north-east end of town, has stock car, motocross and other races from March to November.

Three miles northwest of town, the **Fool Hollow Lake Recreation Area** (☎ 537-3680) has boat ramps, fishing, showers and a campground, and **Show Low Lake**, 4 miles south on Hwy 260 and a mile east on Show Low Lake Rd, has boat rentals (☎ 537-4126), fishing and camping.

The **scenic drive** along Hwy 60 to Globe goes through the Salt River Canyon and is one of the area's most spectacular drives.

### Places to Stay & Eat
Undeveloped free dispersed camping is available in the Apache-Sitgreaves National Forest surrounding town. (The ranger station is in Pinetop-Lakeside.) The USFS campground at *Fool Hollow Lake* offers showers, tent sites for $10 and RV sites with electric hookups for $17, and the one at *Show Low Lake* charges $8/16.

A dozen hotels line Deuce of Clubs. The cheapest, for about $30 to $50, include *Downtown 9 Motel* (☎ 537-4334, 1457 E Deuce of Clubs) and *Thunderbird Motel* (☎ 537-4391, 1131 E Deuce of Clubs). Nicer rooms with refrigerators and coffeemakers are $50 to $80 at the *KC Motel* (☎ 537-4433, 800-531-7152, 60 W Deuce of Clubs), which also offers a whirlpool and continental breakfast.

Five *chain motels* include the Motel 6, Best Western, Days Inn, Sleep Inn and Holiday Inn Express, all with rooms under $100. The last three have indoor pools.

Food in Show Low definitely leans toward standard American, with numerous eateries lining Deuce of Clubs.

### PINETOP-LAKESIDE
☎ 928 • pop 3582 • elevation 7000 feet
Southeast of Show Low, Hwy 260 (White Mountain Blvd) wends its way past three public lakes and passes numerous motels, cabins and stores.

The Pinetop-Lakeside Chamber of Commerce (☎ 367-4290, 800-573-4031), 674 E White Mountain Blvd, is open 9am to 5pm (till 4pm in winter) Monday to Friday, plus 9am to 3pm on summer weekends. Its website is www.pinetoplakesidechamber.com. Other services include the USFS Apache–Sitgreaves Lakeside Ranger Station (☎ 368-5111), 2022 W White Mountain Blvd; the Arizona Dept of Fish & Game (☎ 367-4281, 367-4342), 2878 E White Mountain Blvd; library (☎ 368-6688), 1595 W Johnson Lane; post office (☎ 367-4756), 712 E White Mountain Blvd; police (☎ 368-8802), 1360 Niels Hansen Lane. The hospital is in Show Low.

### Activities
The chamber of commerce has brochures describing scores of White Mountain lakes and streams suitable for **fishing**, and the USFS ranger station and Dept of Fish & Game are also excellent sources of information. Right in town, Rainbow Lake, Woodland Lake and Scotts Reservoir all offer fishing and **boating**, and Rainbow Lake has boat rentals.

Pinetop-Lakeside is a base for **cross-country skiing** and **hiking** as well as other activities in the White Mountains. Thirty miles east of town on Hwy 260, the Sunrise Ski Area (see White Mountain Apache Indian Reservation, later in this chapter) has **downhill skiing**. There are numerous **mountain-biking** trails. Several stores in town sell or rent camping gear, skis or bikes. For **horseback riding**, Porter Mountain Stables (☎ 368-5306) charges from $20 an hour to $75 all day for all levels of experience (minimum age six).

The White Mountains Trail System (☎ 368-6700) is a 180-mile series of loop trails designed for hiking, biking, horseback riding and cross-country skiing.

### Places to Stay
The accommodations are in a forest setting and are more rural than in Show Low. The location brings higher prices and two-day minimum stays may apply during summer.

Pick up a USFS map to find several roads heading northeast into the forest where free dispersed camping is allowed.

Opposite the ranger station, the USFS *Lakeside Campground* (☎ 368-6841) offers more than 80 sites for $10 each, and provides drinking water but no showers or hookups. The *Rainbow Forest RV Park* (☎ 368-5286, 3720 Rainbow Lake Dr), offers a few tent sites for $10 and 44 RV sites with hookups for $15.

Basic motel rooms are priced in the $50s and $60s in summer, more on weekends and holidays, less off-season. The *Nine Pines Motel* (☎ 367-2999, 888-597-4637, 2089 E White Mountain Blvd) has 23 standard rooms; visit their website at www.9pines .com. The *Bonanza Motel* (☎ 367-4440, 888-577-4440, 850 E White Mountain Blvd) has simple rooms and a few more-expensive units with kitchenettes.

The *Mountain Hacienda Lodge* (☎ 367-4146, 888-567-4148, 1023 E White Mountain Blvd) has 24 standard motel rooms with coffeemakers; its website is www.mountain-hacienda.com. The nearby *Timber Lodge Motel* (☎ 367-4463, 1078 E White Mountain Blvd), has 31 rooms, most with microwave and refrigerator; visit their website at www.timberlodge.com.

*Chain motels* include a Super 8 with a swimming pool, and a Best Western, Comfort Inn and Holiday Inn Express with whirlpools.

The following charge $60 to $120 a double. The small *Lazy Oaks Resort* (☎ 368-6203, 1075 Larson Rd), on a quiet street along Rainbow Lake, offers boat rentals and 15 one- and two-bedroom cabins with kitchens and fireplaces. Each sleeps from two to 10 people; its website is www.lazyoaks.com. The 11 cabins at *Hidden Rest Resort* (☎ 368-6336, 800-260-7378, 3448 Hwy 260) have fireplaces, kitchens and porches, and some have hot tubs; visit their website at www.hiddenrest.com. The *Rainbow's End Resort* (☎ 368-9004, 267 Trout Rd) has eight lakeside cabins, all with kitchenettes and some with fireplaces. Boats can be rented; take a look at their website at www.rainbowsendresort.com.

The *Coldstream B&B* (☎ 369-0115), located at the southeast end of Pinetop (call for directions or look at their website at www.wmonline.com/coldstream), rents six rooms with private bath for $95 to $160 double, and provides a hot tub, pool table, bicycles and afternoon tea as well as full breakfast. Several less expensive B&Bs belong to the White Mountain B&B Association – their website is at www.wmbba.com.

*Lake of the Woods* (☎ 368-5353) has two dozen cabins and chalets sleeping two to eight people for $100 to $190. A playground, game room and whirlpool are available, and boat rental is nearby; visit www.privatelake.com. The *Northwoods Resort* (☎ 367-2966, 800-813-2966, 165 E White Mountain Blvd) has 15 pleasant one-to three-bedroom cabins, each with fireplace and kitchen, ranging from $120 to $300 a double in summer; its website is www.northwoodsaz.com.

The area's most upscale accommodations are at *Sierra Springs Ranch* (☎ 369-3900, 800-492-4059, Sierra Springs Dr). Eight fully furnished cabins, including fireplace and kitchen, start at $175 double and go up to $525 for a cabin sleeping 13. The grounds feature fishing ponds, a tennis court, game room, playground and exercise room. website: www.sierraspringsranch.com

## Places to Eat

As in Show Low, the best places serve American food. The following serve good dinners in the $13 to $25 range. *Charlie Clark's* (☎ 367-4900, 1701 E White Mountain Blvd) has been a favorite steak house for decades. The *Christmas Tree Restaurant* (☎ 367-3107, 455 Woodland Rd) has an oddly rustic Christmasy décor; the varied menu is not limited to steak and seafood, offering chicken 'n dumplings as the house specialty. Dine outside in summer.

## WHITE MOUNTAIN APACHE INDIAN RESERVATION

Lying north of the Salt River, this reservation is separate from the San Carlos Apache Indian Reservation, described later in this chapter.

Like the Navajo, with whom they share linguistic similarities, the Apache were relatively late arrivals in the Southwest, arriving in the 14th century from the north. A hunting people, they lived in temporary shelters and moved often, frequently raiding other tribes and, later, Europeans. The White Mountain Apache were willing to accommodate US expansion more than most, and many of the US Army's Apache scouts were secured from this group.

The White Mountain Apache were fairly isolated until the 1950s, when tribal leaders began long-term development to take advantage of modern lifestyles. Building roads and dams, they created some of the Southwest's best outdoor recreation. Over 2500 sq miles of forest offer beautiful hiking, cross-country and downhill skiing, fishing, camping and boating. State licenses for fishing, boating or hunting aren't needed, but you do need tribal permits for these activities, as well as for all outdoor activities. Permits are available from stores on the reservation or from surrounding towns.

**Whiteriver** (population 3800) is the tribal capital, with the tribal offices, a supermarket, bank, post office, restaurant and basic motel ($55).

**Fort Apache**, 4 miles south of Whiteriver, was a US Army post in 1870. It remains in much better condition than most structures from that period. Two dozen remaining buildings give visitors a sense of army life on the Western frontier. Closed in 1922, the fort became an Indian boarding school, which contributed to its preservation. Stop by the Apache Cultural Center (☎ 338-4625), open Monday to Friday 8am to 5pm (with extended summer hours) to learn about the history of the fort and the soldiers and scouts stationed there. The center also has informative exhibits about the tribe's cultural heritage and an excellent display of basketry. Admission is $3 for 15- to 62-year-olds, $2 for seniors and children over five.

## Activities

Sunrise Park Resort has good skiing, excellent summer fishing and a comfortable, if characterless, hotel. The Sunrise Ski Area (☎ 735-7669, 735-7600, 800-772-7669 for a snow report, 735-7518 for the ski school) is the state's largest ski area with 60 runs serv-

iced by seven chair and four tow lifts. Snowboarders are welcome. Two miles from the alpine ski area, the Sunrise Sports Center (☎ 735-7335) has 6 miles of groomed cross-country trails. At 9100 feet, Sunrise Lake has some of the best trout fishing in the area and boat rental is available. Other lakes are close by.

Hon-Dah Casino & Resort (☎ 369-0299, 800-929-8744), 2 miles south of Pinetop-Lakeside at the junction of Hwys 260 and 73, has slot machines and live poker. Hawley Lake is one of the two most developed fishing areas on the reservation. Rent canoes, rowboats and electric motorboats from the marina (☎ 335-7511) from mid-May to mid-October.

## Places to Stay

The Hon-Dah Casino complex includes the *Hon-Dah Resort* (see Activities), with 128 comfortable rooms and a restaurant and lounge with entertainment. Weekend rates are $99, $20 less midweek. *Hon-Dah RV Park (☎ 369-7400)* has 120 sites at $17.

*Hawley Lake Resort (☎ 335-7871, 369-1753)* has about 30 motel rooms and cabins, all with kitchenettes, for $110 to $150; they sleep from four to ten people. Campsites are also available.

The *Sunrise Park Hotel (☎ 735-7669, 800-554-6835)* is by Sunrise Lake and a couple of miles from the ski area. Free shuttle buses run frequently in winter, and the restaurant, swimming pool, whirlpool, sauna and bar – with winter weekend entertainment – keep guests relaxed and happy. During the high season (winter weekends, holidays and mid-December through the first week in January) room prices jump to between $95 and $125, and suites to $300. At other times, rates start around $60. The hotel offers a variety of special packages to tie in with resort activities; call for details. Near the hotel are inexpensive *camping sites*.

## GREER

☎ 928 • pop 100 • elevation 8500 feet

In summer, tiny Greer provides a cool getaway with convenient fishing and shady hikes. Get information about its offerings at www.greeraz.com. In winter the town is a base for skiing, with the Sunrise Park Resort 15 miles away and cross-country skiing, if conditions permit, outside your door. Lee Valley Stables (☎ 735-7454) leads horseback-riding trips in summer, and the Greer Lodge arranges romantic horse-drawn sleigh rides when winter conditions permit. The small Circle B Market (☎ 735-7540) has food, fishing information, maps and cross-country ski rentals. There is no public transportation.

The USFS has two *campgrounds* on Hwy 373. Benny Creek offers 30 sites for $8 with no drinking water. Rolfe C Hoyer offers 100 sites for $14 and has drinking water, electric hookups, lake access and a boat ramp. Both are open mid-May to mid-September.

Most places are pretty rustic, and two-night minimum stays are often required. For basic *motel rooms* from $50, call the Circle B Market. The *Molly Butler Lodge* (☎ 735-7226) opened in 1910, claims to be the oldest lodge in Arizona; it offers simple rooms for $35 to $50 a double and has a good *restaurant*.

The *Greer Lodge* (☎ 735-7216, 888-475-6343) offers eight lodge rooms for $150 a double and some cabins with full kitchens. Most cabins are $120 a double, and two larger ones are $35 per person with a six-person minimum.
website: www.greerlodge.com

The *Snowy Mountain Inn* (☎ 735-7576, 888-766-9971), set back off Hwy 373 amid the trees, has seven log cabins with fire-places, kitchens, TV/VCRs and hot tubs. Two one-bedroom cabins are $150 and five two- and three-bedroom cabins are $165. It also has four homes with three beds and two baths sleeping six to 12 people for $255 to $350.
website: www.snowymountaininn.com

At the far south end of Greer, the attractive award-winning *Red Setter Inn B&B* (☎ 735-7441, 888-994-7337) is a three-story hand-hewn log building. Nine individually decorated rooms with private baths and some with a fireplace, Jacuzzi, deck or patio are $120 to $160 a double, including full breakfast. Smoking and children under 16 are not allowed.
website: www.redsetterinn.com

The *White Mountain Lodge B&B* (☎ 735-7568, 888-493-7568) is in an 1892 farmhouse. Seven rooms with private baths, some with fireplace or whirlpool tub, cost from $85 to $155 a double including full breakfast; six cabins with kitchens and fire-places range from $85 to $100 double, not including breakfast.
website: www.wmlodge.com

## SPRINGERVILLE & EAGAR
☎ 928 • pop 1972; pop 4033 • elevation 7000 feet

These adjoining towns are important ranch-ing centers and the cool climate attracts tourists, anglers and hunters. The area has the added attraction of being close to two archaeological sites currently under excava-tion. West of town, notice over 400 volcanic vents in a 1200-sq-mile volcanic field, the continent's third largest. The chamber of commerce has information about this as well as about the private Renee Cushman collection of European art from the Renais-sance to the early 20th century, in the Springerville Church, which can be viewed on request.

The area has several good fishing and boating lakes, as well as trails for hiking, mountain biking and horseback riding. The USFS and chamber of commerce have in-formation. Fishing permits, supplies and in-formation are available from the Sport Shack (☎ 333-2222), 329 E Main, Springerville, or Western Drug (☎ 333-4321), 105 E Main, Springerville. You can rent skis, snowboards and mountain bikes at the Sweat Shop (☎ 333-2950), 74 N Main, Eagar.

### Information
The Round Valley Chamber of Commerce (☎ 333-2123), 318 E Main, Springerville, is open 9am to 4pm daily; visit their website at www.az-tourist.com. Other services include the Springerville USFS Ranger Station (☎ 333-4372), Mountain Ave at Airport Rd; library (☎ 333-4694), 367 N Main, Eagar;

Springerville Post Office (☎ 333-4962), 5 Main; hospital (☎ 333-4368), 118 S Mountain Ave, Springerville; and police (☎ 333-4240), 418 E Main, Springerville.

## Archaeological Sites

At the **Casa Malpais** site, a kiva, burial chambers, plaza, buildings, two stairways and many rock art panels were created by the Mogollon people in the mid-13th century and abandoned in the late 14th century. The site, 2 miles northeast of Springerville, can be visited only on guided tours from the Casa Malpais Archaeology Center (☎ 333-5375) in the chamber of commerce building. The center has a tiny museum, a short video about the site and a bookstore. Hours are 8am to 4pm daily. In summer, tours are offered at 9 and 11am and 2pm, with fewer departures in winter. Tours are weather dependent, last about 90 minutes, and involve a half-mile walk with some climbing. Fees are $6; $5 for those over 55 or between 12 and 18 years old. Call about the center's participatory archaeological research program.

website: www.casamalpais.com

The **Raven Site** is a Mogollon pueblo built and occupied between AD 1100 and 1450. Over 600 rooms have been identified at this site, about 12 miles north of Springerville. It is closed at time of publication, but is expected to re-open in 2003. Contact the Casa Malpais Archeology Center for the latest information.

## Places to Stay

The USFS office can tell you about campgrounds in the Apache-Sitgreaves National Forest (some of the closest are at Greer, above, and at Big Lake). *Casa Malpais Campground & RV Park* (☎ 333-4632), 1½ miles northwest of Springerville on Hwy 60, offers showers and RV sites with hookups for $16. *Bear Paw RV Park* (☎ 333-4650, 425 E Central, Eagar) offers RV hookups for $13, but lacks showers.

The *White Mountain Motel* (☎ 333-5482, 333 E Main, Springerville) has basic rooms from $45, some with kitchenettes. Friendly *Reed's Lodge* (☎ 333-4323, 800-814-6451, 514 E Main, Springerville) has an outdoor spa, a game room, gift shop, morning coffee, and a few bicycles to loan. It's a pleasant old Western inn, and John Wayne (who owned a ranch nearby) used to hang out here. The owners run a 30 sq mile working ranch, and they offer guests the opportunity to join them as they round up the cattle and work the ranch. If the day's work includes horseback riding, rates are $75/100 for a half/full day; otherwise, rates vary. They only take a couple of families at a time, so it is an intimate way to wee the western ranch life. They also offer hikiing trips. Clean and comfortable older rooms are $30/40 single/double, and newer 'deluxe' rooms are $10 more. Chains include the *Super 8* and *Best Western*.

---

### Archaeology in Action

The Mogollon people left fewer sites than did some other cultures living in the early part of the second millennium, but two that did survive are currently being excavated in the Springerville area. Ever wondered what archaeologists do for a living? You can watch them work at Casa Malpais or Raven Site.

If you really want to get involved, ask about the participatory research programs, but be aware that research procedures are deliberate and painstaking. The archaeologist uses brushes and hand trowels to slowly and gingerly loosen centuries of debris from the sites. Each object found, be it an entire pot or just a tiny shard or scrap of wood, must be carefully labeled and recorded. Archaeologists must know exactly where one piece was found in relation to the next in order to build up an accurate record of the history of the site. A helper who removes an artifact and says 'Look what I found!' is no help at all; archaeologists must know exactly where the item was found and what was underneath, over and next to it. The work requires care and attention but can be very rewarding.

Four rooms in the 1910 *Paisley Corner B&B* (☎ 333-4665, 287 N Main, Eagar) are furnished with antiques, have private baths, and are priced from $75 to $95. Its mailing address is PO Box 458, AZ 85938.

## Places to Eat
In Springerville, *Booga Reds Restaurant & Cantina* (☎ 333-5036, 521 E Main) serves inexpensive Mexican and American food from 5:30am to 9pm daily. *Los Dos Molinos* (☎ 333-4846, 900 E Main) prides itself on its hot homemade salsa, and is open for Mexican lunch and dinner Tuesday to Saturday. The *Safire Restaurant & Lounge* (☎ 333-4512, 411 E Main) opens at 6am daily and serves a good variety of reasonably priced American food, with some Italian and Mexican plates and nightly dinner specials.

## LYMAN LAKE STATE PARK
Lyman Lake was formed when settlers dammed the Little Colorado River in 1915, bringing fine fishing, boating and water sports to an area where, even at 6000 feet, summer temperatures are often over 90°F. A small marina has boat rentals, supplies and a boat ramp. Rangers offer special programs in summer, including tours of nearby petroglyphs and sites. A small herd of buffalo lives in the park. Day use costs $4.

The park (☎ 337-4441), off Hwy 191 about 12 miles south of St Johns, offers tent camping for $10, partial RV hookups for $15, and provides showers.

## CORONADO TRAIL SCENIC ROAD
In 1540 Francisco Vásquez de Coronado (see Coronado National Memorial in the Southeastern Arizona chapter) headed northeast in search of riches and the legendary Seven Cities of Cibola. Highways 180 and 191 between Springerville and Clifton roughly parallel this historic route. Although it is only 120 miles, it takes four hours to drive. The road climbs to 9000 feet before dropping to 3500 feet at Clifton, and many hairpin bends in the descent slow you down to 10mph. Scenic views provide occa-

sional pullouts, but trailers over 20 feet long are not recommended. Fall colors, peaking in September and October, are among the most spectacular in the state, especially on aspen-covered Escudilla Mountain near Alpine. Many unpaved side roads lead into pristine forest for hiking, camping, fishing, hunting and cross-country skiing, but winter snows can sometimes close the road south of Alpine for days. There are several USFS campgrounds along the main road, and others on unpaved side roads. The Apache-Sitgreaves Ranger Stations in Clifton, Alpine and Springerville have information. Remember that there are no gas stations along the 90 miles between Alpine and Morenci.

## Alpine
☎ 928 • pop 650 • elevation 8050 feet
One of Arizona's highest towns, Alpine is an excellent base for outdoor activities in the surrounding Apache-Sitgreaves National Forest. The village is loosely scattered around the junction of Hwy 180 and Hwy 191; visit its chamber of commerce website at www.alpine-az.com. The Apache-Sitgreaves Alpine Ranger Station (☎ 339-4384) is at the junction.

**Hannagan Recreation Area** At over 9000 feet and 20 miles south of Alpine along Hwy 191, the Hannagan Recreation Area is the highest part of the Coronado Trail, and offers summertime mountain biking and hiking, as well as some of the best cross-country skiing and snowmobiling in the state. You can fish in a nearby lake and camp in one of the many campgrounds near the area. Stop at the ranger station to pick up more information. The Hannagan Meadow Lodge is open year-round.

**Places to Stay & Eat** On Hwy 180 near the junction, *Alpine Village RV Park* (☎ 339-1841) has showers ($4) and tent and RV sites with hookups for $5/15. *Meadow View RV Park* (☎ 339-1850), on Hwy 191 south of the junction, has RV sites for $20. Free dispersed camping is allowed throughout much of the forest, and there are many developed USFS campgrounds. The closest ones are *Alpine Divide*, 4 miles north of town on Hwy 180, offering 12 sites for $8 mid-May to mid-September, and *Luna Lake*, 6 miles east on Hwy 180, with sites for $10. Fishing and boat rental are nearby.

Four basic motels or cabin complexes are near the Hwy 191/180 junction. They charge $35 to $55. A couple of simple diners are nearby. The *Tal-Wi-Wi Lodge* (☎ *339-4319*), 4 miles north on Hwy 180, offers 20 rooms ranging from standard motel rooms to rooms with hot tubs and fireplaces for $65 to $95. *Hannagan Meadow Lodge* (☎ *339-4370*), 20 miles south along Hwy 191, provides 16 attractively rustic rooms and cabins from $70 to $100. Its restaurant is open in summer and winter.

## Clifton
☎ 928 • pop 2596 • elevation 3500 feet
Although Clifton is the Greenlee County seat, it is one of the most decrepit towns in Arizona and most of the once-splendid buildings lining historic Chase Street (off Hwy 191 in the center) are boarded up; it's still worth a stroll. The neighboring town, Morenci, was swallowed up by a huge open-pit mine and rebuilt in the 1960s at its present site. Six miles above Morenci, an overlook from Hwy 191 gives dizzying views of the country's biggest producer of copper. As you look down on this open-pit mine 2 miles in length, 200-ton trucks with tires 9 feet in diameter crawl like insects at the bottom. Free mine tours by Phelps Dodge (☎ 865-4521) might be offered. Standard motel rooms are available in the $40s at the *Rode Inn* (☎ *865-4536, 186 S Coronado Blvd*), on Hwy 191 at the south end of Clifton, and in the $70s at the *Morenci Motel* (☎ *865-4111*) on the main street in Morenci.

## SAFFORD
☎ 928 • pop 9232 • elevation 2920 feet
Safford's motels make this the most convenient gateway for the Coronado Trail to the northeast, the San Carlos Apache Indian Reservation to the northwest and

the Swift Trail up lofty Mt Graham to the southwest.

Greyhound stops outside the Cirkle K (☎ 428-1711),1123 W Thatcher en route to Phoenix and Lordsburg, New Mexico.

### Orientation & Information
Safford is mostly spread out along east-west Hwy 70, also called Thatcher Blvd and 5th St in the town center.

The chamber of commerce (☎ 428-2511, 888-837-1841), 1111 W Thatcher Blvd, is open 8am to 5pm weekdays, and 9am to 3pm Saturday; look at www.graham-chamber.com. It has a display on local industries as well as tourist information. Other services include the Coronado National Forest Ranger Station (☎ 428-4150) in the post office building; BLM (☎ 348-4400), 711 14th Ave; library (☎ 348-3202), 808 7th Ave; post office (☎ 428-0220), 504 5th Ave; hospital (☎ 348-4000), 1600 20th Ave; and police (☎ 348-3190, 428-3141), 525 10th Ave.

### Things to See & Do
**Discovery Park** (☎ 428-6260, 888-837-1841), 2 miles south along 20th Ave, has trails, nature exhibits and a short narrow-gauge railway. The highlight is the **Gov Aker Observatory**, with a 20-inch reflecting astronomical telescope, a space-flight simulator and astronomy exhibits. The park is open 1 to 10pm, Tuesday through Saturday. Admission is $4, $3 for children, $6 for the space-flight simulator and $1 for a train ride. This observatory will arrange tours of the observatory at Mt Graham (see the boxed text 'Development on Mt Graham'). The observatory is closed for remodeling at the time of publication; call the park or access their website at www.discoverypark.com for current information on tours.

Several natural mineral **hot springs** are six miles south of town. Two commercial spas charge $5 to use their hot tubs and offer massage and reflexology treatments for $25 and up. Call Essence of Tranquility (☎ 428-9312, 877-895-6810) or Kachina Mineral Springs (☎ 428-7212) for rates and directions.

EAST-CENTRAL ARIZONA

**Roper Lake State Park** (☎ 428-6760), on the east side of Hwy 191, 6 miles south of Safford, offers camping, boating, fishing, swimming and a hot springs. Day use costs $5 per vehicle.

Hwy 366, popularly called the **Swift Trail Scenic Drive** is a paved road up the Pinaleno Mountains almost to the top of 10,713-foot **Mt Graham**. The road begins from Hwy 191 almost 8 miles south of Safford and climbs 34 miles to the summit, all within the Coronado National Forest. The Columbine Visitor Station, more than 20 miles along the Swift Trail, offers maps and information and is open daily 9am to 6pm Memorial Day to Labor Day.

### Places to Stay & Eat

Several **USFS campgrounds** (☎ 428-4150) along the Swift Trail cost $8 to $12 and have water but no showers or hookups. **Roper Lake State Park** charges $10 for tents and

---

### Development on Mt Graham

Mt Graham is one of the 'sky islands' of southeastern Arizona, separated from other summits in the area by lowlands. Because plants and animals living near the top of the mountain have been isolated from similar species living on other nearby ranges, some have evolved into different species or subspecies; this makes these high peaks a living natural laboratory for the study of evolution.

However, because Mt Graham is the highest mountain in the area and a long way from city lights and other sky pollutants, it has been chosen as the site of a major telescope observatory. Currently under construction, the project threatens the habitat of the Mt Graham red squirrel, among other 'sky island' species, and is therefore embroiled in controversy. Mt Graham is also a sacred site for some Apache Indians, an additional conflict. A small exhibit in the Safford Chamber of Commerce describes the astronomy project in glowing terms as a source of more employment and tourism for the area.

---

$17 for RVs with hookups; the campgrounds have showers. *Essence of Tranquility Hot Springs* (see above) allows camping for $10 and has teepees for rent. The teepees come with beds and communal baths and start at $20/30 for a single/double bed. Reservations are required.

For rooms around $30, try the *Motel Western* (☎ 428-7850, 1215 W Thatcher Blvd), which has a small pool. Otherwise, it's mainly **chain motels** including Econolodge, Days Inn, Best Western, Comfort Inn and Ramada Inn.

*Olney House B&B* (☎ 428-5118, 800-814-5118, 1104 Central Ave) charges $80 per couple in three rooms with shared bath and in two cottages with kitchenettes. Email the B&B at olney@zekes.com.

*Casa Mañana* (☎ 428-3170, 502 1st Ave) has been here for half a century and serves tasty Mexican lunches and dinners daily. Standard American fare is offered at restaurants next to all the chain motels.

## SAN CARLOS APACHE INDIAN RESERVATION

About 2900 sq miles of lakes, rivers, forests and desert belong to the San Carlos Apache Tribe. Over 8000 people live here, of whom 3000 live in the tribal capital of San Carlos just off Hwy 70. Cattle ranching is the primary business.

Most tourists come for outdoor recreation or the tribal casino. A maze of unpaved roads penetrates the reservation, leading to scores of little lakes and river fishing areas as well as primitive camping areas. The best known is **San Carlos Lake**, formed by the Coolidge Dam on the Gila River. When full, it covers 30 sq miles and has excellent fishing, including state record-winning catfish, largemouth bass and crappie. Near Coolidge Dam are a marina, convenience store and campground (no phone) with RV hookups, water and tent spaces, but no showers. Fees are $5 a person. Trout fishing on the Black River is good, and big-game hunting is permitted in season; local guides can be hired.

To camp, hike, fish, hunt and drive off the main highways, you'll need a permit from

Tucson is ringed by mountain ranges.

Barrio Historico in downtown Tucson

Kennedy outside the Pima Courthouse

RICHARD CUMMINS

Mission San Xavier del Bac against the sunset sky, near Tucson

RICHARD CUMMINS

Petroglyphs at Signal Hill in Saguaro National Park, near Tucson

the San Carlos Recreation and Wildlife Dept (☎ 475-2343, 888-475-2344), PO Box 97, San Carlos, AZ 85550. The tribal offices (☎ 475-2361) have other information.

The small but informative **San Carlos Apache Cultural Center** (☎ 475-2894) tells of the history and culture of the tribe. The center is near mileage marker 272 on Hwy 70, about 20 miles east of Globe. Hours are 9am to 5pm, but days change so call ahead. Admission is $3; $1.50 for seniors; $1 for students and children.

**Sunrise Ceremonies**, held in the summer, feature traditional dances in honor of young girls' coming of age. Some ceremonies may be open to the public; call the tribal office for details. The tribal **rodeo and fair**, held in San Carlos over Veterans Day weekend (closest weekend to November 11) also features traditional dancing.

The only motel is the ***Best Western Apache Gold Hotel*** (☎ 402-5600, 800-272-2438) near the tribal casino (☎ 425-8000), 5 miles east of Globe. It features a pool, sauna, whirlpool, restaurant and lounge, and 146 rooms in the $50 to $100 range. There is an RV park here as well, and a campground near Coolidge Dam.

## GLOBE
☎ 928 • pop 7486 • elevation 3544 feet
The discovery of a globe-shaped boulder formed of almost pure silver sparked a short-lived silver boom here in the 1870s, followed by the development of a long-lasting copper mining industry. Globe offers the best accommodations in the area, and its various attractions provide a pleasant rural alternative to Phoenix (80 miles west).

Greyhound (☎ 425-2301), 1660 E Ash, has two buses a day to Phoenix and two to Safford and beyond.

## Information
The Globe-Miami Chamber of Commerce (☎ 425-4495, 800-804-5623), 1360 N Broad, is open Monday to Friday 8am to 5pm. Other services include the Tonto National Forest USFS Ranger Station (☎ 402-6200) on Six Shooter Canyon Rd at the south end of town; library (☎ 425-6111), 339 S Broad;

post office (☎ 425-2381), 101 S Hill; hospital (☎ 425-3261), between Globe and Miami south of the Hwy 60/88 intersection, and the police (☎ 425-5752), 175 N Pine.

## Things to See & Do
Behind the chamber of commerce, the Gila County Historical Museum (☎ 425-7385) displays much about Globe's history; hours are 10am to 4pm Monday to Friday, 11am to 3pm on Saturday; admission is free. Ask at the chamber about the many turn-of-the-19th-century buildings lining Broad St south of Hackney Ave – a pleasant stroll with few tourists.

Globe's highlight is the Besh-Ba-Gowah Archaeological Park (☎ 425-0320), 150 N Pine (follow signs south of town). The centerpiece is a small pueblo built by the Salado people in the 1200s and abandoned by the early 1400s. The park also has a museum with a fine collection of Salado pottery and an ethnobotanical garden. Admission is $3 for those over 12 years old.

Wilderness Aware (☎ 425-7272, 800-231-7238) offers one- to five-day Salt River rafting trips. High water is February to April.

## Places to Stay & Eat
Several inexpensive mom 'n' pop motels are found along Hwy 60. The ***El Rey Motel*** (☎ 425-4427, 1201 E Ash) is an old-fashioned motor court surrounding a lawn and barbecue area; this glimpse of Americana has basic but clean rooms for $25/36 with one or two beds. ***Chain motels*** along Hwy 60 include a Days Inn, Comfort Inn, Super 8, Ramada Limited and Holiday Inn Express.

Housed in a renovated school dating from 1907, the ***Noftsger Hill Inn B&B*** (☎ 425-2260, 425 North) has rooms with shared bath or with private bath and king-size beds, most with fireplaces; prices range from $65 to $85. See them on the web at noftsgerhillinn.com. ***Cedar Hill B&B*** (☎ 425-7530, 175 E Cedar) charges $50.

In the old-town center of town, ***La Casita*** (☎ 425-8462, 470 N Broad) serves good Mexican lunches and dinners. Another

EAST-CENTRAL ARIZONA

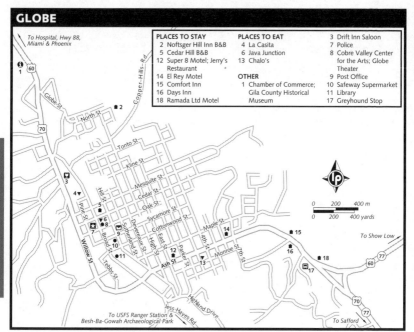

**GLOBE**

To Hospital, Hwy 88,
Miami & Phoenix

**PLACES TO STAY**
2 Noftsger Hill Inn B&B
5 Cedar Hill B&B
12 Super 8 Motel; Jerry's Restaurant
14 El Rey Motel
15 Comfort Inn
16 Days Inn
18 Ramada Ltd Motel

**PLACES TO EAT**
4 La Casita
6 Java Junction
13 Chalo's

**OTHER**
1 Chamber of Commerce; Gila County Historical Museum

3 Drift Inn Saloon
7 Police
8 Cobre Valley Center for the Arts; Globe Theater
9 Post Office
10 Safeway Supermarket
11 Library
17 Greyhound Stop

To Show Low

To USFS Ranger Station & Besh-Ba-Gowah Archaeological Park

To Safford

good Mexican-food choice is *Chalo's* (☎ 425-0515, 902 E Ash). The best coffee in town is at *Java Junction* (☎ 402-8926) at the corner of Broad and Cedar. *Jerry's Restaurant* (☎ 425-5282, 699 E Ash) serves standard American fare 24 hours a day.

Wet your whistle at one of the old bars, such as the *Drift Inn Saloon* (☎ 425-9573, 636 N Broad).

## BOYCE THOMPSON SOUTHWESTERN ARBORETUM

About 28 miles west of Globe on Hwy 60, this arboretum (☎ 520-689-2811) is the Southwest's oldest and is a great place for a quiet garden walk. The visitor center has information about the trails winding through these 35 acres of arid-land plants; dogs are welcome. It's open daily except Christmas; admission is $6; $3 for five- to 12-year-olds.
website: www.arboretum.ag.arizona.edu

## THE APACHE TRAIL

The Apache Trail (Hwy 88) heads northwest of Apache Junction (west of Phoenix), ending at Globe 75 miles later, and is one of the more spectacular drives in the area. A 20-mile section west of the Roosevelt Dam is steep, winding, narrow and unpaved; not recommended for trailers or large RVs. Once you reach Globe, return via the much faster paved Hwy 60. Stop at the arboretum for a good roundtrip from Phoenix.

Almost immediately after leaving Apache Junction, you'll see the **Superstition Wilderness** looming above you to the right. Supposedly home to the fabled Lost Dutchman Mine, this rugged area is filled with hiking trails and mining stories. It is a designated wilderness, so no development or vehicles are allowed. You can hike in on foot and camp anywhere, but be prepared – there's some remote and difficult terrain in here. The area is part of the Tonto National

Forest. Ranger stations in Mesa, Roosevelt and Globe have information.

Nestled under the Superstition Mountains is **Lost Dutchman State Park** (☎ 480-982-4485), 5½ miles northeast of Apache Junction. The park (elevation 2000 feet) has picnic areas and hiking, horse and mountain-bike trails, which are hot in summer. Day use is $5 per vehicle or $1 per individual. A 35-site *campground* charges $10 and has water but no showers or hookups.

Just before the park **Goldfield Ghost Town** (☎ 480-983-0333) has been renovated for tourism. Try your hand at gold panning, eat at the Western steak house, examine old artifacts in the mining museum, take a horse ride or jump aboard the steam-train circling the town. Admission is free, though the attractions charge a few dollars each. A dry *campground* charges $10. A few miles beyond, the 20-mile unpaved section begins.

Fifteen miles from Apache Junction, **Canyon Lake** (☎ 602-944-6504) offers boat rentals, a *restaurant* and *bar*, and *camping* ($12 for tents and $25 for RV hookups). Ninety-minute cruises (☎ 480-827-9144) are $15, $9 for five- to 12-year olds. Given its proximity to Phoenix, it's a busy lake. Two miles beyond, you hit the Wild West at **Tortilla Flat**, once a stagecoach stop and now a touristy but popular stop for drivers on the trail. You can eat lunch in the saloon (10am to 4pm), or spend the night in the *campground* opposite, which offers sites without drinking water for $10. Soon after, the road begins the unpaved section.

Long, narrow **Apache Lake** features the *Apache Lake Resort* (☎ 928-467-2511) where a marina offers a boat ramp and rentals, tent ($5) and RV camping with hookups ($20), and a small lodge with standard motel rooms and rooms with kitchenettes for $60 to $90; visit www.apachelake.com. Also along the lake and the Salt River are several *campgrounds* administered by the Tonto National Forest.

Some 45 miles out of Apache Junction, the road returns to pavement and passes the **Theodore Roosevelt Dam**. Built of brick on the Salt River in 1911, this was the first large dam to flood the Southwest and, at 280 feet, is the world's highest masonry dam. The Roosevelt Lake behind the dam attracts water-sport enthusiasts year-round; swimming, water-skiing and boating are popular activities from spring to fall. The fishing is great throughout the year, and bass and crappie are two favored catches. A visitor center and the Tonto Basin Ranger Station (☎ 928-467-3200) are about 1½ miles east of the dam. The **Roosevelt Lake Marina** (☎ 928-467-2245) has groceries, fishing and camping supplies, a snack bar and a boat ramp; boat rentals range from fishing boats for $50 a day to ski boats for $260 a day.

At the far end of the lake is the *Spring Creek Inn (☎ 928-467-2888)*, where a motel has rooms for $45 or rooms with kitchenettes for $65; rates are a bit more on weekends, and RV sites are $20.
website: www.rooseveltlake.com

## TONTO NATIONAL MONUMENT

About 28 miles northwest of Globe off paved Hwy 88, the monument protects a highlight of the area: a two-story Salado pueblo built in a cave. Like most other pueblos, it was mysteriously abandoned in the early 1400s.

From the visitor center (☎ 928-467-2241), a paved half-mile footpath climbs gently to the site, with good views of the saguaro cactus-studded hillsides in the foreground and Roosevelt Lake in the distance. The visitor center has a museum and water but no food or camping facilities.

The monument is open from 8am to 5pm every day except Christmas, but the trail closes an hour earlier. Admission costs $3 per person over 16 and all passes are honored.

# Tucson & Southern Arizona

When isolated groups of Spanish explorers straggled through in the 1530s, this region of desert, mountain ranges and grasslands was inhabited by the Tohono O'odham (called Papago until 1986) and the closely related Pima Indians, who were perhaps the descendants of the Hohokam people, whose culture disappeared around AD 1400. The

## Highlights

- Picnicking and hiking in the Santa Catalina Mountains

- Birding in the mountains and desert surrounding Tucson, well known for rare birds

- Splurging on a ranch vacation, with horseback riding and other activities

- Eating fiery salsa and enchiladas at the many Mexican restaurants

- Learning about desert critters and flora at the Arizona-Sonora Desert Museum

- Driving and hiking through Saguaro National Park

- Exploring undisturbed Sonoran Desert habitat

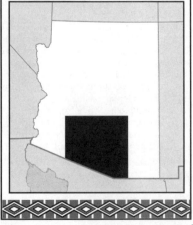

Apache Indians, who arrived later on, lived in the far southeast of present-day Arizona.

The first big Spanish expedition was in 1540, led by Francisco Vásquez de Coronado, who entered the area near present-day Sierra Vista on his way north in search of the 'Seven Cities of Cibola.' His descriptions are the earliest we have of the region, which was largely ignored by the Spanish for well over a century until the Jesuit priest Padre Eusebio Francisco Kino arrived in the late 1600s and spent two decades establishing missions primarily among the Pima people. One of the churches he founded, Mission San Xavier del Bac, south of Tucson, is still used today. It is the finest example of Spanish colonial architecture in Arizona, rivaling the missions of New Mexico for architectural beauty and historical interest. Kino was also responsible for introducing cattle into the area.

With the missions came immigrants: Spanish settlers from the Mexican colonies. They lived in an uneasy truce with the Indians until 1751, when the Pimas rebelled against the unwanted newcomers and killed or forced out many settlers and missionaries. The Spanish authorities sent in soldiers to control the Indians and protect the settlers, building several walled forts, or *presidios*, one of which became the city of Tucson. After Mexico won its independence from Spain in 1821, Tucson became a Mexican town. Thus southeastern Arizona, more than other parts of the state, had both a traditional Indian culture and a rich Hispanic heritage that predated the arrival of the Anglos.

The Gadsden Purchase of 1853 turned southeastern Arizona, on paper at least, from Mexican into US territory. Anglos began to arrive, homesteading the grasslands in the southeastern corner and finding that it made good ranching country. But they failed to realize that the Apaches, who inhabited the desert grasslands and mountains of the far southeastern corner of

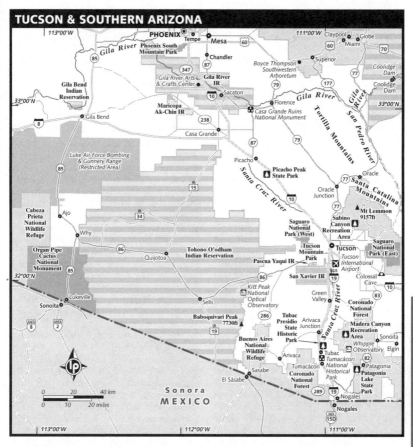

# TUCSON & SOUTHERN ARIZONA

Arizona, didn't much care about the Gadsden Purchase – after all, from their point of view, it was Apache country and not Mexican in the first place. Tensions arising from this difference erupted in conflicts between Indians and Americans. Although such conflicts marked the US expansion from the east through most of the 1800s, the ones in Apache territory were especially fierce. Led by legendary warrior-chiefs Cochise and Geronimo, Apaches were the last holdouts in the so-called Indian Wars, which lasted until the 1886 surrender of Geronimo.

Today, many Apaches live on reservations in east-central Arizona and New Mexico, and what used to be their territory is now cattle ranching and mining country, where rolling vistas of ranchlands are studded with small but steep mountain ranges, the 'sky islands' of southeastern Arizona. The most dramatic are the Chiricahuas, protected in a national monument. The early ranchers and miners begot some of the classic tales of the Wild West, and now tourists flock to small towns like Tombstone and Bisbee, which retain much of their Old Western look (for more on these sights, see the Southeastern Arizona chapter).

West of these ranchlands lies the Arizona-Sonora desert, home of the majestic saguaro cacti, which are a symbol of this region. The Sonoran desert is also home to the Tohono O'odham Indians, who live west of Tucson on Arizona's second largest Indian reservation. And in between is Tucson itself, a major tourist destination both for travelers throughout the year and for the retired 'snowbirds' who enjoy spending several months each winter in the Tucson area, escaping the snows of their northern homes.

# Tucson

☎ 520 • pop 486,699; metro area 843,746 • elevation 2500 feet

Tucson is attractively set in a flat valley surrounded on all sides by close mountain ranges, some of which top 9000 feet. The elevation gives Tucson a slightly milder climate than that of Tucson's northern neighbor, Phoenix. Summers are still hot, however, with frequent days exceeding 100°F. But an hour's drive can take you up to the cooler mountains that are high and accessible enough to afford relief from summer heat. In winter, you can ski on Mt Lemmon, which is the southernmost ski resort in the country. After a day on the slopes, you can drop down to the city where pleasant winter daytime temperatures in the 70s are not unusual. The surrounding Sonoran desert is more accessible from Tucson than it is from Phoenix.

Tucson is Arizona's second largest city. Well over 20% of Tucson's inhabitants are Hispanic, and this is reflected both in the language and the food. Spanish is frequently spoken and Mexican restaurants abound.

Tucson is also the home of the University of Arizona (U of A), which has about 35,000 students and plays an important role in Tucson's economy. Also important to the city's economy are tourism and high-tech industries such as Hughes Missile Systems

Company and IBM Corporation, which employ thousands of Tucsonans. The Davis-Monthan Air Force Base also contributes to the economy. It is one of the largest aircraft storage bases in the country, and if you drive along Kolb Rd on the east side of town, you'll witness the eerie sight of almost 5000 mothballed aircraft lined up as far as the eye can see.

## HISTORY

Visitors to downtown Tucson see 'A Mountain' looming over the city to the southwest. Its proper name is Sentinel Peak, but its nickname comes from the giant 'A' white-washed onto the mountain by students from the U of A in 1915 and now repainted by freshmen as an annual tradition. But the peak's history goes back much farther than 1915. When the Spaniards arrived, the village below A Mountain was known as 'Stjukshon,' meaning 'at the foot of the dark mountain' in the Indian language. The Spaniards pronounced it 'Took Son' and later the Anglos dropped the 'k' sound, giving the city's name its current pronunciation of 'TOO-sahn.'

The first permanent Spanish settlement in Tucson was in 1775, when a large walled presidio was built here to house a garrison that protected settlers from the Indians. The Presidio District is now the most historic in Tucson, though almost nothing remains of the original buildings. Most of the oldest buildings date back to the mid-1800s, when arriving Anglos nicknamed the Hispanic fort 'the Old Pueblo.' The name has stuck and is often heard today as a nickname for Tucson.

Anglos began to arrive in greater numbers after the Butterfield Stage Company started passing through Tucson in 1857. War with the Apaches prompted the construction of Fort Lowell in 1866. The town was a wild place in those days, and soldiers on drinking sprees added to the general mayhem. In 1873, in an attempt to minimize carousing by the army, Fort Lowell was moved to its present location 7 miles northeast of town. It was abandoned

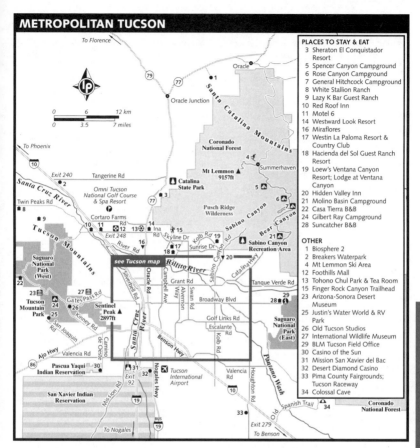

**METROPOLITAN TUCSON**

PLACES TO STAY & EAT
3 Sheraton El Conquistador Resort
5 Spencer Canyon Campground
6 Rose Canyon Campground
7 General Hitchcock Campground
8 White Stallion Ranch
9 Lazy K Bar Guest Ranch
10 Red Roof Inn
11 Motel 6
14 Westward Look Resort
16 Miraflores
17 Westin La Paloma Resort & Country Club
18 Hacienda del Sol Guest Ranch Resort
19 Loew's Ventana Canyon Resort; Lodge at Ventana Canyon
20 Hidden Valley Inn
21 Molino Basin Campground
22 Casa Tierra B&B
24 Gilbert Ray Campground
28 Suncatcher B&B

OTHER
1 Biosphere 2
2 Breakers Waterpark
4 Mt Lemmon Ski Area
12 Foothills Mall
13 Tohono Chul Park & Tea Room
15 Finger Rock Canyon Trailhead
23 Arizona-Sonora Desert Museum
25 Justin's Water World & RV Park
26 Old Tucson Studios
27 International Wildlife Museum
29 BLM Tucson Field Office
30 Casino of the Sun
31 Mission San Xavier del Bac
32 Desert Diamond Casino
33 Pima County Fairgrounds; Tucson Raceway
34 Colossal Cave

## ORIENTATION

Tucson lies mainly to the north and east of I-10 at its intersection with I-19, which goes to the Mexican border at Nogales. Downtown Tucson and the main historic districts are east of I-10 exit 258 at Congress St/Broadway Blvd.

Congress/Broadway Blvd is a major west-east thoroughfare. Most west-east thoroughfares are called streets, and most north-south thoroughfares are called avenues (although there is a sprinkling of Rds, Blvds etc). Stone Ave, at its intersection with Congress, forms

in 1891 and there is a museum and a small historic district on the site today. In 1880 the railroad arrived and the university opened in 1891 – an air of sophistication and coming-of-age descended on the wild city.

Tucson grew slowly until WWII brought an influx of young men to train at the Davis-Monthan Air Force Base. After WWII, many of these trainees came back to Tucson and this, along with the widespread development of air conditioning, ensured Tucson's rapid growth in the latter half of the 20th century.

the zero point for Tucson addresses. Streets are designated west and east and avenues north and south from this point.

Downtown Tucson is quite compact and is best visited on foot, although you have to battle the heat from May to September. Away from downtown, major thoroughfares are at 1-mile intervals, with minor streets and avenues (mainly residential) filling in a checkerboard arrangement.

About a mile northeast of downtown is the U of A campus, with some worthwhile museums, and just over a mile south of downtown is the square mile of South Tucson. This is a separate town inhabited mainly by a traditional Hispanic population with few tourist sites, but it does have some cheap and funky restaurants with tasty Mexican food. The rest of the city is mainly an urban sprawl of shopping malls and residential areas interspersed with golf courses and parks. The main section of the city, between Campbell Ave and Kolb Rd, is known as midtown.

The south end of town is the industrial area with Tucson International Airport, the Davis-Monthan Air Force Base and industrial parks. You'll go past this to visit Mission San Xavier del Bac, Arizona's most impressive Spanish colonial site.

The north end of town is the Catalina Foothills, bounded by the steep and rugged Santa Catalina Mountains and home to the pricier residential districts, resorts and country clubs. Northwest of town, the city oozes around the western edge of the Catalinas into the I-10 corridor to Phoenix. This is where most of the current development is taking place.

East and west of town are wilderness areas, parts of which are protected by the east and west units of Saguaro National Park.

## INFORMATION

The Convention & Visitors Bureau (☎ 624-1817, 800-638-8350), 110 S Church, Suite 7199, is open daily except on major holidays. Ask for its free *Official Visitors Guide.* website: www.visittucson.org

The Coronado National Forest Supervisor's Office (☎ 670-4552), inside the Federal Building at 300 W Congress, is open weekdays. Also, the Santa Catalina Ranger Station (☎ 749-8700), 5700 N Sabino Canyon Rd, at the entrance to Sabino Canyon, is open daily.

The BLM Tucson Field Office (☎ 722-4289) is at 12661 E Broadway Blvd, just before Saguaro National Park (East) and the Arizona Game & Fish Dept (☎ 628-5376) is at 555 N Greasewood Rd.

Foreign exchange is available at most banks; a $5 fee is charged if you don't have an account. The Tucson airport does not offer currency exchange.

The main post office (☎ 800-275-8777) is at 1501 S Cherrybell. The downtown branch is at 141 S 6th Ave and there are numerous other branches.

The main library (☎ 791-4393) is open daily at 101 N Stone Ave. There are many other branch libraries. The U of A libraries (☎ 621-6441) have excellent and extensive collections, including a superb map room open to the general public.

Independent bookstores include Antigone Books (☎ 792-3715), 411 N 4th Ave, with books for, about and by women. Readers Oasis (☎ 319-7887), 3400 E Speedway, No 14, often has readings on weekends.

The local newspapers are the morning *Arizona Daily Star,* the afternoon *Tucson Citizen* and the free *Tucson Weekly,* published on Thursdays. The *Citizen* leans to the right, and the *Star* is more liberal.

Tucson's community radio station, KXCI, at 91.3 FM, is funded by listeners and has an eclectic and excellent range of programs from all over the musical spectrum (with the notable exceptions of classical music and top 40 stuff).

Pima County Medical Society (☎ 795-7985) gives doctor referrals during business hours. There are 10 hospitals and many smaller health care facilities in Tucson. The police (☎ 791-4444, 911 in emergencies) are at 270 S Stone Ave.

## DOWNTOWN TUCSON
### Historic Buildings

The Convention & Visitors Bureau has a brochure detailing a downtown walking tour with more than 40 sites. Some of the more noteworthy ones are mentioned here.

Many of the most interesting and colorful historic buildings are in the **Presidio Historic District**, especially in the few blocks between Franklin and Alameda and Main and Court Aves. This district merits a leisurely stroll. **La Casa Cordova**, at 175 N Meyer Ave, at the northern end of the Tucson Museum of Art (see later) is believed to be the oldest house, dating from 1848, and can be visited during museum hours. Just north of La Casa Cordova is the 1868 **Romero House**, now part of the Tucson Museum of Art School. Behind the museum, buildings dating from 1862 to 1875 feature saguaro-rib ceilings and now house La Cocina Restaurant and six interconnected, good-quality arts and crafts galleries of **Old Town Artisans** (☎ 623-6024), 186 N Meyer Ave.

The **Fish House**, 120 N Main Ave, built in 1868 for political representative Edward Nye Fish, and the roughly contemporary **Stevens House**, 150 N Main Ave, home of Hiram Sanford Stevens, formed the heart of Tucson's social scene during the 1870s and '80s. They now house parts of the Tucson Museum of Art. Restaurants in historic buildings include Tucson's oldest Mexican restaurant, **El Charro Cafe**, 311 N Court Ave, in a 1900 stone house (most of the earlier houses were adobe), and the **Cushing St Bar & Grill**, several lengthy blocks to the south at 343 S Meyer Ave, housed in an 1880s store and displaying many old photographs.

Cushing St is the north end of the **Barrio Historico** district, which was an important business district in the late 1800s. Many of the old buildings around here continue to house businesses. **El Tiradito** is a quirky and crumbling little shrine on Cushing on the west side of Main Ave (south of El Minuto Café). The story behind the shrine is one of passion and murder. Apparently a young herder was caught making love with his mother-in-law and was shot dead by his father-in-law at this spot, where he was buried. Pious locals burned candles here because it was unconsecrated ground. The practice continues today, with candle-burners praying for their own wishes to be granted. If a candle burns throughout the night, your wish will be granted!

Between the Presidio and Barrio Historico districts is the modern Tucson Convention Center (TCC) complex. Only one house survived the construction of the TCC. At the northwest end is hidden the **Sosa-Carrillo-Frémont House Museum** (☎ 622-0956), at 151 S Granada Ave. Built in the 1850s by the Sosa family, it was then bought by the Carrillo family and rented briefly by John C Frémont, Arizona's fifth governor. The restored house is now an 1880s period museum open 10am to 4pm Wednesday to Saturday; admission is free. It is operated by the Arizona Historical Society, which offers guided walking tours (☎ 622-0956 to register) of historic Tucson at 10am on Saturday from November through March ($10).

The downtown area also has several notable newer buildings from the early 20th century. The **Pima County Courthouse**, at 115 N Church Ave, is a colorful blend of Spanish and Southwestern architecture with an impressive mosaic-tile dome. **El Presidio Park**, on the west side of the courthouse, covers what was the southern half of the original presidio and also houses a Vietnam Veterans Memorial. A few blocks south is the elegant, whitewashed St Augustine Cathedral, 192 S Stone Ave, begun in 1896. Stained-glass windows and a Mexican-style sandstone facade were added in the 1920s. Two blocks to the southeast is the **Temple of Music & Art**, 330 S Scott Ave, built in 1927 and gloriously restored as the home of the Arizona Theater Company. A block northeast of it is the **Tucson Children's Museum** (see below), 200 S 6th Ave, housed in a 1901 library designed by the noted Southwestern architect Henry Trost, who also designed several other turn-of-the-19th-century buildings in Tucson. Two still standing are the **Steinfeld House**, 300 N Main Ave, and the **Owl's Club Mansion**, 378 N Main Ave.

### Tucson Museum of Art

The Tucson Museum of Art (☎ 624-2333), 140 N Main Ave, houses a small collection of pre-Columbian artifacts from Latin

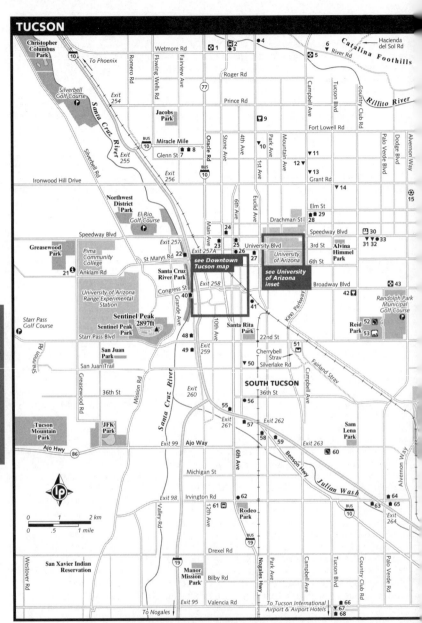

# TUCSON

# TUCSON

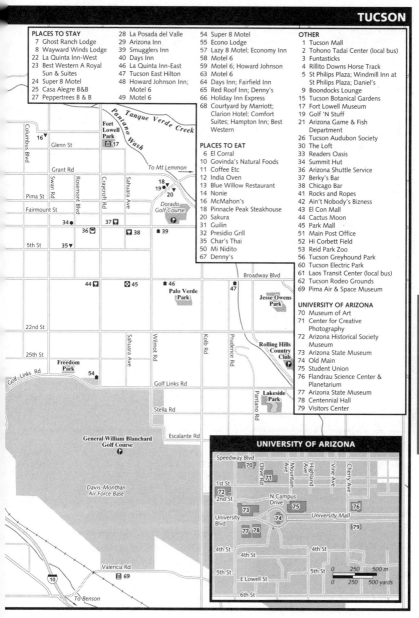

**PLACES TO STAY**
- 7 Ghost Ranch Lodge
- 8 Wayward Winds Lodge
- 22 La Quinta Inn-West
- 23 Best Western A Royal Sun & Suites
- 24 Super 8 Motel
- 25 Casa Alegre B&B
- 27 Peppertrees B & B
- 28 La Posada del Valle
- 29 Arizona Inn
- 39 Smugglers Inn
- 40 Days Inn
- 46 La Quinta Inn-East
- 47 Tucson East Hilton
- 48 Howard Johnson Inn; Motel 6
- 49 Motel 6
- 54 Super 8 Motel
- 55 Econo Lodge
- 57 Lazy 8 Motel; Economy Inn
- 58 Motel 6
- 59 Motel 6; Howard Johnson
- 63 Motel 6
- 64 Days Inn; Fairfield Inn
- 65 Red Roof Inn; Denny's
- 66 Holiday Inn Express
- 68 Courtyard by Marriott; Clarion Hotel; Comfort Suites; Hampton Inn; Best Western

**PLACES TO EAT**
- 6 El Corral
- 10 Govinda's Natural Foods
- 11 Coffee Etc
- 12 India Oven
- 13 Blue Willow Restaurant
- 14 Nonie
- 16 McMahon's
- 18 Pinnacle Peak Steakhouse
- 20 Sakura
- 31 Guilin
- 32 Presidio Grill
- 35 Char's Thai
- 50 Mi Nidito
- 67 Denny's

**OTHER**
- 1 Tucson Mall
- 2 Tohono Tadai Center (local bus)
- 3 Funtasticks
- 4 Rillito Downs Horse Track
- 5 St Philips Plaza; Windmill Inn at St Philips Plaza; Daniel's
- 9 Boondocks Lounge
- 15 Tucson Botanical Gardens
- 17 Fort Lowell Museum
- 19 Golf 'N Stuff
- 21 Arizona Game & Fish Department
- 26 Tucson Audubon Society
- 30 The Loft
- 33 Readers Oasis
- 34 Summit Hut
- 36 Arizona Shuttle Service
- 37 Berky's Bar
- 38 Chicago Bar
- 41 Rocks and Ropes
- 42 Ain't Nobody's Bizness
- 43 El Con Mall
- 44 Cactus Moon
- 45 Park Mall
- 51 Main Post Office
- 52 Hi Corbett Field
- 53 Reid Park Zoo
- 56 Tucson Greyhound Park
- 60 Tucson Electric Park
- 61 Laos Transit Center (local bus)
- 62 Tucson Rodeo Grounds
- 69 Pima Air & Space Museum

**UNIVERSITY OF ARIZONA**
- 70 Museum of Art
- 71 Center for Creative Photography
- 72 Arizona Historical Society Museum
- 73 Arizona State Museum
- 74 Old Main
- 75 Student Union
- 76 Flandrau Science Center & Planetarium
- 77 Arizona State Museum
- 78 Centennial Hall
- 79 Visitors Center

TUCSON & SOUTHERN AZ

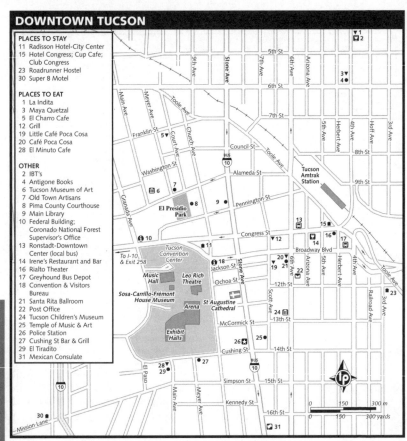

## DOWNTOWN TUCSON

**PLACES TO STAY**
11  Radisson Hotel-City Center
15  Hotel Congress; Cup Cafe;
    Club Congress
23  Roadrunner Hostel
30  Super 8 Motel

**PLACES TO EAT**
 1  La Indita
 3  Maya Quetzal
 5  El Charro Cafe
12  Grill
19  Little Café Poca Cosa
20  Café Poca Cosa
28  El Minuto Cafe

**OTHER**
 2  IBT's
 4  Antigone Books
 6  Tucson Museum of Art
 7  Old Town Artisans
 8  Pima County Courthouse
 9  Main Library
10  Federal Building;
    Coronado National Forest
    Supervisor's Office
13  Ronstadt-Downtown
    Center (local bus)
14  Irene's Restaurant and Bar
16  Rialto Theater
17  Greyhound Bus Depot
18  Convention & Visitors
    Bureau
21  Santa Rita Ballroom
22  Post Office
24  Tucson Children's Museum
25  Temple of Music & Art
26  Police Station
27  Cushing St Bar & Grill
29  El Tiradito
31  Mexican Consulate

America, varied exhibits of 20th-century Western art, a decent little multimedia collection, changing shows and a gift shop with local art. Hours are 10am to 4pm daily except Sunday, when it opens at noon. It is closed on Monday from the last Monday in May to the first Monday in October. Admission is $5, $4 for seniors, $3 for students, and free to children under 12 and to everyone on Sunday.

### Tucson Children's Museum

Hands-on activities for kids and permanent exhibits are featured at this museum (☎ 884-7511), 200 S 6th Ave. Special programs occur frequently. Hours are 10am to 5pm, Tuesday to Saturday and noon to 5pm on Sunday. Admission is $5.50 for adults, $4.50 for seniors and $3.50 for two- to 16-year-olds. On Sundays, a $14 family pass will admit four family members.

### UNIVERSITY OF ARIZONA

This fine campus houses some excellent museums and several notable outdoor sculptures. This is not just a place for students; it's a worthwhile stop for everyone. Note that hours can change during school holidays; call ahead.

TUCSON & SOUTHERN AZ

A visitor center (☎ 621-5130), at the southeast corner of University Blvd and Cherry Ave, is open weekdays. Campus tours are offered during the school year. **Old Main** on University Blvd near the middle of the campus is the original university. The **Student Union**, just northeast of Old Main, has an information desk (☎ 621-7755) as well as various restaurants, art displays, a campus bookstore and the Gallagher movie theater. Note that University Blvd, east of Old Main, becomes a grassy pedestrian walkway called the University Mall.

Parking can be problematic when school is in session, especially if the U of A Wildcats are playing a home game. Large parking garages at the northeast corner of Park Ave and E Speedway Blvd and at Cherry Ave and E 4th charge a few dollars but fill during games. Call the U of A Parking & Transportation Dept (☎ 621-3550) for details.

Other useful campus numbers are the general operator (☎ 621-2211), athletic events ticket information (☎ 621-2287), Centennial Hall cultural events ticket office (☎ 621-3341) and the fine arts box office (☎ 621-1162).

## Center for Creative Photography

This has one of the world's best collections of works by American photographers, as well as some European and other artists. The small public gallery displays images by famous photographers and changing exhibits throughout the year. Most of Ansel Adams's and Edward Weston's work, as well as images by many other photographers, are stored in the archives. Serious photography buffs can call for an appointment to view the works of one or two particular photographers; this is a remarkable opportunity rarely offered elsewhere. The center (☎ 621-7968), 1030 N Olive Ave, is open 9am to 5pm Monday to Friday and noon to 5pm on weekends. Admission is free.

website: www.creativephotography.org

## University of Arizona Museum of Art

Opposite the photography center, this museum (☎ 621-7567) displays changing shows of mainly student works. These exhibits range widely in quality but are always intriguing. There are also fine permanent collections of European art and a variety of sculptures. Hours are 9am to 5pm Monday to Friday and noon to 4pm Sunday during the school year; summer weekday hours are 10am to 3:30pm. Admission is free.

## Arizona State Museum

This anthropological museum (☎ 621-6302) focuses on the region's Indians. One of the permanent exhibits entitled 'Paths of Life: American Indians of the Southwest' is a state-of-the-art representation of the past and present lives of several tribes; it's well worth seeing. The museum is in two buildings on the north and south sides of University Blvd, east of the campus entrance at Park Ave. 'Paths of Life' is in the north hall; admission is free. Hours are 10am to 5pm Monday to Saturday and noon to 5pm on Sunday.

## Arizona Historical Society Museum

This is the society's flagship museum; it also manages the Sosa-Carrillo-Frémont House Museum (see Historic Buildings, earlier) and the Fort Lowell Museum (see Beyond Downtown, later). The museum's collection (☎ 628-5774), 949 E 2nd, is a comprehensive trip through Tucson's history as a Spanish colonial, Mexican, territorial and state city. Anything from colonial silverware to vintage automobiles is shown in this wide-ranging selection of historical artifacts. Changing exhibits keep bringing locals back, too. Hours are 10am to 4pm daily except Sunday (noon to 4pm); closed major holidays. Admission is free, but donations are appreciated.

## Flandrau Science Center, Planetarium & Mineral Museum

At the northeast corner of Cherry Ave and University Mall, the Flandrau (☎ 621-7827) has a permanent collection and many changing shows. Permanent exhibits include a 'walk-in' meteor and a variety of hands-on science displays. The Mineral Museum is in the basement of the Science Center. Minerals, meteorites and gemstones from all over the world are exhibited, with an emphasis on local stones. Varying planetarium shows are shown throughout the day; call for times and titles. Laser rock shows are occasionally featured.

Admission to the science center is $3, and $2 for three- to 12-year-olds. Admission to planetarium shows (including exhibits admission) is $5 for adults; $4 for children. Those under three are not admitted. The science center is open 9am to 5pm Tuesday to Saturday, 7 to 9pm Thursday to Saturday, 1 to 5pm Sunday. The mineral museum is open the same daytime hours, but not in the evenings. Various astronomical events are scheduled throughout the year.
website: www.flandrau.org

### Campus Sculptures

Beginning with *The Flute Player*, commissioned in 1979 and now standing in front of the main library, the U of A has steadily acquired an eclectic collection of about a dozen sculptures scattered throughout the campus. The most controversial? The huge *Curving Arcades (Homage to Bernini)* at the main eastern entrance at University Mall and N Campbell Ave. Visitors' favorite? The whimsical *25 Scientists* in front of the new chemistry and biology building on University Mall, just west of the main library. Ask at the visitor center or the Museum of Art about the others.

### BEYOND DOWNTOWN
### Tucson Botanical Gardens

These quiet and pleasant gardens (☎ 326-9255/686), 2150 N Alvernon Way, cover 5½ acres and focus on native dry-land plants. There is also a small tropical greenhouse, an herb garden and other plant attractions forming a quiet midtown oasis. All paths are wheelchair accessible. Various workshops and events are offered throughout the year, including garden tours (not in summer). There is a gift shop. Hours are 8:30am to 4:30pm daily. Admission is $5, $4 for seniors and $1 for those six to 11.
website: www.tucsonbotanical.org

### Reid Park Zoo

This small but excellent zoo (☎ 791-4022), in Reid Park north of 22nd St, provides a good look at animals from all over the world, including some unusual ones such as giant anteaters and pygmy hippos. All the standard favorites are here, as well as some well-themed exhibits (especially the South American area). The zoo's compact size makes it a great excursion for children because they don't get overwhelmed and tired out. A gift shop and a fast-food restau-

> ## Kids' Stuff
>
> The Tucson Children's Museum, open year-round, appeals to younger kids, while the Flandrau Science Center shows are aimed at older kids and teenagers. The Reid Park Zoo and the Arizona-Sonora Desert Museum are good for the entire family, as is the Pima Air & Space Museum, especially if your kids are plane nuts.
>
> Two places that offer miniature golf, go-carts, bumper boats, batting cages and other fun stuff are Funtasticks (☎ 888-4653), 221 E Wetmore, and Golf 'N Stuff (☎ 885-3569), 6503 E Tanque Verde Rd.
>
> During the summer, water parks offer something a little more exciting than swimming laps. Breakers (☎ 682-2530), 8555 W Tangerine Rd (1½ miles east of I-10 exit 242, 16 miles north of downtown), has a huge wave pool for surfing, as well as water slides and nonwave pools. Hours are 10 am to 6 pm; admission is $15 for adults, $10 for kids under 48 inches tall and free for children under three. Children under 13 must be accompanied by an adult. Justin's Water World & RV Park (☎ 883-8340), at 3551 S San Joaquin Rd (8 miles west of I-19 exit 99 along Ajo Way, then 2 miles north) has swimming pools, toddlers' paddling pools, water slides galore, a tubing area and an 'Atlantis – The Lost Continent' attraction. Hours are 10 am to 5 pm Friday to Sunday and holidays. Admission is $11 with one child under six free with each paid admission.

rant are here. Hours are 9am to 4pm daily. Admission is $4, $3 for seniors and 75¢ for five- to 14-year-olds accompanied by an adult.

Outside the zoo, the surrounding Reid Park provides picnic areas, playgrounds and a duck pond with paddleboat rentals in summer.

### Fort Lowell Museum
After Geronimo surrendered, Fort Lowell's important role in the Indian Wars faded, and the army closed it in 1891. Only weathered ruins remain today, with a museum (☎ 885-3832) housed in reconstructed officers' quarters with furnishings and exhibits of the fort's heyday. Hours are 10am to 4pm, Wednesday to Saturday; admission is free. Fort Lowell Park is off the 2900 block of N Craycroft Rd and also features playgrounds, duck pond and picnic areas. Across Craycroft Rd, a short way north of the fort, Fort Lowell Rd heads west past several early houses in the small Fort Lowell historical district.

### Pima Air & Space Museum
With over 275 aircraft representing a history of aviation, this museum (☎ 574-0462) 6000 E Valencia Rd, is a must-see for aircraft buffs. The museum also operates the Titan Missile Museum (see Green Valley later in this chapter). Hours are 9am to 5pm daily except Thanksgiving and Christmas. Admission is $9.75 for adults, $6 for children. From 10am to 3pm, there are wheelchair-accessible tram tours for another $2.
website: www.pimaair.org

Nearby, note the approximately 5000 mothballed aircraft at Davis-Monthan Air Force Base (see them driving north on Kolb Rd and then west on Escalante Rd). Bus tours of the aircraft 'graveyard' are given several times a day weekdays except holidays, beginning at 9:30am. Reservations (☎ 618-4806) are required well in advance. Tours cost $6, or $3 for those under 13. Discounts are given for combined visits with the Air & Space or Titan Missile museums (see South of Tucson).

### Tohono Chul Park
This small desert oasis, surrounded by encroaching development north of town, is a good place to see desert flora and fauna in a natural setting. There are demonstrations and ethnobotanical gardens, an exhibit room with changing shows, gift shops, plant sales and a tea room. A variety of docent-led tours are offered. The park (☎ 575-8468, 742-6455), 7366 N Paseo del Norte, is open 7am to dusk daily; the other attractions have shorter hours. Admission is free, but a $2 donation is suggested.
website: www.tohonochulpark.org

## SANTA CATALINA MOUNTAINS
The Santa Catalina Mountains, within the Coronado National Forest and topped by 9157-foot Mt Lemmon, form Tucson's northern boundary and are the best loved and most visited of Tucson's many mountain ranges.

### Sabino Canyon
This area is the most popular and accessible part of the Santa Catalinas. A visitor center includes a USFS ranger station (☎ 749-8700), open 8am to 4:30pm weekdays and 8:30am to 4:30pm weekends. Maps, hiking guides and information are available here, and there is a short nature trail nearby. The visitor center is at the entrance of the canyon at 5900 N Sabino Canyon Rd, where there is a large parking lot. Admission is $5 per vehicle, valid also on Mt Lemmon.

Roads continue beyond the visitor center into the canyon, but only shuttle buses (☎ 749-2861 for recorded information) are allowed to drive on these. The Sabino Canyon Rd goes a scenic 3.8 miles up the canyon, crossing the river several times. Narrated shuttle bus tours spend 45 minutes doing the roundtrip and stop at nine points along the way. Tours leave every half hour from 9am to 4:30pm, and ticket holders can get on and off at any point whenever they feel like it. There are several riverside spots and picnic places on the way. At the top is a trailhead for hikers wanting to go high into the Santa Catalinas. Fares are $6; $2.50 for three- to 12-year-olds. Full-moon shuttle tours are given by reservation on the nights around a full moon from September to June. Call ☎ 749-2327 for information.

Another road from the visitor center goes 2½ miles to the Bear Canyon trailhead. A shuttle bus takes hikers there every hour from 9am to 4pm. The fare is $3; $1 for children. From the trailhead a 2.3-mile (one-way) hike leads to Seven Falls, a scenic and popular spot for picnics and swimming, with no facilities (allow 3½ hours roundtrip). From the falls, the trail continues up as high as you want to go.

Bicycles are allowed on the roads only before 9am and after 5pm and not at all on Wednesday and Sunday. Hikers can walk along the roads at any time from dawn to dusk. You don't have to take a shuttle to get to a trailhead; starting from the visitor center, there are plenty of hiking possibilities. The Phoneline Trail, skirting Sabino Canyon high on its southeastern side, is an alternative to taking the road.

Several picnic areas with grills, tables and bathrooms are in the area. Camping is not allowed within those areas. Backpackers can hike into the Santa Catalinas and wilderness camp almost anywhere that is more than a quarter-mile away from a road or trailhead.

## Catalina State Park

This park is in the western foothills of the Santa Catalinas and is popular for hiking, picnicking, bird watching and camping. You'll find both short nature trails and trailheads for long-distance hiking and backpacking. Horseback riding is permitted, and one trail is specifically developed for horses. The Equestrian Center has boarding for horses. Natural swimming holes occur along some of the trails and make good day-hike destinations. Ask the ranger for directions. For more information call Catalina State Park (☎ 628-5798). The park is about 15 miles north of Tucson along Oracle Rd (Hwy 77). Day use is $5 per vehicle.

## Mt Lemmon

Spend a couple of days hiking up to Mt Lemmon's summit along the many trails in the Santa Catalinas, or head east on Tanque Verde Rd, pick up the Catalina Hwy and enjoy the hour-long **scenic drive** to the top. This is a favorite getaway for Tucsonans wishing to escape the summer heat. Along the way are four USFS campgrounds and several pullouts with great views. The road is narrow and winding, however, and requires some concentration, as well as a $5 per vehicle toll. Several hiking trails intersect with the highway. Near the top of the drive is the Palisades Ranger Station (no telephone) with useful information about the area, or call the Sabino Canyon Ranger Station (☎ 749-8700).

At the top is the small village of **Summerhaven** where there are cabins to rent, some restaurants, a picnic area and a ski area (see Skiing). During the summer you can take scenic rides on the chair lift from 10:30am to 5pm for $8 ($4 for three- to 12-year-olds). Families pay $21 for two adults and up to four children. Gas up in Tucson; there's no gas on Mt Lemmon.

## ACTIVITIES

The Convention & Visitors Bureau can provide lists of golf courses, tennis courts and other local attractions. The Summit Hut (☎ 325-1554), 5045 E Speedway, is an excellent source of outdoor gear, including guidebooks (Lonely Planet titles are sold), maps and rental equipment; you can shop online at www.summithut.com.

## Hiking & Backpacking

Tucson is ringed by mountains. The Rincons to the east and the Tucson Mountains to the west are easily explored from Saguaro National Park. The Santa Ritas, topped by 9453-foot Mt Wrightson, are visible in the distance, to the south (see Green Valley).

The Santa Catalina Mountains can be accessed from several trailheads, including the Finger Rock Canyon (Mt Kimball) trailhead at the far north end of Alvernon Way, which leads steeply up past Finger Rock – an obvious point on the northern skyline from many parts of Tucson. (Note that Alvernon stops in midtown Tucson at Fort Lowell Rd. Take Campbell Ave north to

Skyline and then go east to pick up Alvernon again.) Other trailheads are found in Sabino Canyon and Catalina State Park (see earlier).

Take extra precautions hiking around Tucson in summer, when dehydration can be a potentially lethal problem. You should carry water at all times and drink a gallon of water per day. Sunburn can be debilitating, so protect yourself. Also, watch out for those spiny plants. It's worth carrying tweezers and a comb – they help remove cactus spines from your skin.

Backpackers should contact a USFS ranger station about suitable places to camp and where to leave their cars.

### Rock Climbing
Mt Lemmon has good rock climbing – route books are available from the Summit Hut. Rocks and Ropes (☎ 882-5294), 330 S Toole Ave (hard to find; call for directions), is an indoor rock-climbing facility with equipment rental.

### Bird Watching
Bird watchers come here from all over the USA to see birds found nowhere else in the country. While the months between April to September see the most species of hummingbird, there are always a few around. In addition, common desert birds such as roadrunners, gila woodpeckers, elf owls and cactus wrens attract out-of-state birders wanting to add to their life lists.

The best resource for bird watchers is the Tucson Audubon Society (☎ 629-0510), 300 E University Blvd. It has an excellent nature shop with a fine selection of bird guides and related materials. Hours are 10am to 4pm, Monday to Saturday, and to 6pm on Thursday. A research library is also available. Ask here about monthly meetings and slide shows held from September to May, as well as field trips, many of them free. An essential handbook for birders is *Finding Birds in Southeastern Arizona* by William A Davis and Stephen M Russell. A bird-sightings and information hotline (☎ 798-1005) is updated weekly.
website: www.tucsonaudubon.org

### Skiing
Mt Lemmon Ski Area (☎ 576-1400/1321) is the most southerly ski area in the USA and is mainly for intermediate and experienced skiers. Rentals, lessons and food are available. Depending on the weather, the slopes are open from mid-December to late March. Lift tickets are $32.

### Hot-Air Ballooning
Several companies offer hot-air-balloon flights, which usually take place in the calm morning air, last about an hour and finish with a traditional champagne breakfast. Costs are about $150 to $200 per person. Flights may be canceled in windy or very hot weather. Most companies can arrange flights on a day's notice. Experienced companies include Balloon America (☎ 299-7744) and A Southern Arizona Balloon Excursion (☎ 624-3599, 800-524-3599). Or go online and check www.Balloon RidesUSA.com for more information.

### Horseback Riding
Several stables offer excursions by the hour, half day or longer. Summer trips tend to be short breakfast or sunset rides because of the heat. Desert cookouts can be arranged. One of the most reputable companies is Pusch Ridge Stables (☎ 825-1664), 13700 N Oracle Rd, which also offers overnight pack trips. Nearby, Walking Winds Stables (☎ 742-4422), at 10,000 N Oracle in the the Sheraton El Conquistador Resort, offers rides Catalina State Park at the national forest. At the other end of town is Pantano Stables (☎ 298-8980), 4450 S Houghton Rd. Several others advertise locally. Rates start around $20 for the first hour, but are much lower for subsequent hours.

### ORGANIZED TOURS
Gray Line (☎ 622-8811) offers standard coach and van tours of the city and its surroundings as well as excursions all over the state. Tours of Tucson and southeastern Arizona are offered by Off the Beaten Path Tours (☎ 529-6090). Trail Dust Jeep Tours (☎ 747-0323) takes you into the desert in open jeeps. Old Pueblo Tours (☎ 795-7448)

TUCSON & SOUTHERN AZ

specializes in historical tours of Tucson. Note that some tours don't operate in the summer heat.

## PLACES TO STAY

December through April is the high season and May to September is the low. During the Gem and Mineral Show in early February, prices rise way above their already high winter rates, so budget travelers should avoid Tucson then unless they're attending that show. A $99 room in January can be $49 in July and $139 during the Gem and Mineral Show. Prices given below tend towards the winter rates but can only be used as an approximation; rates drop considerably in the summer.

### Camping

The USFS (☎ 749-8700) operates four basic campgrounds on the Catalina Hwy going up to Mt Lemmon. The campground at *Catalina State Park* (☎ 628-5798), about 15 miles north of downtown along Oracle Rd (Hwy 77), has tent/RV sites for $10/15. *Gilbert Ray Campground* (☎ 883-4200), on Kinney Rd a couple of miles east of the Arizona-Sonora Desert Museum (see Around Tucson, later), has 152 sites open year-round, some with electrical hookups. There's water but no showers. Site rates are $8 or $12.50 with hookups. Check the Yellow Pages for long-term RV parks.

### Budget

The friendly *Roadrunner Hostel* (☎ 628-4709, 346 E 12th St), offers dorm rooms ($18 per person) and doubles ($38). Free Internet access, kitchen privileges, TV/video room and coin laundry are included; bicycles can be rented ($15). Check the website (www.roadrunnerhostel.com) for more information. Also downtown, the very popular *Hotel Congress* (☎ 622-8848, 800-722-8848, 311 E Congress), with free Internet access for guests, a hip music club and a café, dates back to the 1920s and has dorm beds ($17 for IYHA members with passport) and singles/doubles for $30/35 in summer. Rates are $62/69 in winter, when reservations are suggested. Rooms can be

loud because of the club.

The *Lazy 8 Motel* (622-3336, 314 E Benson Hwy), with doubles from $58, a pool and continental breakfast, is the best of several independent cheap motels, near I-10 exit 261, though this is not the best of neighborhoods. Nearby, an *Econo Lodge* is in this price range. Also consider *Wayward Winds Lodge* (☎ 791-7526, 628-2010, 707 W Miracle Mile), which has 40 good-sized rooms, and a swimming pool on pleasant grounds. Other cheap but very basic places are southeast along the Benson Hwy.

Rooms are $40 to $65 in Tucson's six *Motels 6s*.

### Mid-Range

**Hotels** The 1940s *Ghost Ranch Lodge* (☎ 791-7565, 800-456-7565, 801 W Miracle Mile) sits in eight acres of cactus-filled desert gardens surrounded by rooms. Some have private patios or kitchenettes. A pool, whirlpool and restaurant are on the premises. Rates are an excellent value at $70 to $100, perhaps because the surrounding neighborhood is run-down. Once you enter the lodge, you can forget about that.

Many *chain motels* offer satisfactory lodging in the $60 to $175 range for a double in winter. Most have a pool and whirlpool; many include continental breakfast. Many of the ones listed in the Facts for the Visitor chapter have at least one, and often three or four, properties in Tucson. See the maps for a selection.

The *Smugglers Inn* (☎ 296-3292, 800-525-8852, 6350 E Speedway Blvd) has attractive gardens and spacious rooms with balconies or patios. Facilities include a pool, spa, putting green, restaurant and bar with room service. Rates are $80 to $125, including weekday cocktails and a continental breakfast.

website: www.smugglersinn.com

The *Windmill Inn at St Philips Plaza* (☎ 577-0007, 800-547-4747, 4250 N Campbell Ave) is in one of the more upscale shopping plazas. In the 120 attractive two-room suites are decorated in Southwestern style and many have microwaves, wet bars and refrigerators. Winter rates are $100 to $150, with newspapers, coffee and pastries delivered to your room every morning. There is a pool, a spa and a lending library of paperback bestsellers as well as bicycles for guest use.

website: www.windmillinns.com

**B&Bs** Tucson has dozens of B&Bs; many are listed at www.bbonline.com/az, or get a listing from the visitors bureau.

*Casa Alegre (☎ 628-1800, 800-628-5654, 316 E Speedway Blvd)* is a peaceful 1915 house that is convenient to U of A and downtown and is decorated with historical memorabilia. Four rooms with baths range from $80 to $135, and there is a pool and spa. *Peppertrees B&B (☎/fax 622-7167, 800-348-5763, 724 E University Blvd)* is a quick walk away from U of A. Three large guest rooms in the 1905 house cost $110, and two guesthouses, equipped with TVs, phones, laundry facilities, full kitchen and two bedrooms, are $185; a smaller one-bedroom casita is $125. Rates are about 15% less in summer. See them on the web at peppertreesinn.com. *La Posada del Valle (☎/fax 795-3840, 888-404-7113,1640 N Campbell Rd)* is also close to U of A and has a beautiful courtyard. It features five rooms with private entrances and bathrooms; rates are $100 to $140. For information on the web, access thesuncatcher.com.

Take Broadway all the way east to the Saguaro National Park and look for signs before the fork in the road to find the luxurious and remote *Suncatcher B&B (☎/fax 885-0883, 877-775-8355, 105 N Avenida Javelina)*. This B&B has four rooms all individually decorated to resemble some of the world's most exclusive hotels. It also has a pool and spa. Rates are $80 to $145.

## Top End
The grand dame of Tucson hotels is the sedate and beautiful *Arizona Inn (☎ 325-1541, 800-933-1093, 2200 E Elm)*, built in 1929. The 14-acre grounds are attractively landscaped and the public areas are elegant and traditional. Swimming, tennis and croquet are available. The rooms, decorated in Southwestern style, are spacious though

the bathrooms are not very large (people spent less time in them in 1929, perhaps). There are 70 rooms and 16 suites with patios or fireplaces. The restaurant is good enough to attract the local citizenry, and you can order room service. The service is friendly and unpretentious, yet professional. Expect to pay $250 to $300 in the winter.

website: www.arizonainn.com

*Casa Tierra B&B (☎ 578-3058, 11155 W Calle Pima)* is just west of the western section of Saguaro National Park. It's a modern-day adobe surrounded by desert, with a hot tub for relaxing. Four rooms, each with private bathrooms, patios, microwaves and refrigerators are between $150 and $200, and a two-bedroom suite is $200. This B&B closes from June through August.

Tucson's ranches and resorts, often destinations in themselves, rival those in the Valley of the Sun for beauty, comfort and diversity of facilities. Rates are in the $200 to $400 a double range, including meals and activities; note that 8% tax and 15% gratuities may be added to ranch rates. Minimum stays are usually required and weekly discounts offered. Ranches may close in summer.

*Lazy K Bar Guest Ranch (☎ 744-3050, 800-321-7018, 8401 N Scenic Drive)* offers horseback riding twice a day on desert and mountain trails. Mountain biking and hayrides are some of the other activities. The style is very much family-oriented with plenty of activities for children and large sit-down dinners with all the guests. The ranch has 23 rooms in adobe buildings, all with air conditioning and private baths.

website: www.lazykbar.com

*White Stallion Ranch (☎ 297-0252, 888-977-2624, 9251 W Twin Peaks Rd)* is a quiet, peaceful, family-style ranch where you can groom your own horse before a ride, let the children roam free in a petting zoo, relax on a patio and listen to the birds or take a challenging hike throughout the desert mountain wilderness. This 3000-acre ranch has 41 rooms.

website: www.wsranch.com

Fifteen miles east of Tucson, *Tanque Verde Guest Ranch (☎ 296-6275, 800-234-*

*3833, 14301 E Speedway Blvd)* sits in the Rincon Mountains, offering plenty of opportunities for hiking, riding and nature walks. For more 'resort-style' activities, there are two pools, five tennis courts, a spa, sauna, exercise room and basketball courts. But 100 head of horses remind you what Tucson ranches are about. This is one of the more famous and comfortable ranches in the area, with 74 well-decorated casitas, attentive service, great food and beautiful surroundings.

website: www.tanqueverderanch.com

Several big resorts center around a top-notch golf course (or two!), along with tennis courts, pools and fitness and relaxation activities galore. All have good, if pricey, restaurants. Winter rates start around $250 for large and comfortable rooms (plus about $100 for greens fees), and go up from there for deluxe rooms and suites. Prices drop in summer. The following golf resorts are highly recommended:

**Lodge at Ventana Canyon** (☎ 577-1400, 800-828-5701) 6200 N Clubhouse Lane
website: www.wyndham.com

**Loew's Ventana Canyon Resort** (☎ 299-2020, 800-234-5117) 7000 N Resort Dr
website: www.loewshotels.com

**Omni Tucson National Golf Course & Spa Resort** (☎ 297-2271, 800-528-4856) 2727 W Club Dr
website: www.tucsonnational.com

**Sheraton El Conquistador Resort & Country Club** (☎ 544-5000, 800-325-7832) 10000 N Oracle Rd
website: www.sheratonelconquistador.com

**Westin La Paloma Resort** (☎ 742-6000, 800-937-8461) 3800 E Sunrise Dr
website: www.westin.com/lapaloma

If you're not looking for on-site golf but do want extensive resort facilities, a good bet is the *Westward Look Resort (☎ 297-1151, 800-722-2500, 245 E Ina Rd)*; visit it online at www.westwardlook.com. Another good top-end choice is *Hacienda del Sol Guest Ranch Resort (☎ 299-1501, 800-728-6514, 5601 N Hacienda del Sol Rd)*, which allows guests to relax in an authentic Southwest setting with lovely views but without all the golf and tennis hoopla. The resort dates

from 1929, and they say that Clark Gable, Spencer Tracy and other stars stayed here. It does offer tennis, croquet, horseshoes, a whirlpool and a small swimming pool, but with only 33 units, everything is much lower key than other resorts. The Hacienda's website is www.haciendadelsol.com.

Finally, if you want to pamper yourself in a dedicated spa and can afford rates starting at $500 a day, including healthy gourmet meals and some treatments, a top choice is the *Canyon Ranch (☎ 749-9000, 800-742-9000, 8600 E Rockcliff Rd)*. Guests normally stay for several days and indulge in numerous spa and health services provided by health, beauty, well-being and fitness professionals. No alcohol is served; for details, check out www.canyonranch.com. Another option, with alternative treatments/lectures such as equine therapy, ayurveda and the intriguingly named 'Zen Bootcamp' accompanying the usual spa activities, are is the highly recommended *Miraval (☎ 825-4000, 800-825-4000, 500 E Via Estancia)* about 20 miles north of Tucson. Alcohol is served; see the resort online at www.miravalresort.com.

## PLACES TO EAT

Tucson has a well-deserved reputation for Mexican food, and if you like it, you'll never be at a loss for a place to eat. If you don't like Mexican food, you'll still find an extensive and varied selection of excellent American and international restaurants, as well as Southwestern cuisine. Note that smoking is not allowed inside Tucson's restaurants.

The popular and busy *Coffee Etc (☎ 881-8070, 2830 N Campbell Ave)* serves breakfast 24 hours a day, as well as burgers, sandwiches, soups, salads, light meals and, of course, a variety of coffees. There is another branch *(☎ 544-8588)* at 6091 N Oracle. Downtown, the *Cup Cafe (☎ 798-1618)*, in the Hotel Congress, has good breakfasts, light meals and, especially, desserts from 7am to 11pm daily. Also good and locally popular is *Grill (☎ 623-7621, 100 E Congress)*, which is open 24 hours.

The *Blue Willow Restaurant (☎ 327-7577, 2616 N Campbell Ave)* serves many vegetarian dishes, has excellent breakfasts, and its soups, salads and sandwiches are both good and an excellent value ($5 to $8). It has an attractive patio with a shade roof and mist-makers to keep you cool. Beer and wine are served. *Govinda's Natural Foods* (☎ 792-0630, 711 E Blacklidge Drive) has Indian-influenced vegetarian food served buffet-style. The atmosphere is meditative, and vegan food is also available. Hours are 11:30am to 2:30pm Wednesday to Saturday, and 5 to 9pm Tuesday to Saturday. *Guilin* (☎ 320-7768, 3250 Speedway) has Tucson's best Chinese dining and numerous vegetarian options ($7 to $14).

For Mexican dining, there are half a dozen good places along S 4th Ave between 22nd and I-10, any one of which provides satisfactory food (most entrées are $6 to $10). *Mi Nidito* (☎ 622-5081, 1813 S 4th Ave) frequently gets the best reviews and there's often a wait; they don't take reservations. Bill Clinton ate here when he was president. Downtown, *La Indita* (☎ 792-0523, 622 N 4th Ave) serves inexpensive and excellent Mexican food, as well as some Michoacan Tarascan Indian dishes.

Mexican food in more upscale environments costs a few dollars more but has some innovative twists and is still an excellent value. Recommended downtown places include the excellent *Café Poca Cosa* (☎ 622-6400, 88 E Broadway Blvd), in the Clarion Hotel, with beautifully presented, freshly prepared, innovative meals and a full bar. The menu changes often and reservations are requested. It closes on Sunday. Around the corner is *Little Café Poca Cosa* (20 S Scott), open 7:30am to 2:30pm Monday to Friday; alcohol is not served.

*El Minuto Cafe* (☎ 882-4145, 354 S Main Ave) has been in business for six decades and is famous for its chiles rellenos, among other dishes. A branch (☎ 290-9591, 8 N Kolb Rd) serves similar food. The oldest place in town is *El Charro Cafe* (☎ 622-1922, 311 N Court Ave), which they say has been in the same family since 1922 and is very popular with tourists and locals alike. Its carne seca used to be dried on the roof in the old days. There are two branches, at 6310 E Broadway (☎ 745-1922) and at the airport, for your last (or first) Mexican meal.

*Maya Quetzal* (☎ 622-8207, 429 N 4th Ave) is a small, friendly place that serves delicious Guatemalan dishes at pequeño prices; closed Sunday. *Miraflores* (☎ 888-4880, 5845 N Oracle Rd) serves authentic Peruvian cuisine daily except Monday ($8 to $14).

The *Tohono Chul Tea Room* (☎ 797-1222, 7366 N Paseo del Norte) has a pleasant patio open 8am to 5pm daily. The menu features both Mexican and American food, and they serve an English-style high tea from 2:30 to 5pm.

*Sakura* (☎ 298-7777, 6534 E Tanque Verde Rd) serves a varied Japanese menu including sushi and *teppan* (fun table-side chopping and pyrotechnics) with prices ($7 to $18) as varied as the menu. *India Oven* (☎ 326-8635, 2727 N Campbell) serves great Punjab food and has an inexpensive lunch buffet. It's very popular; service can be slow. *Char's Thai* (☎ 795-1715, 5039 E 5th St) has super-spicy plates (though mild dishes are also available) and is open weekdays for lunch and daily for dinner.

For recommended, inexpensive Italian food, consider *Gavi*, with three locations in town.

*Cafe Terra Cotta* (☎ 577-8100, 3500 E Sunrise), east of 1st Ave, is the best Southwestern restaurant in Tucson. The menu is innovative, even wild sounding at times, but there are also a few fairly straightforward choices. The appetizers sound so appetizing that many people order two of them and forgo an entrée, supposedly to leave room for one of the divine desserts. Prices are in the teens for most entrées and a good value. Another moderately priced restaurant with a delicious and eclectic Southwestern menu but a decidedly un-Southwestern ambiance is the *Presidio Grill* (☎ 327-4667, 3352 E Speedway Blvd). Reservations are highly recommended.

*Nonie* (☎ 319-1965, 2526 E Grant Rd) is a New Orleans bistro serving authentic French Creole and Cajun cuisine. If crawfish, jambalaya, alligator and fried pickles are your idea of good food, the cooks know how to prepare them here. They also have the world's hottest hot sauce – available on special request only. Prices are reasonable – $5 to $10 for lunch and $8 to $20 for dinner.

There are plenty of steak houses. For those on a budget, *El Corral* (☎ 299-6092, 2201 E River Rd) is a good choice. Service is a little amateurish but aims to please. Prime rib is the specialty of the house and a great deal at about $10. Hours are 4:30 to 10pm daily; reservations aren't taken, and there's always a line outside. The same owners run the *Pinnacle Peak Steakhouse* (☎ 296-0911, 6541E Tanque Verde Rd), where the atmosphere is Wild Western and fun, if slightly touristy. Wooden sidewalks pass dance halls and saloons as you swagger into the dining room. The sign outside warns 'Stop! No Ties Allowed'; if you've got one on, you can donate it to the rafter decorations. The food is inexpensive and good; dinner only.

The *Hidden Valley Inn* (☎ 299-4941, 4825 N Sabino Canyon Rd) has that old Wild West look to bring in the crowds as well as reasonable prices ($6 for hamburgers to $17 for big steaks). It's a great family place with hundreds of animated models of the Old West around the walls – kids can wander around and look at them while waiting for a meal. Open daily for lunch and dinner. The most upscale steak house is *McMahon's* (☎ 327-7463, 2959 N Swan Rd), which has an excellent seafood selection as well.

All the resorts listed under Places to Stay have top-class restaurants.

## ENTERTAINMENT
The free alternative *Tucson Weekly*, published every Thursday, has the most detailed club and bar listings. Also read the Friday Starlight section of the *Arizona Daily Star* and the Thursday Calendar section of the *Tucson Citizen*. Performances are fewer in summer.

### Cinemas
Tucson has many cinema multiplexes showing the year's best and worst movies. *The Loft* (☎ 795-7777, 3233 E Speedway Blvd) is the best bet for alternative or foreign flicks.

### Nightlife
The *Cactus Moon* (☎ 748-0049, 5470 E Broadway Blvd) is loud, brash and the place to see and be seen if you're into two-stepping to recorded music. Come dressed in the latest Western wear. Call if you are interested in dance lessons.

Downtown, 4th Ave near 6th St is a good spot to bar hop. *Club Congress* (622-8848) in the Hotel Congress, has alternative dance music (recorded and occasionally live). For Latin music, try *Irene's Restaurant and Bar* (☎ 206-9385, 254 E Congress). *IBT's* (☎ 882-3053, 616 N 4th Ave) is Tucson's best gay dance club, while *Ain't Nobody's Bizness* (☎ 318-4838, 2900 E Broadway) (in a shopping plaza) attracts lesbians.

Students head to *Chicago Bar*, (☎ 748-8169, 5954 E Speedway Blvd) for blues, rock and reggae. *Berky's Bar* (☎ 296-1981, 5769 E Speedway Blvd) attracts an older crowd and often has decent live bands and dancing; *Boondocks Lounge* (☎ 690-0991, 3360 N 1st Ave) is a pretty good blues venue.

Some older theaters now function as performance venues for musicians playing anything from a cappella through punk to zydeco, and where dancing is sometimes allowed. These include the *Rialto Theater* (☎ 740-0126, 318 E Congress) and the *Santa Rita Ballroom* at 6th Ave and Broadway Blvd.

### Performing Arts
The renovated 1920s *Temple of Music & Art* (☎ 884-4875, 622-2823, 330 S Scott Ave) is the home of the Arizona Theater Company, which produces shows from October to May. The *Tucson Convention Center* (☎ 791-4101, 791-4266, 260 S Church) has a Music Hall, the Leo Rich Theatre and a convention area that plays host to many events, including performances by the Arizona Opera Company (☎ 293-4336) from October to March; the Tucson Symphony Orchestra (☎ 882-8585) November to March; and sporting and theatrical events. The U of A *Centennial Hall* (☎ 621-3341, 1020 E University Blvd) hosts excellent international acts throughout the academic year and presents Ballet Arizona

(☎ 602-381-1096, 888-322-5538) occassionally. Several local theater companies present alternative and avant-garde productions.

On Thursday night, Tucson Arts District (☎ 624-9977) sponsers art walks; call for other art events.

## SHOPPING

Southwestern arts and crafts are of the most interest to travelers. Small but exquisite pieces of jewelry can easily be carried, and bulky items can be shipped.

Some of the best stores are in the Presidio Historic District (see Downtown Tucson, earlier in this chapter). Another good place for quality arts and crafts is St Philips Plaza at the southeast corner of River Rd and Campbell Ave. Prices are high, but so is the quality. Particularly good stores here are the Obsidian Gallery (☎ 577-3598) for crafts and jewelry, Bahti Indian Arts (☎ 577-0290) for varied Native Americana and the Turquoise Door (☎ 299-7787) for stunning jewelry.

For shopping and browsing, you can't beat 4th Ave between University Blvd and Congress St. Here you'll find books and beads, antiques and African art, jewelry and junk, clothes and collectibles, and all sorts of treasures. Then head west along Congress for the Arts District.

## GETTING THERE & AWAY
### Air

Tucson International Airport (☎ 573-8000) is 9 miles south of downtown. It has a few direct flights into Mexico, but international airport facilities are limited to immigration and customs. Many major US carriers have direct flights between Tucson and many large US cities.

The local bus agency, Sun Tran (☎ 792-9222), has buses (No 25) during the day to the Laos Transit Center at Irvington and Liberty Ave, halfway between the airport and downtown. From here you have to connect to another bus. The fare is $1 and a transfer is free. Bus No 11 from the airport goes north through town along Alvernon Way, connecting with many east-west routes. There's information at the airport.

A more convenient option is using Arizona Stagecoach (☎ 889-1000,), which has door-to-door, 24-hour van service to anywhere in the metropolitan Tucson area. The fare ranges from $10 to more than $20 – roughly half of a cab fare.

website: www.arizonastagecoach.com

### Bus

The Greyhound terminal (☎ 792-3475) is at 2 S 4th Ave. Several buses a day run east along I-10 to New Mexico, and northwest along I-10 to Phoenix, connecting to the rest of Arizona and California. Greyhound also connects with vans to Nogales every hour from 7am to 7pm for $6.50 and with Golden State (☎ 623-1675) buses for Douglas ($20), via Sierra Vista and Bisbee, leaving five times a day.

Arizona Shuttle Service (☎ 795-6771, 800-888-2749), 5350 E Speedway Blvd, has hourly vans from three Tucson locations to Phoenix Airport from 4am to 9pm. The fare is $24 with discounts for roundtrips, children and groups.

website: www.arizonashuttle.com

## GETTING AROUND
### Bus & Trolley

Sun Tran (☎ 792-9222) has buses all over the metro Tucson area from early morning into the evening every day, but no buses run past 11pm. Fares are $1 with a free transfer. Passes and timetables are available at many locations; call Sun Tran for the nearest one. There are many park-and-ride lots around town, and some buses have bike racks. Major transit centers are the Laos Transit Center near Irvington and Liberty Ave to the south; the Ronstadt-Downtown Center at Congress and 6th Ave; and the Tohono Tadai Center at Stone Ave and Wetmore Rd to the north.

Sun Tran Trolley is an old-fashioned-looking trolley (fit with air-conditioning) linking U of A (it leaves from Old Main) with the 4th Ave shopping area, Congress and the Arts District, historical downtown, and the Ronstadt-Downtown Center. Trolleys run two or three times an hour from about 10am to 6:30pm weekdays and less frequently on Saturday (no Sunday service). Trolleys run until 11pm on the nights of Downtown Saturday Night and when the U of A has a home game. Trolley fare is 25¢.

## Car

All the main companies have offices in the airport and many have offices in other parts of the valley or will deliver your car.

## Taxi

The fare from the airport to downtown is around $15. Companies include Yellow Cab (☎ 624-6611) and Allstate Cab (☎ 798-1111). Apart from the cab rack at the airport, you need to phone to get a cab – they don't cruise the streets.

## Bicycle

Tucson takes pride in being bike-friendly, with bike lanes on many major roads. Public libraries have free maps of the bike-lane system. Tucson's bike shops can provide you with information, rentals (about $20 a day) and details of mountain biking off the main roads. Try Bargain Basement Bikes (☎ 624-9673), 428 N Fremont Ave. Helmets are required for cyclists under 18.

## AROUND TUCSON
## Mission San Xavier del Bac

Founded by Padre Kino in 1700, this is Arizona's oldest European building still in use. Mostly destroyed in the Pima Indian uprising of 1751, it was rebuilt in the late 1700s and today looks much like it did 200 years ago. The building has been restored and work continues on the frescoes inside. A visit to San Xavier is a highlight of any trip to Tucson.

Nicknamed 'the white dove of the desert,' its dazzling white walls are a splendid sight as you drive south on I-19 (take exit 92). The mission is on the San Xavier Indian Reservation (part of the Tohono O'odham tribe), and the plaza by the mission parking lot has stores selling Indian jewelry, arts and crafts, and snacks.

Catholic masses are held daily. The church itself (☎ 294-2624) is open 7am to 5pm daily, and the church museum and

gift shop is open 9am to 5pm. Admission is by donation. Photography is permitted when religious ceremonies are not taking place.

Colorful religious ceremonies are held on the Friday after Easter, the Fiesta of San Xavier in early December, and Christmas. Call the mission for details.

## Arizona-Sonora Desert Museum

The ASDM (☎ 883-2702), 2021 N Kinney Rd, is a living museum representing the flora and fauna of the Arizona-Sonora Desert and, as such, is more like a zoo than a museum. It is one of the best of its kind in the country and well worth a visit. Almost all local desert animals are displayed, often in quite natural-looking settings. The grounds are thick with desert plants too, many of which are labeled. You'll see scorpions and saguaros, coatis and coyotes, bighorn sheep and rattlesnakes, golden eagles and tiny hummingbirds, javelinas and agaves. It's all here.

Docents are on hand to answer questions about the live animals and to show other exhibits throughout the day – you might get a chance to pet a snake. There are two walk-through aviaries, one dedicated solely to hummingbirds; a geological exhibit featuring an underground cave (kids love that one); an underground exhibit with windows into ponds containing beavers, otters and ducks (found along the riparian corridors of the desert); and much more.

Allow at least two hours (half a day is better) and come prepared for outdoor walking. Strollers and wheelchairs are available, as are a gift shop, art gallery, restaurant and café.

The drive out to the ASDM is about 14 miles west along Speedway Blvd, which crosses over the very scenic Gates Pass and turns into Gates Pass Rd. The narrow and winding Gates Pass Rd is impassable for trailers and RVs, which must take the longer route west along Ajo Hwy. The visit can be combined with Old Tucson Studios, the International Wildlife Museum or Saguaro National Park (West) to make a full-day outing.

The ASDM is open 8:30am to 5pm daily, and from 7:30am from March to September. (On summer Saturdays, it's open until 10pm.) Admission is $9.95 ($8.95 from May to October), and $1.75 for six- to 12-year-olds.

website: www.desertmuseum.org

## Old Tucson Studios

This film set was used in hundreds of Western movie productions from 1939 onward. Unfortunately, 65% of it burned down in 1995, but it has been rebuilt and expanded as a Western theme park, and movies are still shot here. Visitors are treated to shootouts, stagecoach rides, saloons, sheriffs and Wild West events galore; it is one of Tucson's most popular tourist spots. Old Tucson (☎ 883-0100) is on Kinney Rd a few miles southeast of the ASDM. Hours are 10am to 6pm daily, and admission is $14.95 ($9.45 for four- to 11-year-olds) plus tax.

website: www.oldtucson.com

## International Wildlife Museum

Housed in an odd castle-like building at 4800 W Gates Pass Rd (between Speedway Blvd and Gates Pass), this museum (☎ 617-1439) is a taxidermist's delight. Hundreds of animals from all over the world have been killed and expertly mounted. There are various hands-on exhibits and hourly movies about wildlife but no live animals. Hours are 9am to 5pm daily; admission is $7 for adults, $5.50 for students and seniors and $2.50 for six- to 12-year-olds.

## Biosphere 2

This unique 3.15-acre glassed dome was built to be completely sealed off from Biosphere 1 (our planet). Inside, different micro-habitats, ranging from tropical forest to ocean environment, were designed to be completely self-sustaining. In 1991, eight bionauts entered Biosphere 2 for a two-year tour of duty during which they were physically cut off from the outside world. The experiment was criticized because the dome leaked gases and it was opened to allow a bionaut to emerge for medical treatment

and to bring in supplies. The facility is now operated by Columbia University and the public can tour the site and enter parts of the biosphere.

Biosphere 2 (☎ 800-828-2462, 825-1289, 896-6200) is 5 miles northeast of the junction of Hwy 77 and Hwy 79, 30 miles north of Tucson. Hours are 8:30am to 5pm and guided tours are offered all day. Admission is $12.95, $8.95 for 13- to 17-year-olds and $6 for six- to 12-year-olds. Those over 10 can actually enter Biosphere 2 for an additional $10; reservations are required as tours entering the biosphere are limited to 20 people. There is a restaurant, gift shop and the *Biosphere 2 Hotel*, with 27 rooms, all with coffeemakers, mini-fridge bars and balconies, for $100, less in the summer.

website: www.bio2.edu

## Colossal Cave

This dry limestone cave, six stories under the ground, was a legendary outlaw hideout. It's a 'dry' cave with no dripping water: Formations are no longer growing. A half-mile trail takes visitors through several different chambers with many geological formations. The temperature inside is a pleasant $72°F$ year-round.

Colossal Cave (☎ 647-7275) is open every day for tours 9am to 5pm mid-September to mid-March and 8am to 6pm rest of the year. It stays open one hour later on Sundays and holidays. Admission is $3 per vehicle. Cave admission includes a 45-minute guided tour for $7.50; $4 for six- to 12-year-olds. The cave is 8 miles north of I-10 exit 279, about 25 miles southeast of Tucson. Alternatively, head southeast on Old Spanish Trail and follow the signs.

## SAGUARO NATIONAL PARK

This park has two sections, Saguaro East and Saguaro West, about 30 miles apart and separated by Tucson. There are no drive-in campgrounds or lodges and only Saguaro East allows overnight backpacking, but the park is a fine day trip. As its name implies, it preserves large stands of the giant saguaro cactus and associated habitat.

TUCSON & SOUTHERN AZ

## Flora & Fauna

Saguaro seedlings are vulnerable to intense sun and frost, so they often grow in the shade of palo verde or mesquite trees, which act as 'nurse trees.' Saguaros grow slowly, taking about 15 years to reach a foot in height, 50 years to reach 7 feet and almost a century before they begin to take on their typical many-armed appearance.

Saguaros are only part of the landscape. Many birds nest in holes in these giant cacti. Gila woodpeckers and flickers excavate the holes, which form hard scar tissue on the inside of the plant, protecting the nest and the cactus. In subsequent years, owls, cactus wrens, kestrels and other birds may use these nests, which are often 20°F cooler than the outside. On the ground, many other kinds of cacti and a variety of vegetation is home to javelinas, desert tortoises, gila monsters, jackrabbits, coyotes, kangaroo rats, rattlesnakes, roadrunners, tarantulas and many other animals.

Late April is a good time to visit the park, when the saguaros begin blossoming with lovely white flowers – Arizona's state flower. By June and July, the flowers give way to ripe red fruit that has been traditionally picked by desert Indians; they use them both for food (as fruit and jam) and to make saguaro wine.

## Saguaro East

Also called the Rincon Mountain District, this larger and older section of the park encompasses both the desert and mountain country of the Rincon Mountains and their western slopes. The saguaro grows up to about 4000 feet and then the scenery gives way first to oak woodland, then pine and finally, at elevations of more than 7000 feet, to mixed conifer forest.

**Information** The park is open daily from 7am to sunset. The visitor center (☎ 733-5153) at the park entrance is open 8:30am to 5pm daily except Christmas and is the only place with drinking water. It has a bookstore, information, an audiovisual display and exhibits. Ranger-led programs are offered, especially in the cooler months. The

park is 15 miles east of downtown along Old Spanish Trail. Admission is $6 per private vehicle or $3 for walkers and cyclists; all passes are honored.

**Cactus Forest Drive** This paved, one-way, 8-mile loop road gives access to picnic areas (no water), nature trails of varying lengths and views of the saguaro forest. The road is accessible to all vehicles, including bicycles. A 2½-mile trail off the drive is suitable for mountain bikes only.

**Hiking & Backpacking** Of almost 130 miles of trails in Saguaro East, the easiest is the quarter-mile, wheelchair-accessible Desert Ecology Nature Trail, which leaves from the north end of Cactus Forest Drive. Progressively longer trails strike off into the park, including the Tanque Verde Ridge Trail, which climbs steeply from the south end of Cactus Forest Drive up into the Rincon Mountains, where the highest elevation is Mica Mountain at 8666 feet. There are six designated backcountry camping areas, most of which lack water. Campers must have permits, which are available at the visitor center at no charge up to two months ahead of your chosen date. Permits must be picked up by noon on the day you start hiking to allow time to reach the first camping area. Horses are also permitted on trails.

## Saguaro West

Also called the Tucson Mountain District, this is just north of the Arizona-Sonora Desert Museum, and a drive through the area can be combined with a visit to the ASDM. Saguaro West is much lower than Saguaro East, with the highest point being 4687-foot Wasson Peak.

**Information** The visitor center (☎ 733-5158) on Kinney Rd, 2 miles northwest of the ASDM, is open 8:30am to 5pm daily except Christmas, with similar facilities to Saguaro East. The two paved roads through the park (Kinney Rd and Picture Rocks Rd) are open 24 hours a day. Unpaved loop roads and hiking trailheads close at sunset, however. Admission is free but there are plans to adopt Saguaro East's fee structure.

**Bajada Loop Drive** The unpaved, 6-mile Bajada Loop Dr begins 1½ miles west of the visitor center and can normally be negotiated by ordinary vehicles. Apart from fine views of cactus forests, there are several picnic areas as well as trailheads.

**Hiking** Short, paved nature trails are near the visitor center. Longer trails climb several miles into the Tucson Mountains and give access to Indian petroglyphs as well as admirable views. The King Canyon trailhead, just outside the park boundary almost opposite the ASDM, is open until 10pm. Although night hiking is permitted, camping is not. The nearest campground is the Gilbert Ray Campground about 4 miles southeast of the park (see Places to Stay, earlier in the chapter).

# Tucson to Phoenix

Most people barrel through from city to city along I-10 in a couple of hours. It's not a particularly attractive ride, except for the view of Picacho Peak. There are several worthwhile side trips, however, for travelers with a little time.

## PICACHO PEAK STATE PARK
Picacho Peak (3374 feet) is an obvious landmark on the west side of I-10 exit 219, 40 miles northwest of Tucson. The westernmost 'battle' of the American Civil War was fought here, with the Confederate forces killing two or three Union soldiers. The Confederates then retreated to Tucson and dispersed, knowing their forces would soon be greatly outnumbered.

The state park (☎ 466-3183) provides camping, picnicking and two steep hiking trails to the summit. Fixed ropes and ladders are used to aid hikers, but no technical climbing is involved. It's about 2 miles and 1500 feet up to the top. Day use is $5 per vehicle (up to four passengers).

The *campground* has 95 sites open year-round on a first-come, first-served basis. Rates are $10 for tents, $15 for hookups. Drinking water and showers are available. The campground's 1800-foot elevation makes this a hot stop in summer.

## CASA GRANDE & AROUND
The modern town of Casa Grande is a few miles northwest of the I-10 interchange with I-8, on Hwy 238. The archaeological site of Casa Grande (described below) is about 30 miles away.

Indian dances and a powwow are held annually during **O'odham Tash** (☎ 836-4723, fax 426-1731), an annual celebration in mid-February.

Some cheap motels and chains line Florence Blvd, west of exit 194.

### Casa Grande Ruins National Monument
Once a major Hohokam Indian village covering about 1 sq mile, this site was abandoned around AD 1350 and little remains today except for one building, the Casa Grande (big house).

The Casa Grande is quite imposing. About 30 or 40 feet high, it is built of mud walls several feet thick. The mud was made from caliche, the rock-hard soil of the area that is the bane of the modern gardener. A huge amount of work went into constructing the building, which is the most unusual Hohokam structure standing today. Rain and human intrusion have caused some damage, but the general structure of the building remains clear. To prevent further erosion, Casa Grande has been capped by a large metal awning built in the 1930s, an effective, if incongruous, preservation tool. You cannot enter the building itself, though the outside is quite impressive.

The site, about 20 miles north of I-10 exit 212 or 14 miles east of I-10 exit 185, has a visitor center (☎ 723-3172) with a good small museum explaining the general history of the Hohokam and this ruin in particular. There are picnic tables, drinking water and a bookstore, but no overnight facilities. The monument is open 8am to 5pm daily except Christmas. Admission is $3 per person and passes are honored.

## Florence

☎ 520 • pop 17,054 • elevation 1493 feet

Founded in 1866, this is one of Arizona's earliest Anglo towns and is the home of the Arizona State Prison, which replaced Yuma's notorious prison in 1909. The visitor center (☎ 868-4331), 330 Butte, is open 9am to 3pm weekdays and has a brochure describing some of the historic buildings. The most interesting is the 1878 adobe brick courthouse (with assorted later additions) in **McFarland Historical State Park** (☎ 868-5216), Main at Ruggles Ave, which offers exhibits about Florence's past. Hours are 8am to 5pm Thursday to Monday; admission is $2.

## Gila River Arts & Crafts Center

This is named for the Gila River Indian Reservation, Arizona's earliest reservation, established in 1859 for the Pima and Maricopa Indian tribes. Near I-10 exit 175, the center has a museum (☎ 315-3411) about the Pima and Maricopa tribes and a gift shop selling arts and crafts from several Southwestern tribes. Hours are 8am to 5pm. A simple restaurant serves up mainly American food along with a few Indian items.

# West of Tucson

Highway 86 heads west of Tucson toward some of the driest parts of the Sonora Desert. Much of the land is part of the Tohono O'odham Indian Reservation, the second largest in the country, though the reservation itself has little of tourist interest. Highlights of a trip out west are the Kitt Peak Observatory and the Organ Pipe Cactus National Monument.

## BUENOS AIRES NATIONAL WILDLIFE REFUGE LOOP

From Robles Junction, on Hwy 86 about 20 miles west of Tucson, Hwy 286 goes south to the 175-sq-mile Buenos Aires National Wildlife Refuge, good for grassland birding with an ongoing project to reintroduce the masked bobwhite, which became extinct in Arizona about a century ago. The refuge is open daily during the daylight hours, and guided tours are occasionally offered. Backpacking and overnight camping are permitted at about 100 sites, none of which have facilities. Information is available from Buenos Aires NWR Visitor Center (☎ 823-4251) open 7am to 4pm daily.

A few miles east of the refuge is the little village of **Arivaca** with several buildings dating from the 1880s. There is a café but no motel. From Arivaca, you can return to Tucson via the paved road to Arivaca Junction and then I-19, the quickest way, or take the unpaved **Ruby Road** (Hwy 289) to Nogales. This is a scenic route with plenty of border history. The road is passable to ordinary cars in dry weather but should be avoided in rain; it passes through the Coronado National Forest (see Nogales later) where you can camp almost anywhere. There are some small lakes along the way that attract wildlife.

The Buenos Aires NWR and Ruby Road make an interesting trip, which few people make, so you'll get away from the crowds.

## TOHONO O'ODHAM INDIAN RESERVATION

This large desert and mountain reservation of almost 4500 sq miles is home to the Tohono O'odham, traditionally an agricultural people who still practice farming and, since the Spaniards introduced cattle, ranching as well. Maize, beans and cotton are important crops, and naturally growing saguaro fruit is harvested for jams and a kind of wine. Mesquite beans and other naturally occurring plants are also harvested. There are small branches of the reservation around Mission San Xavier del Bac (see Around Tucson, earlier in this chapter) and just north of Gila Bend, but the majority of the land is in the deserts beginning about 25 miles west of Tucson.

Heading west out of Tucson, you'll see humpbacked Baboquivari Peak (7730 feet), the highest in this area and sacred to the tribe. To its north is Kitt Peak (6875 feet), home of the observatory described below. The tribal capital, Sells, 60 miles west of Tucson on Hwy 86, has a couple of places to eat and some stores but no accommodations.

The Tohono O'odham have little interest in tourism except for casinos near Tucson. They are known for their fine basket work, which can be purchased from the gift shop at Kitt Peak and the Gu-Achi Trading Post at Quijotoa, on Hwy 86, 23 miles west of Sells.

The main event is the annual Tohono O'odham All-Indian Tribal Fair & Rodeo, which has been held for over 60 years, attracts Indians from many tribes and is open to the general public. The rodeo is the main attraction, but there are also dances, concerts, Indian food stands and basket work for sale. This is usually held in February. For information, call the Tucson Visitor Center. Other events are held at the San Xavier Mission and the O'odham Tash Indian Celebration in Casa Grande in February.

## KITT PEAK NATIONAL OBSERVATORY

From Tucson you can make out the white telescope domes on top of Kitt Peak, even though it is 40 miles as the crow flies.

This is the largest optical observatory in the world and includes 22 telescopes, one of which is a solar telescope used for studying the sun via a series of mirrors. The largest telescope has a diameter of 4 meters and is housed in a 19-story-high dome.

A visitor center (☎ 318-8726) with a museum, audiovisual presentations, gift shop, but no food, provides information. Guided tours, lasting about an hour and visiting two or three telescopes, leave daily at 10am, 11:30am and 1:30pm. (You don't get to look through the telescopes.) Self-guided tours are available. Hours are 9am to 3:45pm daily except major holidays. A $2 donation is suggested. The nearly 6900-foot elevation often means snow in winter, which may close the steep road up the mountain.

Nightly public stargazing, limited to 20 participants, starts with a sunset snack and is followed by three hours of observation. Rates are $35, or $30 for students and seniors. This is very popular and should be booked well in advance. Call for details. website:   www.noao.edu/outreach/kpout reach.html

## ORGAN PIPE CACTUS NATIONAL MONUMENT

This giant columnar cactus differs from the saguaro in that it branches from its base – both species are present in the monument, so you can compare them. Organ-pipe cacti are common in Mexico, but this national monument is one of the few places in the USA where they are commonly seen. The third species of columnar cactus found here (and nowhere else in the USA) is the senita, which, like the organ pipe, branches from the bottom but has fewer pleats in its branches, which are topped by the hairy white tufts that give the senita its nickname of 'old man's beard.'

The monument is mainly undisturbed Sonoran Desert habitat. Not only do three types of large columnar cacti grow here, but a profusion of other desert flora and fauna also thrive. In spring, in years that have the right combination of winter rains and temperatures, the monument can be carpeted with wildflowers (mid-February to April is the best time). Cacti flower at different times, particularly from late April to early July, although some species can flower in March or as late as October.

Many animals are present, but the heat and aridity force them to use survival strategies such as hiding out in a hole or burrow during the day. Therefore early morning and evening are the best times to look for wildlife. Walking around the desert by full moon or flashlight is another good way to catch things on the prowl, but wear boots and watch where you step.

The monument offers six hiking trails ranging from a 200-yard paved nature trail to strenuous climbs of over 4 miles. Cross-country hiking is also possible, but have a topographical map and a compass and know how to use them – a mistake out here is deadly if you get lost and run out of water. Two scenic loop drives of 21 and 53 miles start near the visitor center and are steep, winding and unpaved. They are passable to cars except after heavy rain, but RVs and trailers are not recommended. Other roads are passable only to 4WD vehicles. Carry extra water in your car in case of a break-down. There are several picnic sites along the way, but no water.

### Information

A visitor center (☎ 387-6849) on Hwy 85, 22 miles south of Why, is open 8am to 5pm daily and has information, drinking water, a bookstore, a small museum and a slide show. Ranger-led programs take place from about October to April. Admission to the monument is $5 per vehicle, or $3 per bike or bus passenger. All passes are honored. There is no charge to drive through the monument on Hwy 85 from Why to Lukeville.

Winter is the most pleasant season to visit. Summer temperatures soar above 100°F most days from June to August, although nights are pleasant, with lows typically 30°F lower than daytime highs. The summer monsoons make July to September the wettest months, although the rains tend to be of the brief, torrential variety and rarely stop anyone for more than an hour or two. Winter temperatures are pleasant, with January, the coolest month, experiencing average highs of 67°F and lows of 38°F.

### Places to Stay

Over 200 sites at the campground by the visitor center cost $10 on a first-come, first-

served basis and are often full by noon from mid-January through March. There is drinking water but no showers or RV hookups. Backcountry camping (no water) is only allowed with a permit ($5) obtainable at the visitor center.

## AJO

☎ 520 • pop 3000 • elevation 1750 feet

Ajo (pronounced 'AH-ho') was once a major copper mining town; a mile-wide open-pit mine can be seen south of town. Falling copper prices closed the mine in 1985, many miners left and housing costs dropped, attracting retirees who revived the town. The town plaza, built in Spanish-colonial style, has several pleasant restaurants and shops.

The chamber of commerce (☎ 387-7742), near the plaza, is open 9am to 4pm Monday to Friday, with reduced summer hours. The **Ajo Historical Society Museum** (☎ 387-7105), in an attractive church close to the copper mine, south of town, is usually open in the afternoon except in summer.

A few miles west of Ajo is one of the most rugged regions in the country, the **Cabeza Prieta National Wildlife Refuge**. You must have a permit from NWR headquarters (☎ 387-6483), 1611 N 2nd Ave, to visit the area. The refuge was set aside as desert bighorn sheep and pronghorn habitat. This is 135 sq miles of wilderness, with no facilities and only rudimentary dirt roads. The summer heat is, literally, a killer.

### Places to Stay

*La Siesta RV Resort & Motel* (☎ 387-6569, 2561 N Hwy 85) has RV hookups and 11 simple rooms from $35 to $60. The little *Marine Resort Motel & RV Park* (☎ 387-7626, 1966 N Hwy 85) has 20 large, clean motel rooms with refrigerators and coffeemakers for about $55 to $65 in winter, less in summer. RV hookups are available.

The 1925 *Guest House Inn B&B* (☎ 387-6133, 700 Guest House Rd) has four comfortable rooms decorated in a Southwestern motif and with private baths for about $90 a double.

# South of Tucson

I-19 due south of Tucson heads to Nogales, on the Mexican border 62 miles away. The distances to freeway exits and speed limits are all in kilometers here. The route follows the Santa Cruz River Valley and has been a trading route since pre-Hispanic times.

## GREEN VALLEY & AROUND
☎ 520 • pop 26,000 • elevation 2900 feet
Green Valley is a retirement community spread around I-19 exits 69, 65 and 63. The chamber of commerce (☎ 625-7575, 800-858-5872), just west of exit 63, is open year-round 9am to 5pm weekdays and 9am to noon Saturdays from September to May. A huge open-pit copper mine can be seen west of the freeway near here.

### Asarco Mineral Discovery Center
Asarco, one of the nation's largest producers of non-ferrous metals, operates four copper mines in Arizona, including the Mission Complex open-pit mine between Tucson and Green Valley. The discovery center (☎ 625-7513) is a mining museum opened in 1998. Hours are 9am to 5pm Tuesday to Saturday; admission is free. Open-pit mine tours lasting one hour cost $6 for adults, $5 for seniors and $4 for five-to 12-year-olds. The last tour leaves at 3:40pm. The center is just west of I-19 exit 80, and the mine is 4 miles farther west.

### Titan Missile Museum
During the Cold War, the USA had many intercontinental ballistic missiles armed with nuclear warheads and ready to fly within a few seconds of receiving a launch order. Fortunately, that order never came. With the SALT II treaty, all the missiles and their underground launch sites were destroyed except for this one, which has been kept as a national historic landmark. The nuclear warhead was removed, but the rest remains as it was during the tense 1960s and '70s, when the push of a button could have started a cataclysmic nuclear war.

The public can tour the entire complex. The museum (☎ 625-7736) is west of I-19 exit 69. Guided tours (reservations recommended, ☎ 625-7736 during business hours) leave every half-hour 9am to 4pm daily except Thanksgiving and Christmas, November to April. From May to October the museum is closed on Monday and Tuesday. The tours involve stair climbing, but wheelchair-accessible tours can also be arranged. Admission is $7.50 for adults, $6.50 for those over 62 or with military ID and $4 for seven- to 12-year-olds. Discount combination admissions with the Pima Air & Space Museum located in Tucson are offered.

## Madera Canyon Recreation Area
This canyon gives access to hiking trails into the Santa Ritas, including two trails up the biggest peak, Mt Wrightson (9453 feet), in the Coronado National Forest (the ranger station is in Nogales, ☎ 281-2296). These trails are 5.4 and 8.1 miles respectively, and there are numerous others. The riparian habitat in the canyon attracts an unusually large variety and number of birds, and this is one of the most popular places for birding in southeastern Arizona. Parking may be difficult to find, especially on weekends, when an early arrival is essential. It's a popular spot; on busy weekends, like Easter or Labor Day, the canyon is closed down once it gets too full! Madera Canyon is about 13 miles east of I-19 exit 63. Day use is $5 per vehicle. The elevation is a pleasant pine-shaded 5200 feet.

The USFS runs the 13 campsites at *Bog Springs Campground* on a first-come, first-served basis. There is water but no showers or hookups. The fee is $10. There is also a USFS-run picnic area.

*Santa Rita Lodge (☎ 625-8746)* has eight rooms and four larger cabins, all with kitchenettes, which are popular with birders and usually booked far in advance from March to May. Rates are $78 for rooms and $93 for cabins. The lodge has hiking information and runs birding tours ($15) and other educational activities.
website: www.santaritalodge.com

TUCSON & SOUTHERN AZ

## Whipple Observatory

A new paved road leads up to the observatory from I-19 exit 56. The multi-mirror telescope atop Mt Hopkins at 8550 feet is one of the world's largest and can be visited only by a bus tour ($7; $2.50 for six- to 12-year-olds) beginning at the visitor center at 9am on Monday, Wednesday and Friday from mid-March through November. Tours last six hours and are limited to 26 participants by reservation only (☎ 670-5707).

Ten miles below the observatory, a visitor center shows a film and has exhibits about the telescope (admission is free). The visitor center is open 8:30am to 4:30pm weekdays. website: http://linmax.sao.arizona.edu/help/FLWO/whipple.html

## TUBAC & AROUND

☎ 520 • pop 1200 • elevation 3200 feet

Tubac is one of the main arts and crafts villages in the Southwest and is also among the most historic. If history and/or crafts shopping interest you, Tubac is definitely a worthwhile stop.

There was a Pima Indian village here before Spanish missionaries arrived in the late 17th century, followed by settlers in the 18th century. A Pima revolt in 1751, which the Indians lost, led to the building of Tubac Presidio in 1752, which fell into disuse when the garrison moved to Tucson in 1776. A Spanish/Pima garrison was established a few years later. Tubac became part of Mexico after 1821, but, in 1848, Apache Indians forced the settlers out again. After the Gadsden Purchase of 1853, Americans revived mining operations and Tubac briefly became Arizona's largest town in 1860. Activities ceased during the Civil War, and then afterwards Tubac became a sleepy farming community. After an art school opened in 1948, Tubac began its transformation into a major artists' community.

## Information

Tubac is east of I-19 exit 34. It's a small village and is easily visited on foot. The chamber of commerce (☎ 398-2704) answers questions during the week or online at www.tubacaz.com. Most of the approximately 80 galleries, art studios and crafts stores in town have a map showing the location of the shopping district and shops, most of which are open from 10am to 5pm daily, year-round.

## Tubac Presidio State Historic Park & Museum

The presidio now lies in ruins, but you can see the 1885 schoolhouse and other historic buildings nearby. The exhibits in the museum (☎ 398-2252) describe the history of Tubac. Hours are 8am to 5pm daily except Christmas, and admission is $2, $1 for seven- to 14-year-olds. The park is at the east end of Tubac and offers picnicking facilities.

## Tumacácori National Historical Park

Three miles south of Tubac at I-19 exit 29 are the well-preserved ruins of the Tumacácori (pronounced 'too-ma-CA-co-ree') Franciscan Church, built in 1800 but never completed. Although abandoned in the late 1800s, the church was protected as a national monument in 1908. It gives the visitor an idea of the Spanish history of the area. A visitor center (☎ 398-2341) features a museum, gift shop and picnic area. Mexican and Indian artists demonstrate their techniques on weekends. Hours are 8am to 5pm daily except Thanksgiving and Christmas. Admission is $2 per person over 16, and all passes are honored.

## Special Events

The Tubac Arts & Crafts Festival is held in early February and lasts several days. Anza Days, on the third weekend in October, features historical reenactments and cultural events.

A mass is said in the Tumacácori Church on Christmas Eve, and a couple of times a year besides. Call the visitor center for information. An Indian arts and crafts fair is held in Tumacácori in early December.

## Places to Stay & Eat

*Tubac Country Inn B&B* (☎ 398-3178), at Plaza Rd and Burruel in downtown Tubac,

RICHARD CUMMINS

Fancy pants at the Tucson Rodeo

ANN CECIL

Indian blanket, pottery and rug, Sedona

RICHARD CUMMINS

Wooden Indians, Scottsdale

Old West justice at the state historic park in Tombstone

Gold King Mine Museum, near Jerome

Rawhide Western Town in Scottsdale

has five large rooms with private baths (two with kitchenettes) opening onto a porch and garden for $85. A two-bedroom/two-bathroom house, perfect for a family, is $240. The *Amado Territory Inn* (☎ 398-8684, 888-398-8684,), near I-19 exit 48, has nine rooms decorated in territorial (19th-century ranch) style, all with private baths and some with patios or decks. Rates are $95 to $135; see the inn and adjoining restaurant online at www.amado-territory-inn.com. The chamber of commerce has details of several other B&Bs.

*Tubac Golf Resort* (☎ 398-2211, 800-848-7893) is a mile north of Tubac. Apart from the 18-hole golf course, there is a tennis court, pool, spa, and a good restaurant and bar. The 45 rooms and suites are all spacious, and some have fireplaces, living rooms or kitchenettes attached. Winter rates are $140 to $195, depending on the size of the room. Summer rates are $80 to $130.

website: www.tubacgolfresort.com

The restaurants adjoining the Amado Territory Inn and the Tubac Golf Resort are both good. There are several quaint eateries in Tubac.

## NOGALES & AROUND
☎ 520 • pop 20,878 • elevation 3865 feet
Nogales (pronounced 'noh-GAH-lez'), Arizona, and Nogales, Sonora, are towns separated only by the USA/Mexico border. You can easily walk from one into the other and many visitors come to shop for Mexican goods. The twin towns are locally called *Ambos Nogales* or 'Both Nogales.' Nogales is Arizona's most important gateway into Mexico and also the major port of entry for the agricultural produce Mexico sells to the USA and Canada.

The Greyhound Terminal (☎ 287-5628), 35 N Terrace Ave, has buses about once an hour during the day and early evening to Tucson ($6.50).

### Information
Steep hills, a dividing railroad, one-way streets, a confusing street system and poor local maps make getting around Nogales

difficult for visitors. It's not a big town, though, so relax and you'll eventually find where you want to go.

The chamber of commerce (☎ 287-3685), in Kino Park off Grand Ave, is open 8am to 5pm weekdays. Other services include the Mexican Consulate (☎ 287-2521), 571 Grand Ave; US Immigration (☎ 287-3609) at the border; Coronado National Forest Ranger Station (☎ 281-2296), near I-19 exit 12; library (☎ 287-3343), 518 Grand Ave; post office (☎ 287-9246), 300 N Morley Ave; hospital (☎ 287-2771), 1171 W Target Range Rd; and police (☎ 287-9111), 777 Grand Ave.

### Pimeria Alta Historical Society Museum
This historical museum (☎ 287-4621), in the old town hall (built in 1914) at 136 Grand Ave, gives a good introduction to the area. Hours are 10am to 4pm, Thursday to Saturday; admission is free.

### Visiting Mexico
Most visitors shop for a few hours and perhaps have a meal in Nogales, Sonora (Mexico). Park on the US side (many lots around Crawford and Terrace Ave charge $4 a day) and walk over into the Mexican shopping district. US dollars and credit cards are accepted and prices are good (though not much cheaper than in Arizona), but the quality varies so shop around. Bargaining is certainly possible. All kinds of Mexican goods are available, such as pottery, stoneware, silver, tin, glass, weavings, leather, basketry and woodcarvings.

From Nogales, buses and trains continue farther into Mexico. Drivers need car insurance, available from Sanborn's (☎ 281-1873), 2921 Grand Ave.

Also see the 'Crossing the Border' boxed text.

### Places to Stay
The USFS-operated *Upper/Lower White Rock* campgrounds are on Peña Blanca Lake, 9 miles west of I-19 exit 12, north of Nogales. There are 15 sites with water (but no showers or hookups) available year-

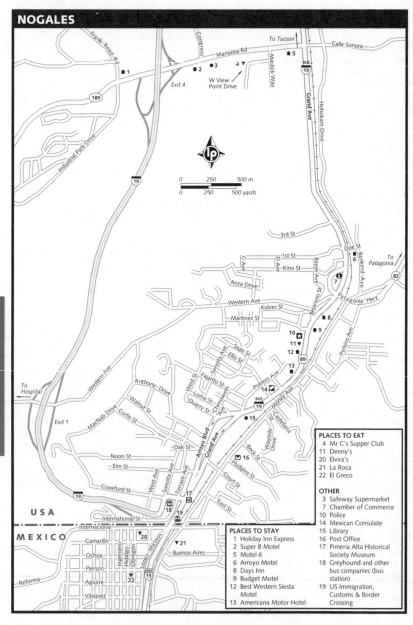

# NOGALES

0   250   500 m
0   250   500 yards

**PLACES TO EAT**
4  Mr C's Supper Club
11  Denny's
20  Elvira's
21  La Roca
22  El Greco

**OTHER**
3  Safeway Supermarket
7  Chamber of Commerce
10  Police
14  Mexican Consulate
15  Library
16  Post Office
17  Pimeria Alta Historical
   Society Museum
18  Greyhound and other
   bus companies (bus
   station)
19  US Immigration,
   Customs & Border
   Crossing

**PLACES TO STAY**
1  Holiday Inn Express
2  Super 8 Motel
5  Motel 6
6  Arroyo Motel
8  Days Inn
9  Budget Motel
12  Best Western Siesta
   Motel
13  Americana Motor Hotel

TUCSON & SOUTHERN AZ

USA
MEXICO

round on a first-come, first-served basis. Sites are $8 and there is fishing and boating.

The cheapest places are the independent *Arroyo Motel (☎ 287-4637, 20 Doe St)*, with basic rooms around $30, or the *Budget Motel (☎ 287-2200, 820 Grand Ave)*. The *Americana Motor Hotel (☎ 287-7211, 639 Grand Ave)* has a restaurant, pool, and 96 good-sized older double rooms from $50 to $60. Otherwise, you have a choice of *chain motels*, with a Motel 6, Super 8 Motel and Holiday Inn Express near I-19, exit 4, and a Best Western and Days Inn on Grand Ave.

### Places to Eat
Mariposa Rd east of I-19 offers the usual assortment of fast-food restaurants and a supermarket.

The best restaurant in Nogales is *Mr C's Supper Club (☎ 281-9000, 282 W View Point Dr)*. Reserve ahead for a window seat with a view. Guaymas shrimp is the house specialty, and American steak and seafood are served from 11:30am to 11pm Monday to Friday, dinner only on Saturday, with dinner entrées mainly in the teens including a visit to the salad bar.

Several Mexican restaurants are found along Grand Ave. Diners on the Mexican side have a reasonable choice of Mexican restaurants. Good choices are *Elvira's (Calle Obregón 1)*, with meals under $10 and a free margarita thrown in; the similar *El Greco (Calle Obregón 152)*; and the slightly pricier *La Roca (Calle Elías 91)*. These clean places have Mexican atmosphere designed with the American visitor in mind.

### PATAGONIA & AROUND
☎ 520 • pop 881 • elevation 4050 feet

Patagonia and smaller Sonoita (elevation 4970 feet), 12 miles northeast, are ranching centers and the hub of Arizona's wine country. Both towns were important railway stops, but since the line closed in 1962, tourism and the arts have helped keep them thriving. Nearby grasslands were the surprising setting of the musical *Oklahoma*.

### Information
Patagonia has area information at its visitor center (☎ 394-0060, 888-794-0060), 307 McKeown Ave, in the Mariposa Book and gift shop, one block off Hwy 82. In front, the town center is a tree-filled park with the 1900 train depot, now the town hall. There is no hospital; call ☎ 911 in emergencies. Many places (including area restaurants) close on Monday and Tuesday.
website: www.patagoniaaz.com

### Patagonia Lake State Park
A dam across Sonoita Creek forms this 2½-mile-long lake (elevation 3750 feet), about 7 miles southwest of Patagonia. The park (☎ 287-6965) is open year-round for camping, picnicking, walking, bird-watching, fishing, boating and swimming. A marina provides boat rentals (no motor boats) and supplies. The campground has showers and hookups and 100 plus sites available on a first-come, first-served basis. Rates are $5 for day use, $10 for camping and $15 with hookups.

### Patagonia-Sonoita Creek Preserve
Managed by The Nature Conservancy, Sonoita Creek is the home of four endangered species of native fish, and the splendid riparian habitat along the creek attracts almost 300 species of birds, including rarities from Mexico. Birding is good year-round. March to September is the very best time, with peaks of migrants in late April and May, and in late August and September. Beware of insects in spring and summer (chiggers are bad in July and August!) and wear long pants and insect repellent.

Reach the preserve by going northwest on N 4th Ave in Patagonia, then south on Pennsylvania Ave, driving across a small creek. The fee is $3 for visitors who are members of The Nature Conservancy, and $5 for everyone else. There is a visitor center (☎ 394-2400) and trails but no camping or picnicking facilities. The preserve is closed on Monday and Tuesday. From April through September hours are 6:30am to 4pm, from 7:30am in other months. Guided tours are given at 9am on Saturdays.

## Wineries

Near tiny Elgin, a few miles east of Sonoita, the Village of Elgin Winery (☎ 455-9309) and Callaghan Vineyards (☎ 455-5322) advertise tours and tastings daily. They may be open weekends only, so call in advance.

## Crossing the Border

You can freely walk across the border into Mexico for shopping or a meal at any of the border towns. Returning from Mexico into the USA, however, is another matter. Foreign travelers need to carry a passport to show the US immigration authorities. US citizens on a day trip don't need passports if they carry their birth certificates (if they were born in the USA) or a naturalization certificate. Although a US driver's license will sometimes suffice, don't count on it. US resident aliens need to carry their resident alien card when returning to the USA.

To enter Mexico for more than a border day trip, bring a passport and a Mexican tourist card, which will be checked a few miles inside the country. The tourist card is available for free at the border upon producing a passport. (US citizens can obtain a tourist card with a birth certificate, but a passport is a more convenient and quickly recognized document and enables you to change money and perform other tasks.) Mexican tourist cards are valid for up to 180 days, but normally much less time is given. Ask for as many days as you will need. A few nationalities require a Mexican visa; recently, these included some European, African and Asian nationals, but the situation changes. If in doubt, check with the Mexican consul in your home country or in Tucson or Nogales. Be warned that even the Mexican consul might not be aware of the latest changes. If you are heading just to Puerto Peñasco, four hours drive from Tucson, you don't need a tourist card.

Travelers into Mexico cannot bring in guns or ammunition without a special permit. This law is very strict – someone with just a few bullets can be imprisoned for weeks.

You can bring almost anything bought in Mexico back into the USA duty-free as long as it's worth a total of less than $400 and doesn't include more than a quart of booze or 200 cigarettes. Many handicrafts are exempt from the $400 limit. Fresh food is prohibited, as are fireworks, which are illegal for personal use in Arizona. Importing weapons and drugs is also illegal, except for prescribed drugs, which are cheaper in Mexico – some visitors without health insurance fill their prescriptions in Mexico.

Traveling by Mexican public transport is a little more adventurous than the equivalent in the USA. However, it's also much more far-reaching and you can get almost anywhere on a bus at reasonable cost. If you prefer to bring your own car, you should get Mexican car insurance; US car insurance is not normally valid in Mexico. Car insurance can easily be bought at one of many places at the border (Sanborn's in Nogales and Tucson are reputable) or through the American Automobile Association. Rates are $10 to $15 a day for comprehensive coverage, but if you buy insurance by the week or month, rates drop substantially. Remember: Mexico's legal system is Napoleonic, that is, you are guilty until proven innocent, and you are likely to be arrested and held after a car accident unless you can show Mexican car insurance covering the accident.

Nogales is the main Arizona/Mexico border crossing and is also the safest. Along the southeastern Arizona border, drug smuggling and international car theft are frequent occurrences, and illegal immigration is a concern. Immigration and customs officials are working to control these problems. Not all officials are honest, however; both Mexican and US officers have broken the law in recent years. This is a recognized problem that both countries are working to solve, but travelers should be aware that a small percentage of officials on both sides of the border are corrupt. The best defense is to make sure that your documents are perfectly in order, to travel by day and to not allow officials to intimidate you for any reason. It is most unlikely that you will have any problems.

## Special Events

The Sonoita Quarter Horse Show is the oldest in the country and runs in early June. Sonoita is home of the Santa Cruz County Fair & Rodeo Grounds with a rodeo over Labor Day weekend and county fair over the fourth weekend in September. Call for these and other events (☎ 455-5553). The Fall Festival, second weekend of October, is Patagonia's largest event, with arts, crafts, music and food.

## Places to Stay & Eat

Patagonia has a hotel, guest ranch and B&Bs. Sonoita has the best restaurants, with oft-changing hours. Call.

The *Stage Stop Inn* (☎ *394-2211, 800-923-2211, 303 W McKeown*) in Patagonia is a modern motel with a Western facade. Over 40 rooms are $70 a double or $89 with a kitchenette, and there is a small pool, restaurant (closed Tuesday in summer) and bar.

The *Circle Z Ranch* (☎ *394-2525, 888-854-2525*) is a working cattle ranch a few miles southwest of Patagonia. From November to mid-May it offers horseback-riding vacations with a three-night minimum. Accommodations are in rustic but comfortable rooms and cabins, and all meals are provided. Rates are about $800 to $1000 per person for a week, including riding, though families can arrange package discounts. website: www.circlez.com

The *Duquesne House* (☎ *394-2732, 357 Duquesne St)*, inside one of Patagonia's first buildings, is the town's longest established B&B. Six old-fashioned units with private bath are $75 per double. The Patagonia visitor center can suggest half a dozen other B&B options.

Eat at the *Velvet Elvis* (☎ *394-2102, 292 Hwy 82)* in Patagonia, which does include a velvet Elvis among its funky artwork and serves designer pizzas, soups and salads. Outdoor tables are available. The restaurant is closed on Tuesdays.

In Sonoita, the non-smoking *Sonoita Inn* (☎ *455-5935)* has 18 rooms from $125 to $140, including continental breakfast. The inn is a celebration of western living, with a decidedly horsey bent; its website is www.sonoitainn.com. Next door, the *Steak-Out* (☎ *455-5205, 3235 Hwy 82)* will please carnivores with meals ranging from 1/3 lb burgers for $7 to 2 lb porterhouse steaks for $31. They serve dinner daily and weekend lunches, and feature live entertainment on weekends.

*Café Sonoita* (☎ *455-5278, 3280 Hwy 82)* is popular and serves dinner Wednesday to Saturday and lunch Friday and Saturday. *Grasslands Natural Food Bakery* (☎ *455-4770, 3119 Hwy 83)* a half mile south of Sonoita, does great vegetarian options 8am to 3pm Friday and Saturday, 10am to 3pm Wednesday to Saturday.

TUCSON & SOUTHERN AZ

# Southeastern Arizona

This is Cochise County – the land of Indians, cowboys, miners, outlaws, ranchers, gunslingers and Western lore. Today cattle ranches are still here, but mining operations have mainly closed down. The Huachuca Mountains and the Chiricahua Mountains provide scenic and natural beauty.

## Highlights

- Visiting the Amerind Foundation museum and archaeology research center, which focuses on Southwestern Indians

- Touring the spectacular Kartchner Caverns, a 2½-mile-long limestone cave discovered in 1974 and opened to the public in 1999

- Wandering around the old Western buildings and watching gunfight reenactments in Tombstone, home to the famous OK Corral

- Relaxing in Bisbee, an old mining town with a Victorian look and an artsy feel

- Exploring the remote Chiricahua Mountains, with their wild and weird rock formations and plentiful wildlife

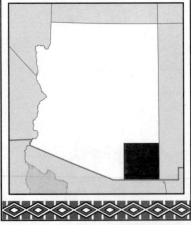

## BENSON

☎ 520 • pop 4711 • elevation 3580 feet

This rural town grew around a railway halt during the 1880s. Today it is a quiet travelers' stop and the nearest to Kartchner Caverns. Book lovers will enjoy the Singing Wind Bookshop (☎ 586-2425), 700 W Singing Wind Rd, 2½ miles north of Benson along Ocotillo Ave and then through a green gate (close it after you). Open 9am to 5pm daily, this ranch house/bookshop has thousands of books, mainly with Southwestern themes. The small San Pedro Valley Arts & Historical Museum (☎ 586-3070), at 5th and San Pedro St, is open 10am to 4pm Tuesday to Friday and 10am to 2pm Saturday October to April; 10am to 2pm Tuesday to Saturday in May, June, July and September (closed in August). Admission is free.

The Greyhound (☎ 586-3141) bus stops at 680 W 4th St on its runs along I-10.

### Information

The chamber of commerce (☎ 586-2842), 249 E 4th, is open 10am to 5pm Monday to Friday and 1 to 5pm Saturday; visit the website at www.bensonchamberaz.com. Other services include the library (☎ 586-9535), 300 S Huachuca; post office (☎ 586-3422), 260 S Ocotillo Ave; hospital (☎ 586-2261), 450 S Ocotillo Ave; and the police (☎ 586-2211), 360 S Gila St.

### Places to Stay & Eat

**Red Barn Campground** *(☎ 586-2035)* and **KOA** *(☎ 586-3977)* are both just off Ocotillo Rd, north of I-10 exit 304. Red Barn charges $14 for tents and $18 for hookups. KOA charges $19 and up and has a pool, hot tub and mini-golf.

Six basic, old motels along 4th St (Hwy 80) offer rooms in the $30s including the **Benson Motel** *(☎ 586-3346, 185 W 4th St)*, with old-fashioned car-garages and the **Sahara Motel** *(☎ 586-3611, 1150 S Hwy 80)*, with kitchenettes and TVs but no phones.

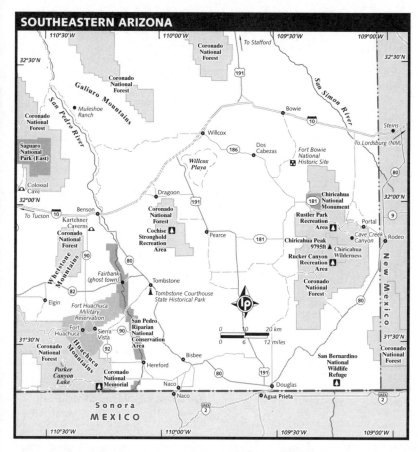

SOUTHEASTERN ARIZONA

*Chain motels* include a Motel 6 and Holiday Inn Express by I-10, exit 302 (en route to Kartchner Caverns) and Days Inn, Super 8 and Best Western by exit 304.

The *Chute-Out Steakhouse* (☎ 586-7297, 161 S Huachuca) serves steaks and seafood and is locally popular; the steaks aren't great but are relatively cheap and the ribs are pretty tasty. It's open for dinner daily. *Ruiz's* (☎ 586-2707, 687 W 4th St) is a decent little Mexican restaurant. *Galleano's* (☎ 586-3523, 601 W 4th St) is a homey place serving Italian and American breakfast, lunch and dinner.

## AROUND BENSON
### Vega-Bray Observatory

This astronomy observatory is on a hill a few miles southeast of Benson. It has a classroom, planetarium and eight telescopes from 6 to 20 inches in diameter, some computer controlled. During the day, filtered telescopes are used for solar observations. A 2-mile nature trail goes to the San Pedro River.

At the observatory is *Skywatcher's Inn* (☎/fax 615-3886), a four-room B&B. All rooms have private baths and guests have the use of two kitchens. Rates are $85 to

SOUTHEASTERN ARIZONA

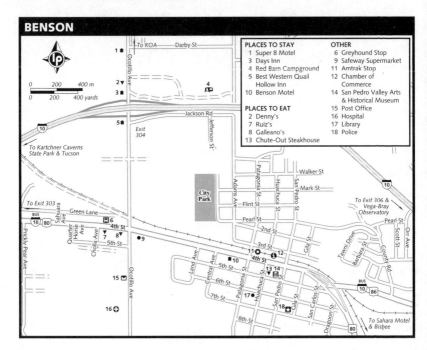

**BENSON**

| PLACES TO STAY | OTHER |
|---|---|
| 1 Super 8 Motel | 6 Greyhound Stop |
| 3 Days Inn | 9 Safeway Supermarket |
| 4 Red Barn Campground | 11 Amtrak Stop |
| 5 Best Western Quail Hollow Inn | 12 Chamber of Commerce |
| 10 Benson Motel | 14 San Pedro Valley Arts & Historical Museum |
| PLACES TO EAT | 15 Post Office |
| 2 Denny's | 16 Hospital |
| 7 Ruiz's | 17 Library |
| 8 Galleano's | 18 Police |
| 13 Chute-Out Steakhouse | |

$120 (one or two people). A four-hour guided introductory astronomy session for up to five people is $85, and other sky-watching packages for beginners to professionals can be arranged. Reservations are necessary.

website: www.communiverse.com/skywatcher

### Amerind Foundation

This excellent museum and archaeology research center (☎ 586-3666) is in Dragoon, near I-10 exit 318, 15 miles east of Benson. The exhibits of Native American archaeology, history and culture cover many tribes from Alaska to South America, with a special focus on Southwestern Indians.

Don't miss the Western-art gallery in a separate building, featuring a small but superb collection of artists of the past century including some Indian painters whose works have been exhibited internationally. Hours are 10am to 4pm daily September to May, closed Monday and Tuesday in summer and major holidays. Admission is $5; $4 for seniors and 12- to 18-year-olds.

### Kartchner Caverns State Park

This spectacular limestone cave was almost completely undamaged and unexplored when discovered. The moist cave is 2½ miles long and the geological features within it are still growing. Cavers stumbled across it in 1974, but the location of this spectacular spot was kept secret until 1988, when state park protection could be assured. It opened to the public in 1999. State-of-the-art trail, lighting and misting systems protect this unique and fragile living cave. All equipment and tours have to go through air locks to minimize contaminating the cave, touted as one of the world's 10 best living caves. Thousands of examples of several different kinds of formations are seen, being formed imperceptibly, drop by drop, by water.

A visitor center introduces visitors to the cave with a film and other exhibits. A half-mile wheelchair-accessible trail within the cave can be visited on guided tours only. Twenty-five daily tours (except Christmas) leave between 8:30am and 4:40pm, take 75 minutes, and are limited to 20 people. A new tour is in the planning stages. Admission to the park is $10 per vehicle and reserved guided tours cost $14, $6 for seven- to 13-year olds. Reservations (☎ 586-2283) are strongly recommended because the tours sell out months in advance, especially during the busy cooler months and holidays. Each morning, 100 walk-up tickets are available for that day. Cars begin lining up before dawn and visitors are often turned away even if they arrive before the park opens. Photography and all food and drinks are not allowed within the cave, which is a comfortable 70°F year-round.

The park (☎ 586-4100) is open from 7:30am to 6pm. Outside the visitor center is a wheelchair-accessible hummingbird garden trail, and 2- and 4½-mile hiking trails into the nearby Whetstone Mountains. A campground with showers and RV hookups has 60 sites for $20, including the $10 park entry fee. The park is 9 miles south of I-10, exit 302.

## SIERRA VISTA

☎ 505 • pop 37,775 • elevation 4623 feet
Sierra Vista was founded in the 1950s as a service center for Fort Huachuca (see below) and makes a good base from which to visit Cochise County's attractions.

## Information

The chamber of commerce (☎ 458-6940, 800-288-3861), 21 E Wilcox Dr, is open 8am to 5pm Monday to Friday, and from 9am to 4pm on Saturday; visit www.visitsierra vista.com. Other services include the Coronado National Forest Ranger Station (☎ 378-0311), 7 miles south at 5990 Hwy 92; library (☎ 458-4225), 2600 E Tacoma St; post office (☎ 458-2540), 2300 E Fry Blvd; hospital (☎ 458-4641, 458-2300), 300 El Camino Real; and the police (☎ 458-3311), 911 N Coronado Dr.

## Fort Huachuca Military Reservation

Founded in 1877 by the US Army during the wars with the Apaches, Fort Huachuca has had a colorful history. In 1913 it was a training ground for the famous Buffalo Soldiers, made up entirely of African American fighting men. Today, the military reservation is one of the largest employers in Arizona. The Fort Huachuca Museum (☎ 533-5736) has free displays explaining the history of the fort. Hours are 9am to 4pm weekdays and 1 to 4pm on weekends. Register at the main gate at the west end of Fry Blvd and the guard will give directions to the museum, three miles west of the main gate.

## Places to Stay

Several motels in the $30s are found along Fry Blvd, including the **Western Motel** (☎ 458-4303, 43 W Fry Blvd), which has a microwave and refrigerator in every room. The **Motel 6** (☎ 459-5035, 1551 E Fry Blvd) has 103 rooms in the $40s. Other **chain motels** in the $45 to $90 range include a Super 8, Best Western and Comfort Inn & Suites.

**Sun Canyon Inn** (☎ 459-0610, 800-822-6966, 260 N Garden Ave), just off Fry Blvd, has a pool and Jacuzzi, microwaves and refrigerators in every room, continental breakfast and charges $66 for a double; visit www.suncanyoninn.com. The **Windemere Hotel** (☎ 459-5900, 800-825-4656, 2047 S Hwy 92) has a pool, Jacuzzi, lounge, restaurant with room service and 149 good-size rooms with coffeemakers, microwaves, refrigerators and hair driers. Rates are about $90, including hot breakfast buffet and complimentary evening cocktails. Two suites are about $150; get details at www.windemere hotel.com. **Sierra Suites** (☎ 459-4221, 800-852-2430, 391 E Fry Blvd) has 100 large rooms with refrigerators and microwaves for $70 to $100. There is a pool, whirlpool and fitness room, and continental breakfast is provided; send email to sierrasuites@earthlink.net.

## Places to Eat

There are plenty of good restaurants to choose from all along Fry Blvd. *Caffé-O-Le*

(☎ *458-6261, 400 E Fry Blvd*) is open for breakfast and lunch and has a great coffee selection. Decent Mexican food is served at *La Casita* (☎ *458-2376, 465 E Fry Blvd*).

For American steak and seafood, the best place is 7 miles south at *The Mesquite Tree* (☎ *378-2758, 6398 S Hwy 92*), open for dinner daily except Sunday. Dinner entrées range from $10 to $18. For a more continental menu, the casually elegant *Outside Inn* (☎ *378-4645, 4907 S Hwy 92*) serves weekday lunch salads and sandwiches for $6 to $8. Dinners, served Monday to Saturday, cover a spectrum of veal, lamb, beef, chicken and seafood, all including a soup or salad, in the $10 to $18 range.

### Getting There & Around

America West Express flies several times daily between Phoenix and Sierra Vista's Fort Huachuca Airport. Golden State (☎ 458-3471), a Greyhound subsidiary at 28 Fab Ave, has buses on Douglas-Bisbee-Sierra Vista-Tucson-Phoenix runs.

Enterprise and Monty's (☎ 458-2665) rent cars. AA Cab (☎ 378-2100) and ABC Cab (☎ 458-8429) have 24-hour taxi service.

## AROUND SIERRA VISTA
### Ramsey Canyon Preserve

At 5500 feet in the Huachuca Mountains to the south of Sierra Vista, this Nature Conservancy-owned preserve is famous throughout the birding world as one of the best places in the USA to see up to 14 species of hummingbird. The highest numbers are seen from April to September, but there are some year-round. Trogons and other rarities from Mexico are also seen in the wooded riparian habitat in the canyon in summer. Also protected is the Ramsey Canyon leopard frog, found nowhere else in the world. Visitors are quite likely to see deer, and sightings of coatis, ringtails, javelinas, mountain lions and black bears are reported regularly.

Entrance to the preserve (☎ 378-2785, 378-2640) is limited by the 23 spaces of the parking lot, at the end of a very narrow and winding road along which parking is illegal. There's no room for RVs or trailers. Spaces are first-come, first-served.

Preserve hours are 8am to 5pm March to October and from 9am in other months; the preserve is closed major holidays. A $5 donation is requested from non–Nature Conservancy members, $3 for members. A visitor center features a gift- and bookshop, and hummingbird feeders are hung on the grounds to attract the birds. Two trails lead up into the canyon. The 0.7-mile nature loop is quite easy, and the longer Hamburg Trail climbs high into the Huachucas. Register at the visitor center to use the trails. At 9am Tuesday, Thursday and Saturday March to October, guided nature walks are offered.

website: www.tncarizona.org

For overnight stays, the *Ramsey Canyon Inn B&B* (☎ *378-3010*) has two housekeeping cabins (up to four people, $158) and six B&B rooms (two people, $121 to $145). These are often booked a year ahead for the peak summer season, and reservations are always necessary. Minimum two-night stays are required in the busy season. If the inn is full, Sierra Vista is just 10 miles away. No smoking is allowed in the inn or the preserve.

### Coronado National Memorial

This commemorates the first major European expedition into the Southwest when Francisco Vásquez de Coronado, accompanied by hundreds of Spanish soldiers and Mexican Indians, passed through in 1540 on his way from Mexico City, searching for gold in the Seven Cities of Cibola. Coronado is credited with introducing horses to the Indians.

The memorial is at the southern end of the Huachuca Mountains on the Mexican border, 20 miles south of Sierra Vista on Hwy 92. The visitor center (☎ 366-5515), open daily except Thanksgiving and Christmas, features exhibits on Coronado's expedition and the area's wildlife. The memorial itself is open during daylight hours, and admission is free.

The road from Sierra Vista to the visitor center is paved. West from the visitor center (at 5230 feet), a graveled road climbs the 6575-foot-high Montezuma Pass, offering great views. A 3.3-mile hiking trail also links these two points. From the pass, a 0.7-mile trail climbs to Coronado Peak (6864 feet) with great views into Mexico. West of the pass, the road continues through the Coronado National Forest emerging at Nogales, about 50 miles away. This road is passable to cars except after rain.

The memorial has no camping, but you can camp for free almost anywhere in the Coronado National Forest to the west. *Lakeview* is a developed USFS campground at **Parker Canyon Lake**, reached by driving west from the memorial or south from Sonoita on Hwy 83. The lake has a marina (☎ 455-5847) with boat rentals and fishing supplies. A five-mile hiking trail encircles the lake. There are 65 camping sites with water but no hookups for $10, available on a first-come, first-served basis. Day use is $5.

## San Pedro Riparian National Conservation Area

About 95% of Arizona's riparian habitat has disappeared, victim to poor grazing practices, logging for firewood, dropping water tables and development. Loss of this habitat has endangered many species' existence, and about 10% of the more than 500 species on the Endangered Species List are found along the San Pedro River. Clearly, this is valuable habitat. Almost 400 bird species, over 80 mammal species and nearly 50 species of reptiles and amphibians have been recorded along the 40-mile stretch of the San Pedro within the conservation area. This is the healthiest riparian ecosystem in the Southwest, and the San Pedro is also the longest remaining undammed river in Arizona.

The conservation area is managed by the BLM (☎ 458-3559) in Sierra Vista. Highway 82 crosses the river at **Fairbank**, a ghost town with interpretive signs, a picnic area, several hiking trails and a volunteer BLM host. Highway 90 crosses the river at San Pedro House, a 1930s ranch that now houses an information center (☎ 508-4445) and bookshop. It's open 9:30am to 4:30pm daily. Again, hiking trails are nearby.

Further south, there's a parking area where Hereford Rd crosses the river. All hiking trails are ideal for birding. The Southeastern Arizona Bird Observatory (SABO; see Bisbee, later in this chapter) does **birding tours** of the area.

Permits for **backcountry camping** cost $2 per day and are available at self-pay stations at parking areas. You must camp at least a mile away from roads and parking areas. Undocumented migrants pass through the area, so don't leave gear unattended.

The closest accommodations are at *Casa de San Pedro B&B* (☎ 366-1300, 8933 S Yell Lane), near the river off Hereford Rd. It has 10 comfortable nonsmoking rooms with private bath for $110 to $140 a double (two-night minimum), including full gourmet breakfast. The inn is popular with birders. website: www.naturesinn.com.

The rustic *San Pedro River Inn* (☎ 366-5532, 8326 S Hereford Rd) has four nonsmoking housekeeping cottages about 2 miles east of the river. The 20-acre property is also good for birding. Rates (two-night minimum) are $105, including continental breakfast.
website: www.sanpedroriverinn.com.

## TOMBSTONE
☎ 520 • pop 1504 • elevation 4539 feet

Despite friends' warnings that all he would find would be his own tombstone, prospector Ed Schieffelin braved the dangers of Apache attack and struck it rich. The year was 1877, and a rip-roaring, brawling, silver-mining town appeared very quickly. In 1881, when the population reached 10,000, 110 saloon licenses were sold, and there were 14 dance halls for the entertainment of the get-rich-quick miners. The famous shootout at the OK Corral also took place in 1881, during which the brothers Earp and Doc Holliday gunned down three members of the Clanton cowboy gang. This was one of dozens of gunfights in Tombstone, but it so caught people's imagination that it now is perhaps the most famous shootout in history.

Tombstone was typical of southwestern mining towns of the late 1800s. Saloons,

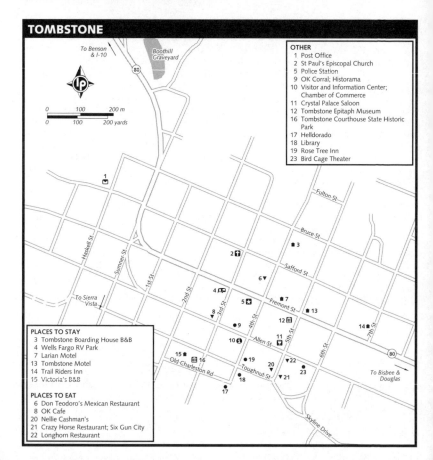

## TOMBSTONE

To Benson & I-10

Boothill Graveyard

**OTHER**
1  Post Office
2  St Paul's Episcopal Church
5  Police Station
9  OK Corral; Historama
10  Visitor and Information Center;
    Chamber of Commerce
11  Crystal Palace Saloon
12  Tombstone Epitaph Museum
16  Tombstone Courthouse State Historic
    Park
17  Helldorado
18  Library
19  Rose Tree Inn
23  Bird Cage Theater

To Sierra Vista

**PLACES TO STAY**
3  Tombstone Boarding House B&B
4  Wells Fargo RV Park
7  Larian Motel
13  Tombstone Motel
14  Trail Riders Inn
15  Victoria's B&B

**PLACES TO EAT**
6  Don Teodoro's Mexican Restaurant
8  OK Cafe
20  Nellie Cashman's
21  Crazy Horse Restaurant; Six Gun City
22  Longhorn Restaurant

To Bisbee & Douglas

gambling halls and bordellos made up a good portion of the buildings, but there were, as always, a sprinkling of sober citizens running newspapers, businesses and banks. The silver-mining boom was short-lived and declining silver prices and floods in the mines closed down the last operation in the early 1900s. Most other boomtowns became ghost towns, but Tombstone, the 'Town Too Tough to Die,' continued to be a commercial center.

After WWII, Arizona's growing population gave Tombstone a new vitality; the old county courthouse opened as a museum in the 1950s and Tombstone became a national historic landmark in 1962. Tombstone now attracts large crowds of tourists who visit the town's old Western buildings, many of which are now gift shops. Reenactments of gunfights and other late 1800s events provide entertainment.

There are no bus services to Tombstone. Visitors either come in their own vehicle or on a guided tour.

### Information

The visitor and information center (☎ 457-3929, 800-457-3423) at the corner of 4th and

Allen Sts, is open 9am to 4pm and 10am to 4pm on Sunday. Other services include the library (☎ 457-3612), at 4th St and Toughnut; post office (☎ 457-3479), 100 Haskell St; and the police (☎ 457-2244), 339 E Fremont St.

## The OK Corral

Site of the famous gunfight, the OK Corral (☎ 457-3456), on Allen St between 3rd and 4th Sts, is the heart of both historic and touristic Tombstone, as well as the first stop for many visitors. It's open 9am to 5pm daily; admission is $2.50 (free for children under six), and it has models of the gunfighters and numerous other Western exhibits; email for details at okcorral@ ok-corral.com. The most interesting is CS Fly's early photography studio. Next-door is **Historama**, with 26-minute presentations of Tombstone's history using animated figures, movies and narration (by Vincent Price). This is an additional $2.50, and showings are on the hour between 9am and 4pm. At 2pm daily there is a reenactment of the gunfight ($4.50).

Wyatt Earp

## Tombstone Courthouse State Historic Park

Built in 1882, abandoned in 1931, and rehabilitated in the 1950s, the courthouse displays thousands of artifacts relating to the town's history, including a 19th-century gallows, which will (for better or worse) pique children's interest. Staffed by knowledgeable state-park rangers, this museum deserves a visit. The courthouse (☎ 457-3311) at 3rd St and Toughnut is open 8am to 5pm daily. Admission is $2.50, $1 for seven-to 13-year-olds.

## Other Attractions

The **Bird Cage Theater** (☎ 457-3421, 800-457-3423), 517 E Allen St, got its name from the 14 bed-sized, draped cages suspended from the ceiling, used by prostitutes to entertain their clients. A bordello, gambling den, dance hall and saloon during the 1880s, this was the wildest place in the West, and you can see it for $4.50, $3 for six- to 18-year olds. Hours are 8am to 6pm daily.

Antique 1880s furniture and the world's largest rosebush can be seen at the **Rose Tree Inn** (☎ 457-3326) at 4th St and Toughnut. The white banksia rose bush arrived as a shoot sent from Scotland to a young emigrant wife in 1885; now over 8600 sq feet, the bush is especially pretty in April when the white flowers bloom. Hours are 9am to 5pm; admission costs $3 for those 14 and over.

The **Tombstone Epitaph Museum** (☎ 457-2211), at 5th and Fremont Sts, houses the presses of the town's first newspaper. Hours are 9:30am to 5pm daily; admission is free. It costs $1 for a replica of the October 27, 1881, edition of the *Tombstone Epitaph*, which reports the gunfight at OK Corral and contains various period ads, including one for **GF Spangenberg**, a gun dealer at 4th and Allen Sts. This business still operates today, selling both modern and antique weapons.

One of the few places you can see for free in this tourist town (though you have to enter through a gift shop) is the **Boothill Graveyard**, with the graves of many of Tombstone's early desperadoes. Some of the headstones' epitaphs make interesting reading:

Here lies

Lester Moore

Four slugs from a .44

No Les

No more.

The graveyard is off Hwy 80 just north of town and is open to visitors from 7:30am to late afternoon.

**St Paul's Episcopal Church** at Safford and 3rd, is the oldest non-Catholic church in Arizona, dating from 1882.

## Staged Shootouts

A prime tourist attraction, the shootouts are reenacted by various acting troupes in town. Most charge about $4 for the show ($1 for six- to 12-year-olds), though this varies. Apart from the daily 2pm show at the OK Corral (which sells out early on busy days), there are shows at Helldorado at 11:30am, 1 and 3pm daily. At Six Gun City, you can eat an outdoor lunch at the Crazy Horse Restaurant while enjoying shootouts several times a day. Shootouts, some at no charge, occur spontaneously at other times, especially during special events.

## Special Events

Tombstone's events revolve around weekends of Western fun with shootouts, stagecoach rides, chili cook-offs, fiddling contests, mock hangings and melodramas. The biggest event is Helldorado Days over the third weekend in October. Others are Territorial Days (in March), Wyatt Earp Days (Memorial Day weekend), Vigilante Days (second weekend in August) and Rendezvous of the Gunfighters (Labor Day weekend).

## Places to Stay

One and a half miles north on Hwy 80, **Tombstone Hills** (☎ 457-3829) has a pool, showers, laundry and over 80 tent and RV sites from $22 to $28. **Wells Fargo RV Park** (☎ 457-3966), near 3rd and Fremont Sts, allows tents and has about 60 sites with hookups at $22.

Motels raise their rates during special events, when reservations are recommended. Summer rates are the lowest.

The friendly **Larian Motel** (☎/fax 457-2272, 410 E Fremont St) has 14 very clean rooms with coffeemakers, most with two beds and many with mini-fridge and microwave, for $40 to $59 a double; go to www.tombstonemotels.com. The **Trail Riders Inn** (☎ 457-3573, 800-574-0417, 13 N 7th St) has 14 plain but reasonably sized rooms with two beds for $45 to $60 for two to four people in winter, $5 less in summer. The **Tombstone Motel** (☎ 457-3478, 888-455-4578, 502 E Fremont St) has 12 decent rooms at $45 to $55 single and $50 to $70 double in winter, $10 less in summer; visit their website at www.tombstonemotel.com.

The most comfortable motel is the **Best Western Lookout Lodge** (☎ 457-2223), on Hwy 80 a mile north of town, which has a pool, nice views and 40 good-size rooms for $65 to $90, including continental breakfast.

The visitor center can point out about eight B&Bs. **Tombstone Boarding House B&B** (☎ 457-3716, 108 N 4th St) is in two restored 1880s adobe homes. Six bedrooms with private baths and entrances are furnished with period pieces and rent for $60 to $80 double. Its breakfast is reputedly the best in town. A restaurant serves dinner daily except Monday, and a Sunday champagne brunch. Find out more on the web at tombstoneboardinghouse.com.

**Victoria's B&B** (☎ 457-3677, 211 Toughnut), dates from 1880 and has a checkered past featuring gamblers, judges and ghosts. Nowadays, it has a private wedding chapel (!) and the owner will arrange for a minister if you bring a partner and the wedding license. Three rooms with private bath rent for $65 to $75 double.

website: www.tombstone1880.com/vsbb

## Places to Eat

**Nellie Cashman's** (☎ 457-2212), near 5th St and Toughnut, dates from 1882. Nellie was a tough Irishwoman who stood no nonsense but helped out many a miner down on his luck. This no-alcohol establishment serves home-style meals 7am to 9pm daily in the quietly charming dining room. Huge hamburger plates are around $6 and varied dinner entrées are in the $9 to $19 range. For something a little wilder, cross the street to the *Crazy Horse Restaurant* (☎ 457-3827), which serves good, reasonably priced Western food outside during the daily shootouts, and quieter dinners.

The popular *Longhorn Restaurant* (☎ 457-3405), near 5th St and Allen, serves American and Mexican breakfast, lunch and dinner. Tourists line up outside the door at lunchtime. *Don Teodoro's Mexican Restaurant* (☎ 457-3647, 15 N 4th St), has inexpensive lunches and dinners, the latter accompanied by a flamenco guitarist Thursday to Saturday. For buffalo, ostrich and emu burgers and other American delights, the *OK Cafe* (☎ 457-3980, 220 E Allen St) is open 7am to 2pm daily.

### Entertainment
Several bars along Allen St have old Wild West ambiance. The best kept of these is the *Crystal Palace Saloon* (☎ 457-3611), near 5th and Allen Sts, dating from 1879. Nearby, *Big Nose Kate's* (☎ 457-3107) has live music Saturday night. There's little to do in the evening but go on a pub crawl – or make that a saloon stagger.

## BISBEE & AROUND
☎ 520 • pop 6090 • elevation 5300 feet
Bisbee, 24 miles south of Tombstone, shares a similarly wild early mining history. The difference was that Tombstone had silver, which fizzled out in the 1890s, while Bisbee had copper, which became Arizona's most important industry. By 1910 Bisbee had 25,000 inhabitants, making it the biggest city between El Paso, Texas, and San Francisco, California. Residents built elegant Victorian brick buildings, reminiscent of the East Coast and reasonably suited to the cooler elevation. Built in a narrow canyon, the town soon had no room for further construction. Today, Bisbee has more of a Victorian feel to it than any other town in Arizona. Copper mining declined after WWII and the mine closed in 1975, when production became unprofitable.

Bisbee's pleasant climate and old-fashioned ambiance attracted artists and the artistically inclined, and now the town is an intriguing mix of aging miners and gallery owners, ex-hippies and artists. It has more of an upscale air than Tombstone. Whereas Tombstone thrives on gunfight reenactments, Bisbee offers mine tours.

One World Travel (☎ 432-5359), 7 OK St, sells tickets for buses between Douglas and Tucson (via Sierra Vista).

### Orientation & Information
The steep canyon walls make Old Bisbee's layout rather contorted; Bisbee wasn't set up on the typical Western grid-like formation. East of Old Bisbee is the Lavender Pit Copper Mine, over a mile wide (a pullout on Hwy 80 has good views) followed by the traffic circle at Lowell (a useful landmark) and the suburb of Warren, 3 miles southeast of Bisbee. Warren has many Victorian homes and the local hospital. The modern district of San Jose, about 3 miles southwest of Warren, has the golf course.

At the chamber of commerce (☎ 432-5421, 866-224-7233), 31 Subway St, staff can reserve space for a mine tour, and they keep track of available lodging; visit www.bisbeearizona.com. Other services include the library (☎ 432-4232) and post office (☎ 432-2052), both at 6 Main St; hospital (☎ 432-5383), on Bisbee Rd at Cole Ave, Warren; and the police (☎ 432-2261).

### Bisbee Mining & Historical Museum
Housed in the 1897 office building of the Phelps Dodge Copper Mining Co, the museum (☎ 432-7071), at Copper Queen Plaza, has a fine display depicting the first 40 years of Bisbee's history, along with exhibits about mining. It also has a history and mining research library and is associated with the Smithsonian Institute. Hours are 10am to 4pm daily; admission is $4, free for kids under 16.

### Organized Tours
The **Queen Mine** (☎ 432-2071), in Old Bisbee, can be visited in underground mine

# BISBEE & AROUND

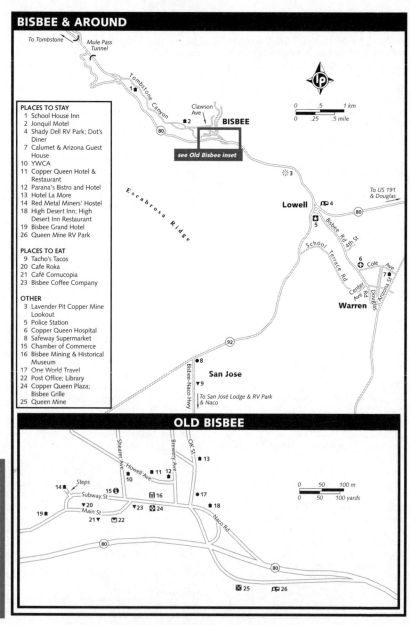

To Tombstone
Mule Pass Tunnel

Tombstone Canyon

Clawson Ave

**BISBEE**

see Old Bisbee inset

Escabrosa Ridge

**Lowell**

To US 191 & Douglas

Bisbee Rd
4th St
School Terrace Rd
Center Ave
Douglas
Cole Ave
Arizona St

**Warren**

**San Jose**

To San José Lodge & RV Park & Naco

Bisbee-Naco Hwy

**PLACES TO STAY**
1 School House Inn
2 Jonquil Motel
4 Shady Dell RV Park; Dot's Diner
7 Calumet & Arizona Guest House
10 YWCA
11 Copper Queen Hotel & Restaurant
12 Parana's Bistro and Hotel
13 Hotel La More
14 Red Metal Miners' Hostel
18 High Desert Inn; High Desert Inn Restaurant
19 Bisbee Grand Hotel
26 Queen Mine RV Park

**PLACES TO EAT**
9 Tacho's Tacos
20 Cafe Roka
21 Café Cornucopia
23 Bisbee Coffee Company

**OTHER**
3 Lavender Pit Copper Mine Lookout
5 Police Station
6 Copper Queen Hospital
8 Safeway Supermarket
15 Chamber of Commerce
16 Bisbee Mining & Historical Museum
17 One World Travel
22 Post Office; Library
24 Copper Queen Plaza; Bisbee Grille
25 Queen Mine

# OLD BISBEE

Shearer Ave
Howell Ave
Brewery Ave
OK St
Steps
Subway St
Main St
Naco Rd

cars. Reservations are suggested. Tours, given by retired miners, last about an hour and leave at 9 and 10:30am, noon, 2 and 3:30pm daily. Participants wear hard hats and go deep into the mine, which is a chilly 47°F; bring warm clothes. The price is $10 for adults, $3.50 for seven- to 15-year-olds and $2 for three- to six-year-olds. Guided van tours of the **Surface Mines & Historic District** leave at 10:30am, noon, 2 and 3:30pm for $7 per person over age two.

**Southeastern Arizona Bird Observatory** (SABO; ☎ 432-1388), a conservation, research and education program, offers various birding tours and workshops. There are weekly guided walks (three hours, $10) along the San Pedro River and Huachuca Mountains during the spring migration (April and May). Evening owl walks, hummingbird-banding programs and other birding tours are offered – contact SABO for details.

website: www.sabo.org

## Special Events

Art fairs and other events take place regularly; dates and programs are subject to change. The biggest events are the Spring Arts Festival on the second Sunday in May; Underground Film Festival at the end of June; Fourth of July parade (said to be the oldest in the state); Brewery Gulch Daze over Labor Day weekend; and a Home Tour over Thanksgiving weekend.

## Places to Stay

Most beds are full on weekends and you definitely need reservations for special events or holiday weekends. Most accommodations are historic hotels or B&Bs in older houses; there are no modern chain motels. Call the chamber of commerce for details of numerous other places in and around town.

**Camping & Hostels** Near the Queen Mine, ***Queen Mine RV Park*** (☎ 432-5006) has 25 RV sites with hookups for $19. ***San Jose Lodge & RV Park*** (see Motels & Hotels) has 50 RV spaces with hookups for $15. Several others are a few miles from Bisbee.

The ***YWCA*** (☎ *432-3542, 26 Howell Ave*) has 12-person women's and men's dorms for $10 per person. You must bring a sleeping bag; there is no kitchen and doors lock at 9pm. The funky, arty ***Red Metal Miners' Hostel*** (☎ *432-6671, 59-N Subway St*) sleeps up to 12 folks at $18 in dorms or $40 in private rooms, has Internet access, kitchen, laundry and bike rental.

**Motels & Hotels** The ***Jonquil Motel*** (☎ *432-7371, 317 Tombstone Canyon*) has seven older but clean nonsmoking budget rooms at $40 to $70. Budget rooms are also available at the ***San Jose Lodge & RV Park*** (☎ *432-5761, 1002 Bisbee-Naco Hwy*), with 45 modern rooms, a seasonal pool and a restaurant. Rates are $65 to $85 for a double.

In Old Bisbee, the 1902 ***Copper Queen Hotel*** (☎ *432-2216, 800-247-5829, 11 Howell St*) was Bisbee's most famous hotel. It retains its turn-of-the-century feel, especially in the public areas. The 47 rooms are furnished with antiques but have modern amenities, vary in size and comfort, and rent at $75 to $136. An outdoor pool, an old-fashioned saloon and a good dining room provide all you need.

website: www.copperqueen.com

---

### Vintage Vacation

One of the most unusual places to stay in Bisbee is the **Shady Dell RV Park** (☎ 432-3567, 1 Douglas Rd) at the Lowell traffic circle, which rents seven antique aluminum camping trailers. Among the lineup are a 1949 Airstream, a 1951 Spartan Royal Mansion and others from the 1940s and 1950s. They have been restored and fitted with refrigerators and propane stoves; dishes and bedding are provided. Most of them do not have their own showers and bathrooms. Trailers will sleep from one to four people and rent for $35 to $75. If you have your own rig, a few RV hookups are available and tent camping is possible.

The **High Desert Inn** (☎ 432-1442, 800-281-0510, 8 Naco Rd) has five comfortable rooms ($75 to $100) in contemporary European style with modern amenities, housed in what was the county jail back in 1901. Its website is www.highdesertinn.com.

Similarly modern rooms are found in the **Parana's Bistro and Hotel** (☎ 432-1832, 1 Howell Ave), also in a renovated 1901 building.

**B&Bs** The **Bisbee Grand Hotel** (☎ 432-5900, 800-421-1909, 61 Main St) is of the Victorian red-velvet and stuffed-peacock school of elegance. A billiards room and a Western saloon provide relaxation. Eight rooms, all with private baths, range from $75 to $150 double, and six suites are $100 to $150, including full breakfast.
website: www.bisbeegrandhotel.com

The **Hotel La More** (☎ 432-5131, 888-432-5131, 45 OK St) is a 20-room hotel built in 1916, when rates were $2 a night. Renovated in 1996, the antique-filled hotel now charges $65 to $80 a double for 16 rooms with private bath, or $55 for four rooms with shared bath, and $120 to $165 for three suites. The delicious breakfast is an all-you-can-eat buffet.

The **School House Inn** (☎ 432-2996, 800-537-4333, 818 Tombstone Canyon), built in 1918 as a school, now has nine attractive guest rooms following themes such as the Principal's Office and the Writing Room. Rates are $60 to $90 a double with full breakfast. All rooms have private baths.

In the historical suburb of Warren is the **Calumet & Arizona Guest House** (☎ 432-4815, 608 Powell), a grand house built in 1906. Now it features six spacious, old-fashioned but comfortable rooms, two with private bath and four sharing two baths, for $60 to $80 double with a full breakfast. A whirlpool, library and fireplace add cozy touches; send email to timbersj@juno.com.

## Places to Eat

The attractive **Bisbee Grille** (☎ 432-6788), in Copper Queen Plaza, serves moderately priced lunches and dinners (breakfast on the weekends). Near this plaza, **Bisbee**

**Coffee Company** (☎ 432-7879) serves mainly coffees and some sandwiches from 7am to 7pm daily, 'til 9pm on Friday and Saturday. For excellent soup, salad and sandwich lunches daily excep, stop by **Café Cornucopia** (☎ 432-4820, 14 Main St).

For Mexican food, the best is **Tacho's Tacos** (☎ 432-7811, 115 Bisbee-Naco Hwy). **Cafe Roka** (☎ 432-5153, 35 Main St) serves excellent and innovative dinners Wednesday to Saturday. The changing menu is a limited gourmet American selection in the $13 to $20 range, including soup and salad. Jazz is played on Friday and Saturday.

The **Copper Queen Hotel** serves good meals all day. Also check out the **High Desert Inn Restaurant** with fine and highly acclaimed dinners served Thursday to Sunday, and **Le Chêne Bistro**, with genuine and fresh French country dinners served daily in the $15 to $30 range.

## Shopping
Galleries in Old Bisbee exhibit and sell local artists' work. The quality is mixed, but a discerning eye may discover an as-yet-undiscovered artist here.

## DOUGLAS & AROUND
☎ 520 • pop 14,312 • elevation 4000 feet
Once a copper town, Douglas, along with its much larger sister city of Agua Prieta (pop 100,000) in Mexico, has become a ranching and manufacturing center. The downtown area looks pre-WWII without the hoopla of Bisbee or Tombstone.

Golden State (☎ 364-2233), on 2nd at S 4th Ave, has buses to Tucson and Phoenix; they connect with Greyhound.

## Information
The chamber of commerce (☎ 364-2477), 1125 Pan American Ave, is open 9am to 5pm Monday to Friday; visit www.ci.douglas.az.us. Other services include the Coronado National Forest Ranger Station (☎ 364-3468, 364-3231), on Leslie Canyon Rd; library (☎ 364-3851), at 560 10th St; post office (☎ 364-3631), 601 10th St; hospital (☎ 364-7931), 4 miles west of Douglas; and the police (☎ 364-8422), 300 14th St.

## Things to See & Do

Established in 1907, the **Gadsden Hotel** (see Places to Stay) is on the National Register of Historic Places. The lobby is one of the most opulent early-20th-century public areas in Arizona. A white Italian marble staircase and marble pillars with gold-leaf decorations, a superb 42-foot Tiffany stained-glass Southwestern mural, and vaulted stained-glass skylights combine for an elegant surprise. It's well worth a visit even if you aren't staying here.

The **John Slaughter Ranch** (☎ 558-2474) was one of the largest and most successful ranches of the late 1800s. The buildings have been restored and the ranch is on the National Register of Historic Places. Photo exhibits and a video show what life was like on the property a century ago. The ranch is 16 miles east of Douglas (leave town via 15th St) along a gravel road paralleling the border. Hours are 10am to 3pm Wednesday to Sunday, and admission is $3 for those over 14. The ranchlands are now a wildlife refuge (☎ 364-2104).

**Agua Prieta,** across the border, can be entered on foot. In daylight, the atmosphere is much more leisurely and relaxed than in Nogales and you'll find a selection of gift shops (no bargaining) and restaurants. From the international border, walk south six blocks to Calle 6 and turn left for two blocks to the church and plaza, which are pleasant. At night, this area becomes a major illegal crossing place for undocumented aliens; expect to see border patrols and to be asked for identification.

**Special events** celebrating the town's Mexican ties are Cinco de Mayo, celebrated on or near May 5th, and Douglas Fiestas in mid-September.

## Places to Stay & Eat

The rooms are nowhere near as fancy as the lobby in the *Gadsden Hotel* (☎ 364-4481, 1046 G Ave), but they are comfortable enough and the price is right. There are 160 rooms and suites ranging from $45 to $85; most are under $65. The rooms contain an eclectic grouping of styles and amenities,

but just sitting in the lobby makes this a great value.

website: www.theriver.com/gadsdenhotel

Otherwise, there are a few basic mom 'n' pop places and a *Motel 6* (☎ 364-2457, 111 16th St) with a pool and rooms around $40.

The restaurants in the Gadsden Hotel are good, or you can eat Mexican and American food across the street in the *Grand Cafe* (☎ 364-2344, 1119 G Ave).

## WILLCOX

☎ 520 • pop 3733 • elevation 4167 feet

Settled in 1880 as a railroad camp, Willcox quickly became a major shipping center for southeastern Arizona's cattle ranches. Today Willcox is also famous as a fruit-growing center, and people drive from all over southeastern Arizona for the apple harvest. Willcox is the boyhood home of cowboy singer and movie actor Rex Allen (1920–99). Nearby is a playa – a lake that dries in summer – which is the wintering ground of thousands of sandhill cranes, a spectacular sight for bird watchers.

Greyhound (☎ 384-2183) buses stop at the Lifestyle RV Resort (622 N Haskell Ave) several times a day on their runs along I-10.

## Information

The chamber of commerce (☎ 384-2272, 800-200-2272), by I-10 exit 340, is open 8am to 5pm Monday to Saturday and 10am to 2pm on Sunday. Other services include the library (☎ 384-4271), 207 W Maley St; post office (☎ 384-2689), 200 S Curtis Ave; hospital (☎ 384-3541), 901 W Rex Allen Dr; and the police (☎ 384-4673), 151 W Maley St.

## Things to See & Do

The **Rex Allen Arizona Cowboy Museum** (☎ 384-4583), 155 N Railroad Ave, is in an 1890s adobe building in the Willcox Historic District. Exhibits interpret the lives of pioneers as well as Rex Allen. Hours are 10am to 4pm daily except some Sundays and major holidays; admission is $2 per person, $3 for a couple and $5 for a family. Nearby, the Willcox Commercial Store dates to 1881

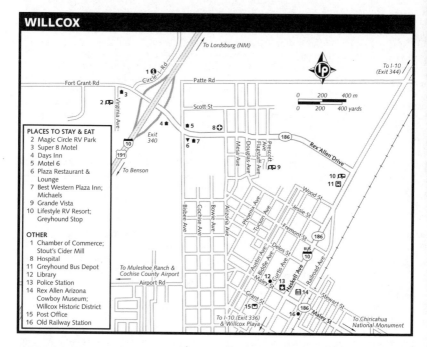

**WILLCOX**

PLACES TO STAY & EAT
2  Magic Circle RV Park
3  Super 8 Motel
4  Days Inn
5  Motel 6
6  Plaza Restaurant &
   Lounge
7  Best Western Plaza Inn;
   Michaels
9  Grande Vista
10 Lifestyle RV Resort;
   Greyhound Stop

OTHER
1  Chamber of Commerce;
   Stout's Cider Mill
8  Hospital
11 Greyhound Bus Depot
12 Library
13 Police Station
14 Rex Allen Arizona
   Cowboy Museum;
   Willcox Historic District
15 Post Office
16 Old Railway Station

and is the oldest continuously operating store in Arizona. Other old buildings can be visited.

South of town, the huge **Willcox Playa** is the winter home of approximately 10,000 sandhill cranes. Drive southeast on Hwy 186 a few miles and then take the left fork for Kansas Settlement. At dawn, the birds fly out of the playa and land in the corn stubble around Kansas Settlement, where they feed during the day, flying back to the playa at sunset.

On the third weekend in January, Wings Over Willcox Sandhill Cranes Celebration has guided tours to good viewing sites near Willcox Playa and offers related birding activities. In late summer and fall, there are pick-your-own apple orchards, roadside fruit and vegetable stands, and often an apple harvest festival in December. Rex Allen Days, with rodeo and other events, is the first week in October.

## Places to Stay & Eat

*Magic Circle RV Park* (☎ 384-3212), at I-10 exit 340, has 80 RV sites with hookups at $24; *Lifestyle RV Resort* (☎ 384-3303, 622 N Haskell Ave) has 60 RV sites with hookups for $22. *Grande Vista* (☎ 384-4002, 711 N Prescott Ave) charges $15.50 for 50 RV sites with hookups.

The cheapest places are small mom-and-pop establishments along Haskell Ave charging in the $20s and $30s. Otherwise, choose from a *chain motel* at I-10 exit 340. These all have pools and include a Motel 6, Days Inn, and Super 8, with rooms in the $40 to $60 range. Also at exit 340 is Willcox's most comfortable hotel: the *Best Western Plaza Inn* (☎ 384-3556), with a pool, whirlpool, lounge and restaurant with room service. Rooms feature coffeemakers and some refrigerators; six have whirlpool baths as well. Rates are $70 to $90 a double.

The best restaurant is **Michaels** in the Best Western, open 6am to 9pm daily and serving moderately priced American and Mexican food, ranging from $5 to $17. Otherwise, there's the **Plaza Restaurant & Lounge** (☎ 384-3819) next door, open 24 hours, and a slew of fast-food places. By the chamber of commerce, **Stout's Cider Mill** (☎ 384-3696) sells every imaginable apple concoction.

## MULESHOE RANCH

Cooperatively managed by the Nature Conservancy, BLM and USFS, the ranch is a good place for birding and wildlife observation. It's about 30 miles northwest of Willcox (leave town via Airport Rd) in the foothills of the rugged Galiuro Mountains, which are the watershed of seven permanently flowing streams – an important ecosystem.

At ranch headquarters (☎ 212-4295) is a visitor center, nature trail, five cabins with kitchens for rent by reservation (at least two weeks in advance, $95 to $140 double occupancy, $15 for additional people). Cabins require a two-day minimum stay and are closed in summer. Primitive backcountry camping is allowed by permit, and there are hiking and horse trails. Call about road conditions – the road here is unpaved. Another contact is Tucson's Nature Conservancy office (☎ 622-3861).

## CHIRICAHUA MOUNTAINS & CHIRICAHUA NATIONAL MONUMENT

The strangely eroded volcanic pinnacles and balanced rocks of the Chiricahua Mountains are unlike any others in Arizona. The Chiricahua National Monument contains the wildest and weirdest of the formations. This is one of the smaller and more remote NPS areas in the Southwest, but the scenery alone makes it a worthwhile trip. It is surrounded to the north, east and south by the Coronado National Forest (see the Douglas and Sierra Vista sections, earlier, and the Safford section in the East-Central Arizona chapter,

for the nearest USFS offices), which also has interesting rock formations as well as camping.

The remoteness of the area makes it attractive to wildlife – a jaguar was recently recorded near here! There is a good chance of seeing deer, coatis and javelinas. Mountain lions, bobcats and bears are sighted many times a year on the hiking trails within the monument. The Chiricahuas are the nearest high mountains to the Mexican mountain ranges, and several Mexican bird species are found here. The highest peak is 9795-foot Chiricahua Peak, just south of the monument in the national forest.

History and architecture can be found at Faraway Ranch, built in the early part of the 20th century. Tours of the now-restored ranch are led by monument rangers.

### Orientation & Information

The monument is almost 40 miles southeast of Willcox by paved road (no gas along this route). The visitor center (☎ 824-3560) has a slide show about the Chiricahuas, a small exhibit area and a bookstore. Ranger-led programs are sometimes offered. The monument is open 24 hours but offers no gas, food or lodging facilities (except camping). Admission is $5, and all passes are honored.

The closest food supplies are in Sunizona, 24 miles away.

**Climate & When to Go** March, April and May are by far the busiest months, due in part to the pleasant spring climate. Summers are hot and July through early September are the wettest months, with frequent storms. Beware of flash floods after summer storms. Freezing overnight temperatures are normal late November through February, and the trails, though open year-round, may be snow-covered in winter.

### Bonita Canyon Scenic Drive

This paved 8-mile road climbs from the entrance gate (at about 5000 feet) to Massai Point at 6870 feet. The visitor center is 2 miles along this road from the entrance station. There are several scenic pullouts and trailheads and views from Massai Point are spectacular.

## Faraway Ranch

Originally a pioneer's cattle ranch begun in 1888, it became one of Arizona's earliest guest ranches in the 1920s. The ranch is near the monument entrance. To enter, you must go on a ranger-led tour, offered several times a day during the busy season, less often in other months.

## Hiking

More than twenty miles of hiking trails range from easy, flat loops of 0.2 miles to strenuous 7-mile climbs. The short, flat trails west of the visitor center and campground are the easiest and are good for birding and wildlife observation. The trails east of the visitor center lead into rugged mountain country with the most spectacular geology. A hikers' shuttle bus leaves daily from the visitor center at 8:30am, going up to Massai Point (free). Hikers return by hiking downhill.

## Places to Stay

The **Bonita Campground**, with 24 sites just north of the visitor center, has water but no hookups or showers. During the busy months, the campground is often full by noon. Sites cost $12 on a first-come, first-served basis. Note that wilderness camping is not permitted.

If the campground is full, there are numerous campgrounds in the Coronado National Forest south of the monument. Rangers will give you a map (there's one outside the visitor center if the center is closed) showing where the campgrounds are. These usually have space available.

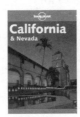

# Index

## Text

### A

AAA 70
Abbey, Edward 33
accommodations 44–7. *See also individual locations*
  B&Bs 45
  cabins 46
  camping 44, 54–5
  guest ranches 46
  hostels 27, 44–5
  hotels 45–7
  lodges 46
  motels 45–6
  reservations 46–7
  resorts 46
activities 53–62. *See also individual activities*
agaves 22
agriculture 23–4, 154
Agua Prieta (Mexico) 274, 275
AIDS. *See* HIV/AIDS
air travel 63–6, 69
  airlines 63–4
  airports 63
  regional & local 69
  security 34, 65
  tickets 64–5
Ajo 254
alcoholic drinks 49
Allen, Rex 275
Alpine 222–3
American Automobile Association (AAA) 70
Amerind Foundation 264
Amtrak 67, 69
amusement parks 87
Anasazi. *See* Ancestral Puebloans
Ancestral Puebloans 11, 12–3, 169, 188–9, 204, 208–9
Anglo culture 24
Antelope Canyon 130

antiques 214
Apache Lake 227
Apache Trail 226–7
Apaches
  history 13, 15–6, 199, 218–9, 228–9
  population 24
  reservations 24, 218–9, 224–5
Apache-Sitgreaves National Forest 222
The Arboretum 179
archaeology 32, 221
archery 88–9
architecture 84, 169–70
Arcosanti 169–70
Arivaca 252
Arizona Fish & Game Department 40
Arizona Hall of Fame 80
Arizona Mining & Mineral Museum 80, 82
Arizona Museum for Youth 87
Arizona Science Center 76
Arizona State Capitol Museum 80
Arizona State Museum 237
Arizona State University 85
Arizona Strip 121–7
Arizona Trail 54
Arizona-Sonora Desert 18, 21–2, 230, 248
Arizona-Sonora Desert Museum 248–9
art 24, 52. *See also* crafts; galleries
Asarco Mineral Discovery Center 255
astronomy. *See* observatories; planetariums
ATMs 29
auto racing 100, 217

### B

B&Bs. *See* accommodations
Bacavi 213
backpacking. *See* hiking & backpacking
ballooning, hot-air 61, 88, 241
banks 41
bars 49
baseball 50–1, 100
basketball 51, 99
baskets 52, 253
Benson 262–3, **264**
Betatakin 208
bicycling 57–8, 72, 112–3, 126. *See also* mountain biking
Biosphere 2 249
Bird Cage Theater 269
bird watching 10, 22, 60, 123, 156–7, 241, 252, 255, 259, 266, 267, 273, 276, 277
Bisbee 271–4, **272**
Bisbee Mining & Historical Museum 271
bites 36–7, 40–1
boat tours 130, 145
boating 58–9, 133–5, 145, 151, 217, 222
books 31–3, 53
Boothill Graveyard 269–70
border, US-Mexican 257, 260, 275
Boyce Thompson Southwestern Arboretum 226
Bright Angel Point 124, 125
Bright Angel Trail 110–1
Buckskin Mountain State Park 151
Buenos Aires National Wildlife Refuge 252
Bullfrog Marina 134
Bullhead City 146–8, **147**

**Bold** indicates maps.

## N

## O

**Bold** indicates maps.

Bold indicates maps.

---

## Boxed Text

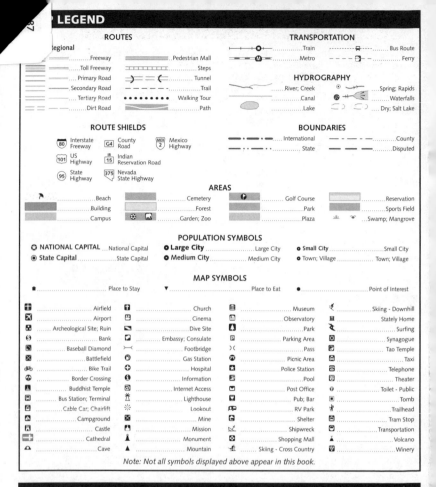

### ROUTES

**Regional**

| | |
|---|---|
| Freeway | Pedestrian Mall |
| Toll Freeway | Steps |
| Primary Road | Tunnel |
| Secondary Road | Trail |
| Tertiary Road | Walking Tour |
| Dirt Road | Path |

### ROUTE SHIELDS

| | | |
|---|---|---|
| 80 Interstate Freeway | G4 County Road | MEX 2 Mexico Highway |
| 101 US Highway | IR 15 Indian Reservation Road | |
| 95 State Highway | 375 Nevada State Highway | |

### AREAS

| | | | |
|---|---|---|---|
| Beach | Cemetery | Golf Course | Reservation |
| Building | Forest | Park | Sports Field |
| Campus | Garden; Zoo | Plaza | Swamp; Mangrove |

### TRANSPORTATION

| | |
|---|---|
| Train | Bus Route |
| Metro | Ferry |

### HYDROGRAPHY

| | |
|---|---|
| River; Creek | Spring; Rapids |
| Canal | Waterfalls |
| Lake | Dry; Salt Lake |

### BOUNDARIES

| | |
|---|---|
| International | County |
| State | Disputed |

### POPULATION SYMBOLS

| | | |
|---|---|---|
| ✪ NATIONAL CAPITAL ... National Capital | ● Large City ... Large City | ● Small City ... Small City |
| ◉ State Capital ... State Capital | ● Medium City ... Medium City | ● Town; Village ... Town; Village |

### MAP SYMBOLS

| ■ ... Place to Stay | ▼ ... Place to Eat | ● ... Point of Interest |
|---|---|---|

| | | | |
|---|---|---|---|
| Airfield | Church | Museum | Skiing - Downhill |
| Airport | Cinema | Observatory | Stately Home |
| Archeological Site; Ruin | Dive Site | Park | Surfing |
| Bank | Embassy; Consulate | Parking Area | Synagogue |
| Baseball Diamond | Footbridge | Pass | Tao Temple |
| Battlefield | Gas Station | Picnic Area | Taxi |
| Bike Trail | Hospital | Police Station | Telephone |
| Border Crossing | Information | Pool | Theater |
| Buddhist Temple | Internet Access | Post Office | Toilet - Public |
| Bus Station; Terminal | Lighthouse | Pub; Bar | Tomb |
| Cable Car; Chairlift | Lookout | RV Park | Trailhead |
| Campground | Mine | Shelter | Tram Stop |
| Castle | Mission | Shipwreck | Transportation |
| Cathedral | Monument | Shopping Mall | Volcano |
| Cave | Mountain | Skiing - Cross Country | Winery |

*Note: Not all symbols displayed above appear in this book.*

## LONELY PLANET OFFICES

### Australia
Locked Bag 1, Footscray, Victoria 3011
☎ 03 8379 8000  fax 03 8379 8111
email talk2us@lonelyplanet.com.au

### USA
150 Linden Street, Oakland, California 94607
☎ 510 893 8555, TOLL FREE 800 275 5555
fax 510 893 8572
email info@lonelyplanet.com

### UK
10a Spring Place, London NW5 3BH
☎ 020 7428 4800 fax 020 7428 4828
email go@lonelyplanet.co.uk

### France
1 rue du Dahomey, 75011 Paris
☎ 01 55 25 33 00 fax 01 55 25 33 01
email bip@lonelyplanet.fr
www.lonelyplanet.fr

**World Wide Web: www.lonelyplanet.com *or* AOL keyword: lp**
**Lonely Planet Images: lpi@lonelyplanet.com.au**